Modification of Child and Adolescent Behavior

Third Edition

Garth J. Blackham
Arizona State University

Adolph Silberman
Private Practice

Wadsworth Publishing Company
Belmont, California
A Division of Wadsworth, Inc.

Education Editor: Roger S. Peterson
Production Editor: Anne D. Kelly
Designer: Detta Penna
Cover photo: Elizabeth Crews

Printed in the United States of America

1 2 3 4 5 6 7 8 9 10—84 83 82 81 80

Library of Congress Cataloging in Publication Data

Blackham, Garth J.
  Modification of child and adolescent behavior.

  Bibliography: p.
  Includes index.
  1. Behavior therapy. 2. Child psychotherapy.
3. Adolescent psychotherapy. I. Silberman, Adolph,
joint author. II. Title.
RJ505.B4B55   1980   618.9′28′914   79-9313
ISBN 0-534-00725-2

To our children:
Janet and Paula,
Caryn, Scott, and Marc

Contents

Preface

Behavior modification is now recognized as a viable system for promoting development and inducing behavior change. Respondent, operant, and social learning principles are widely used to alter many types of maladaptive behavior in children and adults. With the broad dissemination of behavioral principles and procedures, behavior change can no longer be regarded as the exclusive province of therapists. Teachers, child care workers, and parents can act as agents of change. And individuals familiar with behavioral principles can better manage or direct the course of their own lives.

This third edition of *Modification of Child and Adolescent Behavior* reflects some of the newer developments in behavior modification and applies behavioral principles and procedures to a variety of child and adolescent problems. One chapter has been completely rewritten to provide the reader with a more comprehensive discussion of the methods used to assess behavior and evaluate treatment effects. Two new chapters explain and illustrate the use of behavior modification both in the regular classroom and with special groups of children and adolescents. Many more specific child and adolescent problems are discussed. We have expanded several sections and added new sections and case illustrations to reflect some of the growing edges of behavior modification. Finally, a completely new section discusses some of the important theoretical, ethical, and legal issues involved in behavior change.

We are indebted to a number of people for their assistance in preparing this book. For their permission to paraphrase or adapt material, we wish to thank the following authors and publishers: Josef Cohen, *Operant Conditioning and Operant Behavior* (Chicago: Rand McNally, 1969); Lloyd Homme, Attila P. Csanyi, Mary Ann Gonzales, and James Rechs, *How to Use Contingency Contracting in the Classroom* (Champaign, Ill.: Research Press, 1969); Ellen P. Reese, *The Analysis of Human Operant Behavior* (Dubuque, Iowa: Wm. C. Brown Company, 1966).

Several reviewers contributed many helpful suggestions that have been incorporated in this edition. Among them are Lee Swanson, School of Special Education and Rehabilitation, University of Northern Colorado; Bruce E. Bailey, Department of Psychology, Stephen F. Austin State University; and Richard T. Owens, Department of Education, Morningside College, Iowa. Roger Peterson, Education Editor at Wadsworth, was very helpful in facilitating the revision. Our families were tolerant of our absences and provided needed support at crucial times. We express our gratitude to all.

Garth J. Blackham
Adolph Silberman

Chapter One

Introduction

Those entrusted with the responsibility of socializing and educating children perform many important roles. Perhaps the central, most significant role is influencing, shaping, and changing child behavior. Although its importance is widely recognized, many perform the role reluctantly because of the connotation of the term "influence." The idea of influencing others is often viewed as contradictory to the humanitarian ideal of freedom of choice. Thus, many accept their influential position halfheartedly, relinquish the role entirely, or choose instead to let their influence operate without design. Such decisions reflect not only an awesome value judgment but also one's concept of development and behavior change.

To illustrate how beliefs, values, and assumptions affect the process of promoting and changing behavior, we will visit a modern American family. The Lander family has three members: Bob, age twenty-nine; his wife Susan, age twenty-seven; and their son Jimmy, age eight. Bob and Susan Lander are sincere, loving, and responsible parents who cherish the freedom-of-choice ideal and believe in performing their parental roles well and encouraging the development of happy, healthy children. They are college educated, have read books on child rearing, and try to implement their concepts in rearing Jimmy. At an early stage they granted

rather complete autonomy to Jimmy, including the right to make choices. All through infancy, they took pride in his expressions of individuality and worked hard to respond to his every need. Almost total permissiveness characterized the relationship; few, if any, limits were imposed. His parents had infinite faith in the directionality provided by the genetic blueprint; expressions of the hereditary endowment would ultimately lead to an orderly, socialized, responsible, and happy life for the child. Their major role was to allow him to grow, interact with him in a way that "felt right," and love him freely.

From birth Jimmy was a finicky eater. There were many occasions when he steadfastly refused to eat the food his parents prepared. Although this part of Jimmy's behavior irritated his mother, she was not overly concerned. Both Bob and Susan Lander assumed that if a well-balanced diet was provided, Jimmy's physical requirements would lead him to obtain proper nutrition. As Jimmy got older, he displayed distinct preferences about his bedtime and eating schedule, and he did not toilet train easily. Of course, his parents became impatient and even distressed. Was it just a phase he was going through? Was it normal? Such questions fleetingly crossed their minds, but they had faith he would eventually outgrow these behaviors and

1

exhibit others more appropriate. After all, they believed much of his behavior was a manifestation of his individuality and freedom of choice.

Jimmy was not always certain how his parents wanted him to behave. Because they rarely insisted on anything, Jimmy knew that if he persisted, he would eventually get his way. However, there were times when Jimmy noted his parents were upset, for their faces would redden even though their voices remained relatively calm. These nonverbal expressions of anger often frightened Jimmy, and he learned to watch for them anxiously.

As Jimmy's world expanded and he began to play with other children in the neighborhood, his demanding behavior led to many skirmishes with his playmates. Many times they hastily dispatched him home. On these occasions his mother comforted him, and placed little credence in the idea that Jimmy's behavior caused the rejection. Consequently, Jimmy saw little need to behave differently. When people did not yield to his demands, he invoked a whole repertoire of aggressive behaviors. As time passed, he found few welcome mats out for him in the neighborhood. His parents' concern mounted, and they intensified their family reasoning sessions with him. However, the sessions often ended in arguments, and finally only mild restrictions were imposed. But Jimmy had a strong sense of individuality and debated endlessly the reasonableness of even these restrictions. If he could not make his point verbally, he used more forceful means such as slamming doors, breaking toys, and cursing.

With only slight variation these events were repeated year after year until Jimmy had well-defined behavior patterns. He became even more demanding; conflicts with peers and arguments with his parents became more frequent. During Jimmy's eighth year, the Landers began to question their parental roles. They felt considerable apprehension and guilt, and, recognizing their failures, they began to devalue themselves. They realized that Jimmy had more than normal problems; his behavior was launched on an inappropriate course.

This example may appear a little overdrawn, but it is quite typical of many parents who have sought help from the authors. They ask: "What went wrong? How could dedicated, sincere, and loving parents promote such behavior in a child? Isn't love freely given enough?"

The answers to these questions depend on one's theory of behavior. In our analysis of Jimmy's behavior, we will try to specify the Landers' apparent assumptions and then discuss them from a behavioral point of view. In later chapters we will explain the concepts and principles used and show how they apply in actual practice.

Bob and Susan Lander assumed (implicitly or explicitly) that Jimmy's genetic endowment would *naturally guide* wholesome, socially adaptive behavior. In a sense, the genetic endowment was seen as a "game plan" which would guide the young quarterback for every play. Since the attributes ascribed to genetic endowment push toward self-actualization and monitor behavior in socially appropriate ways, the moment-to-moment effects of behavior are considered less important. The Landers considered the genetic endowment primary; the effects produced by and on the environment, secondary.

Although the body does have certain built-in mechanisms which operate automatically to avoid aversive stimuli (extremes of cold, heat, noise, etc.), it is questionable whether there exist innate mechanisms to guide socially adaptive behavior. Rather, we suggest that the genetic endowment provides a certain *potential* for response, but how a person responds is a function of the stimulus that elicits the behavior, the response repertoire of the person, and the consequence of the response. If the consequence is positive, the response is likely to be repeated; if the consequence is unpleasant or painful, the individual will inhibit the response or attempt to escape or avoid the aversive stimulus. If there is *no* consequence, he will continue to behave as he did in the past, or try different responses until he produces the desired effects by trial and error.

The Landers were inconsistent in the type of consequences used. Because they employed positive and negative consequences inconsistently, Jimmy had few guidelines for learning socially appropriate responses. Instead, he was left on his own to figure out the parents' hidden agenda. For example, on the occasions when he was sent home after a skirmish with his playmates, Jimmy understood his mother's tendency to "take his side" as a positive consequence, and he continued to behave in the same manner.

Obviously, the Landers were unintentionally influencing Jimmy's behavior. When parental appeals to reason ended in heated arguments and as a result Jimmy won his demands, he learned that arguing paid off. By conceding, the parents increased the probability that the arguments would be repeated. And since Jimmy's arguing was aversive to the parents, conceding to his demands amounted to a positive consequence for them; stopping the arguments removed the aversive stimulus. Thus, not only were the parents influencing Jimmy's behavior, he was influencing their behavior as well.

Bob and Susan Lander did care and express affection for Jimmy. However, the effects of their love cannot be assessed by abstract methods. When people love each other they *do something* to express it. They attend, smile, listen, hug, comfort, speak words of appreciation and endearment; loving is not only a state of mind but also a type of response. An affectionate response usually acts like any other positive consequence: it increases the probability that the behavior will be repeated. Because loving responses are

rarely expressed 100 percent of the time, they act selectively to promote the behavior occurring at the time they are given. To determine their impact on Jimmy, it is necessary to specify *how* and *when* affectionate responses were exhibited. If we carefully analyzed the parents' thousands of affectionate responses, we would probably discover that they were given somewhat indiscriminately. The result was the promotion of at least as much undesirable as desirable behavior. It may be said that the Landers reduced their positive impact on Jimmy's behavior by not clearly understanding how their behavior influenced him.

The analysis raises a very important question: "Doesn't loving selectively actually amount to withholding love or giving conditional love?" The obvious answer is "Yes." However, whether it is good or bad, desirable or undesirable, should be based on the effect it has on the child. Of course, there is no absolute standard of goodness; goodness is a relative matter. Is unconditional love good if it promotes maladaptive behavior or makes a child unhappy? This question, of course, needs no answer; the results must be accepted on their own merit.

One final aspect of the Landers' child-rearing practices deserves comment: the autonomy and freedom-of-choice issue. Philosophically, there is little question about the desirability of extending autonomy and freedom of choice to everyone; the problem is determining when and how much. The ability to act independently and make wise and appropriate choices is *learned* just as is any other facet of behavior. Children cannot make choices for which there is no basis in experience. Allowing a two-year-old to make choices about his own safety is unwise, because he has only a vague comprehension of what is dangerous. He must learn a great deal about his environment before permitted such decisions. We dare not let a very young child "find out for himself," for he may not have another chance if his decision is wrong.

Perhaps the example we have used is an extreme one. Let us consider another. Suppose a five-year-old child decides that he does not wish to attend kindergarten. If his parents are willing to abide by the decision and legal authorities do not subsequently intervene, he may not choose to go to school for one, two, or even three years. Since he has no basis in experience for knowing the significance of his decision and the effects of it are likely to be delayed, he may think he has made a wise choice. Yet, if he holds out for two or three years before he decides to go to school, he may abruptly realize he has made a decision that seriously affects his present as well as future welfare. It is difficult, if not impossible, to make up what he has lost by not attending school.

A child needs not only experience but the right kind of experience. And he needs a wise guide who can steer him clear of danger and who encourages, prompts, and reinforces behavior that is adaptive and successful. Of course, a child does learn from unaided trial and error, but such learning is often slow and unproductive. It is much more efficient and humane to guide the child's learning until he has acquired the ability to make the choices himself. He will be spared the pain, anxiety, and low self-esteem that inevitably result from failure.

With proper assistance, Jimmy Lander's socially nonadaptive behavior can be changed. Just as he *learned* the maladaptive behavior, he can also *unlearn* the behavior. Briefly, a two-phase process is involved. First, the undesirable behavior must be decreased in strength or eliminated. Second, the desirable behavior must be clearly specified and increased in strength or frequency. How these objectives may be accomplished and the psychological principles involved will be the central focus of the remainder of the book.

Some Theoretical Issues

Our historical efforts to explain and modify human behavior raise some interesting theoretical questions. We will discuss them briefly now and give them more complete attention in various sections that follow.

Human beings have often invoked "inner" causes as explanations for human behavior. These inner causes or agents have owned many labels: spirits, devils, willpower, instincts, motives, and intentions (Skinner, 1971). Attributing an act to a motive, for example, assumes that the act was caused by the motive. Yet, how do we know that a motive was present? Usually, we infer it afterward from the behavior exhibited. If a person acts overly aggressive, we infer that he had an aggressive motive which produced the act. But have we enhanced our understanding or uncovered ways by which the behavior can be modified?

Consider another example. "Self-concept" is frequently used to explain a variety of behaviors. Inadequate self-concept is often cited as the cause of poor academic performance, and shy, withdrawn behavior. But may we expect a person with an inadequate self-concept to exhibit all, some, or just one of these behaviors? Is a *very* inadequate self-concept required before some or all of these behaviors are manifested? How is it determined whether a person has an adequate self-concept or an extremely inadequate self-concept? In other words, if the self-concept degree or magnitude cannot be evaluated, how much explanatory power does the construct have? To be useful, an *observable* relationship must exist between the degree of inadequacy and the performance of the behavior.

Inner processes (needs, thoughts, motives, expectations) do seem to have an effect on behavior. However, until methods are devised to observe and measure these processes directly, we can only speculate on what they are and how they influence behavior. We are better advised to concentrate our explanations on observable behavior rather than inner processes.

The theories utilized to explain behavior influence what is done to promote and change it. Theories vary widely in their specificity and in the extent they can be subjected to controlled experimentation. When relationships among variables can be experimentally confirmed, we may know how one event is related to or determines another. For example, a child says "damn" and his parents laugh; parent laughter is soon followed by a great increase in the number of "damns" the child says. An obvious relationship exists between parent laughter and the child's behavior. We can decrease the number of undesirable responses by decreasing parent laughter or not attending to the child when he utters the word. When such dependable relationships are found, we are then able to predictably change behavior.

Identifying Behaviors to Promote or Change

If the essential tasks of those charged with training and educating children are promoting desirable behavior and changing nonadaptive or self-defeating behavior, the forms of behavior to be enhanced or changed must be identified. Cursory examination suggests that it may be relatively easy to identify undesirable behavior, and, in part, this is true. It is certainly not difficult to determine that a child who exhibits an unnatural fear, is excessively inhibited or aggressive, cannot adequately attend to learning, or fails in academic work needs assistance in changing his behavior. These behaviors cause distress to the child, create alarm reactions in others, and ultimately deter healthy personality development. However, we do not wish to imply that behavior distressing to a parent or teacher is *sufficient* criterion for effecting a change. The real problem may not reside in the child's behavior but rather in the person who so labels it. Consider, for example, a parent who does not feel comfortable until *all* expressions of aggressiveness are eliminated from the child's behavior. In this instance, the real problem resides with the parent, not the child, for a certain amount of aggressiveness is necessary to adapt adequately to our society.

The decision to change a child's behavior should involve at least three criteria. First, the behavior presumed to be maladaptive occurs with sufficient frequency. For example, an occasional fight might be typical for most children, but when a child fights every day the behavior is maladaptive. Second, the behavior, if continued, ultimately results in harm to the child and/or environment. For example, a child who has a severe reading disability should not be kept idle in the hope that he will "outgrow" the problem, for reading facility is basic to progress in most academic areas. Third, the behavior impedes subsequent adaptation and healthy development. For instance, a child's tendency to cry every time minor frustration is experienced may pose serious problems at later ages or developmental periods. The child is likely to be avoided by peers or be called a "baby."

We recognize that different societies, social classes, ethnic groups, and subcultures value very different behavior. Acceptable behavior in one society may be socially or legally condemned in another. Adaptive behavior must be socially appropriate. Behavior that is not socially appropriate evokes all manner of negative consequences and ends up being punishing to the offender. However, there is a limit to the application of this criterion: individuals who learn the approved behavior in one social context may find it quite alien in another.

Some may object to the terms "healthy" and "maladaptive" because they seem to imply an absolute standard of desirable behavior. Others criticize their apparent relation to the medical concept of disease. Still others object on the grounds that norms of desirable behavior vary from culture to culture. Each is a valid criticism according to a particular view of human nature.

Theories vary regarding the extent to which human development is directed or controlled by genetic determinants; that is, the roles of heredity and environment are given different emphasis, depending on the theory one chooses. For example, Freudian theorists postulate that two basic instincts direct human behavior: sexuality and aggression. Since both are innate instincts, constantly striving for expression, Freudians view human behavior as attempts to regulate expressions of sexuality and aggression. One's basic nature is regarded as "evil." Although the environment plays a role in development, it is secondary to the directionality and control exercised by the two primary instincts. Thus, in this view, development, personality, and behavior are functions of these inner instinctual determinants.

Rogerians[1] conceptualize human nature quite differently. Although internal genetic determinants provide major direction and control of behavior, one's inherent drives are presumed more wholesome and socially acceptable. One is not enslaved by sexual or aggressive instincts,

but rather is motivated to fulfill the master drive, the "self-actualizing tendency." Since the self-actualizing tendency is hypothesized to be innately "good," the best environment is one that interferes least. Further, the extent to which "significant others" (people with whom one interacts frequently and upon whom one depends for psychological nutrients) provide facilitative conditions for growth is considered important for the enhancement of self-actualization strivings. Significant others must display unconditional positive regard for the individual to achieve self-worth and self-actualization. However, because the specific behaviors presumed to convey positive regard are not clearly defined, it is difficult to evaluate to what extent behavior is a function of genetic or environmental determinants.

In contrast to the Freudian and Rogerian points of view, behaviorism does not postulate genetically determined instincts or drives. Although it is recognized that human beings have certain predetermined response tendencies to pain, extremes in body temperature and chemistry, and physiological deprivation, nothing analogous to drives, needs, or motives is postulated. Instead, behaviorists focus attention on external events that strengthen, maintain, or change behavior. Behavior is viewed as a function of stimulus-response-consequence relationships. Since behavior is not primarily directed or controlled by inner determinants, man has no predetermined goals or destiny to fulfill. In a moral sense, human beings are neither good nor bad. Learning and/or conditioning history will determine personality development, values, and the effectiveness of adaptation to the social environment.

Thus, what is considered maladaptive or deviant is obviously related to one's theoretical orientation. Differences in theoretical viewpoint determine not only the extent of maladaptive behavior, but also the causes for it. Consider, for

---

[1] Carl Rogers is a distinguished American psychologist who developed an approach to therapy that is commonly referred to as "client-centered." His approach to therapy assumes that every individual strives toward psychological health and self-direction. Such self-actualization occurs quite naturally and need not be forced, coerced, or directed. The Rogerian therapist does not direct or guide the client but accepts the client totally regardless of what he or she is or says. The therapist's role is to help the client clarify and understand his or her concerns and feelings. By so doing, the client is able to alter his or her own behavior and overcome problems.

instance, an excessively shy and inhibited child. A Freudian practitioner would tend to consider the behavior a disturbance resulting from the inhibition or repression of aggression. A Rogerian practitioner might interpret the behavior as a temporarily detoured self-actualization, rather than a manifestation of disturbance, or might suggest that significant others have been only conditionally regarding. A behaviorist would probably not consider the behavior disturbed but simply a manifestation of inappropriate or faulty learning. Although he may view the behavior as nonadaptive, it exists because it enables the child to escape certain unpleasant situations.

If the three practitioners treated the child's difficulties, their theoretical differences would become very clear. The Freudian would encourage the child to express or channel appropriately the aggressiveness underlying the shyness and fear. The Rogerian would also encourage the child to express the fear, but, in addition, might suggest that the parents love the child unconditionally. The behaviorist, on the other hand, would specify the exact socially adaptive behavior and encourage the parents to reinforce it, with the aim of extinguishing the excessive shyness and fear through simple nonreinforcement.

Although each school has its own conception and explanation for atypical or nonadaptive behavior, the extent to which certain behavior is *excessive* or *deficient* is a useful criterion for all. Regardless of theoretical emphasis, each would carefully evaluate and assess (1) the extent to which intellectual processes are appropriate, (2) the type and intensity of emotional reactivity or distress, (3) the presence of physical complaints, and (4) the situational appropriateness of the person's behavior. Indeed, psychological problems are likely to be expressed in any or all of these aspects of behavior.

There will be further discussion of nonadaptive behavior in subsequent sections. However, we will suggest here that adaptive behavior might well be determined by the extent to which a person is successfully meeting the realistic demands, responsibilities, and expectations of varied roles. If the person is performing effectively, he or she is likely to feel personal satisfaction, self-esteem, accomplishment, and interpersonal harmony.

What Behavior Should Be Promoted?

Most people who care for, work with, or teach children have ideas about the ultimate goals of human development. The goals considered desirable are not only related to one's concept of development but also to one's concept of the "good life." We may call upon a theory to help promote the desirable behavior, but the goals of the behavior are part of the valuing process. What is good, right, or desirable is a value choice. We do not presume to be able to decide what are desirable values. Therefore, we will simply make reference to some important theoretical statements regarding developmental goals and comment on their relevance to the promotion and change of behavior.

For purposes of illustration and analysis, let us consider Maslow's (1954) statement regarding self-actualization as an ultimate goal of human development. He suggests that the self-actualized individual has the following characteristics:

1. An efficient and clear perception of reality

2. The capacity to accept self, others, and nature

3. Spontaneity, naturalness, and lack of artificiality in behavior

4. Capacity to problem center: interest in, and

acceptance of, the responsibility of solving problems outside oneself

5. Capacity for objective detachment and affinity for privacy and solitude

6. Autonomy and independence from the culture and environment for basic and extrinsic satisfactions

7. A richness of subjective experience

8. A deep feeling of identification and sympathy for humanity

9. Capacity to commit, invest, and enjoy deep interpersonal relationships

10. A democratic personality structure

11. Ability to make clear distinctions between right and wrong and to discriminate between means and ends

12. A philosophic and noninjurious sense of humor

13. Creativeness

Maslow's statement is thoughtful, and the goals are appealing; no doubt the world would be infinitely richer if all its inhabitants exhibited these characteristics. However, because they are general and not longitudinally charted, sequentially arranged, or defined in behavioral terms, they are difficult to translate into successive developmental steps. We need to know how each characteristic may be developed and the behavioral criteria to know when they have been attained.

Havighurst (1953) and Erikson (1963) arranged chronologically what they considered desirable developmental acquisitions. They specified a general time sequence for the emergence of each desired behavior acquisition, and Erikson suggested some facilitative conditions to promote the developmental stages. The contributions of these theorists are worthy of study or review and are recommended to the reader.

Assuming that the theoretical formulations mentioned provide some general orientation to ultimate developmental goals, the problem still remains of specifically defining the behavior one wishes to promote. Behavior cannot be promoted if it is only vaguely defined. For example, to promote "creativity" in a child, we must first define creativity and identify all those observable behaviors that are manifestations of it. This is simply a way of stating desired outcome behavior operationally. In this regard, Mager (1962) has suggested that an operationally stated outcome has two essential ingredients. First, the desirable terminal behavior must be stated in terms that are *overtly* observable and measurable. Second, behavioral outcomes must identify behaviors to be performed and the exact conditions in which they are expected to occur.

Let us return to the case of Jimmy Lander. The description of his behavior suggests that he is *excessively* argumentative, aggressive, and disobedient and is inclined to be somewhat self-centered. Since these behaviors appear to create considerable personal and family distress and tend to alienate his peers, they are desirable to change. However, to be certain that the behaviors are in fact problematic, we would ask the parents to describe exactly how they are expressed and in which situations. The parents would be asked to state what Jimmy *does* and *says* when he is behaving undesirably. If it is possible, we may want to observe Jimmy in the situations in which he exhibits the problem behavior. Once we have clearly specified the problem behavior, we are ready to state the target behavior.

Suppose we have learned from talking with the Landers that Jimmy expresses his disobedience by (1) failing to carry out parental requests, (2) calling his parents uncomplimentary names when he cannot persuade them to withdraw the request, and (3) procrastinating as long as two hours before performing some requests. Then, the desired target behavior might be stated as follows: *Jimmy will carry out all parental requests without arguing or name calling within ten minutes after the request is made.* In this statement the target behavior is described in observable actions. Disobedience is not subject to idiosyncratic interpretation; it is possible to determine whether the desirable behavior is or is not being performed. Also, the exact conditions for the target behavior are specified (e.g., all parental requests are to be carried out within ten minutes). Once the target behavior has been clearly specified, it is possible to develop strategies to promote it.

As the previous example shows, defining outcomes or desired behavior in operational terms has much to recommend it. If it is not done, one is never quite sure whether the desired learning outcome has been achieved. An excellent illustration of how learning outcomes can be stated operationally is contained in the work of Valett (1969). He has identified and operationally defined fifty-three basic learning abilities in six major areas of psychoeducational development: (1) gross motor development, (2) sensorimotor integration, (3) perceptual-motor skills, (4) language development, (5) conceptual skills, and (6) social skills. In each of these areas the basic learning abilities are clearly defined, the measurement of each ability is specified, and instructional activities to promote each ability are discussed.

Theoretical, Ethical, and Legal Questions Regarding Behavior Change

In a society where individuality, freedom of choice, and the right to self-determination and dissent are highly cherished values, it is not surprising that the development of effective and predictable behavior change methods would raise questions about the unethical manipulation and control of human behavior. Obviously, if psychological methods can be employed that produce predictable changes in behavior, and they are not used humanely, freedom of choice and self-determination may appear to be in jeopardy. Such concerns may further increase when the nature or form of change procedures seem to control behavior externally and bypass or overthrow the rational and/or thinking processes of individuals.

With the advent of behavior modification and the empirical reports of its efficacy, some feared that the day of the "robotized human" had arrived. Unfortunately, those who entertain these fears overemphasize the power of behavioral methods and appear not to recognize that all types of helping relationships involve some form of social influence, manipulation, and control (Bandura, 1969). Indeed, if therapeutic methods do not have the capacity to induce or produce appropriate change in self-defeating, dysfunctional, or maladaptive behavior, they can hardly be considered viable treatment methods. However, treatment methods can be misused, and the interest and welfare of clients must be humanely served.

Much of the concern regarding the use of behavior change procedures may be stated in three questions. Do some change or treatment procedures manipulate and control while others do not? To what degree is an individual's behavior under his or her conscious control, and to what extent can a person's behavior be changed without his or her knowledge and participation? What safeguards are necessary to protect people from unethical behavior-change agents? Let us consider each of these questions.

The Manipulation and Control Issue

As already noted, regardless of the change procedures used it is now accepted that all forms of social influence involve some type of manipulation and control. Over ten years ago, Skinner (1966) noted that child training and socialization, education, persuasion, and moral discourse are all forms of manipulation and control. All of these methods have as their aim the changing of a person's behavior in ways consistent with certain norms, values, and belief systems. In achieving these aims, various forms of negative manipulation and control may be used. However, these forms of control are acceptable only when they *partially* control a person's behavior. Typically, the encroachment on freedom objected to by those who protest manipulation and control is the result of severe or coercive forms of control. What is often being questioned by objectors is the *amount* of control. That is, if the form and amount of control do not completely restrict one's choices and independence of action, it is often viewed as acceptable manipulation.

Studies show that even the most humanistically inspired, client-centered therapists — selectively expressing empathy and warmth — implicitly control and/or affect the behavior of their clients. For example, Truax and Mitchell (1971) analyzed Carl Rogers's interactions with one of his schizophrenic patients. Specifically, Truax and Mitchell were interested in determining the extent to which Rogers selectively used empathy, nonpossessive warmth, and directiveness in promoting change in nine classes of patient behavior. Analysis of segments of eighty-five recorded therapeutic interviews revealed that Rogers did respond selectively by expressing higher levels of empathy, warmth, and directiveness. In the five classes of behavior to which he did respond selectively, the behavior changed significantly. Of the other four classes to which he did *not* respond selectively or reinforce, there was significant behavior change in only one. By reinforcing some patient behavior and not others, he therapeutically manipulated — whether intentionally or unintention-

ally — the patient's behavior toward goals that were presumed desirable.

Perhaps one of the major reasons why behavioral methods are sometimes viewed as undesirably manipulative is that these procedures are often not completely understood. As a result, several misconceptions have been perpetuated regarding their use, effects, and presumed misuse. One of the most frequently mentioned misconceptions is that behavior modification is essentially a form of bribery. Bribery is usually defined as giving something to another for performing an unethical act before the act has been executed. Behavior modification uses positive reinforcement to increase appropriate or adaptive behavior, not undesirable behavior, and reinforcement is administered after the target behavior is performed (Gambrill, 1977).

A second type of misconception regarding behavior modification is that people become dependent on the external incentives that are used to promote the desired behavior. Of course, it is possible that an individual can develop the expectation that continued reinforcement should be received for the performance of a particular behavior. However, the well-informed behavior therapist does use intrinsic reinforcers; and, once a target behavior has increased to an appropriate frequency or strength, an *intermittent reinforcement schedule*[2] is employed (Gambrill, 1977). Also, tangible reinforcers such as candy, pop, toys, etc. are eventually terminated, and social reinforcers (e.g., praise) are used to maintain the desired behavior. Social reinforcement is more "natural" and probably maintains a substantial part of everyone's behavior.

---

[2] An intermittent reinforcement schedule is a form of reinforcement in which a response is reinforced noncontinuously and somewhat unpredictably. These terms and other concepts introduced in this section will be explained in a later section.

A third misconception is that behavior modification makes excessive use of aversive or punitive procedures. This notion is incorrect since behavior modification is essentially the systematic application of behavioral (especially operant conditioning) principles (Gambrill, 1977). While negative and positive consequences may be used in combination, negative consequences are rarely used as the only type of intervention. The use of aversive procedures alone is difficult to defend on empirical or ethical grounds.

A final misconception and often mentioned objection is that the use of behavioral methods is presumed to imply "acceptance of a specific value system" (Gambrill, 1977, p. 18). Any developed technology, be it splitting an atom or using specific procedures to modify behavior, does not have inherent guidelines specifying its use. Any method can be used for humanitarian or unethical purposes. However, the unethical use of a method does not necessarily condemn the method; it simply reflects the morality of the user (Gambrill, 1977).

It should be apparent from our discussion that behavioral methods, like other types of change procedures, are a form of social influence. Although behavior modification may appear to be a dramatic departure from other change methods, the differences are not that marked. Indeed, if there are real differences, they are reflected in the care with which clients' problems are specified, the precision of the methods that are used to resolve them, and the evidence that is required to decide whether the change procedures are successful (London, 1975).

The Freedom-of-Choice Issue

Central to the freedom-of-choice issue is the question we raised earlier: To what extent is an individual's behavior under his or her conscious control? How this question is answered relates to one's view of the variables that are assumed to influence or determine human behavior. For example, some humanistic theories assume that human beings are capable of being aware of themselves and their responses. To the degree that this awareness is subjected to rational thought, one is able to make wise choices. Freudian theory, on the other hand, espouses the notion that much of human behavior is controlled by unconscious motivation. Therefore, freedom to choose or direct one's behavior is severely limited. Behavioral psychology conceives human behavior as largely a function of the overt and covert consequences that follow a response. To the degree that a person is aware of the contingencies or consequences that maintain his or her behavior, and the contingencies are not imposed coercively or without consent, a wide range of choice and self-direction is possible.

An analysis of the theoretical statements discussed above suggest that while a particular theoretical model may grant more or less freedom to choose, there are important qualifiers in each position. Processes are mentioned, the function and regulation of which are not precisely known. That is, since empirical data has not defined the degree to which a person is aware of his or her responses, the contingencies that influence such responses, or the individual's conscious regulation of responding, it is difficult to give an unequivocal answer to the freedom-of-choice question. What is presently known suggests that there are restrictions on a person's freedom of choice.

A person's capacity for self-direction and free choice is related to several personal and cultural variables. For example, a phobic individual may be restricted from participating in a number of activities, while another person with extreme self-critical tendencies may severely limit what he attempts or what he believes he is capable of doing. Second, a person may have certain behavioral or intellectual deficits that restrict future choices and available opportunities. Third, a person's social position permits some choices and limits others. Fourth, every society has norms, mores, and laws that restrict the rights and freedoms of its members. Therefore, while the selection of particular choices or behavioral options is itself a result of certain determinants, a person can exercise some control over the variables that regulate one's choices. Freedom of choice is clearly not an either-or proposition, but a matter of degree (Bandura, 1969).

Bandura (1969) has indicated that "all behavior is controlled and the operation of psychological laws cannot be suspended by romantic conceptions of human behavior" (p. 85). Any social influence or behavior change process essentially involves the replacement of "new controlling conditions" for those that have operated in the past. Perhaps the main criterion for determining the rightness of a social influence process is the extent to which it promotes freedom of choice (Kelman, 1965).

There is another important question that should be raised regarding the freedom-of-choice issue: To what extent can a person's behavior be changed without his knowledge and participation? If individuals are unaware of the contingencies influencing their behavior, and consequences are imposed without their consent or control, their behavior can be modified to some degree. However, behavioral psychologists recognize that the most rapid and permanent changes in behavior are attained when the client knows the reinforcing contingencies and actively participates in the treatment plan (Bandura, 1969). Behavioral psychologists consider it desirable to have client participation throughout all phases of the change process. Client and practitioner jointly determine the behavior change goals. Reinforcement contingencies that will be used to

modify client behavior are clearly specified, and throughout treatment clients are helped to learn and use behavior principles so they can wisely direct the course of their own lives (Gambrill, 1977).

Legal and Ethical Safeguards

With the development of more effective treatment procedures and the recognition that all types of helping relationships involve some form of influence, the need to protect the client's rights became more apparent. This need was further highlighted by reports that rights of inmates in certain institutional settings were being abused. For example, in some institutions inmates were being denied appropriate treatment; in others, patients were being deprived of certain basic human requirements (e.g., a bed or clothing) until particular tasks had been performed or a certain level of functioning had been achieved. In still other instances, institutional inmates were subjected to unwarranted aversive procedures or were required to perform institutional maintenance tasks that had few redeeming therapeutic benefits (Nay, 1976). What seems to have happened is that some poorly trained paraprofessionals misused behavioral principles and procedures and some professionally trained individuals seemed much too interested in imposing questionable behavior modification procedures on captive audiences.

The recognition of these abusive practices led the courts to take appropriate corrective action. For example, in the case of Donaldson vs. O'Connor (1976) the client's right to appropriate treatment was upheld. Donaldson had been committed to a Florida mental institution, but for religious reasons, he would not accept the first two therapies offered him. Following his refusal, he was offered little if any therapy for the next fifteen years. Donaldson pressed his case in court, demanding that he had a right to treatment or should be released. The federal court ruled that he had a constitutional right to treatment that would improve his mental condition (Gambrill, 1977).

In the Wyatt vs. Stickney (1972) decision the court ruled that institutionalized clients have the right to (1) adequate staff, (2) an individualized treatment program that specifies the standards by which achievement of treatment objectives will be judged, and (3) clearly defined criteria that determine release to a less restrictive environment or discharge from the institution. The court further ruled that all involuntary patient labor involving institutional maintenance and operation was prohibited. Patients may engage in voluntary institutional work of a therapeutic or nontherapeutic type only if they are compensated at a minimum wage. Institutional administrators were required to provide nutritionally adequate meals and comfortable living space and to allow patients to see visitors, wear their own clothing, have clothes washed, attend religious services, have appropriate exercise, and be outside at regular intervals. The right of a patient "to the least restrictive conditions necessary to achieve purposes of commitment" was also guaranteed (Wyatt vs. Stickney, 1972).

Recent court decisions have more clearly defined the conditions in which aversive procedures can be used in public institutions. Depending on the procedure used, or the length of time it is employed, some aversive methods may be interpreted as "cruel and unusual punishment." These forms of treatment are prohibited by the eighth amendment of the Constitution. Consequently, clients must be provided with due process (Nay, 1976). Due process must be provided (1) before institutional clients are moved from a less to a more restrictive environment (Williams vs. Robinson, 1970); (2) prior to being subjected to a special treatment program separated from the regular institutional environment (Clonce vs. Richardson,

1974); and (3) before severe punishment procedures are administered (Wyatt vs. Stickney, 1972).

The rights of juveniles have also been clarified in court decisions. For example, whenever actions are taken against juveniles that may be construed as depriving them of certain liberties, due process is required. In the Gault case (Re Gault, 1967), a fifteen-year-old adolescent boy was confined in an industrial school because he had made obscene phone calls. He contested the action by proposing that the juvenile hearing did not provide full due process rights. The state contended that since the action was taken for the benefit of the boy, due process was not required. The Supreme Court ruled that the preplacement hearing amounted to a "potential loss of liberty" and required that Gault receive complete due process rights. That is, he had the right to (1) know the charges against him, (2) be represented by counsel at a hearing, (3) question his accusers, (4) refuse to testify against himself, (5) have a transcript of the hearing, and (6) retain the right of appeal (Martin, 1975, p. 170).

To ensure that clients are not forced to accept any form of treatment a behavior change agent might impose, courts have ruled that client participation must be voluntary. That is, "informed consent" of the client must be secured before treatment is given. Several things are involved in obtaining client consent. First, prior to undertaking any assessment or treatment activity, the client's voluntary consent must be secured without duress. The client is assumed to have the capacity to consent when he or she has "a sound mind and sufficient age to be able to act in one's own behalf" (Martin, 1975, pp. 27–28). If a client does not meet these requirements for consent, the consent of a parent or guardian is required.

A second requirement of informed consent is that the client must have adequate information to make an intelligent decision and must have the capacity to understand the various alternatives presented. A client has the right to refuse any recommended procedure and to withdraw from participation in treatment at any time. The specific benefits, risks, and potential success of the treatment procedures must be fully presented. Ordinarily, this information should be presented in written and oral form in the native language of the client (Martin, 1975; Nay, 1976).

The third requirement of informed consent is that if the procedures to be used are not those that a majority of reasonable practitioners would employ with the client, the benefits should substantially outweigh the risks. Moreover, the treatment procedures must be rendered in a form that allows accurate evaluation (Martin, 1975; Nay, 1976).

There is one final area of judicial decisions that is especially relevant for helpers in public institutions. It involves the duty of employees to provide needed services appropriate to the problems and disabilities of children. These legal decisions are especially relevant because of the temptation to ignore the hard-to-handle cases to avoid legal entanglements. Court rulings handed down in Pennsylvania and New York have now established the precedent that appropriate services must be provided to all who are entitled to them. For example, retarded children must be provided with programs that will increase their functioning to a point that enables them to enter the mainstream of education. The treatment or educational program offered must not worsen and should preferably enhance the child's condition (Martin, 1975).

It should be apparent from the various legal decisions we have discussed that there is a growing need for a more definitive code of ethics for all people in the helping professions. Recognizing this need, both the psychological and legal professions have begun to formulate more specific guidelines for behavior change agents.

One of the more definitive statements appeared in *Law and Behavior* (1976). It is briefly summarized below:

1. The behavior change agent should make a behaviorally specific description of the client's problems and needs.

2. Intervention or treatment goals should also be stated in behavioral terms with a suggested timetable for their attainment. The goal statements should contain sequentially arranged intermediate goals so that progress toward ultimate objectives can be determined before treatment is concluded.

3. The intervention plan should be described in sufficient detail to provide the client with an adequate basis for giving his or her consent. Possible risks, benefits, and side effects of treatment should be clearly indicated.

4. The relationship between each goal and each element of the intervention plan should be carefully explained to the client. This requirement tends to ensure that the intervention plan has been formulated to meet each change objective and guards against the possibility of overtreatment.

5. The intervention plan should describe how individuals from the client's environment will be included. The plan should also describe how restraints or limits imposed on the client will be withdrawn as the client improves and how the client's significant others will be given increasingly more responsibility for treatment and/or rehabilitation of the client in the natural environment.

6. The person or persons responsible for conducting each element of the treatment plan should be clearly delineated. Such a

procedure tends to ensure some degree of accountability to the client and the client's immediate family.

7. The intervention plan should be reviewed and appropriately revised on a monthly basis. Periodic reviews tend to make the plan relevant and are more likely to ensure positive treatment effects.

Although these recommendations were formulated as guidelines for professionals working with clients in public institutions, they might well be used by every practitioner in any institution, school, clinic, or private setting.

Public Law 94-142, the Education for All Handicapped Children Act of 1975, now mandates many of the suggested guidelines described above. The act

. . . assures all handicapped children (ages 3 to 21) have available to them . . . a free public education which emphasizes special education and related services designed to meet their unique needs, to assure that the *rights of handicapped children and their parents or guardians are protected,* to assist States and localities to provide for the education of all handicapped children, and to assess and assure the effectiveness of efforts to educate handicapped children (PL 94-142, p. 3).

PL 94-142 further mandates that an individualized educational program be developed by a qualified local educational agency that is specifically designed to meet the unique needs of the child. The individualized educational program must include (1) an indication of the child's present level of educational performance; (2) a "statement of annual goals, including short-term instructional objectives" (p. 4); (3) the specific type of services to be provided and the extent of the child's participation in the regular school program; (4) a projected date of the beginning of the program and the estimated length of time services will be provided; and (5)

proper evaluation of the child's progress each year to determine whether instructional objectives are being realized.

As is apparent from our brief description, PL 94-142 is a legislative landmark in special education. It not only requires but enables public schools to provide comprehensive educational programs for a portion of the population that has been seriously neglected and underserved.

Basic Concepts and Definitions

We have previously discussed behavior acquisitions that are important to enhance, ways of thinking about and identifying behavior that may be desirable to change, and some theoretical, ethical, and legal questions relating to the manipulation and control of behavior. It is appropriate, therefore, to discuss some terms that we will use as central concepts. In a subsequent section, the concepts will be more completely examined.

Respondent Behavior

A person's behavior may be classified into two categories: *respondent* (unlearned) and *operant* (learned) behavior. Respondent behavior is sometimes thought of as being reflexive since it occurs automatically in response to a specific stimulus. The shedding of tears in response to peeling onions, the knee jerk in response to a tap on the patellar tendon, and the contraction of the pupil of the eye in response to changes in light intensity are all examples of respondent behavior. Respondent behavior is always elicited automatically by a specific stimulus; it is not under voluntary control and appears when a specific stimulus condition is present. The capacity for this type of response is part of the innate equipment of the human organism (Keller, 1969; Reese, 1966). The role that respondent behavior and conditioning assumes in influencing behavior, the ways in which respondent conditioning takes place, and its importance in human affairs will be discussed more fully later.

Operant Behavior

Operant behavior, in contrast to respondent behavior, is under voluntary control. It is influenced and controlled by events or consequences that follow its occurrence. Operant behavior includes all behavior that "operates on," changes, or affects the outside environment (Keller, 1969). Almost any movement under the voluntary control of an individual may be appropriately classified as operant behavior. Picking up and bouncing a ball, writing a letter to a friend, and conversing with an associate are examples of such behavior.

Because higher animals, including man, are much less instinct controlled, they exhibit more emitted (operant) behavior than elicited (respondent) behavior (Cohen, 1969). Consequently, operant behavior and operant conditioning assume a more decisive role in the manipulation and control of human behavior, and we shall give more complete attention to it.

Operant behavior is determined by the conditions or consequences that follow it. Consequences of a response that increase the probability of its occurrence are referred to as *reinforcers* (Keller, 1969). A reinforcer may be something edible, a smile, a reassuring word, or a friendly pat on the back—anything that increases the probability that the response it follows will be emitted again. The response is strengthened by an increase in the frequency of its appearance. And, when the consequences that follow a response have increased the frequency of that response, conditioning has occurred. The strength of a response decreases when reinforcement is terminated. If rein-

forcement is completely withdrawn for a period of time, the response rate tends to return to the preconditioned rate or *operant level*. The decrease in response strength is referred to as *extinction* (Reese, 1966).

Positive and Negative Reinforcement Reinforcers are often classified as either positive or negative according to the state of the organism after they have been employed. Hence, a positive reinforcer is sometimes described as a type of rewarding stimulus that leads to comfort and a desire to repeat the response. However, some behavioral scientists object to the use of terms such as "comfort" or "desire" because they are subjective states which must be inferred and cannot be precisely measured.

Operationally defined, a *positive reinforcer* is any stimulus that increases the probability of the response it follows. A *negative reinforcer* may be defined as any stimulus which, by its *removal*, increases the probability of the response that follows it (Keller, 1969).

In positive reinforcement the response is strengthened by the *addition of something* that follows its occurrence. Positive reinforcers may be grouped into three general categories: (1) social reinforcers, (2) tokens and tangible reinforcers, and (3) intrinsic reinforcers. Praise, approval, and affection are examples of *social reinforcers*. *Tangible reinforcers* refer to material items that can be experienced with the senses, that is, eaten, touched, seen, played with, etc. Food, candy, toys, and games are all examples of tangible reinforcers. *Tokens* may assume the form of check marks, points, plastic strips, or just about anything that can be exchanged for tangible reinforcers or reinforcing events. *Intrinsic reinforcers* refer to satisfactions inherent in performing an activity itself. These satisfactions typically involve curiosity, novelty, and pride resulting from achievement.

In negative reinforcement response probability is increased because something is *removed* or withdrawn (Skinner, 1953). The removal or withdrawal of almost any aversive stimulus after a response to it, typically acts as a negative reinforcer. Suppose, for example, that you are listening to the radio, and it suddenly emits a long wave of loud, continuing static. You reach up and turn off the radio. This act terminates the noise (aversive stimulus) and increases your comfort; you have been negatively reinforced.

Let us consider another example. Suppose you have just placed your four-year-old child in her room for some misbehavior. After she is isolated in her room, she begins to cry. You respond to the crying by saying: "When you stop crying, I will let you come out of the room." If you follow through immediately upon the cessation of the crying and allow the child to come out of the room, you have employed negative reinforcement. The response "to not cry" has been strengthened because you have removed an aversive condition (being confined in a room). We should note, however, that these acts may not have any desirable effects on the earlier misbehavior. To enable you to do something to strengthen appropriate behavior, the child must make the desirable response before positive reinforcement is administered.

Children may perform many aversive behaviors that lead to negative reinforcement of undesirable behavior. Underachievers and maladjusted children will frequently exhibit an "I can't" cry or have a temper tantrum as a way of escaping performance demands. If the teacher withdraws the performance demand because it prompts the aversive behavior, the behavior becomes negatively reinforced and the next time the child is faced with an unpleasant learning task he will be prone to exhibit the same behavior.

It can be seen, then, that negative reinforcement produces its influence by removing a host of aversive stimuli. That is, we act to terminate an aversive stimulus or we act to remove it by performing an avoidance or escape response. When we act to remove or terminate a loud noise, a bright light, or even a disturbing thought, negative reinforcement is operating. Under certain conditions, the avoidance of punishment may be negatively reinforcing. If a response results in termination of or avoidance of punishment, that response is strengthened. However, as Travers (1977) has indicated, the use of punishment *reduces* response frequency or strength by the application of an aversive stimulus. Moreover, we should note that the effects of punishment are not predictable.

Positive reinforcement, negative reinforcement, and punishment are all used in operant conditioning. However, for obvious reasons, positive reinforcement is used most often to promote desirable behavior. Negative reinforcement and punishment are used to promote and extinguish certain forms of behavior.

The distinctions that are made from a behavioral point of view among positive reinforcement, negative reinforcement, and punishment are illustrated in Table 1. This table should clarify the differences, as well as introduce some possible uses of positive and negative reinforcement. In Chapter 2 the use of reinforcement in changing behavior will be discussed at greater length.

Primary and Secondary Reinforcement Reinforcers may be further classified as primary or secondary. *Primary reinforcers* are stimuli that have biological significance and/or satisfy a physiological need. Thus, water, food, and sexual release may be designated primary reinforcers. *Secondary* or *conditioned reinforcers* refer to stimuli that have *acquired* reinforcement properties by being associated or paired with primary reinforcers or stimuli that have established power. The types of stimuli that may function as secondary reinforcers are incalculable since *any stimulus that is paired with and precedes a primary reinforcer may acquire such properties.* Consequently, a sound, light, word, or smile may all function as secondary reinforc-ers. The stimuli that do, in fact, acquire second-ary reinforcement properties are related to a person's life history (Skinner, 1953; Lundin, 1974; Travers, 1977).

Stimuli that have been paired with *more than one* primary reinforcer acquire the attri-butes of *generalized reinforcers*. These are stimuli that have reinforcement properties re-gardless of the conditions operative at the time. A good example of a generalized reinforcer is money. It acquires a generalized reinforcement property when it is used to obtain and satisfy primary needs. Further, even apart from oper-ative primary need (or, in this case, financial condition), money may continue to have rein-forcement property. For example, it has been demonstrated that money has reinforcement

Table 1   Illustration of Positive Reinforcement, Negative Reinforcement, and Punishment

Behavior Desired	Verbal Prompting Statement	Method of Reinforcement	Type of Reinforcement
1. Completion of homework	"Complete your homework and I'll give you a quarter."	Reward presented	Positive
2. Completion of homework	"If you don't do your homework, you will lose your allowance."	Reward withdrawn	Punishment
3. Completion of homework	"Do your homework and you can leave your room."	Punishment withdrawn (aversive condition terminated)	Negative
4. Completion of homework	"If you don't complete your homework, I will spank you."	Punishment presented	Punishment
5. Termination of thumb-sucking	"If you don't suck your thumb, I will give you a toy truck."	Reward presented	Positive
6. Termination of thumb-sucking	"If you suck your thumb, I will take away your toy truck."	Reward withdrawn	Punishment
7. Termination of thumb-sucking	"If you don't suck your thumb, you may leave your room."	Punishment withdrawn	Negative
8. Termination of thumb-sucking	"If you suck your thumb, I will spank you."	Punishment presented	Punishment

Adapted from J. Cohen, *Operant Behavior and Operant Conditioning*, © Rand McNally, Chicago, 1969, with permission.

strength even if the amount received has no economic significance to the person. Rich people sometimes work hard to make more money even though they have no economic need for it.

Other stimuli may also function as generalized reinforcers, since they have frequently been paired with more than one primary reinforcer. Particularly significant stimuli of this type are attention, approval, and affection. Each of these stimulus conditions appears to acquire these reinforcement properties by its position as prelude to satisfaction of a physiological need. For example, in a typical feeding situation, attentive and/or affectionate behaviors are directed by the mother toward the child before feeding. The giving of attention and affection prior to the satisfaction of many other infant needs probably takes place thousands of times in the early months of the child's life. Consequently, these generalized reinforcers acquire great strength that is maintained in subsequent years because of their constant association with primary-need gratification.

With the exception of primary reinforcers, stimulus conditions have no inherent capacity to reinforce. The capacity to reinforce is acquired. Therefore, one cannot assume that certain stimulus conditions will automatically reinforce a person's behavior. The only sure way of finding out is to study the individual's past history carefully and observe those stimulus conditions that increase the response rate.

Self and Covert Reinforcement Up to this point we have discussed reinforcement that is administered externally by others. However, there are forms of reinforcement that operate internally and are self-administered.

Images, thoughts, and recalled experiences often have positive and negative qualities associated with them. When we recall an image, thought, or experience that has a positive con-

notation, we are likely to make approach responses in closely related situations. In fact, just thinking about a positive experience might lead us to involve ourselves in the same experience again. On the other hand, if an image or thought has negative connotations, we tend to avoid the thought and the situation to which it refers. Therefore, if thoughts can invoke positive and negative feelings and lead to approach and avoidance responses, it may be said that thoughts, images, and symbols have positive and negative reinforcement properties.

Individuals are constantly evaluating their moment-to-moment performance, and their evaluations appear to influence the occurrence of certain behavior. For example, when a person performs inappropriately or unsuccessfully, he is prone to evaluate his behavior in negative terms. Similarly, when his behavior meets performance requirements, he is inclined to use positive terms to evaluate his performance and himself. The process by which individuals evaluate their behavior in positive or negative terms and permit or restrict themselves from accepting certain rewards is referred to as *covert* or *self-reinforcement*. As we have noted, these self-administered reinforcements appear to increase or inhibit the performance of certain behavior. Bandura (1969) has suggested that self-administered reinforcement may be *more* influential in determining some types of behavior than externally administered reinforcement.

Self-reinforcing processes are established by adopting the standards of significant socializing agents. For example, if parents consistently reinforce a child for high standards of performance, the child is likely to reinforce himself only when the high standards have been achieved. If the child frequently fails in meeting the high achievement standards, he will tend to evaluate his performance and himself very negatively; that is, he will tend to use self-critical and devaluing terms. He may think: "I do not deserve a reward, because my performance or behavior is very bad." On the other hand, the less stringent the parents' performance or behavior standards, the more likely the child is to meet them and reinforce himself positively for his behavior. Thus, a child's self-esteem may be regulated by adopting standards that have been reinforced and modeled by adults. Once a self-monitored reinforcement system has been established, it may be highly resistant to change. Bandura (1969) has noted that adopted standards of self-evaluation tend to be maintained by associating with others that hold similar standards, for the reference group members reinforce and tend to maintain the self-prescribed standards.

Individuals who adopt liberal, or frequent, self-reinforcement standards are inclined to more positive self-evaluative statements. Individuals who adopt high standards that are difficult to attain may make exorbitant self-demands, express feelings of worthlessness, and exhibit considerable depression. Extreme cases of self-punishment may be similarly explained.

The experiences of most people readily confirm that thoughts and images have positive or aversive qualities. Therefore, they should have the capacity to promote or inhibit certain overt behavior. Indeed, Cautela (1970) has demonstrated that a reinforcing stimulus presented in imagination functions in a manner similar to externally presented reinforcing stimuli. He has systematically utilized such inner mental experience to modify homosexual and avoidance (inhibitions or phobias) behavior.

Cautela's procedures involve a series of steps. First, reinforcing stimuli (both overt and covert) are identified by having a client complete the *Reinforcement Survey Schedule.* Then, deficient approach behaviors and nonadaptive avoidance behaviors are specified. If a deficient approach behavior is identified as the target behavior, the client is asked to imagine a situation involving the performance of the approach behavior. Suppose, for instance,

that an adolescent boy would like to date girls but is unable to ask a girl for a date. In therapy, Cautela would likely instruct his client in the following way:

"Close your eyes and relax. I am going to describe a scene. When the scene is clearly in your imagination, I will ask you to raise your right index finger. I will then say to you 'reinforcement.' When I say 'reinforcement,' imagine the scene we practiced before."

(The latter reinforcement scene has been previously invoked in practice sessions. The therapist then begins systematic covert reinforcement to encourage step-by-step the desirable approach behavior.)

"Imagine you are home. It is Saturday and you are thinking about Debbie. You would like to ask her for a date. When you have the scene clearly in mind, raise your right index finger." [The therapist then says, "Reinforcement."] *"Was the delivery of the reinforcement clear? . . . Good, let's proceed. You decide to call Debbie. You go to the phone and dial her number. Raise your right index finger when this is clear."* [The therapist then says, "Reinforcement."][3]

The client is guided through the entire sequence until he has executed in imagination the desired approach behavior. When the therapist says "reinforcement," the client imagines a scene that is positively reinforcing to him. For example, the therapist might say: "Imagine yourself on the beach and the breeze is blowing gently off the lake. You are lying in the sand, drinking a beer. You feel great. You say to yourself, 'Life is wonderful.'" The entire sequence may be practiced three or four times in the therapy session, and then the client is asked to practice several more times at home before the

---

[3] Adapted from J. R. Cautela, "Covert reinforcement," *Behavior Therapy,* 1970, *1,* 33–50.

actual behavior is performed. By successively approximating the desired approach behavior and systematically using covert reinforcement at each step, the client is subsequently able to perform the behavior in the actual situation.

The effectiveness of covert reinforcement in changing the self-concepts of emotionally disturbed children was demonstrated in an experiment conducted by Krop, Calhoon, and Verrier (1971). The children were diagnosed as disturbed and resided in a state hospital. One group of disturbed children was overtly reinforced (with tokens and gumdrops) for making responses associated with a positive self-concept. A second group was given covert reinforcement when they performed responses associated with a positive self-concept. A third group was given no reinforcement for exhibiting positive self-concept responses. Comparisons of treatments and groups revealed that only the covert reinforcement treatment group made significant changes in self-concept. Apparently, covert reinforcement may prove more potent than externally administered reinforcement in positively modifying certain types of behavior.

Generalization   Behavior that is learned in one stimulus situation tends to be expressed in other situations. Consider, for example, a very young child who has learned to fear the neighbor's dog. This fear is not likely to be restricted to the neighbor's dog but directed to many, if not all, dogs. As a matter of fact, the fear of the neighbor's dog may spread to toy dogs. The spreading or transfer of a learned response to one stimulus (or stimulus complex) to other similar stimuli is called *generalization*. The more similar the two stimulus situations, the more likely the response is to generalize.

The process of generalization in learning does provide some dividends, but it may be advantageous or disadvantageous depending on the situation. In the example described above, the generalization of the child's fear of the neighbor's dog greatly restricts the child's desire to explore the environment. To the extent that the fear generalizes to many similar objects and situations, the child is likely to be very inhibited in exploration of unfamiliar situations.

Generalization is also advantageous. Behavior learned in one situation may be readily employed in other similar situations in which it is appropriate. Consequently, in each new situation, one does not have to resort completely to trial and error to know how to behave. Once a child has learned to relate to a teacher in an acceptable manner, he may employ the same manner of relating to other teachers and be assured that his behavior is acceptable.

Discrimination and Differential Reinforcement   There are occasions when overgeneralization leads to difficulty. For example, the student who responds to a strict teacher in the same manner that he responds to a permissive one is likely to find his behavior inappropriate. If he is to spare himself some discomfort, he will have to learn to *discriminate* between the expectations of each and behave accordingly.

We learn to make appropriate discriminations when behavior is reinforced in the presence of one stimulus situation and is not reinforced in another. Thus, the teacher with strict discipline noted above may help the child behave according to her expectations that no one talk without permission by reinforcing the pupil for remaining quiet when it is desired and reinforcing him for asking permission before he talks. In this way, through the use of *differential reinforcement*, the child soon learns to make appropriate discriminations of the situations in which talking is permitted. However, if the teacher is not consistent in enforcing her own rule of no talking without permission, the discrimination is more difficult for a pupil to learn.

When an individual has learned to perform a particular response in the presence of specific stimulus conditions, *stimulus control* is demonstrated. That is, when a person learns to make a specific response only when a particular stimulus is present, the presence of that stimulus (usually referred to as a *discriminative stimulus* or S^D) tends to prompt or prime that response. To behave efficiently, literally thousands of such stimulus-response associations must be learned.

Although differential reinforcement is essential in promoting stimulus control, other procedures may be required to establish it. For example, suppose a young child is having difficulty learning to recognize two letters, *b* and *d*. Since the usual verbal instruction has failed to help the child recognize the two letters, you might begin by asking the child to watch you write each of the two letters as you comment on the distinctive characteristics of each. You might say:

"Both the b *and the* d *are made by drawing two straight lines [demonstrating by drawing two straight lines] and a part circle or hump. Notice that the* b *has a hump on the right side of the straight line and the* d *has a hump to the left of the straight line [drawing the humps as you instruct]. Now you might think of the straight line as a skinny person standing up [pointing]. The* b-person *is pushing a ball [pointing to the partial circle] and the* d-person *is pulling a ball [pointing].*

"Now let's see if you can do it. I will help you by guiding your hand as you make each letter. To make a b *we must first draw a straight line [moving the child's hand down in a vertical direction]. Very good. Now, let's put a hump on the right side [moving the child's hand to make a partial circle so it is touching the straight line]. That's fine. Now let's make the letter* d."

Similar instructions and demonstrations are used in guiding the child's hand in making a *d*. When the *b* and *d* have been executed, the child is asked to make each letter by herself. As the child begins the *b* you might instruct her by reminding her to begin by drawing a straight

line and putting a hump on the right side so the *b-person* can push the ball. *Prompts* (physical or verbal clues) are given as required, and each correctly executed movement is reinforced. As each letter is formed correctly, and the child identifies the letters by name, reinforcement is given. Subsequently, as the child's success in naming each correctly drawn letter increases, the prompts and drawing procedures are gradually decreased or *faded*, and the child is asked to identify each letter on visual presentation only.

In the above example, several procedures have been used to facilitate stimulus control. First, *modeling* and *verbal instructions* were used to focus the child's attention on the distinctive features of each letter. Modeling is a form of demonstration that is useful in helping a person learn responses not in his or her behavioral repertoire. Pointing out the distinctive cues eliminates unnecessary trial and error and draws attention to topographical features that are essential to make correct discriminations. Second, to ensure that the child made the correct movements initially, *guided participation* was used. Third, to further direct or guide responding, *verbal prompts* (e.g., humps on the right or left side) were used. Fourth, to help the child associate the present learning task with previous learning, an analogy was used (e.g., the *b-person* pushing the ball). Fifth, differential reinforcement was used to help the child make appropriate stimulus-response associations. Finally, prompts were gradually decreased as each letter was correctly recognized on visual presentation.

These and other concepts and procedures can be further illustrated by the use of a case example. Ray, an eight-year-old boy, was referred to one of the authors because of his inability to read. In three years of school attendance, he had not learned any sight words and was unable to recognize a single letter of the alphabet. Although he received additional teacher instruction and assistance, these efforts did not achieve the desired results. To get a better understanding of Ray's difficulties and to identify possible causes for Ray's failure, a psychological evaluation was done. The evaluation revealed that he had a Wechsler I.Q. of 89, a visual problem which had recently been corrected by prescriptive eyeglasses, and a history of considerable family conflict. Ray appeared to be concerned about the stresses in the family and was resistant to, and poorly motivated in, most learning activities. Because Ray responded so unproductively to remedial instruction, his teachers thought he might have a psychological block.

Probably, a number of variables together produced the reading problem. When he was first introduced to formal reading, Ray had a visual problem which was not discovered until he was seven years old. His intellectual development was proceeding at a slow rate. The stresses and strains in the family appeared to make it difficult for him to concentrate and give his undivided attention to learning. No doubt, Ray felt a sense of defeat because his attempts to read had not been successful. However, with the correction of his visual difficulty (which had impaired Ray's visual-perceptual functioning), it was assumed that he could learn to read if the proper learning conditions were established.

A series of individualized instructional sessions were arranged. When Ray arrived for the first session, the author indicated that he was aware of his difficulty in learning to read. Ray was asked if he would like some assistance in learning to read. Although his response was not enthusiastic, he reluctantly agreed to come in for assistance. Ray was then asked to think of a word he would like to learn. After a moment's reflection, he said "baby." The author took out a sheet of lined paper and asked the boy to watch him write the word. He was immediately given two M & M's for paying attention while the word was written. He was then told that he would be helped to write the word *baby*. His hand was guided in forming each letter until the

word was written. Upon completion of the task, he received two more M & M's. Ray was then asked to look at the model word the author had written and write it himself. His reproduction was correct except for the last letter. Because he wrote the word incorrectly, he was not reinforced. Instead, he was asked to compare his word with the model word to see if he could determine where he had erred. He was able to discover his error. He was reinforced with two more M & M's and praised for his work. Once again, he was asked to write the word *baby* unassisted. He did so correctly, and received two more M & M's and an exuberant "terrific" from the examiner. This procedure was continued until he was able to write and recognize three words.

In subsequent sessions similar procedures were used, but several modifications were introduced. As Ray made correct writing or word-recognition responses, points, pennies, and praise were paired with M & M's. After the fifth session, the following modifications in procedure were introduced:

1. At the end of each session, small assignments were given. The words Ray had practiced in the session were written on cards, and he was asked to study and remember them. In the following session, he was given a penny for each word he could recognize by sight.

2. Points could be exchanged for inexpensive toys which Ray desired.

3. Words selected for study were ones Ray wanted to learn and words from the Dolch Basic Sight Vocabulary list.

4. To ensure that the words studied became sight words, all were periodically reviewed. Words that Ray recognized correctly on presentation earned him a penny. Words he did not recognize instantly were further

studied, and correct responses were reinforced with points and praise.

5. The sessions were divided into a word study period and a play therapy period. The word study period always occurred at the beginning of each session, followed by the play therapy session.

6. Ray's regular classroom teacher and his special reading teacher were asked to present not more than one new word a day and to review frequently the words previously taught. The reinforcers were praise and points, which could be exchanged for privileges in the classroom and for various activities around the school.

7. When Ray had difficulty learning a word, in addition to following the writing procedure previously mentioned, the author "wrote" the word on Ray's back and in the palm of his hand. After these three different methods were presented and he recognized the word, he was reinforced.

8. As Ray began to acquire a stable sight vocabulary, the schedule of reinforcement was changed. Instead of reinforcing each correct learning trial, *variable reinforcement* was used. That is, instead of reinforcing every correct response, every third, eighth, or thirteenth response was reinforced.

During the play therapy sessions, Ray was given the opportunity to select the activities. Although he liked hand-puppet play and drawing, he often selected the dart game, which allowed him the opportunity to express his feelings about competition and failure, as well as giving him the chance to practice eye-hand coordination. During these activities, the therapist reinforced (1) his successes in throwing the darts and winning the games, (2) his acceptance of occasional losses, and (3) his positive statements about himself and his performance. On the occasions when Ray discussed his concerns and conflicts with his family, the therapist helped him clarify them and proposed and encouraged constructive solutions.

Ray made steady progress. In a period of twelve weeks he mastered about 150 sight words and read two primers. Even Ray's classmates were surprised and spontaneously praised him when he read orally. His participation in peer activities increased considerably. His parents reported a change in his attitude at home. His withdrawn, resistant behavior was replaced by more spontaneity in the sharing of his concerns and in his activities. Apparently, Ray's sense of frustration and incapacity changed to a belief in his capacity to learn.

Ray's case is instructive because a number of important concepts and principles were used in helping him. When the tutor-therapist first wrote the word *baby,* and Ray was asked to match or reproduce the word in writing, *modeling* was being used. (As will be noted in a subsequent chapter, it is an effective procedure when there is some question about the learner's ability to perform a specific behavior.)

Each correct modeled response was strengthened initially by the use of *primary reinforcers* (M & M's). Later, when praise, points, and pennies preceded the M & M's, these stimuli began to acquire reinforcement properties and became *conditioned reinforcers*.

Ray was taught to make appropriate *discriminations* in two ways. First, when he made an error in writing a word, he was instructed to find the error by comparing his written word with the model word. If he had difficulty discovering his error, the therapist *prompted* him by suggesting a procedure for finding it. Once he had discriminated the difference between his word and the model word, he was asked to verbalize the difference. When the difference was correctly articulated, he was reinforced for making the appropriate discrimination. In other words, he was *differentially reinforced,* that is, reinforced for correct discriminations and not reinforced for incorrect discriminations. Second, Ray was asked to identify a spoken word from among a list of three or four printed words. When he identified the spoken word from the list, he was reinforced. Also, when Ray was able to look at a printed word and verbalize it, the configurational cues became *discriminative stimuli.* A discriminative stimulus is a stimulus with which an operant response has become associated as a result of reinforcement. The discriminative stimulus does not elicit or cause the operant response. Rather, when the stimulus is present, it serves as a cue and triggers the response. Discriminative stimuli prime the organism to respond or not respond, depending upon the presentation or withholding of reinforcement (Cohen, 1969).

Other principles were used in working with Ray. Initially, Ray was reinforced for each correct response, and these responses were approximations of reading, the ultimate behavior change objective. The instruction was presented in small steps to ensure that he could successfully perform the behavior. As he learned to recognize words by sight, the objectives for each instructional period were increased. Also, as we mentioned, his initial learning trials were reinforced *continuously.* As he became more successful, reinforcement was *varied;* that is, he did not receive reinforcement for each correct trial, but rather for every third, eighth, or thirteenth correct response. *Variable reinforcement* was used to increase the durability of the reinforced behavior. Variable reinforcement makes the behavior resistant to extinction because the subject never knows when he will be reinforced. He will continue to respond for a long time in an anticipation of the reinforcement.

The concepts and principles that were used and illustrated in Ray's case will be elaborated further in Chapters 2 and 3. However, before we conclude this chapter we wish to state an assumption implicit in the material that follows: The behavior that people exhibit, be it adaptive or nonadaptive, is primarily a product of learning. Adaptive behavior can be systematically promoted, and nonadaptive behavior can be unlearned when appropriate conditions are properly implemented. It is assumed that human behavior is a function of lawful relationships. And, although all of the laws which govern human behavior have not been discovered, many learning-theory-based principles have now been demonstrated to have utility in altering human behavior (Dollard and Miller, 1950; Skinner, 1953; Grunbaum, 1966).

In our discussion of principles and methods for promoting or changing behavior it may appear that we are segmenting the child and losing sight of him as a unified whole. This is not our intention. We recognize that we work with children who exhibit certain problems or deficiencies. The *child* is primary; the problem is secondary. No technique or method should be used that does not promote the child's welfare.

Most of the principles we will discuss are laboratory derived, but their applications in promoting behavior change are based primarily on their use with human subjects reported in the literature. The authors have used many of these principles in their own work with children and adolescents. As a result, we are cautiously optimistic and hope that future research and clinical application will extend and further validate their utility.

Summary

1. The assumptions and theories that we use to explain behavior influence what we do to promote and change it. Theories vary regarding the nature of human beings, the explanatory concepts used, the type of data on which they are based, and their utility in promoting behavior

change. Theoretical concepts that relate stimulus-response-consequence relationships appear to be most useful in predictably modifying behavior.

2.   Speculations regarding inner psychological processes as determinants of behavior have been of limited value. Constructs such as will, need, or motive are impossible to observe, difficult to measure, and cannot be systematically related to overt behavior.

3.   What is considered nonadaptive or deviant is related to one's values and theoretical orientation. However, the decision to modify a child's behavior might appropriately be based on three criteria: (a) the nonadaptive behavior is excessive and occurs with high frequency, (b) the continuance of the behavior will hurt the child and/or other people, and (c) the continuance of the nonadaptive behavior will impede subsequent adaptation and healthy development of the child.

4.   All types of helping relationships involve some form of social influence, manipulation, and control. To avoid unwarranted influence and manipulation of clients, behavior change agents should (a) recognize clients' rights and involve them in the definition and determination of behavior change goals, (b) clearly specify and explain the procedures that will be used to promote the behavior change goals, (c) describe the apparent benefits and risks involved in the treatment procedures used, (d) obtain informed consent from the client and/or guardian, and (e) periodically evaluate progress to determine whether change goals are being achieved and client interests are being humanely served.

5.   It is difficult to promote or modify behavior until the behavior to be changed is stated in operational terms. An operationally defined change objective (a) is stated in terms that are observable and measurable and (b) specifies the behaviors to be performed and the exact conditions in which they are expected to occur.

6.   Two types of learning are basic to the acquisition of behavior: respondent and operant conditioning. Respondent behavior occurs automatically in response to a specific stimulus and is usually not under voluntary control. Operant behavior is under voluntary control and is a function of the consequences that follow its occurrence.

7.   Stimuli that increase response probability or strength are known as reinforcers. Positive reinforcers generally increase approach behavior; negative reinforcers promote avoidance and escape behaviors. Secondary reinforcers (praise, approval) and generalized reinforcers (attention, affection) acquire the reinforcement property by being paired with primary reinforcers (food, drink, sex). All of the above types of reinforcers are used to maintain and modify behavior.

8.   Self-reinforcement is a process by which individuals evaluate their behavior positively or negatively and permit or restrict themselves from receiving certain rewarding events. It has been shown to be intimately involved with the development and maintenance of certain forms of depressive and self-injurious behavior. Under some circumstances, self-reinforcement may be more influential in determining behavior than external reinforcement.

9.   Fantasies and imagery of previous experiences may have positive or negative qualities. Such mental experiences have been demonstrated to maintain, increase, or decrease certain types of overt behavior. Covert reinforcement, the use of imagery to increase or decrease responses, has been used successfully to modify overt approach and avoidance behaviors.

10.   Differential reinforcement is used to help the learner discriminate and perform appropri-

ate responses. This is done by selectively reinforcing the desired response and omitting reinforcement when an inappropriate response is made. When a person learns to make a particular response in the presence of a specific stimulus, stimulus control has been established. A response learned in one situation tends to generalize or transfer to other similar stimulus situations. Generalization is advantageous in that one need not learn a different response to each new situation. It may be disadvantageous when a fear response overgeneralizes, leading to avoidance of situations that are not inherently dangerous.

Chapter Two

Methods for Promoting Behavior Change: Strengthening Appropriate Behavior

Historically, two basic propositions have served as theoretical cornerstones for promoting behavior change—that is, behavior is learned for two reasons. First, behavior is learned in order to terminate a condition that is noxious, distressing, or painful. Second, behavior is learned in order to induce positive sensations or lead to some satisfying state (Ford and Urban, 1963).

When we say that behavior is learned in order to terminate conditions that are noxious or distressing, we mean that responses are performed that reduce anxiety or enable us to avoid physical or psychological pain. There are many examples of this in everyday life: A burnt child avoids a hot stove; a child with a hypercritical parent stops "hearing" the parent; a soldier rapidly forgets (suppresses or represses) a terrifying combat experience.

The second proposition, that behavior is learned in order to induce positive sensations, satisfaction, or pleasure, is a familiar notion, since it is involved in reinforcement. It is simply another way of indicating that we learn behavior that is positively reinforced.

Each of these principles will be illustrated and applied in a variety of ways in the material that follows. To do this, we will want to discuss again respondent and operant conditioning as they apply to behavior change. Other principles of learning used to enhance and change behavior will also be discussed. At appropriate points

practical applications will be made and studies reported that illustrate the concepts, principles, and procedures.

Respondent Conditioning

Respondent behavior, we indicated, refers to behavior (involuntary muscle reactions and glandular activity) elicited automatically by a particular stimulus. Respondent conditioning utilizes these stimulus-response relationships by greatly extending the range of stimuli that will elicit a particular response.

Respondent conditioning involves two types of stimuli. One stimulus is originally neutral—that is, not sufficient to elicit the involuntary response until learning has taken place. It is referred to as the *conditioned stimulus*. The other stimulus, which is adequate to automatically elicit the response, is referred to as the *unconditioned stimulus;* learning does *not* have to take place before a response is elicited by it. The response is designated in two ways: (1) prior to conditioning it is appropriately called the *unconditioned response;* and (2) once conditioning has taken place, it is called the *conditioned response* (Gladstone, 1967).

As is well known, Pavlov (1927) was the first to report systematically on classical (respondent) conditioning. He discovered that by presenting a bell followed by food a salivary response was elicited in a dog. After repeated pairings of the two stimuli, the bell alone elicited salivation. By this experimentation, he demonstrated that a neutral stimulus (bell), not originally adequate to elicit a specific response (salivation), could in fact do so if paired appropriately with an unconditioned stimulus (food). It can be seen that Pavlovian conditioning essentially involves the pairing of a neutral stimulus and an unconditioned stimulus periodically (eight to ten pairings, usually) until the response is elicited by the conditioned—although originally neutral—stimulus. Thus, Pavlovian (classical) conditioning consists primarily of substituting one stimulus for another. Consequently, a great range of neutral stimuli, not originally adequate to elicit a response, will evoke the reflexive behavior. This is why Pavlovian conditioning is referred to as *stimulus substitution*. Some of these relationships are illustrated in Figure 1.

It is well to note that the extent to which and the rate at which a neutral stimulus may be conditioned to elicit a response is governed by *when* it is presented in relationship to the eliciting (unconditioned) stimulus. The neutral stimulus must be presented *before* the eliciting (unconditioned) stimulus. Moreover, for most

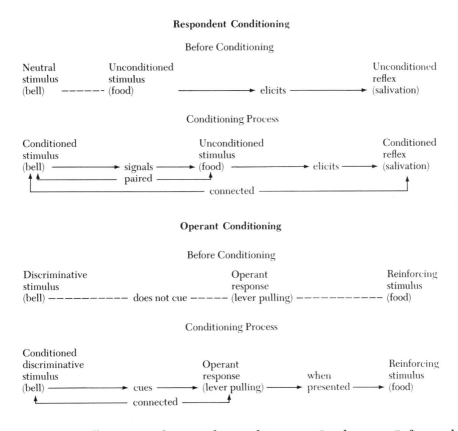

Figure 1 An Illustration of Respondent and Operant Conditioning Before and After Conditioning Has Taken Place

rapid conditioning the neutral stimulus must be followed by the eliciting stimulus within seconds.

One of Pavlov's important discoveries was the process of *extinction*. He observed that if the unconditioned stimulus was omitted in a series of conditioning trials, the conditioned response began to decrease and eventually disappeared. As we described above, in his conditioning experiments with dogs, a bell (conditioned stimulus) was sounded a short time before food (unconditioned stimulus) was presented. As we can predict, the dog salivated when the bell sounded. However, if the bell was rung repeatedly without food present, salivation decreased and ultimately stopped. Although the food may appear to act as a reward, Pavlov did not conceptualize it in those terms. He considered the food as the evoking stimulus and as a "reinforcing stimulus" in that it was a "strengthener," but he did not speak of it in terms of its rewarding properties (Bugelski, 1964).

Even though a response has been extinguished, after a period of time it may reappear. The return of the previously extinguished response, referred to as *spontaneous recovery*, explains why an undesirable behavior in a child, thought to have been extinguished, makes a somewhat mysterious reappearance after the initial extinction. Also, as we will indicate later, spontaneous recovery may have other practical implications when conditioning procedures are used to change behavior.

Pavlov's experimentation and discoveries did not end with the ideas we have already presented. He experimented extensively with the process of *generalization*. He found that once a response had been conditioned to a particular stimulus, it was unnecessary to present that exact stimulus for the response to occur. Slight variations of it and/or similar stimuli would also evoke a response. This tendency to give a specific response to similar stimuli is called generalization. Pavlov was able to demonstrate this by conditioning a dog to salivate to a metronome. After a dog had been conditioned to respond to a metronome beating at sixty times a minute, the rate was accelerated or decreased, and the dog would still respond (Bugelski, 1964).

Pavlov did rather extensive experimentation with discrimination learning and discriminative stimuli. It was in this connection that Pavlov discovered he could induce *experimental neurosis* in dogs. A dog was first conditioned to salivate when a luminous circle was presented on a screen. The animal was then trained to discriminate between a circle and an ellipse. When appropriate discrimination had been established, the ellipse was gradually changed to more closely approximate the circle. The dog continued to make appropriate discriminations, but as the two stimuli began to more closely approximate each other, discrimination became poor. At this point, the dog began to get very restless and to struggle and squeal. Ultimately, the dog became violent and resisted going into the experiment room (Deese and Hulse, 1975). The dog had developed an experimental neurosis.

The experimental neurosis developed because of the dog's inability to know when to respond and when the response was inappropriate. Conflict apparently developed because the discrimination problem was too difficult for the animal. Deese and Hulse (1975) have also indicated that similar conflict may develop if an animal is required to delay a conditioned response too long after the presentation of a conditioned stimulus.

Respondent conditioning has been demonstrated in dogs, sheep, worms, cockroaches, and humans. In humans, this type of conditioning influences reactions mediated by the autonomic nervous system. Hence, smooth-muscle and glandular response, and activities which they influence, such as changes in heart rate, blood pressure, stomach and bowel activity, adrenal secretion, perspiration, and salivation, may all be involved. Since some of these reactions are intimately involved in the experiencing of emotional states (i.e., anxiety, fear, etc.), it is readily apparent how respondent conditioning may influence many aspects of our emotional behavior (Lundin, 1974).

The process by which emotional reactions are conditioned is illustrated by the classical study of Watson and Raynor (1920). An eleven-month-old boy who displayed approach reactions to a white rat was taught to fear it by the following procedure. A white rat (neutral or conditioned stimulus) was presented to the child, and at the moment his hand touched it, an iron bar was struck. The striking of the iron bar created an unexpected, loud noise. The noise (the eliciting or unconditioned stimulus) evoked a start and what appeared to be a fear response in the child. The pairing of the noise with the presence of the rat was repeated seven times. A strongly conditioned (fearful) emotional reaction to the rat had been established. Albert's fear generalized (spread) from the rat to a rabbit, a dog, a Santa Claus mask, a fur coat, and even Watson's hair.

In much the same manner, a first-grade teacher who presents fear-eliciting stimuli may come to be feared by his students. And, in accordance with the principle noted above, the fear of the first-grade teacher may generalize to other teachers or to any stimulus or object in the school situation. Indeed, some first graders' aversion to reading might well be explained according to the same principle. Obviously, a first-grade teacher should behave in a way to ensure that he is regarded with positive feeling, for first graders are then more likely to generalize their positive feeling to learning and stimulus objects in the school environment.

An experience that occurred with one of the author's children illustrates the principle equally well; it demonstrates the effect of generalization of stimulus words rather than objects. The event occurred when the author's daughter experienced her first practice fire drill at school. When the teacher announced to the class that they were going to have a fire drill, the child became very frightened. She rose from her seat and quickly ran out the back door of the classroom. The teacher was perplexed and later discussed the incident with the author. Upon investigation of the incident with the child, several interesting facts emerged. The child apparently had associated the words "fire drill" with a dentist's drill that shot flames of fire. She had assumed that all children in the classroom would be subjected to tooth repair with the fire drill. Recognizing the pain previously associated with the dentist's drill, she found the added element of fire indeed a frightening prospect. A brief discussion with her regarding various types of drills helped her to quickly discriminate the difference. Subsequent fire drills at school created no further fear reactions.

In this episode, the pain from the dentist's drill might be considered the eliciting or unconditioned stimulus, and the words *fire* and *drill* (once neutral stimuli) became associated with pain and now evoked fear. Consequently, any stimulus that is labeled *fire* or *drill* may now evoke a fearful response. It can be seen, therefore, how words themselves may evoke fear by having been associated with stimuli adequate to elicit fear. Indeed, thinking itself may evoke considerable fear.

It is apparent from these examples that any stimulus that precedes and is appropriately paired with an eliciting stimulus adequate to evoke fear (or any negative effect) may acquire the capacity to automatically provoke certain emotional states in a person. The pairings may take place without the person's awareness. Yet, on subsequent occasions, in the presence of the conditioned stimulus, the person may experience the emotional state without understanding it or knowing why. This has been labeled clinically as free-floating anxiety. If the conditioned fear is intense, avoidance of situations involving the conditioned stimulus may be complete.

Vicarious Conditioning

The acquisition of a fearful reaction to a neutral stimulus by direct respondent conditioning is not the only way that fears and inhibitions may be acquired. Many avoidance or phobic reactions arise not from direct experiences with the phobic object but by *watching others* be hurt or respond fearfully to certain things. It has been shown that observers who watch another person being aversively conditioned to a neutral stimulus may also express similar fear reactions. It has also been demonstrated that emotional reactions exhibited by one person can serve as aversive stimuli and produce emotional reactions in others; that is, a person who observes another person exhibit fear may also experience a degree of fear (Bandura, 1969).

Why does viewing another's emotional reaction lead the observer to respond emotionally? Probably because emotional expressions of others are often followed by negative consequences for the observer. For example, when a parent is angry, he is more likely to be punitive to a child. The parent's expression of anger serves as a signal that something unpleasant is likely to follow. Hence, recognition of parental anger is enough to set off a fearful reaction in the child.

Changing Conditioned Emotional Responses

Undesirable emotional reactions such as inhibitions, fear, or phobias can be changed. Essentially, it involves a process of *counterconditioning* by which a person learns a new response to the aversive conditioned stimulus. Three procedures have been used. First, *desensitization* is used to overcome the inappropriate avoidance reaction. This is accomplished by pairing the fear-provoking stimulus to responses that are antagonistic to it. For example, a fearful person is taught to relax and while relaxed the fear-producing stimulus is presented repeatedly. The second procedure, *modeling,* is also used to overcome undesirable avoidance reactions. A model performs the fear-provoking behavior in front of the observer without experiencing negative consequences. To obtain the best results (1) the model's performance must be slowly graduated to avoid intense emotional arousal in the observer, (2) the model must perform the fear-provoking behavior repeatedly and safely under a variety of conditions, and (3) the model's emotional expressions must be positive while performing the phobic behavior (Bandura, 1969). Third, *aversive counterconditioning* is used to change inappropriate approach responses. The usual practice is to prompt the undesirable approach behavior and immediately present an aversive stimulus to the client. For example, an adolescent boy with a fetish for women's undergarments might be counterconditioned by pairing a woman's undergarment, or a picture of it, with electric shock.

Counterconditioning may also utilize *covert sensitization* (Cautela, 1966). This treatment procedure requires the client to visualize himself performing the inappropriate response, immediately after which he is asked to visualize an extremely repugnant scene. For instance, an alcoholic may be asked to visualize himself drinking liquor. When he has the smell and taste of alcohol clearly visualized, he is asked to imagine that the bottle contains yellow, diseased, crawling worms.

The reader will note that covert sensitization is opposite in its effect on behavior to covert reinforcement. Covert sensitization promotes an avoidance of an undesirable behavior while covert reinforcement tends to promote more desirable approach and socially adaptive behavior.

Kolvin (1967) used covert sensitization to treat a fourteen-year-old boy who, under certain circumstances, was sexually aroused by the sight of a young woman wearing a skirt. Sometimes he felt compelled to approach a woman and run his hand under her clothes. On three occasions the boy was charged with indecent assault.

Study of the boy revealed him to be rather serious, reserved, and somewhat inarticulate. He acknowledged some anxiety and guilt about masturbation and reported frightening dreams. He reported a compulsion to commit the undesirable behavior. Because the boy was somewhat limited intellectually and appeared inaccessible to traditional therapeutic procedures, covert sensitization was used.

A list of situations and experiences the boy viewed as unpleasant were identified. Two such experiences containing aversive imagery were dreams of falling and looking down from a high or precarious place. In treating the boy, the therapist encouraged him to practice visualizing scenes according to stories devised by the therapist. When the boy was able to vividly imagine a scene, the therapist told an erotically toned story, involving falling or heights.

Over a period of three weeks, the boy was treated in seven thirty-minute sessions using the techniques described. These sessions were supplemented by discussions of the biology and psychology of normal sexual behavior and socially desirable heterosexual relationships. The treatment proved effective. The boy reported no additional compulsive urge to make improper sexual advances. A follow-up seventeen months later indicated that the improvement had been maintained.

Operant Conditioning

The conditioning of an operant response is achieved when positive reinforcement im-mediately follows the appropriate execution of the response. Three major steps are generally involved in the conditioning of the operant response. First, a measurement of the operant level or baseline is taken. Second, a reinforcer is presented each time the response is performed until the operant rate has clearly increased. Third, the reinforcer is withheld to permit the conditioned response to become extinguished. If the conditioned response is extinguished, then there is some certainty that appropriate variables have been identified (Reese, 1966).

Although these three sequential steps may appear to be very simple to perform, this appearance may be deceptive. Therefore, it is desirable to elaborate on the additional procedures that are required in operant conditioning.

Basic Procedures in Conditioning Operant Behavior

At least six basic procedures are considered essential in conditioning operant behavior. They are stated below (Reese, 1966):

1. *Define and state operationally the behavior to be changed.* The target behavior (i.e., the behavior to be changed) should be described in terms of the observable behavior the subject is to perform, the standard(s) by which you will consider the performance acceptable, and the conditions under which the behavior is expected to occur. You will recall that Jimmy Lander (Chapter 1) had difficulty carrying out parental requests, called his parents uncomplimentary names, and procrastinated excessively. We stated the target behavior in the following way: Jimmy will carry out all parental requests without arguing or name calling within ten minutes after the request is made. The statement leaves no doubt about what Jimmy should do, how frequently he should do it, and under what conditions.

2. *Obtain a baseline or operant level of the behavior that is considered desirable to promote or change.* Once target behavior has been stated operationally, its frequency or magnitude should be determined before the behavior is reinforced or treated. Subsequently, it will be possible to determine the effects of the treatment and whether any treatment procedures need to be changed. (Methods of observing and recording behavior in a variety of situations are discussed in Chapter 4.)

To get a baseline of Jimmy's behavior, we might ask the parents to record for three days (Monday, Wednesday, and Saturday) every request they make of him and the number of times he carries them out without arguing within ten minutes. Suppose we found that he carried them out 30 percent of the time during baseline. Then, after treatment has been in effect for six weeks, we record his behavior again and find that he carries out requests 80 percent of the time. It is apparent that treatment has been effective and has increased his performance of parental requests by 100 percent.

3. *Arrange the learning or treatment situation so that the desirable behavior will occur.* Before reinforcement is administered, it is necessary to determine whether the individual can perform the desired response. If one is attempting to increase the strength or frequency of academic responses, it is necessary to determine present performance level and reinforce those responses the subject can execute easily.

A response in the subject's repertoire can often be prompted by a verbal request which specifies the desired behavior and the reinforcement given. For example, we might say: "When you have finished working the five arithmetic problems, you may play with the toys quietly in the back of the room." Or, a situation may be arranged so that the desired response has a high probability of occurrence. Suppose you want to increase a child's tendency to say

"Thank you." Set up a situation in which the child is reinforced with something he desires, and the "Thank you" will most likely follow.

To illustrate, let us refer again to the hypothetical case of Jimmy Lander. We know that Jimmy can execute the target behavior because the baseline observation reveals that he carries out parental requests 30 percent of the time. To prompt the response of carrying out requests appropriately, either of two procedures might be used. The parents can initiate a request and reinforce him immediately upon its proper execution. However, this may not be as effective as a second procedure. The parents could tell Jimmy that they are starting a new program at home. Each time he carries out a parental request within ten minutes he will receive five cents. When he has earned one dollar, he will receive a bonus, and have the opportunity to participate in a special activity of his own choosing. When the child is aware of all the incentives beforehand, the probability is high that he will perform the target response with little urging.

4. *Identify potential reinforcers.* Before most people will *do* something, they must *want* something. With the possible exception of primary reinforcers and some aversive stimuli, a stimulus has no inherent reinforcement property. We must determine the reinforcement property of a stimulus (that is, its capacity to increase response probability). Although it is possible to increase the probability that a stimulus will tend to be reinforcing by first depriving a child of something (say, extend the length of time since he last had something to eat), such a procedure is not desirable. It is more feasible to capitalize on the conditions operating at the moment. For example, if a child has been sitting at his desk for two hours with little or no opportunity to move around, the possibility of participating in a "fun game" may have great potential reinforcement value.

Fortunately, some stimuli—for example, attention and affection—function as generalized reinforcers and may often promote the type of response that is desirable. Such generalized reinforcers may not function equally well with all children, and it may be desirable to establish their reinforcement properties by pairing them with primary reinforcers (see Chapter 1).

Perhaps the most useful method of all for identifying potential reinforcers is to observe a child (or person) in his free-choice activities. What a child does when he has the opportunity to do what he wishes usually reveals the type of stimuli or events that have reinforcing properties for him. In a subsequent section, the authors will present the products of their attempts to identify potential reinforcers.

5. *Shape and/or reinforce the desired behavior.* If a child is able to perform the desired response, reinforce it on its first and every subsequent appearance until it has assumed appropriate strength. Once the response is being performed with high frequency, the reinforcement schedule may be changed to ensure its durability. For example, when Jimmy is carrying out parental requests 80 percent of the time, we may want to switch the continuous reinforcement schedule to a variable schedule. We would not reinforce him each time he carries out the request but every third, fifth, or seventh time. As we will discuss later in this chapter, both variable-ratio and variable-interval schedules promote behavior that is resistant to extinction.

If a child is unable to perform the terminal (desired) behavior, successive approximations of the behavior must be identified and appropriately reinforced. Since the reader will be introduced to this concept in the section that follows, we will not discuss it here. It is sufficient to indicate that shaping essentially involves identifying and reinforcing step-by-step the responses that ultimately lead to the desired behavior.

Finally, it is important to mention that as the terminal behavior is being shaped and/or reinforced, a variety of reinforcers must be used to avoid satiation. Popcorn may be very reinforcing for making a response the first ten or twenty times; after that, one's appetite for popcorn greatly diminishes.

6. *Maintain records of the reinforced behavior to determine whether response strength or frequency has increased.* To determine whether the reinforcement contingencies have been effective, longitudinal records must be kept. Comparison of each experimental or treatment session with the baseline rate quickly reveals whether the reinforcement has promoted the response considered desirable. If the reinforcement procedures are not producing the desired result, it is necessary to determine why and to make appropriate adjustments.

To determine empirically if the reinforcement or treatment procedures have produced an increase in the desired behavior, extinction procedures may be instituted. A reduction in the frequency of the target response would suggest that the reinforcement or treatment has been responsible for the increase in the desired behavior. In the hypothetical case of Jimmy, terminating the money or the bonus special privilege when he carries out parental requests will likely lead to a reduction of his responsiveness to parental requests to near the 30 percent baseline after three days. If that occurs, we know that the reinforcement system we have been using has increased the target behavior.[1]

The use of operant conditioning is illustrated in a study by Dickinson (1967). He was interested in increasing the academic performance of a child who rarely completed school as-

---

[1] For obvious reasons, reversal of the reinforcement contingencies is done only in experimental situations. It should not be done in clinical, school, or other applied situations unless it is part of an experiment.

signments. Dickinson initiated the procedure by inviting the child into his office and asking him to solve some arithmetic problems. Ten problems, appropriately graded in difficulty, were presented individually to the child. As he solved each problem correctly, candy corn, poker chips (to be traded for candy after school), and verbal reinforcements were given. When the child had correctly calculated each of the ten problems, the reinforcement schedule was changed: The child was reinforced only after he had correctly calculated five problems. The fixed-ratio reinforcement procedure continued until the child was correctly calculating problems at a reasonably high rate. At this point, the responsibility for reinforcement was transferred to the teacher in the classroom. The teacher reinforced the arithmetic-calculating behavior with poker chips and praise, and after three weeks, check marks were substituted for poker chips.

Conditioning was terminated by the experimenter after eighteen days, at which point the child's performance dropped sharply. But during the third week after termination, performance began to increase; during a twenty-week period, the child failed to complete arithmetic assignments only six times.

Besides illustrating the potential value of operant methods to a child's school problem, Dickinson's experiment demonstrates other important operant features. He began by using primary reinforcers with reliable reinforcement properties. But, since he also presented poker chips and gave verbal approval simultaneously with a primary reinforcer, they acquired reinforcement properties. When the desirable behavior was fairly well established, immediate primary reinforcement was delayed. Also, once the desirable behavior was being performed at a higher rate, the schedule of reinforcement was changed. Reinforcement was given for the correct solution of five problems (fixed-ratio reinforcement) instead of one (regular reinforce-

ment). This type of schedule establishes behavior more resistant to extinction. Finally, to get a transfer of the appropriate response to the classroom, the teacher maintained reinforcement in the classroom where school assignments should be done.

Prompting, Shaping, and Fading

The steps enumerated above are typically employed when the operant behavior occurs with reasonable frequency, but what do we do if the behavior rarely occurs? We can

1. Instruct the subject to perform the response, hoping he will follow our request

2. Shape and/or reinforce successive approximations of the terminal behavior

3. Arrange or fade stimulus conditions so that there is a high probability the subject will give the desired response

4. Request the subject to watch someone perform a response and then ask him to imitate it

5. Present a contingency contract: "If you perform behavior A, you will get to engage in behavior B"

6. Use punishment to inhibit the performance of an undesirable behavior and reinforce the opposite or desirable behavior

Of course, some of these procedures may prove more effective than others, depending on the subject's history and behavior repertoire. All of the procedures involve some form of prompting to initiate a predetermined response. We will discuss procedures 2 and 3 here and the others later in the chapter.

Shaping is a procedure by which a desired behavior is evoked by reinforcing successive approximations of that behavior. Suppose you wish to increase the social participation of an extremely shy five-year-old child. Using praise, candy, or tokens as reinforcers, several steps might be employed. The child would be reinforced for

1. Looking at a group of children involved in some activity

2. Standing within ten feet of a group of children

3. Standing within five feet of a group of children

4. Sitting with a group of children

5. Imitating any action of a group member

6. Participating in any activity with the group

7. Making a one-word verbal response to any question of a group member

8. Responding with a verbalization of three or more words to a group member's question

9. Initiating a conversation with others

10. Initiating any activity with another or a group

11. Playing cooperatively with a group

12. Playing cooperatively and talking with a group involved in an activity

At first glance, shaping might appear amazingly simple; however, the procedure requires that certain rules be followed. First, the successive approximations must be identified and stated in behavioral terms. Second, the behavioral approximation must be reinforced immediately upon execution or the wrong response might be reinforced. Cohen (1969) has indicated that in some instances a delay of one-twentieth of a second may lead to the reinforcement of the wrong response. Third, the successive approximations of the desired behavior must be appropriately reinforced. If an approximation is reinforced for too long a period, it may become so well established that further, closer approximations of the desired behavior may not occur. Moreover, if the shaping process is too slow, the subject may tire or refuse to execute the response. On the other hand, if shaping proceeds too rapidly, the earlier shaped behavior may become extinguished (Reese, 1966).

Another procedure similar to shaping for prompting a desired response is *fading*. As we noted, shaping is a procedure in which approximations of a target response are successively reinforced until the desired behavior is performed. When *fading* is used, *the stimuli are successively varied* until a response made in one situation is made in another situation. Shaping involves a successive response change, while fading involves a gradual change in the stimulus presented to a subject. With fading the subject may continue to make the same response to different stimuli, but the subject is reinforced for making a response to successive approximations to the target stimulus.

Whaley and Malott (1971) utilized fading to help a retarded eight-year-old girl (Betty) to recognize her printed name. The experimenters took the white letters B, e, t, t, y and put them on a white card. Although the letters were white and placed on a white background, they were clearly distinguishable. The letters S, u, s, a, n, cut out in white, were placed on a card with a black background. Then, Betty was asked to select the card with her name on it. Although she initially picked up cards indiscriminately, she was reinforced with candy when she picked up the card with her name on it. Within a few trials she was consistently picking up the correct card.

After forty correct trials, the letters in Betty's name were removed from the white background and placed on a card that was slightly more gray in color. She selected correctly between the two cards and was immediately reinforced with candy. After forty correct trials, Betty's name was transferred to a slightly darker card. The same procedure continued with eleven cards of successively darker shades. Finally, the card with Betty's name had the same background color as the card with Susan's name. Betty was able to make the appropriate discriminations.

It can be observed that the original card with Betty's name and the card with Susan's name differed on two stimulus dimensions: (1) the backgrounds on which the letters were placed (white and black) and (2) the letters on each card. One of these stimulus dimensions was gradually faded out until the crucial stimulus dimension was the only one that varied.

Chaining

From the discussion of operant conditioning, the reader may have gleaned the impression that behavior is a simple matter of learning separate stimulus-response units. In part that is true, since stimulus-response units must be first learned before more complex learning can take place. However, most human behavior is characterized by a series of stimulus-response (S-R) units connected together in a sequence. The connection of two or more previously learned S-R[2] units in a sequence as a result of learning is called *chaining*. These chains of connected S-R units may involve both motor responses and verbal responses or verbal chains (Gagné, 1970).

An example may help clarify the concept of chaining. One of the authors has a small, lovable dog of pekingese and poodle parentage. The dog has been taught a number of tricks involving the chaining of separate motor response units. For example, when prompted by the request, "Give me a love, Ebbie," she will jump up into your lap and lay her head on your shoulder. In the performance of the trick, it is apparent that at least two separate S-R units are involved. The initial learning of the S-R units demonstrates clearly how the process of chaining takes place.

The dog was first taught to jump into the trainer's lap when the command "jump" was accompanied by the trainer's patting of his knee. Since the dog was accustomed to jumping into the trainer's lap, this was relatively easily executed by the dog. When the action was performed, she was reinforced.

Once the first S-R unit had been learned, the next S-R unit was taught. After the dog had executed the first S-R unit, and while still on the lap of the trainer, the request was given to "Give me a love, Ebbie" while the trainer was patting his shoulder. As the dog performed an appropriate approximation of the desired response, she was reinforced. After a series of training sessions, the dog was able to perform the appropriate terminal behavior upon verbal command. With this accomplished, the dog had chained (or connected) two separate S-R units in a sequence.

As the reader will note, in the initial learning sessions, two types of stimuli were presented: (1) verbal stimulus (statement) and (2) visual stimulus (the trainer's patting of his knee and later his shoulder). However, as the dog began to perform each S-R unit with high frequency, only the verbal stimulus was presented. Consequently, the dog learned to execute the

---

[2] Stimulus-response units are typically designated as Ss-R to denote that part of the stimulus complex is proprioceptive, or internal, resulting from muscle activation. In chaining, a symbol is added to designate response-produced cues as each response is performed sequentially: A small *s* is added to the R. Thus, it appears Ss-Rs-Ss-Rs, etc. For ease of presentation, the S-R is used in the text.

two S-R units in sequence only to the verbal command "Give me a love, Ebbie." The verbal command now appears to function as a discriminative stimulus.

The reader may be wondering how chains of S-R units get to be connected. In some instances, the connecting of the S-R units may be explained by contiguity; that is, because the stimulus is rapidly followed by a response, the two become associated. In other S-R chains (much like the example cited above), reinforcement appears to be operative (Staats and Staats, 1963). There are additional explanations, among them this: It is quite generally accepted by experimental learning theorists that the response element in the S-R unit produces stimuli which may serve as a cue for the response that follows. Each stimulus produced by a response is referred to as a *response-produced cue or stimulus*. It seems to function in the following manner. When a motor response is performed, the sensory receptors in the muscles and tendons are activated. The stimuli accompanying these movements, proprioceptive stimuli, appear to cue or trigger the next response in the chain (Staats and Staats, 1963).

In human beings, the learning of response chains is greatly facilitated by external stimuli, particularly by verbal instructions that direct us to perform certain behaviors in sequence. For example, consider how such instruction facilitates learning how to kick a football. We may direct our young learner to perform the appropriate sequence of acts by saying, "Extend the football with both hands as far as you can in front of you. As you begin to drop the ball, move your right leg into the air in front of you to meet the football as it falls." After our young learner has had a few practice trials (and if he can perform the separate motor acts involved in the sequence), he will have learned motor response chains. Besides the proprioceptive stimuli produced by the motor responses, he may self-instruct his own actions — that is, he may talk to himself as he sequentially performs the motor responses. He engages in thinking responses which also produce stimuli. Such thinking-produced stimuli become involved in verbal chains. For example, the child who is learning to kick a football may instruct himself to (1) "hold the football in front," (2) "drop the football straight down," (3) "raise your right foot as the ball drops," and (4) "kick the football before it hits the ground." However, once the chains of motor responses have been learned, the response-produced stimuli allow him to execute the response chain with ease. With the forming of the response chain, the actions may be performed independent of the original evoking stimulus (Staats and Staats, 1963).

The role of response-produced stimuli in learning response chains is clearly seen by the difficulty people have in performing certain learned responses in reverse order. A dramatic test of this is to try to recite the alphabet backwards or to count in reverse. The central importance of the response-produced stimuli in cueing each of the S-R units in the chain is clearly revealed by the difficulty a person has in starting at the middle of the sequence and performing the remaining responses from that point on. It is difficult indeed, but if asked to go back to the beginning of the sequence, the person can perform the responses with much greater ease.

Children must acquire hundreds or even thousands of response chains to approximate the complex behavior characteristic of adults. In the primary grades of elementary school, skill learning requires the acquisition of many motor-response chains. Examples of simple motor chains are buttoning a coat or dress, tying one's shoes, and using scissors. More complex chains are involved in learning to print or write. In the higher elementary grades, the learning of response chains involving various types of procedures is required (Gagné, 1970).

The Conditions for Learning
Response Chains

If it is true that much of the behavior people exhibit in daily life is composed of response chains, it is important to know the basic conditions for learning them. Gagné (1970) describes five essential conditions. First, the separate S-R units or links must be learned before they can be chained. In the example of the child learning to kick a football, he must be able to (1) hold the football in front of him, (2) simultaneously drop the football and begin to raise one leg, (3) make contact with the football before it hits the ground, and (4) kick the ball in the right position to increase distance.

The second essential condition is that the learner must execute each link in the proper sequence. Perhaps the most effective way to achieve this is to prompt or verbally instruct the learner in the proper execution and sequence of response, as in the example of the child learning to kick the football.

The third condition requires that S-R units (or links) be performed in "close time succession" to ensure that the links are chained together. If there are long delays between the execution of each link, it is difficult to establish the chains.

The fourth condition requires that the sequence be repeated until the desired learning has been achieved. Since one cannot always assume that the individual links have been adequately mastered or that the instructional prompting has been entirely effective, it is generally necessary to repeat the sequence. Repetition tends to polish the performance into a smoothly executed sequence. Also, the better it is learned the more resistant it is to being forgotten.

The final condition is that reinforcement must be present in the learning of chains. The execution of the final link must lead to the proper effects. The reinforcement must be immediate. If reinforcement is not given upon the execution of the final response unit in the chain, the terminal link is extinguished, and the chain is not maintained.

While the discussion of chaining may appear to have little relevance to the practical tasks of initial learning or behavior modification, it is quite relevant. Too often, one suspects, we attempt to teach children a response chain without knowing whether the child can perform the S-R units involved. If such is the case, it is important to break the chain into performable S-R units and help him master those first. Even more important, it may be well to make such an analysis before any instruction is attempted to help the child acquire response chains (or skills).

Schedules of Reinforcement

The quickest way to increase the frequency or strength of a response is to reinforce it each time it is performed. That is, the response is reinforced regularly or *continuously.* However, once responding has increased to an acceptable rate and if one wishes the response to endure, a different type of *reinforcement schedule* is desirable.

There are two basic ways in which reinforcement can be administered: (1) *ratio* schedules and (2) *interval* schedules. When a ratio schedule is used, a certain number of responses must be emitted before reinforcement is given. If the ratio is *fixed*, a response is reinforced after a specified number of responses are performed. If the fixed ratio is 5 (FR 5), reinforcement is given immediately after every fifth, tenth, fifteenth, etc., response. When a *variable* ratio is employed, the number of responses that must be made varies; that is, reinforcement could be given after the third, seventh, eighth, eleventh, etc., responses. The reinforcement on a variable schedule is not entirely predictable (Reese, 1966; Cohen, 1969).

Reinforcement based on an interval schedule is primarily a function of the passage of time. When a *fixed-interval* schedule is used, a specified amount of time must pass between each reinforcement. If the fixed interval is 4 (FI 4), an interval of four minutes must transpire before reinforcement is given. When a *variable-interval* schedule is used, the length of time varies from one reinforcement to another.

Ratio Schedules   Behavior, as we have noted, is maintained or changed as a result of its consequences: that is, behavior is a function of reinforcement. Ratio schedules, like interval schedules, tend to promote a patterning of response peculiar to them. Thus, knowing the basic features of each type of reinforcement schedule assumes considerable importance in promoting certain types of response and extinguishing or decreasing others. Failure to develop a certain pattern of response through inadequate knowledge of reinforcement schedules occurs with considerable frequency. For example, more than a few parents have been dismayed to find that offering a dollar for every 'A' on a report card often fails to promote the 'A'-getting behavior. The long delay between one reporting period and another makes this offer an ineffective way to utilize reinforcement for a low-probability behavior (behavior that occurs infrequently). Hundreds of appropriate responses have to be made between the two reporting periods to attain the desired achievement level. Only a few of those responses, near goal attainment, can be influenced by this type of reinforcement.

Ratio schedules are generally characterized by a high rate of responding—if the ratio is reasonably low: that is, if the number of nonreinforced to reinforced responses is small (e.g., nonreinforced 15:1 reinforced). With variable-ratio reinforcement, responding is maintained at a high rate. This also tends to be true with fixed-ratio schedules, but typically there is a pause following reinforcement with a somewhat sudden change to a high, stable rate of response (Skinner, 1953; Lundin, 1974).

When one employs a *fixed ratio*, and the ratio is low and then increased slowly (from 5:1 to 10:1 to 15:1) a very high ratio may ultimately be used (400:1). Response usually diminishes immediately after reinforcement, but rapidly builds up as the next reinforcement is about to be given. Fixed ratio has demonstrated superiority over both continuous-reinforcement and fixed-interval schedules (Lundin, 1974).

Extinction under fixed-ratio schedules is characterized by a high rate of response for a short period of time after termination of reinforcement, followed by a somewhat sudden drop. Sometime after the drop, responding may again increase for a while but is subsequently characterized by rather sudden termination.

Fixed-ratio schedules operate in many areas of human activity. Since reinforcement is contingent upon the number of responses given, any work paid according to quantity produced illustrates this type of schedule. Money paid for piecework completed, arithmetic problems successfully solved, or errands performed are excellent examples of fixed-ratio schedules. It can be seen that when reinforcement is administered for a number of behaviors properly executed, incentive to stick to a task is high.

Variable-ratio schedules are characterized by a relatively steady rate of responding without sudden or marked changes. Because reinforcement is not exactly predictable, an animal or a person is likely to continue to respond in anticipation that the reinforcement will be given at any time. The anticipation of reinforcement on variable ratios is aptly illustrated by the persistent interest in and involvement of large numbers of people in games of chance or gambling. And even though the spacing of the variable reinforcement is wider than the gambler would like, he continues to entertain the notion that he will be lucky and win a large sum of money.

A remedial reading teacher with whom one of the authors is acquainted used variable-ratio reinforcement to greatly enhance pupil attention and reading behavior. Pupils in the remedial reading class had not been attending well during periods of oral reading, and when they were called upon to read, they had often lost their places. She began continuous reinforcement (with candy) each time a pupil who was called upon to read knew the proper place. After a short period of reinforcement of this type, she switched to variable-ratio reinforcement and increased attending responses to about a 100 percent accuracy. Certainly this is a much more effective way of getting desired behavior than scolding a child every time he loses his place.

The use of variable-ratio reinforcement has real virtue because the behavior so established and maintained is quite resistant to extinction. When extinction procedures are implemented, rate of response is well maintained, punctuated by pauses. As extinction proceeds, pauses increase in length, and the overall rate is reduced (Lundin, 1974).

Interval Schedules   When interval schedules are used, the rate of response is much lower than with ratio schedules. Of course, the rate of responding varies according to the size of the interval. If the interval is long, the rate of response is low. Compared with ratio schedules, interval schedules tend to have an overall response rate that is low.

In the initial phases of conditioning with a *fixed-interval schedule*, there is rapid responding immediately following reinforcement, followed in turn by a general slowing down until the next reinforcement. As conditioning continues, and the organism begins to develop time discrimination, reinforcement is followed by minimal responding. The response rate rapidly increases as time for the next reinforcement comes near (Lundin, 1974).

Fixed-interval schedules are quite commonly found in human affairs. Perhaps the best illustration of fixed-interval schedules is the payment of wages or salary by intervals of time. Elementary school teachers use a fixed-interval schedule when they use a reinforcing activity such as reading a favorite story to their class at a specific time each day. It can be observed in this situation that as the time approaches for the favored activity there is a general increase in appropriate pupil behavior. However, it should be noted that this type of schedule does not have much positive effect on the pupils' activities in the morning. If the interval is too long between reinforcements, desirable behavior is not readily maintained.

Extinction under fixed-interval schedules is characterized by more regular response than is true with continuous reinforcement. Behavior established with such a schedule tends to be quite resistant to extinction (Reese, 1966).

While conditioning with fixed-interval reinforcement schedules tends to be characterized by ultimate slowing down and pauses after reinforcement, *variable-interval schedules* are typified by a steady rate of responding, although the rate is dependent on the length of time intervals utilized. Activities that operate on this type of schedule are well illustrated by fishing and hunting; and bonuses in industry have the same effect (Lundin, 1974). Because reinforcement is a function of variable time intervals and appears to the recipient to occur at random, motivation would appear to be maintained by anticipation of a reinforcement at almost any time.

Teachers can use variable-interval schedules to good advantage. By using intermittent reinforcing activities or bonuses throughout the day, pupil performance and interest in learning can be maintained at a steady rate for long periods of time. However, the reinforcing stimuli must be properly interspersed to prevent long periods of time without reinforcement.

As the reader may have already inferred, behavior maintained on a variable-interval schedule is very resistant to extinction, continuing for a long period of time before any noticeable decrement. As Lundin (1974) has suggested, variable-interval schedules probably explain why some people will continue to try in the face of failure. As a matter of fact, steady, even predictable behavior may well be a function of this type of schedule.

Besides being extremely resistant to extinction, interval schedules have the added advantage of being much easier to administer. Ratio schedules require that response rates be counted or tallied. Interval schedules require timekeeping. Obviously, timekeeping is much easier to do than tallying response rates. Thus, interval schedules can be applied with much greater facility to groups than is true of ratio schedules.

Figure 2 shows the expected type of response when the four basic schedules are used. Inspection of Figure 2 shows that under a fixed-ratio schedule there is a high rate of response with brief pauses after the delivery of reinforcement. When a variable-ratio schedule is operative, there is a high sustained response rate with no pauses after reinforcement is given. Under a fixed-interval schedule, there is a low overall response rate with an obvious pause after reinforcement is given. When a variable-interval schedule is used, there is a low sustained rate of response with no pausing after reinforcement is administered.

Contingency Management

The discussion of schedules of reinforcement pointed out how the pattern of reinforcement specifically affects behavior. The rate at which

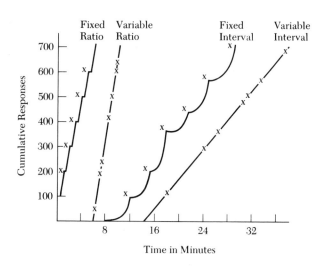

Figure 2 A Typical Record of Responding Under Four Basic Schedules of Reinforcement: The x's indicate points of reinforcement, and the slope of the lines give an approximation of various response rates. (Adapted from E. P. Reese, *The Analysis of Human Operant Behavior.* Wm. C. Brown, Dubuque, Iowa, 1966, p. 16, with permission.)

behavior is acquired and changed, as well as its durability, is intimately related to the schedule of reinforcement. The nature of the consequence and the timing and frequency with which a consequence is contingent upon a response has important effects on the response.

The procedures by which the environment is arranged to make reinforcement dependent upon the performance of certain behavior is called *contingency management*. A contingency is the type of consequence that is dependent upon and follows a response. Contingencies may be either positive or negative. In the terminology of contingency management, a *positive contingency* is a desired consequence that follows, or is contingent upon, a certain act. For example, if a parent says to a child, "When you have emptied the garbage, you may go out and play," a positive contingency is operating. A *negative contingency* usually involves a threat of an undesirable consequence unless a certain act is executed. A parent utilizes a negative contingency when he says: "You will be grounded for a week if you get home late tonight." (Homme and Tosti, 1971).

In the two examples above, a "contractual" element is stated. When a contingency manager says: "When you do A, then consequence B will follow," a promise or contract is operating between the two parties. When a person is informed that if he performs in a certain way he will *escape* or *avoid* an undesirable consequence, the stated condition is a *negative contingency contract*. On the other hand, when an individual is informed that if he performs in a certain way he will acquire something he desires, a *positive contingency contract* is operating. The positive contingency contract is designed to influence the execution of a desired behavior. The negative contingency contract is intended to prevent the occurrence of an undesirable behavior. Both types of contingency contracts may achieve the intended outcomes, but a

positive contingency contract is preferable in most situations.

It may appear as if contingency management is simply another way of discussing positive and negative reinforcement by coining a new terminology. In part, that is true, since similar theoretical principles are used in both. However, there is one major difference between operant conditioning and contingency management. In operant conditioning, a response is strengthened or inhibited by the presentation of certain *tangible* stimuli which act as reinforcers or punishers. In contingency management, reinforcing conditions take the form of *events or activities;* that is, opportunities to perform desired activities are used to reinforce infrequently performed responses. In this sense, we can say that *reinforcing responses* (rather than *reinforcing stimuli*) increase the frequency or strength of the desirable responses. For example, when a person is permitted to engage in behavior A when he has executed behavior B, the opportunity to perform behavior A reinforces behavior B.

The opportunity to engage in a desired event or activity has long been known to have motivational properties. However, the idea was not clearly formulated as a principle until Premack (1959). The essence of the *Premack Principle* is that any low-probability behavior can be reinforced by an opportunity to engage in a high-probability behavior. As Homme and Tosti (1971) have suggested, our grandmothers intuitively used the principle to reinforce desired behavior. When grandmother said: "Eat your meat and vegetables, then you may have dessert," she was a contingency manager.

Although contingency management may be used to promote social behavior, the principles and procedures have been most extensively used in educational settings to promote academic achievement. Homme, Csanyi, Gonzales, and Rechs (1969) have worked out a sys-

tematic set of procedures for enhancing classroom learning. The main elements of the system
are briefly summarized below:

A. Motivation management

1. Specify the desired learning objectives
   and/or task behaviors.

2. Identify appropriate reinforcing
   activities and events (high-probability
   behaviors).

B. Development of an appropriate
   instructional program

1. Assess the student's achievement in
   each curricular area.

2. Prepare individual task assignments,
   graduated in difficulty, in each
   curricular area. Each task assignment
   should have a progress check to
   determine sufficient mastery of task
   objective. Programmed materials are
   often used to individualize the
   instruction.

3. Clearly indicate for each task
   assignment the beginning of the task
   and the criteria by which successful
   completion of the task can be
   determined.

C. Formulation of the contract

1. Write in simple terms the task to be
   performed, specifying the amount of
   work to be done and criteria for
   completion.

2. Indicate the reinforcing events for
   successful completion of each task
   assignment. (For example, "When you
   have worked ten arithmetic problems
   correctly, you may engage in the
   activity chosen from the Reinforcing
   Events Menu for five minutes.")

3. Arrange the reinforcing events (RE's) so
   they are given frequently and
   immediately upon the execution of the
   task behavior.

4. State the contract positively. Use the
   reinforcing events to promote the
   desired behavior; avoid the use of
   negative contingencies to promote the
   desired behavior.

D. Specify the reinforcing events (RE's) and
   arrange an RE area in the classroom

1. Design an RE menu on which highly
   desirable reinforcing events are listed
   or pictured (for younger children). The
   menu should consist of activities that
   can be used in the classroom. The RE's
   may be activities like working with
   puzzles, reading comics and mystery
   stories, drawing, playing with clay,
   playing games such as tic-tac-toe, cards,
   or chess.

2. Permit students to engage in RE's for
   not less than three but not more than
   ten minutes.

3. Encourage students to work in the task
   area and to engage in reinforcing events
   in the RE area.

4. Use sign-in and sign-out sheets to
   regulate RE activities. Students who
   overstay earned RE time may be
   deprived of RE time equal to the
   amount overstayed.

E. Implementing the program

1. Show the RE area to the students and
   explain how RE's are obtained.

2. Explain the RE menu and the specific
   rules for completing tasks. Discuss
   progress checks, going to and signing

into the RE area, and returning to the task area.

3. Give the students a trial run, going through each step of the procedure. The student is given a record sheet, shown his diagnostic profile and presented a task assignment. When the task is completed, the teacher makes a progress check. If performance is adequate, the student selects an RE from the RE menu, goes to the RE area, and engages in the reinforcing event.

Homme and his associates have worked out rather complete procedures for utilizing contingency management in the classroom. As we noted earlier, the theoretical principles may be adapted for promoting behavior in a social setting also. An example will help to clarify the application.

Suppose a parent consults us regarding her daughter's difficulties in performing certain tasks at home. Susy does not hang up her clothes and procrastinates about doing her homework assignments. To promote the desired behavior, we must first discover reinforcing activities or events (high-probability behaviors) for Susy. Upon questioning the mother, she indicates that Susy likes playing with her neighborhood friends, enjoys helping mother in the kitchen, and is an avid television watcher. To promote the low-probability behaviors, access to the reinforcing events must depend upon the performance of hanging up clothes and completing homework. We might suggest that a system be set up whereby, after she has hung up her clothes, Susy is permitted to watch a television program for fifteen minutes before going to school. When she arrives home from school, changes, and hangs up her clothes, she is permitted to play with her friends for thirty minutes. After supper, Susy might be required to complete all her homework before being given the opportunity to watch an hour of television. We would encourage the mother to be absolutely consistent in following through with the contingencies, to grant the reinforcing event immediately upon the performance of the low-probability behavior, and to use no threats or criticism in carrying out the procedures. After the program has been in operation about two days, we would ask the mother to call and give a progress report. If things are not proceeding according to plan, adjustments would be made quickly, and the mother would be reinforced (verbally) for what she has done correctly.

Negative Reinforcement

Even though we have talked at some length about positive control using reinforcement, we have not exhausted the uses of operant conditioning. Strengthening desirable behavior may be accomplished by using negative reinforcement. This form of behavior control is not as widely used, however, because aversive stimuli are involved.

In our earlier discussion of positive and negative reinforcement, it was noted that when a response is performed that removes an aversive stimulus, that response or behavior is strengthened. That is, we perform a response (or a set of responses) that allows us to escape the aversive stimulus. Escape and avoidance behaviors are similar to one another in that we succeed in keeping the aversive effects of a stimulus away from us; they are different, however, in that with avoidance behavior a response is performed *to prevent the onset* of the aversive stimulus. With escape (or negative conditioning) a response is performed that *removes* an aversive stimulus.

Negative conditioning functions in many areas of everyday life experiences. Our behavior is greatly controlled in that we behave in ways that allow us to remove or escape the effects of aversive stimuli. For example, a child who has a very demanding mother will act to remove the aversive stimulus by leaving the house or ceasing to hear his mother when she makes one of her numerous demands; or during the winter we escape the cold by going inside.

When negative conditioning is used clinically to strengthen a response, obviously one must use some type of noxious or aversive stimulus. Typically, in experimental and clinical situations with people, electric shock and uncomfortable (but not injurious) noise have been used as aversive stimuli. These types of aversive stimuli are used because they are relatively easy to use and tend to induce a minimum of physical discomfort and few, if any, side effects.

The role that negative reinforcement has in maintaining *inappropriate* behavior is illustrated by an experiment by Flanagan, Goldiamond, and Azrin (1958). They were interested in determining the effects of aversive stimulation on stuttering. In the first experimental condition (the aversive period), three stutterers were asked to read aloud, and each occurrence of stuttering was immediately accompanied by a one-second blast of 105 decibel white noise in the subject's earphones. In the second experimental condition (the escape period), the aversive auditory stimulation was continuous but could be terminated for five seconds when stuttering occurred. The second experimental condition was essentially a negative reinforcement procedure.

The results indicated that the response-contingent aversive stimulation terminated stuttering almost completely in one subject and substantially decreased speech blockage in the other two subjects. In the second experimental condition (the negative reinforcement condition), which allowed the subject to escape the aversive auditory stimulation for five seconds each time he stuttered, the frequency of stuttering increased. However, when stuttering did

not enable the subjects to escape from the aversive stimulation, the speech blockage decreased. Apparently, stuttering was maintained because it enabled the subject to escape an aversive stimulus.

Modeling

The tendency to imitate, or perform responses similar to those of a model, plays an exceedingly important role in learning. Indeed, every parent is well aware of the extent to which a young child's behavior is a reflection of his or her own. If the imitations are reflections of the behavior we like in ourselves, we proudly applaud this acquisition. But we are occasionally chagrined when the child has imitated too well a behavior we have exhibited in an unguarded moment. It is also easy to observe the frequency of the uttered phrase "Show me how" as our young learners are busily engaged in the acquisition of new response patterns.

We have seen in our discussion of operant conditioning that before a response can be learned through such procedures, the behavior, or an approximation of it, must exist in the person's repertoire. A response that is not performed cannot be reinforced. If the behavior to be learned is complex and involves many elements, the probability that it will occur and thus can be reinforced may not be great. Thus, operant methods may be useful in controlling behavior that already exists, but inefficient in promoting new behavior.

Operant conditioning may not be as efficient as modeling in another respect. When it is desirable to teach behavior or to train people in skills that involve elements of danger, trial and error may be risky. Rather, appropriate models that exhibit the behavior may greatly reduce trial and error and provide real dividends in learning (Bandura, 1965).

A number of different terms have been used to describe observational learning. For example, the terms *modeling, imitation,* and *copying* are used interchangeably by some, while others use them in a more definitive way. But, as Bandura (1969) has suggested, the distinctions may not be of great importance since a number of studies indicate that *matching responses* (responses made by the imitator that are the same as the model's) as well as more complete behavior repertoires appear to be determined by similar antecedent conditions. Perhaps it is unnecessary to make distinctions if we keep in mind that all three terms refer to learning acquired by an observer as a result of watching a model perform certain specific responses; the observer may perform the modeled activities during, immediately after, or some time after the model's performance. Also, depending on how the modeling activities are arranged and the learning situation constructed, observational learning may involve a live human model or a symbolic model (a picture or film-mediated version) with or without reinforcement for performance of specific responses by the observer.

Theories of Modeling

Several theories have been proposed to explain observational learning or modeling. An associative and classical conditioning conception was espoused by Holt (1931), the essence of which was that modeling occurs when modeling stimuli and matching responses by the imitator occur together in a short interval of time. Sometime later, Miller and Dollard (1941) proposed that modeling tends to result when an adequately motivated observer is positively reinforced for matching the appropriate responses of a model in a situation that is initially trial and error. More recently, on the basis of considerable evidence, Bandura (1969) has formulated a contiguity-mediational theory to explain model learning that occurs when no overt responses are exhibited by the observer of the modeled responses.

Bandura (1969) suggests that observational learning involves two processes and/or representational systems: imaginal and verbal. Images of the model's responses are formed as a result of sensory conditioning. That is, modeling stimuli induce perceptual responses in the observer that are sequentially associated and integrated as a result of temporal contiguity of the modeling stimuli. And even though perceptual processes induced by modeling stimuli are transitory, they tend to endure in the observer and can be retrieved at a later time. Subsequently, the recalled images of the modeled activities or responses function as mediators to direct the reproduction of the imitative, or matching, responses by the observer.

A second type of cognitive process is also involved in observational learning. As the modeled stimuli induce images in the observer, a type of verbal coding of the observed stimuli takes place. An example will illustrate what this process involves. Several years ago, the nine-year-old daughter of one of the authors accompanied him to the university to pick up his mail that had accumulated during a holiday. His daughter observed as he opened his combination-lock mailbox. When he had completed the sequence, his daughter remarked, "That is an easy combination. All you need to remember is the first two letters of our last name [BL] and then add three to B and five to L." The combination was, in fact, three past B and around to five past L in a clockwise direction. Very quickly she had verbally coded the combination. The author was surprised by her incidental observation of the modeled activities. He asked her if she would like to open the mailbox. This she did, without error, to the delight of both parties.

This account also illustrates other elements that Bandura considers important in his formulation of observational learning. The child had made an appropriate attentional investment, discriminated the important modeled cues, and retrieved, as a result of symbolic representation (coding), the modeled events.

Observational learning may occur without external reinforcement. For example, children imitate their favorite television characters without knowledge that their accurate imitations will be rewarded. However, not all behavior of the model is imitated; obviously, the modeled behavior must have some relevance to the observer. The anticipation that one will be positively reinforced for learning the modeled behavior facilitates attention and retention of what is observed. Reinforcement has a facilitating effect; it is an important condition for the *performance* of the modeled behavior but is not required for the *acquisition* of the modeled behavior. In other words, observers may learn the modeled behavior but not exhibit it until reinforcement has been administered. Moreover, the reinforcement need not be externally administered; the reinforcement may be vicariously experienced or self-administered (Bandura, 1971b).

Positive reinforcement of the observer is not the only condition that facilitates modeling behavior. Reinforcement of the *model* for the performance of certain behavior tends to facilitate the learning of the modeled behavior in the observer. However, imitation of the modeled behavior is decreased when either the model or the imitator is punished directly or vicariously (Bandura, 1969). For example, suppose a child of seven years of age is very shy. The child is exposed to a child model who exhibits active, outgoing social behavior. As the child model behaves in this way, she is socially reinforced by an adult for her extroversive behavior. The shy child who observes the model being socially reinforced for extroversive behavior is more likely to imitate the modeled behavior than would be true if the model were not reinforced.

The implications of these findings for the practitioner are obvious. If one wishes to increase imitative behavior in an observer, one must (1) specify the behavior that is desirable for the observer to learn, (2) have an appropriate model perform the desired behavior, (3) reinforce the model for performance of the desired behavior, and (4) reinforce the observer for appropriate imitation of the modeled behavior.

Types of Behavior Learned Through Modeling

If observation of modeled behavior is an important form of learning, what types of behavior can most efficiently be acquired in this way? Studies tend to indicate that observational learning affects three general classes of response. First, modeling has demonstrated utility in the acquisition of new (i.e., not previously in the repertoire) or novel (i.e., unique or unusual) responses. Second, modeling may have an inhibiting or disinhibiting (liberating) effect on previously acquired responses, depending of course upon the behavior exhibited by the model. Third, observing a model may evoke or trigger in the learner a response that has assumed a somewhat neutral status in his repertoire. For example, a child who is not, say, particularly aggressive may upon observing an aggressive model become more aggressive.

The effects of modeling are not limited to motor response. Modeling activities of certain specific types may affect cognitive competencies, interpersonal relationships, and coping behavior. Certain kinds of affective or emotional reactions can be modified. From a model who exhibits particular affective reactions, the observer may acquire the same or similar emotional responses. Avoidance or fearful reactions may be eliminated by observing the model's approach behavior toward fearful objects that does not result in negative consequences (Bandura and Walters, 1963; Bandura, 1969).

The use of modeling procedures to strengthen desirable behavior and to inhibit the undesirable has been clearly demonstrated by Bandura (1967). In one of his experiments, children with fear of dogs were placed in four experimental groups. Group I watched a child without fear of dogs interact, in a party setting, with a dog. Children in Group II watched a child without fear interact with a dog in a nonparty setting. Group III children watched a dog in a party setting without a child model interacting with the dog. Group IV children joined in party activities but were not exposed to a dog or child model. The results indicated that those children who had received modeling treatment (Groups I and II) lost their fear of dogs. At a later time, the experiment was duplicated in essential detail, with a film rather than the real-life version used previously, but with similar results.

Bandura (1965) has also demonstrated that physical and verbal aggression can be strengthened by using film-mediated models. In this type of experimental paradigm, one group of children viewed an aggressive model being punished, a second group watched the aggressive model rewarded, and a third group saw no consequences of the model's aggression. In posttest evaluations, subjects in the reward and no-consequence groups exhibited significantly greater numbers of imitative responses.

In order to determine the variables responsible for the learned imitative responses, Bandura followed the posttreatment evaluations by offering children in all groups incentives (rewards) for reproducing the model's responses. The use of incentives completely removed observed performance differences. Equal amounts of imitative learning appeared to have taken place in the group that saw the model rewarded, the model punished, and the model experience no consequence. Apparently, the imitative responses were learned as a result of modeling *and not as a consequence of reward.* Reinforcement seemed to provide the conditions by

which the learning that had been acquired could be demonstrated.

It can be seen that film-mediated models may be as effective as real-life models for inducing the acquisition or change of certain behaviors. Nonhuman cartoon characters in films appear to have less dramatic modeling effects, although they are still useful (Bandura, 1965). Baer and Sherman (1964) have also shown that certain types of imitative behavior increased as a consequence of social reinforcement from a puppet.

These studies demonstrate the potent effects of real life and symbolic models in promoting behavior change. Specifically, modeling has demonstrated effectiveness in modifying certain types of prosocial (that is, appropriately social) and deviant behavior, nonadaptive emotional behavior, play patterns, standards of self-evaluation and self-reinforcement, language learning, and the enhancement of the ability to postpone gratifications (Bandura, 1969).

Modification of Behavior Through Modeling

The extent to which behavior may be acquired or changed through modeling is related to characteristics of the learner, characteristics of the model, and the modeled activities. We noted that the acquisition of the modeled responses involves four basic processes. First, the learner must attend to and perceive the distinctive cues of the modeled performance. Second, the observer must retain the modeled behavior by coding it verbally or imaginally. Third, the observer must be able to reproduce motorally the modeled responses, using symbolic representation of the modeled behavior to guide his performance. Fourth, proper incentive and/or reinforcement conditions must be present to ensure that the observer will in fact perform the modeled behavior. If conditions in the learner or learning situation interfere with these processes, the modeling effects are not likely to occur.

Imitation of the modeled performance increases when the learner (1) has a previous history of receiving reward for imitating the behavior of others, (2) considers the modeled behavior exemplary, (3) manifests low self-esteem, (4) is highly dependent, and (5) is incompetent (Zinzer, 1966; Goldstein, Heller, and Sechrist, 1966; Bandura, 1971b).

The characteristics of the model also determine the extent to which modeling occurs. Models who are warm and nurturant and have prestige, power, and competence are more likely to be imitated. When the observer is a child, a model of the same sex tends to enhance modeling effects (Goldstein, Heller, and Sechrist, 1966; Bandura, 1971a).

In addition to the influence of model and learner characteristics, specific elements in the modeled activities act to facilitate imitative behavior. As Bandura (1971a) has noted, imitation is greatly facilitated when (1) the model is reinforced, (2) the model's status is enhanced as a result of the behavior he exhibits, (3) the modeled activities help the learner discriminate those situations in which the modeled behavior is appropriate and likely to be reinforced, and (4) the modeled activities are sequentially graduated.

Various types of modeled activities can be used to promote the desired behavior change. Modeled performances may be presented by live models, films of live models, cartoon characters in films, puppets, or real-life model enactments followed by *participant modeling* by the observer(s). The type or form of modeling used is, of course, dependent on the specific behavior one wishes to change and the situation of the practitioner.

Suppose we wish to modify the inhibited and socially avoidant behavior of an eight-year-old girl. We might first analyze and/or ask the child to identify the social situations and social behavior that give her the most difficulty. The socially deficient behaviors are arranged in a hierarchy from least to most difficult to perform. If a series of films is available in which the social behavior is appropriately modeled, we might present them in the hierarchical arrangement to our client. After each presentation of a specific social skill, the client is reinforced for performing matching behaviors. These activities could be videotaped and replayed with both therapist and client present. During the replay, the therapist would verbally reinforce performance of the desired social behavior in the tape and provide constructive feedback to enhance the client's role enactments. If necessary, the situation may be reenacted until the appropriate social behaviors are skillfully performed. To encourage generalization, significant adults may be encouraged to reinforce the desirable behavior of the client whenever it occurs.

Simpler modeling procedures can be used with our hypothetical eight-year-old client. After the deficient social behavior is specified, a child model with high status and prestige enacts the desirable social behavior, beginning with a behavior that is simplest to perform. The therapist is also involved by assuming the role of a person with whom the model interacts. As the model enacts the socially desirable behavior she is reinforced, and the client is reinforced for performing the appropriate matching responses. Subsequently, each successive desirable social behavior is enacted by the model and then the observer, and both are reinforced. When the desired social behavior is appropriately performed in the therapeutic situation, generalization may be encouraged by reinforcing the client for performing the appropriate behavior as it occurs in a social context.

Similar procedures were used by Gittelman (1965) to modify undesirable aggressive behavior in children. The children were asked to discuss situations in which they usually behaved aggressively. A hierarchy of these aggression-arousing situations was constructed from the least to most provocative. The children in the group were then asked to enact or role play them and rehearse nonviolent ways of handling them.

As the Gittelman study suggests, modeling procedures can be used with groups as well as individuals. For example, Ritter (1968) involved in group modeling procedures forty-four preadolescent boys and girls who were fearful of snakes. The treatment consisted of two thirty-five-minute sessions. In the first session, the subjects observed fearless peer models interact with a snake. In the second session, they watched the experimenter positively interact with a snake and subsequently imitated the model's approach responses. Both procedures proved statistically significant in reducing snake avoidance behavior in the subjects. However, the second treatment, the *participant modeling* procedure, proved more effective. Considering that the treatment time involved for both modeling procedures was seventy minutes, the powerful effects of modeling become immediately apparent.

The potent effects of film-mediated modeling procedures in changing social isolate behavior in nursery school children were similarly demonstrated by O'Connor (1972). He was interested in comparing the relative efficacy of shaping and modeling procedures in enhancing socially adaptive behavior of thirty-three nursery school children. The identified social isolates were randomly placed in four different treatment conditions. The first (modeling-shaping) group was shown a modeling film and was verbally reinforced for successively approximating desirable social interactions with peers. A second (modeling) group was shown the modeling film but did not receive external reinforcement. A third (shaping) group, shown no film, was verbally reinforced for successively approximating desirable social interaction. A fourth (control) group was shown a film about

dolphins. Groups receiving *shaping*, or successive approximation procedures, received about five hours of treatment time during a two-week period, although this amount varied within the groups.

Each group was assessed for levels of social interaction at four different times; approximately three weeks intervened between assessments. Analysis of the data indicated an initial increase in social interaction for all three treatment groups. However, in the final and follow-up assessment period, the *modeling-only group* clearly surpassed the shaping group and the modeling-shaping group. The modeling-shaping group did maintain, however, a significantly high level of social interaction. Thus, in this experiment modeling was shown to be a much more effective procedure than shaping, and behaviors learned through modeling were more durable.

The therapeutic utility of modeling procedures is aptly documented in the experimental and clinical literature. The studies reviewed in this chapter suggest only a few of the many therapeutic applications of modeling in modifying undesirable behavior. Other applications are discussed in various sections of this book.

Summary

1. Behavior is learned for two basic reasons: (a) to obtain positive consequences or reinforcement, and (b) to terminate noxious stimulation that is physically or psychologically painful.

2. Respondent conditioning is a process by which a previously neutral stimulus — by repeated pairing with an unconditioned stimulus that automatically elicits an unconditioned response — becomes a conditioned stimulus and elicits the conditioned response by itself. Extinction of the response will occur if the conditioned stimulus is not periodically paired with the unconditioned stimulus. A conditioned response that has been extinguished tends to reappear (spontaneous recovery) after a period of time.

3. Emotional reactions are learned primarily through a process of respondent conditioning. When a person evokes a fear reaction in a child, any stimulus that is present and paired with the fear-provoking person will later tend to elicit the same fear reaction in the child.

4. Emotional reactions may also be acquired by vicarious respondent conditioning. Fearful reactions may be learned by simply watching others be hurt or respond fearfully to certain objects or situations.

5. Undesirable conditioned emotional reactions may be changed by a process of counter-conditioning. Three basic procedures have been used: (a) a person may be desensitized by being trained to relax in the presence of the fear-provoking stimulus or situation; (b) the fearful or avoidant subject may watch a model perform the fear-provoking behavior without negative consequences; or (c) undesirable approach responses may be changed by presenting the approach response in imagination and pairing it with an aversive stimulus. Electric shock and nausea-producing drugs have often been used as aversive stimuli, and, more recently, the visualization of an extremely repugnant scene has also been used.

6. Many, if not most, of our responses are learned and maintained by positive and negative reinforcement. Positive and negative reinforcement act to strengthen behavior, while punishment tends to suppress it. Approach behaviors are usually learned by positive reinforcement, and escape and avoidance behaviors are often the result of negative reinforcement.

7. Operant behavior is typically promoted by using a series of steps described in the operant paradigm. To promote operant behavior (a) define and state operationally the behavior to be changed, (b) obtain a baseline or operant level of the behavior you wish to promote, (c) prompt or arrange the learning situation facilitative for the target response, (d) identify potential reinforcers, (e) shape and/or reinforce desired behavior immediately and continuously upon its occurrence, and (f) keep records of the reinforced behavior to determine if the reinforcement procedures increase the strength or frequency of the target behavior.

8. Adaptive and/or desired behavior may be promoted by (a) reinforcing successive approximations of the target behavior (shaping); (b) arranging and varying stimulus conditions so that the desired behavior occurs (fading); (c) observing and imitating the responses of a model; (d) using contingency management to increase a low-probability behavior by following its occurrence with the opportunity to participate in a high-probability behavior; and (e) using punishment to inhibit the undesirable behavior and simultaneously reinforcing the desirable behavior.

9. Most of the behavior people exhibit in their daily lives is composed of a series of response chains. Chaining essentially involves (a) learning separate S-R units, (b) executing each of the S-R units in proper sequence and in close time succession, and (c) reinforcement of the final response link immediately after its occurrence. The learning of response chains can be greatly enhanced by using modeling and by providing verbal instructions to direct sequential performance of the behavior.

10. Operant behavior may be promoted most effectively by positively reinforcing the response immediately and continuously each time it occurs. Once the desired behavior is performed at a high rate, reinforcement can be varied in terms of time (interval schedule) or on the basis

of the number of responses that are performed between reinforcements (ratio schedule). Interval schedules may be fixed or varied according to the time interval that is used between reinforcements. Similarly, ratio schedules may be fixed or varied. A fixed-ratio reinforcement schedule is an intermittent reinforcement schedule in which reinforcement occurs after a fixed number of responses. A variable-ratio reinforcement schedule is one in which reinforcement occurs after a variable number of responses are performed.

11. The reinforcement schedule has varied effects on the behavior. Ratio schedules are characterized by a high rate of responding—the number of nonreinforced to reinforced responses is small. Both fixed- and variable-ratio schedules maintain a high response rate, but with fixed ratios there is a postreinforcement pause. Response rate is usually much lower with interval schedules, depending, of course, on the size of the time interval. Fixed-interval schedules produce rapid responding immediately after reinforcement, with a subsequent slowing until the next reinforcement. However variable-interval schedules tend to maintain steady responding somewhat better than fixed-interval reinforcement schedules. Intermittent or variable reinforcement tends to maintain and enhance the durability of the response.

12. Negative reinforcement acts to strengthen avoidance or escape behavior by preventing the onset of, or by removing, the aversive stimulus, respectively.

13. Observation of modeled performances is a highly efficient form of learning. It is useful in (a) the acquisition of new or novel responses, (b) strengthening or weakening inhibitory responses, and (c) facilitating the responses in a person's repertoire. When an observer watches a live or film-mediated model perform behavior considered desirable in the observer, those behaviors are, in fact facilitated in the observer. Through the use of modeling procedures, avoidance and fearful reactions can be eliminated and adaptive interpersonal behaviors may be greatly enhanced. Modeling effects appear to be enhanced when (a) the modeled activities are graduated and enhance the status of the model; (b) the model is prestigious, warm, and powerful and is reinforced for his performance; and (c) the learner is dependent, incompetent, or lacking self-esteem and receives reinforcement for appropriate matching responses.

Chapter Three

Methods for Promoting Behavior Change: Weakening Inappropriate Behavior

In this chapter we will discuss methods useful in decreasing or eliminating undesirable behavior. Some of these procedures (extinction, physically aversive stimulation, response cost, and time-out) produce their effects through the systematic manipulation of negative consequences or the withdrawal or termination of positive reinforcement. Other methods which utilize different principles to reduce undesirable behavior (satiation, negative practice, and systematic desensitization) will also be discussed.

The Nature of Extinction

We have stated that behavior is maintained by either positive or negative reinforcement. Consequently, to change behavior the reinforcing stimuli must be withheld. When we stop reinforcing the behavior, it tends to be extinguished. For example, if an indulged child makes unreasonable demands, the behavior will tend to decrease in strength when the parents stop conceding to (reinforcing) the demands (Lundin, 1974). However, it may take many nonreinforced trials before the demanding behavior is extinguished.

It was noted in the previous chapter that the rate at which behavior is extinguished is a function of the reinforcement schedule by which the behavior was learned and/or maintained. When behavior has been reinforced on a continuous schedule (100 percent reinforcement), extinction takes place rapidly. Responses learned with ratio schedules extinguish less rapidly; usually, responding continues at a high rate but drops off rather dramatically when the behavior is about to be extinguished. To extinguish behavior maintained with interval schedules is extremely difficult; after withdrawal of reinforcement, responding continues at a low but persistent rate.

Obviously, if one wishes to change behavior that is considered undesirable, it is important to know something about the reinforcement history. The reinforcement history and schedule generally indicate how long the extinction procedures may take; the person implementing the extinction procedures will not be too inclined to terminate prematurely or give up in the belief that the procedures "will not work." Lack of consistency and persistence in withholding reinforcement may result in reinstating the behavior at full strength. And, for the disbeliever, this may amount to the actualization of a self-fulfilling prophecy. What the disbeliever wanted all along may take place because a reinforcement "just happened" to be given.

It should also be noted that there is an increase in responding after reinforcement has been removed. Consequently, the undesirable behavior one is attempting to remove may, for a while, become worse. However, if one persists in withholding the reinforcement, the behavior will eventually be extinguished (Sulzer, Mayer, and Cody, 1968).

The use of extinction procedures has been effectively demonstrated by Harris, Wolf, and Baer (1964). The subjects of their experimentation were children three and four years of age who exhibited various types of undesirable behavior, such as excessive crying, passivity, isolated play, etc. Illustrative of the extinction procedures used are those employed with a four-year-old boy who tended to cry excessively from mild frustration. Observations of the behavior revealed that the boy averaged approximately eight "crying episodes" each morning at school. The episodes consistently obtained teacher attention, interest, and concern. The teacher was instructed to simply ignore the behavior; for ten days the child's crying was ignored while attention was given for self-help behavior. During the last five days of the ten-day period, crying was observed only once.

To ascertain whether reinforcement had previously maintained the crying behavior, crying was once again reinforced (by giving attention to it). The crying behavior quickly returned to a rate approximating the original baseline. However, with the implementation of the extinction (ignoring the crying) for another ten-day period, the behavior decreased to near zero.

The effectiveness of extinction in decreasing frequency of an undesirable behavior is clearly demonstrated by the Harris et al. study. It should be noted, however, that the procedures used involved both nonreinforcement of the undesirable behavior as well as the *reinforcement of the desirable behavior.* Such a procedure seems to be more efficient than simply withholding the reinforcement for the undesirable behavior.

The treatment of tantrum behavior in a twenty-one-month-old boy by the use of the withdrawal of reinforcement has been reported by Williams (1959). The boy, who had received much care during a rather severe illness during his first eighteen months, continued to make excessive demands for care upon his recovery. When these demands were not responded to, particularly at bedtime, he exhibited extreme temper tantrums.

When the child was put to bed, a routine performed alternately by the parents and an aunt, the child would have a tantrum unless they remained in his room until he had gone to sleep. The child, who obviously had considerable control over the parents, would protest loudly if the parents read while waiting for him to go to sleep.

In order to extinguish the behavior, the parents were instructed to put the boy to bed in a relaxed, unhurried way. Once the child was in bed, the parents left the room and closed the door. Initially, the exit of the parents from the bedroom was greeted with intense crying. The parents were instructed not to return, however. After ten such sessions, the child no longer cried or seemed upset.

Unfortunately, a week later, the boy began to exhibit his crying behavior, and the aunt reinforced the behavior by remaining in the room until he went to sleep. This necessitated the implementation of the extinction procedures again. After nine sessions, the crying behavior once again returned to zero. No undesirable side effects from the treatment were observed.

It would be fortunate if all behavior were susceptible to extinction as the two case reports indicate. Behaviors that can be extinguished usually are ones maintained by positive reinforcement, administered more or less continuously. There are, however, many responses or behaviors that have been induced by successful avoidance of aversive stimulation. That is, the behavior has been negatively reinforced. Such behavior is powerfully resistant to extinction. Obviously, when a response is performed that leads to the avoidance of or escape from an aversive or painful stimulus, it has important survival value. For example, Skinner (1953) cites the case of a saleman who rang a doorbell that caused the back end of a house to explode. Apparently, gas had escaped in the kitchen, and when the doorbell was rung sparks were generated to cause the explosion. Although Skinner does not comment on the behavior changes in the salesman, the incident no doubt changed his doorbell-ringing behavior.

Unusual resistance to extinction, as well as the potentially damaging effects that avoidance-learned responses have, is revealed in a well-known experiment with monkeys. Two monkeys were placed side by side in chairs that restrained them. The first, or executive monkey, was given an electric shock every twenty seconds, which he could delay by pressing a button. The second monkey was shocked in similar fashion, but button pressing did not delay the shock. Consequently, the executive monkey had the responsibility of postponing the aversive shock. The second monkey was not able to assume a similar managerial role, since his button pressing did not delay the shock. These procedures continued for many days and were alternated by six-hour periods of avoidance training and rest (Cohen, 1969).

After twenty-three days, the executive monkey died. Autopsy revealed perforations and lesions in the duodenum wall. The other monkey did not reveal similar physical or physiological damage. Subsequent experiments with other monkeys revealed similar devastating results in executive-type monkeys, although physical damage was even more severe. Apparently, the stress (fear) experienced by the executive monkey was the cause of his demise. This is a powerful demonstration indeed of the dangerous effects of constant stress on an organism (Cohen, 1969).

Once animals and humans have learned to perform responses to avoid aversive stimuli, these responses will be executed literally hundreds of times even though the aversive stimuli are no longer present. Apparently, intense aversive stimuli create automatic fear reactions that evoke instrumental responses to escape from or avoid the aversive stimuli. Such instrumental responses are so powerfully energized that one continues to perform them rather than take a chance of being reexposed to the physical or psychological pain. Subsequently, the fear reaction associated with the aversive stimulus maintains the avoidance behavior because the fear is reduced when the avoidance response is performed. Consequently, one will not take the necessary steps to confront the feared situation, which may no longer be present or which can now be more readily coped with. Such is the case of people who exhibit various types of behavior disorders.

Satiation and Negative Practice

Most of us are acquainted with the well-known remedy of deterring a child's interest in and experimentation with smoking by buying him a box of cigars and encouraging him to smoke "to his heart's content." After he has smoked his way through a box of cigars, his appetite for smoking generally tends to decrease markedly. One way of explaining his decreased interest and experimentation with smoking is that the abundant provision of cigars leads to satiation. But another explanation is that after ten or fifteen consecutive cigars, smoking may have become an aversive stimulus.

The use of satiation and its opposite, deprivation, have demonstrated value in changing behavior. As illustrated in the cigar-smoking example, *satiation* is induced by providing such an abundance of a stimulus that its reinforcement properties are lost (Ullmann and Krasner, 1965). The abundant presentation, or in the case of food the massive consumption, of the stimulus leads to a marked decrement in its appeal.

A close cousin to the stimulus satiation procedure is that of *negative practice*. When this method is used, the person who exhibits an inappropriate response (nail biting, stammering, cursing, etc.) is encouraged to repeatedly perform the response. That is, the person is requested to perform, for example, the stammering response over and over. Eventually, the stammering stops for three basic reasons: (1) the response is extinguished because anxiety is no longer associated with it; (2) the fatigue that accumulates by its repetition makes the performance of the response painful and/or aversive (Ullmann and Krasner, 1965); and (3) the person is made more aware of the successive steps involved in the performance of the behavior and the sequence is interrupted.

At first glance it may appear that satiation and negative practice are really the same thing. However, there is a subtle difference. Although each may (in some instances) involve the performance of a particular response repeatedly, when satiation is used a stimulus is always involved. The repeated presentation or exposure of the stimulus eventually makes it aversive. In negative practice, a person is requested to perform an inappropriate response repeatedly, but no stimulus is involved. The repetition of the response in mass practice sessions leads to a decrease in its frequency.

A simple illustration of the use of negative practice was reported by a school psychologist colleague of one of the writers. A teacher asked the psychologist what she might do to terminate the behavior of a third-grade boy who frequently performed imitations of various animal sounds. The psychologist instructed the teacher to place the child in an empty room adjacent to the classroom and direct him to make the imitations for ten minutes. If the child stopped the imitations, the teacher was instructed to have the child continue by the verbal direction "Please continue." After a few series of ten-minute imitation periods, the teacher reported no more difficulty with animal imitations in the classroom.

Another example of the use of negative practice in eliminating undesirable behavior was brought to the attention of one of the authors quite incidentally at a special school where he serves as a consultant. A child who attends the school was well known for his frequent use of foul language. He cursed almost continuously regardless of the situation but especially when riding to and from school on the bus. After tolerating it for many weeks, the bus driver felt compelled to do something about it. One morning the youngster's language was particularly abusive. Upon arrival at school, the driver immediately ushered the boy to a vacant room. He instructed him to say all the dirty words he knew. He insisted that the boy shout them as loudly as he could for at least five minutes. After two or three minutes, the boy was ready to go to class, but he was urged to continue for about five minutes. After he complied with the request, the youngster was permitted to go to his classroom.

Several days after the incident, the driver apparently began to feel guilty about what he had done and requested an audience with one of the authors. The driver described the incident and indicated that he had used it previously with good results. However, in this instance it was so dramatically effective, he wondered whether he had produced some unobserved side effects that he was unable to discern. Apparently, the boy had not cursed in the driver's presence since the incident and had become much easier to live with. Inquiries were made into the child's classroom and playground behavior to determine whether his foul language had decreased or other undesirable behavior had appeared. Indeed, the cursing had sharply decreased, and no other negative side effects were observed.

Punishment

Punishment is a frequently used form of behavior control. Parents are often observed spanking, scolding, withdrawing their approval, or withholding privileges, when a child has acted in an undesirable way. Polls taken of teachers indicate that a large percentage favor the use of punishment at school. Moreover, as lawlessness increases in our society, many citizens express the need for more severe penalties for lawbreakers. Yet, even though punishment is used frequently, many oppose its use on the grounds it is inhumane. Because of the intense debate on this issue, we will want to examine the utility of punishment as a behavior change method and consider any undesirable side effects that may accompany its use.

Punishment may be defined as the act of presenting an aversive stimulus (spanking, hair pulling, scolding) or withdrawing a reinforcing stimulus event (withdrawal of approval or a privilege) during or after the performance of an undesirable behavior. While the goal of positive and negative reinforcement is to *strengthen* behavior, the aim of punishment is to *stop or suppress* behavior. Although some implicitly assume punishment alone will encourage the desired behavior, it rarely does so.

As the definition suggests, punishment may be administered in several ways. The use of an aversive experience, such as spanking, is the form usually employed. A second type of punishment, sometimes referred to as *response cost*, is used when positive reinforcing stimuli or events are removed. For example, a child is denied the privilege of participating in an appealing activity because of some undesirable behavior he has exhibited. A third type of punishment, often referred to as *time-out*, involves isolating the subject from all sources of reinforcement for a specific period of time (Sherman, 1973). A fourth type of punishment, *over-correction*, requires an individual who has performed an inappropriate act to restore the environment to a better state than existed before the disruptive act occurred (Sulzer-Azaroff and Mayer, 1977). We will consider response cost, time-out, and overcorrection in subsequent sections.

In the past ten years, the effects of punishment on behavior have been studied rather extensively. In substance, the research suggests that the extent to which punishment is effective in suppressing undesirable behavior depends on (1) the intensity, duration, frequency, and dispensation of the aversive consequences; (2) when punishment is administered; (3) the strength of the punished response; (4) alternate responses available; and (5) the extent to which the opposite or desired behavior is reinforced (Bandura, 1969).

To be effective, the administered punishment must be sufficiently intense and last long enough to be experienced by the subject as unpleasant or aversive. It must be administered *every time*, and *during* or *immediately after* the undesirable behavior has occurred. Research suggests that it is more effective to administer punishment as soon as the undesirable behavior begins than to wait until it has run its course (Parke, 1969). If the undesirable behavior is well entrenched, greater intensity and frequency of punishment is required to inhibit the behavior. Also, to achieve positive results, an alternate, more desirable response should be available to the subject, and it should be frequently reinforced. That is, the undesirable behavior should be punished, and the socially appropriate behavior should be adequately reinforced at the same time (Bandura, 1969).

Threats of punishment that are not carried out have little capacity to terminate the undesirable behavior. However, if a threat is discharged immediately, it is likely to be effective. Executing a punishment threat not only helps to inhibit the undesirable behavior in the offender, but may have a similar effect on others who watch the administration of punishment (Bandura, 1969).

Possible Side Effects of Punishment

Studies tend to show that punishment, if used properly, need have no undesirable side effects. Unfortunately, the guiding principles often go unheeded, and side effects do occur. For example, repeated punishment of an aggressive behavior may not only inhibit the aggression but all forms of assertiveness as well. To avoid such undesirable generalization effects, the punished behavior should be clearly specified and the desirable behavior frequently reinforced. These distinctions can be more clearly understood by a child if the times and places that specific behaviors are appropriate or inappropriate are clearly indicated.

A second possible side effect of punishment is that it may lead to avoidance of the punisher and/or others similar to the punishing agent. If this happens, they may lose the ability to be positively reinforcing and thus promote desirable behavior.

A third potential side effect is that punishment may lead to escape and avoidance behaviors undesirable in and of themselves. For example, a child, in fear of punishment, may lie to escape it. Teenagers often attempt to escape from severe punishment by running away from home.

A fourth possible undesirable result of punishment is that the punisher might act as an aggressive model to be imitated by the punished subject. Rather than performing the desired behavior, the punished child may perform the behavior of the punisher. For example, boys who have physically punitive fathers may often be observed acting physically aggressive in play activities with their peers.

Punishment need not lead to unsought consequences. [For example, Lovaas, Schaeffer, and Simmons (1965) and Risley (1968) have effectively used response-contingent shock to appropriately modify the behavior of autistic children. No adverse side effects seemed to accrue from the use of such procedures.] However, it must be emphasized that if punishment is used alone without reinforcement of the desirable behavior, the punished behavior may be inhibited only temporarily; it may return and sometimes with even greater strength.

Many of the harmful side effects of punishment may be avoided if contractual arrangements are formulated in advance which clearly specify both the desirable and undesirable behavior (Bandura, 1969). In the classroom, for example, the teacher should indicate at the beginning of the year permissible and nonpermissible behavior and indicate the consequences for both. The children will then have clear guidelines for behavior. Of course, once the contingencies are set up, they must be consistently enforced.

Let us briefly summarize guidelines to avoid undesirable side effects from punishment:

1. Use punishment infrequently and never as the only method for controlling or eliminating undesirable behavior.

2. Specify clearly the acceptable and unacceptable behavior and the consequences for each. When a child is punished, he or she should know the reasons for the punishment.

3. Punish the undesirable behavior as soon as it appears; do not wait until the behavior has run its course.

4. Provide desirable behavioral alternatives for the child.

5. While punishing the undesirable behavior, reinforce the behavior you wish to promote.

6. Be consistent in punishing behavior you wish to eliminate. Inconsistent punishment may make the undesirable behavior more durable.

Aversive Therapy

The clinical application of punishment, *aversive therapy*, is frequently used to decrease or eliminate behavior that has undesirable long-term effects, such as overeating, smoking, excessive alcohol consumption, drug abuse, and various types of sexual deviation. Because the reader is already acquainted with classical conditioning, the procedures involved in aversive therapy can be readily understood. Aversive therapy involves the pairing of a noxious stimulus (usually electric shock) with the maladaptive behavior or a stimulus object associated with the maladaptive behavior. In the case of fetishism (sexual arousal in the presence of a specific object), the subject holds the fetish object, looks at pictures of it, or imagines that he or she is touching or holding it, and while doing so, the subject is shocked electrically. With repeated pairings of the fetish object and shock, the subject begins to feel uncomfortable and anxious. The uncomfortable, anxious feelings become associated with the fetish object and the undesirable behavior; subsequently, the maladaptive fetish behavior is avoided.

Aversive therapy appears to have promise for eliminating maladaptive approach behavior. However, the evidence seems to suggest that such behavior may be only temporarily suppressed, unless initial treatment is followed by additional noxious stimulation and reinforcement of the adaptive behavior (Sherman, 1973).

The use of aversive therapy in combination with reinforcement and response cost is illustrated by a case report of a nine-year-old psychotic boy (Tate and Baroff, 1966). Sam, the institutionalized psychotic boy, was partially blind

and entered into a variety of self-injurious behavior. He would bang his head against immovable objects and punch his face and head with his fists. Because it was feared that his self-injurious behavior might lead to total blindness, effective intervention steps had to be taken immediately.

Previous observation of Sam's behavior suggested that he enjoyed physical contact and disliked being left alone. Consequently, initial sessions consisted of twenty-minute walks around the hospital grounds, Sam clasping the hands of the two experimenters. Anytime Sam withdrew his hands and hit himself, conversation and physical contact were terminated for three seconds. After this interval, Sam was permitted to hold the experimenters' hands again, and the walk continued. With the use of this response-cost procedure, his self-injurious behavior decreased considerably. However, because the self-injurious behavior was not completely eliminated and the risk of Sam destroying the retina of his right eye was considerable, another procedure was implemented: Whenever Sam performed self-injurious behavior in his room, a cattle prod delivered a painful shock to his right leg. At the same time, noninjurious behavior was reinforced with praise. This procedure was used for 167 days and resulted in the complete elimination of the self-injurious behavior. Favorable side effects were also reported. Sam's eating behavior improved, and he became much more spontaneous in play.

The case of Sam indicates how aversive therapy can be used effectively with other procedures to eliminate extreme forms of self-injurious behavior. However, the use of a cattle prod does raise some important ethical questions. Did the prospect of Sam's destroying his eyesight warrant the use of aversive shock? Should other less aversive procedures have been employed first? Was parent consent secured before the aversive shock was used? Did the experimenters secure other expert professional opinion to determine the treatment of choice?

The experimenters might have used aversive auditory stimulation, but it is questionable whether it would have been as effective as noxious shock. Research of various noxious stimuli (shock, nausea-producing drugs, noxious auditory stimulation) suggests that electric shock is much easier to manage and much more predictable in its effects (Mikulas, 1972).

Since we do not have complete information on the case and do not know the exact circumstances the experimenters faced, it is unwise to make judgments about case handling. However, it is important to indicate that when change agents deal with clients who exhibit self-injurious or other serious maladaptive behavior, it is important to secure informed consent, solicit other professional opinions, and consider potential side effects before an extreme or aversive treatment procedure is employed.

Covert Sensitization

A form of aversive therapy that appears less objectionable is the *covert sensitization* procedure used by Cautela (1966). You will recall from Chapter 2 that the procedure essentially involves use of imagined scenes as the noxious stimuli. First, the therapist specifies the maladaptive behavior that the client wishes to change. Then, the therapist uncovers experiences or conditions that the client considers unpleasant or repugnant. The client is asked to imagine himself executing the maladaptive behavior under certain conditions described by the therapist. When the client has a clear image of the scene, he is immediately asked to invoke an image that is extremely repugnant, and the therapist aids him with a vivid description of the noxious situation. Several practice trials are given under the guidance of the therapist. By

associating the undesirable behavior with the repugnant scene, the client begins to perceive the undesirable behavior as repugnant and eventually stops performing it.

Covert sensitization has much to recommend it because its application is limited only by the client's ability to imagine the appropriate scenes. Although covert sensitization has been frequently used with adults to modify undesirable social behavior (alcoholism, sexually deviant behavior), it appears to have utility in changing such undesirable adolescent behavior as exhibitionism and voyeurism. For the most part, covert sensitization is less objectionable on moral grounds than other forms of aversive therapy and appears to be very effective when used properly.

Response Cost

The removal or withdrawal of reinforcing stimuli and events upon the performance of an undesirable behavior is referred to as *response cost*. It is a well-known and frequently employed technique to depress undesirable behavior.

As the name implies, the undesirable response "costs" the individual something because a desired object, opportunity, or privilege is withdrawn or removed. For example, suppose a group of children are deeply engrossed in a game of Monopoly. As the trading and buying of property becomes more excited, one of the boys says, "Damn it." The boy's mother hears him and deducts five cents from his weekly allowance. Presumably, the response-contingent withdrawal of reinforcement (five cents) reduces the tendency to say "Damn it."

Studies suggest that response-cost contingencies can rapidly decrease some problem behaviors. Winkler (1970) found token fines to be very effective in reducing noise and violent behavior of psychiatric patients. Barrett (1965) used termination of reinforcing music to substantially decrease a tic in a thirty-eight-year-old man. Wolf, Hanley, King, Lachowicz, and Giles (1970) reduced the frequency of the out-of-seat behavior of an intractable child by contingent withdrawal of points for each incident of inappropriate behavior.

Although response cost has been shown to be effective in suppressing inappropriate behavior in several studies, the results are not unequivocal. And, some researchers have raised the question of undesirable side effects. Meichenbaum, Bowers, and Ross (1968) used a token reinforcement system to modify the classroom behavior of female delinquents. When a response-cost contingency was added to the system, there was a decrease in the mean number of appropriate classroom behaviors. As a matter of fact, even threats of fines generated quite negative reactions. Bucher and Hawkins (1971) specifically studied the disruptive effects of response cost (a fine) on their subjects. The imposed fine did not lead to an increase in disruptive behavior. Schmauk (1970) studied the side effects of shock, response cost, and disapproval on normal and sociopathic subjects. Shock produced greater autonomic arousal than response cost or disapproval, but there were no differences in the subjective ratings of anxiety among the three punishment procedures. Apparently, emotional side effects to response cost may occur, but the extent to which the effects are negative may be a function of the individual's problems and/or history (Kazdin, 1972).

Kazdin (1972) did an extensive review of response-cost studies and concluded that this procedure has demonstrated utility in suppressing a variety of inappropriate behaviors in children and adults. The behavior that is suppressed when response cost has been employed *usually* does not recover. Moreover, the side effects associated with other forms of punishment are not usually found with response cost. However, more long-term studies need to be conducted before a definitive statement can be made re-

garding treatment durability and side effects resulting from response-cost procedures.

Given the above discussion, what can be done to enhance the effects of response-cost procedures? First, response cost is most likely to suppress inappropriate behavior when alternate or incompatible responses are reinforced (Azrin and Holz, 1966). Second, the client's history should be studied to determine whether response-cost procedures are likely to produce undesirable negative reactions. In the absence of such indications, response cost should be employed experimentally for a short time to assess positive and negative effects. Third, the withdrawn reinforcement must be something the client values. For example, if an eleven-year-old boy is an enthusiastic baseball player, the loss of the opportunity to play in a coming game may be quite effective in suppressing an inappropriate behavior. The value of the withdrawn reinforcement, rather than the specific amount, may be an important variable in the effectiveness of response cost (Kazdin, 1972).

Overcorrection

Overcorrection is a mild form of punishment that is used to modify behavior that is disruptive to the environment. It has two forms. The first, *restitutional overcorrection*, requires an individual who has performed an inappropriate act to restore the environment to a better state than existed before the disruptive act occurred. For example, if an angry child throws water all over her desk, she is not only required to wipe up the water she has spilled on her desk, but also to wipe off her chair and the floor around her desk. The response the child is asked to perform not only reverses the results of the previous act but restores the environment to a better condition than existed previously (Sulzer-Azaroff and Mayer, 1977).

The second type of overcorrection is referred to as *positive practice overcorrection*. When this procedure is used, an individual who has performed a disruptive act is required to perform a positive and corrective action repeatedly. For example, if a disruptive student has thrown spitballs around the classroom, he would be asked to pick up all the thrown spitballs and to perform an additional positive behavior such as dusting the desks or sweeping the floor of the classroom. The action the student is asked to perform not only corrects the results of the original disruptive behavior but restores the environment in a way that is not necessarily associated with the previous inappropriate behavior (Sulzer-Azaroff and Mayer, 1977).

A good illustration of the utility of the overcorrection procedure is reported in a study by Azrin and Weslowski (1974). The study was conducted with thirty-four severely and profoundly retarded adults residing in an institution. All of the subjects had previously exhibited a high incidence of stealing on the ward, at mealtime and during a between-meal commissary period. The incidence of stealing was so high during the between-meal commissary period, some consideration was being given to discontinuing it.

To modify the stealing, an experiment was designed to determine the effectiveness of simple correction and overcorrection in dealing with the behavior. When one of the subjects took something from another person during the commissary period, the trainer required the offender to return the stolen item. If part of an edible item was already consumed before intervention was taken, the remainder of the item was washed and returned to the owner. This simple correction procedure continued for five days, and all incidents of stealing were recorded.

During the second experimental condition, all subjects were exposed to an overcorrection procedure. Each of the subjects, one group at a time, was allowed to select and eat an item during the between-meal commissary period.

Each time a theft occurred the trainer required the offender to return the stolen item and to give an additional identical item to the victim. The overcorrection condition also continued for five days, and each incident of stealing was recorded.

The incidence of stealing during each experimental condition was compared to determine which of the two procedures was most effective. During the simple correction condition there were twenty stealing incidents each day. With the implementation of the overcorrection procedure, thefts decreased by 50 percent to ten incidents the first day and by 90 percent to two incidents the third day. No stealing incidents occurred after the third day, or during the subsequent sixteen-day observation period. Obviously, the overcorrection procedure was the most effective.

Compared to other more aversive punishment procedures, overcorrection has some distinct advantages. First, overcorrection is less likely to produce withdrawal and negative self statements. Second, since the behavior change agent does not inflict pain or provide an aggressive model in applying the procedure, counteraggression is less likely to occur. Third, the procedure appears to have more rapid and enduring effects in reducing aggressive-disruptive behavior than time-out or verbal and physical punishment. Finally, overcorrection not only reduces inappropriate aggressive-disruptive behavior but provides an appropriate model that is likely to enhance more desirable social behavior (Foxx and Azrin, 1972; Sulzer-Azaroff and Mayer, 1977).

Time-Out

Time-out is used to terminate an undesirable behavior by removing an individual from a situation in which reinforcement is operating. It differs from response cost in that the *individual is removed* from the reinforcing situation, rather than withdrawing the reinforcing stimulus from the individual.

The procedure usually requires the use of a time-out room or area. When a child behaves undesirably, he is immediately taken to the time-out room. He is told that his behavior was unacceptable, and he will remain in the "quiet room" for a short period of time to help him gain control. Confinement is usually limited to a period of ten to fifteen minutes. Because the room is devoid of all reinforcing stimuli, the child is not permitted the opportunity to engage in any interesting or reinforcing activities. When the child has regained control and is ready to behave appropriately, he is allowed to resume his previous activities.

Teachers may feel that the time-out procedure is difficult to use because a time-out room is not readily available. However, there are usually a number of vacant areas in the school building (e.g., a book storage room or an empty cove near the principal's office) that can be converted for such purposes. A child may be placed in the back of the classroom and positioned so that he cannot observe ongoing classroom activity. However, when time-out arrangements are devised, two cautions should be emphasized. First, the time-out area should not have inherent fear or phobic provoking qualities; that is, it should not be a dark dungeon that would likely elicit intense fear in a child. Second, the time-out area should be arranged so that the child is not likely to be reinforced while being there. For example, placing a child in the hall or outside the principal's office (where he may have the opportunity to talk with others or view their activities) is likely to be highly reinforcing and should be avoided.

The use and potential effects of time-out are well illustrated in the study reported by Tyler (1965). Tyler was interested in controlling the behavior of several delinquent adolescent boys interned in a treatment center. The undesirable behavior for which control was sought had been exhibited around a pool table (scuffling, throwing cue balls, bouncing balls on the floor, etc.).

The study had three phases. In phase one (seven weeks long), previously defined misbehavior resulted in immediate confinement to a time-out room for fifteen minutes. When specific misbehavior was manifest, without warning, discussion, or argument the boys were moved to the time-out room with the explanation, "You fouled up."

In phase two, a no-punishment (no removal to the time-out room for misbehavior) condition was instituted, lasting thirteen weeks. The purpose of this phase was to observe the effects of verbal reprimand on behavior. When the boys misbehaved they were given various warnings or threats, such as, "I'm warning you," or "Now cut it out," or "Don't let it happen again." Misbehavior seemed to increase rapidly, and the punishment condition was resumed.

In phase three (twenty weeks), the time-out procedure was reinstated. With the resumption of time-out, cumulative records of misbehavior decreased. It was concluded that swift, brief confinement was a useful method in controlling misbehavior.

As Tyler's study demonstrates, time-out can be useful in reducing undesirable behavior when it is used properly. Besides the ones already discussed, further cautions should be noted. First, unless the child is receiving generous reinforcement for appropriate behavior in the usual setting, the potential effectiveness of the time-out procedure is greatly reduced. Second, it is generally undesirable to lecture, scold, or criticize the child during the time-out procedure. Third, placement in the time-out room should be restricted to a period of ten or fifteen minutes. If longer periods are used, the child might develop extreme negative reactions to the whole procedure and markedly decrease any positive results.

Systematic Desensitization

Systematic desensitization is a procedure used to assist individuals to overcome irrational fears or phobias. The method is based on the assumption that phobic behavior is learned and thus can be unlearned or inhibited. Anxiety-eliciting events are presented in temporal contiguity to responses that are antagonistic to anxiety; that is, if a person can learn to give assertive or relaxed responses to stimuli or situations that usually elicit anxiety, the anxiety is reduced. One cannot be relaxed and anxious at the same time; relaxation is incompatible with anxiety.

Based on the systematic desensitization principle, Wolpe and Lazarus (1966) and Wolpe (1969) have developed a procedure for relieving individuals of many anxiety-produced behaviors. Three steps are usually involved. First, the person is trained to relax by methods developed by Jacobson (1938). Second, a list of phobic or anxiety-producing stimuli are identified and arranged in an intensity hierarchy. Third, the client is asked to imagine or visualize the least disturbing item in the hierarchy until anxiety is no longer induced; each item is eliminated systematically in this manner until no anxiety is elicited by any of them.

Although systematic desensitization may appear to be remarkably simple, each step must be executed with great care. Let us consider each step in more detail. Training the client to relax involves a series of exercises whereby the client learns to differentiate between feelings of tension and relaxation in various muscles. With practice, the client is able to become completely relaxed in a short period of time.

At the same time the relaxation training is in progress, the therapist investigates the background and present status of the phobic reaction. The client is asked to identify stimuli and/or situations in which the phobic reaction occurs and rate the intensity of anxiety that each situation or event evokes on a scale from 0 to 100. From these ratings, the therapist builds the anxiety hierarchy and arranges the phobic situations from least to most threatening. To ensure that the items are appropriately graduated, it is desirable that consecutive items not differ by more than five points (Sherman, 1973).

When the first two phases have been completed, desensitization is begun. The client is helped to relax by specific suggestions of the therapist. (Because the client has been trained in relaxation, this step is usually achieved in a short period of time.) The client is then asked to imagine the least anxiety-producing situation. When the scene is clearly in mind, the client is asked to maintain the image for ten or fifteen seconds. Since the first item is presumed to elicit anxiety of a low magnitude, the client's state of relaxation should circumvent most of the anxiety ordinarily elicited by the imagined scene. As necessary, the scene is imagined repeatedly until anxiety is close to zero. Each item is presented consecutively, in the same manner, until the client is counterconditioned.

In the process of working through the items, it is not unusual for the client to experience some anxiety. When anxiety occurs, the client is instructed to signal and request to stop imagining the scene. The scene is repeated in modified form and/or for a shorter period of time. The length of time required for the entire systematic desensitization procedure varies with the severity of the phobic reaction. For some phobias, five individual sessions may suffice; others require as many as fifteen or twenty.

Wickramaserkera (1968) has reported the use of systematic desensitization with a twenty-five-year-old exhibitionist. The patient had been arrested for exposing himself in a public place. Just prior to the arrest, exhibitionism had begun to increase considerably, so that he was exposing himself as much as ten times a week.

The case history data revealed that the patient was fearful of any type of sexual contact with adult females. His preferred sexual objects were young females approximately eight to fourteen years of age. Although he had earlier achieved some relief from his exhibitionistic urge by masturbation, such behavior had become progressively less reinforcing.

The treatment plan had three basic features: (1) transfer of sexual approach responses from young females to female adults, (2) increase of reinforcement associated with actual physical contact and intercourse, and (3) enhancement of a feeling of relaxation rather than agitation in the presence of sexual stimuli.

The patient was trained to relax with a tape recording in three one-hour sessions, combined with distributed practice of relaxation exercises for about an hour and a half each day between clinic sessions. The patient was also instructed to construct at home an anxiety hierarchy beginning with social contact involving himself and other adult females that terminated in sexual contact. In addition, he was asked to construct a similar anxiety hierarchy involving young females.

Systematic desensitization proceeded in the usual manner until the seventh session. At this point, it was considered desirable to shape responses incompatible with the anxiety precipitated by female adult sexual stimuli. Reading assignments were given that exposed the patient to progressively more erotic content involving adult females. This was done to direct the patient's thoughts and verbal behavior into areas of sexual stimuli with female adults. Reading sessions were approximately ten minutes in length, during which time the therapist administered continuous verbal reinforcement. By the twelfth session, the patient was reading highly erotic material without reinforcement from the therapist.

Starting with the twelfth session, the cooperation of the patient's fiancée was obtained in order to enhance appropriate approach responses regarding adult female sexual stimuli. The fiancée was encouraged to reinforce certain specified approach responses. However, beyond a predetermined point, certain sexual approach responses were strictly forbidden.

The results indicate that the patient did not expose himself after the fourth session, and his relationship with his fiancée improved. There appeared to be no symptom substitution or regression to earlier exhibitionism. A follow-up conducted at six and at ten months disclosed that the patient was married to his fiancée, and the relationship was described as "extremely satisfying."

An interesting application of systematic desensitization is reported by Lazarus and Abramovitz (1962). They treated nine phobic children by using emotive imagery rather than relaxation. That is, hierarchies of most-feared to least-feared situations were established. The child was then asked to imagine a sequence of anxiety-arousing events into which were woven a story of the child's favorite heroes. When imagination and emotion were appropriately aroused, the experimenters introduced, as part of a narrative, anxiety-arousing items in the hierarchy. Of the nine children treated between the ages of seven to fourteen, seven recovered in a mean of 3.3 sessions. Follow-up studies done twelve months later revealed no lapses or symptom substitution.

A procedure similar to systematic desensitization is Cautela's (1970) covert reinforcement discussed in Chapter 1. It is mentioned again to indicate its application to the reduction or elimination of avoidance behavior.

To illustrate the procedure let us assume that a client becomes anxious whenever he is asked to talk or present something to a group. Cautela would first identify a series of graduated scenes that successively approximate the target behavior of speaking before a group. He would also identify scenes or images that the client is able to call to mind that are very pleasant. These pleasant scenes or images are used as reinforcers. When the treatment is started, the client is asked to image a scene that is the first approximation of the target behavior. Since the first approximation of the target behavior induces little anxiety, the client is able to get a clear image of it without feeling great discomfort. When the image is clear in the mind of the client, the therapist asks the client to immediately induce a *pleasant scene that has reinforcement properties.* The therapist then presents another approximation of the situation the client avoids and when the image is clear, the client is asked to induce another image that is pleasant and reinforcing. Step by step the client imagines approximations of scenes until he imagines himself performing the behavior that he avoids. Covert reinforcement (imagining a pleasant scene that is experienced as satisfying) is used at each step to promote in imagination approximations of the avoided behavior. When these procedures have been used for a while in therapy, the client is asked to practice the procedure by himself at home. Subsequently, the client is encouraged to perform the avoided behavior in real life.

Covert reinforcement differs from systematic desensitization in three basic ways: (1) exercises to induce relaxation are not used, (2) an anxiety hierarchy is not constructed, and (3) covert reinforcement is used. However, both procedures do rely on the induction of scenes in imagination that are successive approximations of the feared or avoided behavior.

Systematic desensitization has been most frequently used with neurotic phobic reactions. Wolpe (1969) did follow-up studies on 249 neurotic cases he treated. The data revealed that "from two to fifteen years after treatment, only 4 of the 249 cases acquired new symptoms" (p. 37). He reports success also with problems of sexual inadequacy, stuttering, some types of psychosomatic disorders, and character neurosis.

While systematic desensitization procedures appear effective in greatly decreasing or eliminating anxiety reactions to imagined situations, the anxiety may appear when the individual is confronted with the phobic situation in real life. However, as Sherman (1973) has suggested, transfer may be accomplished if the individual is exposed to the real-life situation during treatment.

In this connection, it is instructive to review Ritter's (1968) study. She compared the relative effectiveness of *group vicarious desensitization* and *contact desensitization* in eliminating children's snake phobias. Forty-four preadolescent boys and girls, five to eleven years of age, were assigned to one of three groups (two treatment groups and one control group) on a random stratified basis. An equal number of boys and girls were assigned to each group, and before treatment the groups were equated on a snake avoidance test. The control group, of course, received no treatment. The two experimental groups participated in two thirty-five-minute treatment sessions spaced two weeks apart.

The children in the vicarious desensitization group observed the experimenter and five peer models perform various activities with a harmless, four-foot gopher snake. The examiner first initiated activity with the snake and then encouraged the peer models to involve themselves in the same activity. Peer models were asked to pet the snake with a gloved and bare hand, to put the snake on a towel with bare hands, and finally to lift the snake within five inches of their faces. The subjects were simply asked to watch the demonstration.

The children in the contact desensitization group were first asked to observe the experimenter taking the snake out of the cage, sitting with the snake, and petting it. When a child appeared interested in touching or handling the snake, he was encouraged to perform a series of graduated tasks: place a hand on the experimenter as she stroked the snake, hold the snake with a gloved hand, and finally hold it with a bare hand.

Analysis of the data revealed that both treatments were statistically significant in reducing snake avoidance when compared with the control group. Contact desensitization was superior to vicarious desensitization. As a matter of fact, children in the contact desensitization group successfully performed 80 percent of the tasks on the snake avoidance posttest, which involved handling the snake in a variety of ways.

It is apparent from Ritter's study that the contact desensitization procedure was highly effective, and that four major variables were probably responsible for the reduction of fearful reactions: (1) graduated exposure to the snake, (2) observing the experimenter-model's fearless handling of the snake, (3) watching bold peer models initiate contact with the snake, and (4) actual contact with the snake.

The studies and procedures we have discussed in this section lead to several tentative conclusions we wish to highlight:

1. Irrational fears may be counterconditioned by inducing a state of relaxation nonsupporting to anxiety, arranging a graduated series of anxiety-provoking events in a hierarchy, and systematically presenting them in the phobic client's imagination.

2. Successive approximation of, or gradual exposure to, the real phobic object or situation is helpful in reducing the client's fearful reaction. Initial exposure to the phobic situation in imagination followed by graduated real-life exposure may be even more effective than either procedure alone.

3. Watching models engaged in activities with the phobic object or situation substantially reduces the fearful reactions in the client.

4. The combination of all three procedures — modeling, graduated

exposure to the real-life phobic event, and positive reinforcement — may be most effective in the reduction of phobic reactions.

Summary

1. A number of methods are useful in modifying maladaptive and/or undesirable behavior. Some (extinction, physically aversive stimulation, response cost, overcorrection, and time-out) produce effects by the systematic manipulation of negative consequences or the removal of positive reinforcement.

2. Extinction is used to eliminate behavior by the complete termination of the reinforcement maintaining it. The rapidity with which a behavior can be extinguished appears to be a function of the previous reinforcement schedule and the extent to which the behavior is maintained by positive or negative reinforcement. Behavior maintained by a continuous, positive reinforcement schedule is extinguished rapidly. Negatively reinforced behaviors (escape or avoidance responses) are more resistant to extinction. Escape or avoidance behavior may be extinguished more rapidly when termination of reinforcement of the undesirable behavior is accompanied by positive reinforcement of the socially adaptive behavior.

3. Satiation and negative practice are similar in that a form of saturation is involved in both procedures. Satiation involves the flooding of the individual with a stimulus until its reinforcement properties are lost. Negative practice involves the massive execution of the undesirable behavior. Negative practice appears to produce its effects by (a) inducing fatigue; (b) decreasing the anxiety associated with some responses (for example, stuttering); or (c) making the person more aware of the successive steps involved in the performance of the behavior and interrupting the sequence.

4.   The aim of punishment is to stop or depress behavior that is undesirable. It has three forms: (a) response-contingent aversive stimulation; (b) removal of reinforcing stimuli and events when the undesirable behavior occurs (response cost); and (c) removal of the subject from all sources of reinforcement when the individual behaves inappropriately (time-out).

5.   Unwise use of punishment may lead to (a) generalized inhibition of behavior similar to the punished response; (b) avoidance of the punisher and others similar to the punishing agent; (c) undesirable behavior (secrecy, lying) to escape and avoid the punishment; (d) reduction of the punisher's ability to positively reinforce desirable behavior; and (e) modeling of the punisher's aggressive behavior, thereby increasing aggressive behavior in the punished.

6.   Punishment can be used effectively to decrease undesirable behavior without negative side effects. To achieve the desired objectives (a) specify the acceptable and unacceptable behaviors and identify the consequences of each, (b) punish the unacceptable behavior immediately and consistently, (c) never threaten to punish an unacceptable behavior without following through, (d) accompany punishment of the un-acceptable behavior with positive reinforcement of the desirable behavior, (e) use punishment infrequently and never as the only means of eliminating the unacceptable behavior, and (f) liberally reinforce all desirable and/or adaptive behavior.

7.   The simultaneous pairing of physically and mentally noxious stimulation with the maladaptive behavior has proven effective in eliminating it. However, when aversive therapy is used, follow-up sessions may be needed to permanently suppress the maladaptive behavior. While aversive procedures are being used to eliminate the maladaptive behavior, adaptive behavior should be simultaneously reinforced.

8.   Three procedures have been used to countercondition irrational fears and excessive avoidance behavior: (a) systematic desensitization, (b) gradual exposure to the real phobic situation, and (c) observation of a model performing the feared behavior. Combinations of these procedures may ultimately prove to be more effective than any one procedure used alone. *Gradual exposure* to the feared situation or object in imagination or real life probably accounts for some of the positive treatment effects in each method.

Chapter Four

Observing, Recording, and Evaluating Treatment Effects

In earlier chapters we alluded to the importance of specifying the behavior we want to change, observing and recording the target behavior before, during, and after treatment is implemented to determine the effects of intervention. In this chapter we want to give more concerted attention to each of these dimensions.

Specifying the Change Objectives

We noted in Chapter 1 that a well-stated objective has three essential characteristics. First, the target behavior must be stated in terms that are observable and/or measurable. Second, the performance standards by which the target behavior can be judged must be precisely stated. Third, the conditions or situation in which the target behavior will be exhibited must be clearly stated (Mager, 1962). Let us illustrate each of these steps by using a brief case example.

Jon Jones, a nine-year-old third grader, has been exhibiting problems at school. His teacher was consulted and she gave the following account of Jon's difficulties:

Jon is one of the most disruptive children in the class. He loves to stick his nose into other people's business and wanders around the class without permission. When I ask a question of another child, Jon always shouts out a reply. When he is walking around the room, he appears to get a good deal of delight in tapping other children on the head or jabbing them in the back with his pencil. He's really hyperactive. He is constantly looking around the room, talking to other children, or playing with things in his desk rather than working on class assignments. He rarely completes his work, and when he does, it is often messy and incorrect.

On the playground, Jon also has his problems. He tends to boss other children and attempts to dominate group games. He's very creative in making up his own rules and is verbally abusive if he is not given his own way.

Jon does have some good qualities. I know he has good ability and could make normal school progress. Occasionally, I've noticed that he can be very kind and supportive to other people. If I have been out of school ill, when I return he usually asks about my health and seems glad to see me. He's a puzzle, and I'm not sure how to help him.

From the teacher's account of Jon's behavior it is apparent that he is exhibiting several problems. Some of them are easily specified because the teacher has described the actual behavior he exhibits that she considers inappropriate. For example, Jon

1. Leaves his seat, talks and walks around the room without teacher permission

2. Taps other children on the head and jabs them in the back with his pencil

3. Does not complete assigned work (although we are not certain whether this refers to some or all school assignments)

4. Hands in work that is messy and incorrect

The teacher also described other problem behavior. However, because she did not describe what Jon was doing or saying that was considered inappropriate, it is difficult to state the problems in behavioral terms. To do so, additional information is needed. For example, what does Jon do or say that leads the teacher to infer that he bosses and dominates other children in group games? What specific behavior does Jon exhibit when he is creating his own rules? Once we have acquired this kind of information, we can proceed to specify problems behaviorally in each of these areas.

Why have we labeled particular behaviors that Jon exhibits as problems? First, his behavior is disruptive, infringes on the rights of his classmates, and is potentially harmful to himself and others. If he continues to behave as he does, his learning and that of his classmates will be negatively affected. Second, Jon's behavior reflects some deficits in self-control. If he does not learn more appropriate ways of behaving, he is likely to turn the environment against him and jeopardize his future adaptation. Third, based on the teacher's account, particular behaviors are of sufficient frequency to consider them inappropriate.

Specifying the Performance Standard

Once we have specified the problem behavior, we are ready to formulate the behavior change objectives. Three questions are relevant in making this determination. What do we want our client or subject to do or say that will be a definitive indication of a positive change in behavior? By what standards will we judge the achievement of the change objectives? Under what conditions, or in what situations, should the desired behavior occur? We will consider the first two questions in this section and discuss the third in the following section.

Performance standards are usually expressed in terms of *frequency, intensity, duration,* and *accuracy.* By frequency we mean the number of times a particular behavior is emitted in a specified time period. The intensity of a response refers to its strength, force, or acuteness (for example, loudness, softness, and so on). The duration of a response is defined as the length of time it is exhibited (such as an hour, a week, and so on). By accuracy we mean the standard of goodness or correctness by which a response will be judged. As you will note from the illustration below, the utility of each criterion varies with the behavior change objective being considered.

Each of these performance standards can be illustrated using Jon's behavior as a referent. Using frequency as the criterion, an appropriate change objective might be to have Jon *complete 30 percent of the class assignments.* The extent to which this would be a desirable performance standard is related to the frequency with which Jon is completing class assignments before intervention procedures are initiated. If the baseline measurement confirms the teacher's observation that he is not completing any assignments, then a 30 percent completion rate would likely be an appropriate objective at this time.[1]

The change objective can be further defined by specifying the accuracy and duration of the target response. Therefore, we might revise the change objective to read: *Jon will complete 30 percent of the assignments for three weeks with*

---

[1] Baseline measurement will be discussed in a subsequent section of this chapter.

not more than 15 percent incorrect responses on any assignment. This modified objective specifies how long Jon should exhibit the target behavior and a standard of correctness by which an assignment can be judged.

The criterion of intensity is not particularly applicable to the assignment completion objective stated above. However, if we were to state an objective relating to Jon's oral participation in class, intensity would be a useful criterion. For example, we might state a change objective like: *Jon will speak when given permission and only with enough volume to be heard by the person(s) to whom he is speaking.* This change objective expresses the intensity dimension by specifying the loudness of his oral responses.

Specifying the Conditions or Situation

The assignment completion objective we formulated for Jon is missing one final element: the conditions under which he will make the response and/or the situation(s) in which he will make the response. Will Jon be asked to complete assignments in all subject areas? Will he be required to complete arithmetic assignments during the arithmetic period? The change objective must be specific enough to answer these kinds of questions.

The change objective may now be stated in final form. It might be stated in the following way: *Given adequate time to complete assignments in each class period, Jon will complete 30 percent of the daily assignments in arithmetic and reading for three weeks with not more than 15 percent incorrect responses on any assignment.* As the behavior change objective is now stated it is easy to determine when Jon has achieved it.

Although the assignment completion objective has been stated in terms of behavior that is desirable to increase, a change objective may sometimes be stated in terms that specify a decrease in a maladaptive or inappropriate behavior. However, when a change objective is stated in terms of behavior to be decreased, the appropriate or adaptive behavior to be learned may be overlooked or not made the object of specific intervention. Ultimately, the effects of our change efforts are directed not only toward decreasing or eliminating a self-defeating or maladaptive behavior but also toward helping an individual acquire or increase behavior that is productive, personally satisfying, and interpersonally adaptive. Therefore, when possible, it is usually preferable to state change objectives in terms of behavior to be enhanced.

Behavior Observation and Recording

The specification of change objectives leads naturally to the next step of the behavior change process—the measurement of behavior. Observing, measuring, and recording of behavior involve six basic steps:

1. Determine the setting in which the behavior will be observed.

2. Decide on the method to be used to observe and record the behavior.

3. Decide the interval of time the behavior will be observed.

4. Observe and record a baseline level of the behavior to be changed.

5. Plot the behavior data on a graph.

6. Continue to observe and record until the desired behavior change has occurred.

We will discuss each step briefly and give more detailed attention to observational and recording methods in subsequent sections.

1. In applied settings, the behavior observed is usually the maladaptive behavior in which change is desired. Therefore, the maladaptive behavior is observed in those situations in which the behavior should be modified. For example, suppose an adolescent uses profane language in the classroom, cafeteria, and school grounds. If it is considered desirable to change this behavior in the classroom and cafeteria, the problem behavior is stated operationally, and observation is done in those situations and not on the school grounds.

2. Observational data is usually coded in a manner efficient to record and use. For example, MacDonald (1971) used four different symbols to code and record four classes of student behavior:

(d)   A student is disruptive and attempts to distract one or more students in class.

(dd)   A student daydreams.

(w)   A student works from his book or on a lesson.

(ws)   A student talks to another student.

There is no uniform system of coding that can be used in all situations. However, it should be as simple as possible and tailor-made to the specific kind of observation. For example, if only one behavior is being observed, one might use an X to record the performance of the behavior during a specific time interval and an O if it does not occur.

If more than one observer is used, the coding system must be uniform. To determine the consistency of rating among the observers, the reliability between raters is usually determined by computing the percentage of agreement between the raters (Sulzer-Azaroff and Mayer,

1977). The percentage of agreement should probably be 75 percent or higher.[2]

3. When a method for coding the behavior observations has been devised, the next step is to determine the length of time for obtaining baseline data and effects of treatment. Practices vary, but experimental studies reported in the literature typically use a five-day baseline observational period. Daily observation time varies. For most purposes, forty-five minutes each day for five days appears adequate. The forty-five-minute observation period, distributed throughout the day, is conducted in situations where undesirable behavior is to be altered. Periodic time sampling provides a representative sample of a child's typical behavior during the day.

4. A *baseline* is a measurement of the inappropriate or maladaptive behavior before intervention procedures have been implemented. The central purpose of a baseline is to collect data on the client's pretreatment behavior to use as a standard by which treatment effects can be compared and evaluated (Sulzer-Azaroff and Mayer, 1977). The assumption is made that if a reliable and valid measure of the client's typical behavior is taken prior to intervention, the change in the client's target behavior after intervention can be attributed to the treatment.

In experimental situations, a second baseline observation (double-baseline approach) is often used and usually takes place after treatment is temporarily terminated and treatment effects have been noted. If data obtained at the second baseline are the same or similar to the first, it is assumed that the intervention procedures have produced the changes noted during treatment.

---

[2] Methods of determining agreement between observers will be discussed in a later section.

The double-baseline approach is rarely used in educational and clinical settings. Obviously, once a certain treatment has produced change in the maladaptive behavior, it would be undesirable to stop it. However, temporary cessation of the treatment procedures is sometimes useful in these settings. One of the authors employed this procedure with a teacher who felt that the author's behavior modification techniques were not responsible for the behavior change noted in a youngster with whom he was working. Instead, she attributed the behavior change to her "firm talk" with the child. To demonstrate the effectiveness of the behavior modification procedures, the reinforcement system used was temporarily terminated. The child's out-of-seat and name-calling behavior returned rapidly to the first baseline level. Needless to say, shortly after the cessation, the teacher was pleading with the author to reinstate the behavior modification procedures.

An alternative to the double-baseline approach is the multiple-baseline procedure used by Baer, Wolf, and Risley (1968). First, a maladaptive behavior that occurs frequently in a variety of settings is identified. Baseline data of the behavior is then recorded in each of the settings. After a specified number of days, the behavior modification is employed in one of the settings, while observation continues in the others. When the behavior modification procedures have been used for a sufficient period of time in one setting, they are extended to another situation in which the deviant behavior has been continuously observed; eventually the behavior modification procedures are applied to all of the settings. By this approach, the effects of treatment can be clearly determined.

An example of the multiple-baseline method is contained in a study by Hall, Cristler, Cranston, and Tucker (1970). They were interested in decreasing the number of students who came late to class. A baseline rate was ob-

tained for students coming to class late from recesses in the morning, at noon, and in the afternoon. After recording baseline data for fourteen days, the experimenters put the names of the children who arrived on time from noon recess on a chart hanging in the classroom. No experimental treatment was used for the morning and afternoon recess. Analysis of the data indicated that the experimental procedure decreased the number of children who came in late from the noon recess, while the morning and afternoon recess remained the same. On the twenty-second day of observation, students were required to be on time from both morning and afternoon recess before their names were placed on the chart. A reduction in the number of students coming to class late from both recesses was noted. On the twenty-eighth day, the children had to arrive on time from all three recess periods before their names were placed on the chart. With the extension of the treatment to the third time period, a reduction in the number of children arriving late from the three recesses was also noted.

The Hall et al. study clearly shows how the multiple-baseline approach makes it possible to ascribe specific changes in behavior to the treatment procedures. Also, it has the advantage of introducing the treatment measures gradually and avoids the problems associated with the double-baseline approach.

5. Data obtained during the baseline period, during and after treatment, are usually plotted on a graph, a pictorial method for presenting the results. The line and bar graphs are the two most commonly used. Both kinds of graphs have vertical and horizontal axes. The horizontal axis usually identifies the time period the experiment covers; it is typically divided into days, weeks, or months. The vertical axis usually denotes the criteria used to evaluate treatment effects: increase or decrease in the number of

maladaptive responses, number of time-outs used, or the number of points earned during treatment. Sufficient space should be allowed on both axes to accommodate the highest frequency of responses and longest time period that may be required during the treatment. The space given to each measurement interval on both axes should be large enough to convey visually the behavioral changes taking place during treatment.

Both line and bar graphs are used frequently to report the results of experimental studies. Either type of graph can be used to illustrate relationships when only one or two variables are involved. For example, to plot the number of times a child gets out of his seat or talks inappropriately during a specific time period, either a line or bar graph might be used. If a line graph is used, a broken line would illustrate out-of-seat behavior, and a solid line would indicate inappropriate talking. The same data could be plotted on a bar graph using a checkered bar and a solid bar. When more than two variables are involved, a line graph is preferable because it is less confusing. In most cases, the decision to use one or the other is based on ease of construction and the manner in which the relationships can be best illustrated pictorially. Examples of both types of graphs are presented in a subsequent section of this chapter.

6. The final step is to continue observation and recording of the deviant behavior until the desired behavior change has taken place. If the expected behavior change does not take place within a reasonable period of time, treatment procedures are altered and the effects of the new procedures on the behavior are carefully observed. Usually, well-designed behavior modification programs produce immediate change in the deviant behavior. Small day-to-day fluctuations are expected and should not create alarm; over a period of time, an effective treatment program will produce the desired behavior change, and a continuous observational record will indicate it.

Observation and Recording Procedures

For purposes of applied behavior analysis, behavior may be observed and evaluated in two basic ways. First, we can observe and evaluate permanent products that result from a person's activity. Common examples of such products are arithmetic problems completed on a sheet of paper, student projects completed in art class, or things constructed from wood by a student in a shop class. Second, we can observe and measure actual responses performed (using frequency, intensity, or duration as criteria) or events in which a person engages. This type of observation and measurement is illustrated by recording the number of times a student speaks without permission, how frequently a student is absent, or the intensity or duration of a temper tantrum (Sulzer-Azaroff and Mayer, 1977).

The measurement of permanent products is usually done by using frequency counts and/or evaluating the quality of the product by using preestablished standards. The measurement and recording of transitory behavioral events is typically done using frequency counts and time-sampling procedures.

Frequency Measures Frequency counts are typically employed when one wants to determine the number of times a person performs a discrete response or produces a particular product. By a *discrete response* we mean a response that occurs during a relatively constant time period and has a definite beginning and end. Examples of discrete responses are verbalized curse words, spit balls thrown, oranges eaten, questions answered, or pages read in a book. Measures of frequency are useful in noting changes in rate during short and long observation periods. Such measures are also useful in determining the amount of behavior displayed over a period of time (Gambrill, 1977; Sulzer-Azaroff and Mayer, 1977).

Frequency counts are done by simply recording the number of times a response is exhibited during a specific time period. Such counts may be done by recording the behavioral incidents on a sheet of paper, or by using any type of accurate hand or wrist counter or a pocket-size computer. If more than one behavior is being observed at the same time, a recording sheet may be used which specifies the behavior being observed, the time of observation, and the days of the week. Figure 3 is an example of a form that can be used to record discrete behaviors or products.

Observation and measurement are usually subject to some error. Therefore, it is often desirable to establish the reliability of observed behavior by computing the degree of correlation or agreement between observers. For example, suppose two observers are recording the number of times Jon Jones gets out of his seat during a specific time period each day for one week. One observer records a total of 14 and a second observer obtains a total of 16. The reliability of the two observers can be deter-

mined by dividing the smaller total (14) by the larger total (16). The reliability of the two raters is 0.88 (Sulzer-Azaroff and Mayer, 1977). An estimate of reliability of 0.88 is adequate for most purposes — if we can be assured that the observers are recording the same instances of out-of-seat behavior. That is, it is possible for two observers to come up with similar totals but record different frequencies of the same behavior during a particular time interval.

One way to determine whether the observers appear to be recording the same behavior incidents is to determine the extent to which each observer has the same or similar number of recorded incidents of out-of-seat behavior for each observation period. For example, consider the recorded data obtained by two other observers, as shown in Table 2.

Table 2 A Frequency Count of Out-of-Seat Behavior

	M	**T**	**W**	**Th**	**F**	**T**
Observer A	3	5	2	1	3	14
Observer B	1	6	0	3	2	12

Student _____ Observer _____

				Time of Observation					
Behavior	M		T		W		Th		F
Talking without permission	///	10:00 to 10:45	/	11:15 to 12:00	////	1:00 to 1:45	//	9:00 to 9:45	/X/	2:00 to 2:45
Out of seat without permission	///	10:00 to 10:45	/X/	11:15 to 12:00	0	1:00 to 1:45	///	9:00 to 9:45	//	2:00 to 2:45
Assignments completed	0	10:00 to 10:45	//	11:15 to 12:00	/	1:00 to 1:45	///	9:00 to 9:45	//	2:00 to 2:45

Figure 3 A Form for Recording Behavior Frequency

The frequency totals of the two observers would result in a high observer agreement (0.86), but there is considerable variation during several of the time observation periods.

To avoid such problems, Sulzer-Azaroff and Mayer (1977, p. 56) recommend that the percentage-of-agreement method be used. To use this method the observers must use a recording form that is divided into small observation intervals with the incidence of behavior being observed and tallied in each time interval. To determine the extent of agreement and disagreement, a line or check mark is placed in each time interval for each evidence of agreement. A circle is placed in each time interval for each evidence of disagreement. The agreements and disagreements are then totaled separately. The percentage of agreement is computed by the following formula:

$$\frac{\text{agreements}}{\text{agreements} + \text{disagreements}} \times 100$$

The resulting figure indicates the percentage of agreement between the observers.

The method can be illustrated by using the data obtained by two observers regarding Jon's out-of-seat behavior (see Figure 4). The sum of the tallies is 9 (number of agreements), and the sum of the circles (disagreements) is 8. Using the formula we discussed, the percentage of agreement between observers would be computed as follows:

$$\frac{\text{agreements}}{\text{agreements} + \text{disagreements}} = \frac{9}{17}$$
$$= 0.529 \times 100$$
$$= 52.9\%$$

It is apparent from the percentage of agreement of 52.9 that the reliability between the observers is too low to be used. The observers disagree almost as frequently as they agree. For applied or research purposes, the index of agreement should be at least 75 percent.

When observer agreement is this low, three things might be done to improve the degree of consistency between the observers. First, the behavior being observed should be stated in more specific and/or operational terms so that both observers can readily recognize when the behavior occurs. Second, the length of the time observation interval should probably be decreased to ensure that the observers are not getting bored or being distracted by other events. Third, the observers probably need additional training to ensure they have no confusion regarding the behavior to be observed or the method of recording it.

Duration Measures   There are occasions when frequency measures do not provide the best measure of the behavior to be observed. Duration measures are particularly useful for observing behaviors that are continuous rather than discrete. For example, when the problems that students exhibit involve resistance, or difficulty applying themselves to or completing tasks, duration measures are particularly useful. Also, there are occasions when the problem behavior (e.g., thumb sucking or temper tantrums) is not performed with great frequency, but when it is exhibited, it continues for a long time. In such cases, duration measures provide a better indication of the extent to which there is a problem

	M	T	W	Th	F
Observer A	OO ///	O ///	OO //	OO /	O ///
Observer B	/	//// /	—	///	//

Figure 4   Computation of the Number of Agreements and Disagreements

as well as a more accurate measure of it (Gambrill, 1977).

Duration measurement is easy to do as long as sufficient preparatory work is done before the observation begins. Suppose we are interested in determining the amount of time Jon takes to begin working on an assigned school task. First, we must specify the behavior that we will accept as an indication that he is working on the assigned task. The beginning-of-work behavior might be specified thusly: *Jon will sit in his chair facing the front of the classroom with both hands on his desk looking at study materials required to perform the assigned task.* Second, an instrument that keeps accurate time needs to be secured. Although any watch or clock that has a minute and second hand can be used, a stopwatch is preferred. Third, the directions necessary for Jon to do the assignment are given, and the stopwatch is started. The watch is stopped when Jon exhibits the specified target behavior. Jon is observed and timed in the same way on subsequent occasions until a representative sample of his beginning-to-work behavior has been obtained.

Time-Sample Measurement   Interval time-sample measurement is used when the behavior to be observed is discontinuous, is not distinct, or does not have a definite beginning and ending. Emotionally handicapped children often exhibit this type of behavior by engaging in a series of disruptive acts that appear to occur simultaneously. For example, a child may curse, knock over his desk, and kick someone near him in a period of a few seconds. The behaviors occur so rapidly it is difficult to know when one action stops and another begins. In such instances, some form of interval time sample may provide the most accurate measure of behavior.

An interval time-sample measure is a type of observation and recording method in which the presence or absence of target behaviors is recorded—if they occur during a specific time interval. There are three basic types of interval time-sampling methods: (1) whole-interval time sampling, (2) partial-interval time sampling, and (3) momentary time sampling (Sulzer-Azaroff and Mayer, 1977).

Whole-interval time sampling is a method of observation in which the target behavior must occur throughout the time interval to be recorded. This type of recording is most useful when it is important to know whether the target behavior occurs continuously and/or without interruption. It is essentially a measure of response duration. Suppose we are interested in obtaining a measure of six-year-old Susie's crying behavior. To record the crying behavior, we would devise a recording form that is divided into a series of thirty-second (or longer) time intervals. A series of observation times would be set up (when the target behavior is most likely to occur), and for each thirty-second time interval the child cries a check mark would be placed in that time interval. If the child does not exhibit the crying behavior for an entire interval, a zero would be placed in that time interval (Sulzer-Azaroff and Mayer, 1977). Figure 5 shows how the behavior would be recorded.[3] It will be noted from Figure 5 that Susie cried for a total of 210 seconds during a period of 270 seconds.

Partial-interval time sampling is a method of recording that is used to observe behavior that persists for short time periods. This form of recording is often used to obtain measures of behavior such as cursing and obscene gestures. When this form of recording is used, the target

Susie's crying behavior

Figure 5   Whole-Interval Time Recording of a Six-Year-Old's Crying Behavior

---

[3] A period of five seconds is usually taken after each time interval to record the presence of the target behavior.

behavior is recorded if it occurs at any time during the specific time interval.

Momentary time sampling is used when the target behavior is less fleeting or continues for a longer period of time than behavior recorded using partial-interval time sampling. For example, a parent may wish to use this method of recording to check on a child's study behavior. A timer is set at random time intervals during the evening, and each time the son is studying when the timer goes off, a check mark is registered on a recording form. This form of recording is convenient because it does not require the observer to watch the subject continuously over a long period of time (Gambrill, 1977; Sulzer-Azaroff and Mayer, 1977).

There are many occasions at school and home when several behaviors must be observed and recorded at the same time. To simplify the observation and recording, coded interval recording is often used. For example, suppose Ms. Patrick wants to obtain a measure of a student's swearing, obscene gestures, and out-of-seat behavior. She has observed that while these behaviors occur with fair frequency, their duration is relatively brief. Hence, she decides to use a partial-interval time sample as a good measure of it. Once she has stated each of these behaviors operationally, she would want to construct a coded interval type of form. Figure 6 illustrates the type form that might be used.

Self-Monitoring The procedures used for self-observation are very similar to the types of recording we have already discussed. One of the simplest types of self-observation is to keep a behavioral diary. This form of self-observation not only enables a person to determine the frequency of a particular behavior but also provides the opportunity to gather information about the circumstances in which the target response occurs. For example, a recording form can be devised which notes the date, time of day, situation, antecedent stimuli, and consequences attending the emission of the target response. This type of information not only provides a record of response frequency but may also provide information that is helpful in understanding variables that prompt and/or maintain the target behavior (Mahoney and Thoresen, 1974).

When the target response is discrete and a simple frequency count is desired, a mechanical counter can be employed. As we noted earlier, hand or wrist counters or golf counters are useful for such purposes. These counters are relatively inexpensive and are easily obtained.

Time-sampling self-monitoring is usually preferred method of recording when the target response is not discrete or occurs with high frequency. Frequency counts do not provide accurate measures of nondiscrete behaviors, and the recording of responses that occur with high frequency can be both laborious and annoying. In

Student:____Jimmy Swift_____   Observer:____Jill Patrick____

Day and Time of Observation:_____February 14, 9:00-9:20_____

| S̸ G Ø | 20 | S̸ G O | 20 | S G Ø | 20 | S G̸ Ø | 20 | S G̸ Ø | 20 | S G Ø | 20 |
| S G̸ O | 30 | S G O | 30 | S G Ø | 30 | S G Ø | 30 | S̸ G O | 30 | S G Ø | 30 |

S = Swearing
G = Obscene gestures
O = Out-of-seat

Figure 6   An Example of a Coded Interval Recording Form

such instances, an "all-or-none" type of recording is most feasible. For example, suppose you want to obtain a measure of a client's tendency to engage in self-devaluative thinking. This type of response is not entirely discrete because it is difficult to discern when such a thought begins and ends. To obtain a measure of it, a ten-hour observation period each day might be set up. Each hour would be divided into twenty-minute time intervals. The observer would place a check mark in an interval upon the occurrence of at least one self-devaluative thought. If more than one self-devaluative thought occurred during a twenty-minute interval, only one check mark would be placed in that interval. If a self-devaluative thought does not occur in an interval, it is left blank. The resulting self-observation data provides a rough indication of frequency and a good indication of the time periods one tends to be self-critical (Mahoney and Thoresen, 1974).

A somewhat different type of self-observation procedure was devised by Sherman and Cormier (1972) to record reactions to interpersonal situations. They developed a subjective-units-of-irritation scale (SUI) that can be used by teachers to record their emotional response to students. The name of each student is written on a three-by-five index card. The teacher records his or her degree of irritation by rating each student from zero (a nonirritating model student) to 100 (the worst possible student). Students are periodically rated on the scale to give teacher reactions over time. Decreases in subjective units of irritation denote improvement and correlate well with overall decreases in disruptive classroom behavior.

Self-observation and recording have been used with elementary school children of various ages. For example, Broden, Hall, and Mitts (1971) had an elementary school student record her own study behavior in a history class. A self-observation form was devised consisting of

three rows with ten boxes in each row. The student was requested to place a "+" in the appropriate box when she observed herself studying and a "−" when she was not studying. The counselor reviewed the self-observations with the student each week and praised her for increases in study behavior. During the period of the study, the student's study time increased from 30 to 78 percent.

Broden, Hall, and Mitts (1971) found, as have others, that accurate and reliable self-recording is more likely to occur when it is systematically reinforced. This is especially true of children. When children are involved, it is usually desirable to verify the child's self-recording with the recording of another observer. When there is an adequate degree of correspondence between the two records, the child should be reinforced. Also, if one wants to promote change in the target behavior being observed, it is necessary that the target behavior be systematically reinforced.

Illustrative Observational and Recording Methods

To illustrate the observational and recording procedures we have discussed previously, several studies have been identified from the research literature. The selected studies provide a variety of observational and recording systems that have been used to analyze (1) teacher-student interaction, (2) teacher classroom behavior, and (3) child and adolescent behaviors that are of particular interest to helping professionals.

Attending and Deviant Behavior

Werry and Quay (1969) have presented a method for observing and recording students' classroom behavior. They defined three categories of behavior, two of which are described here. (One of the categories relates to teacher behavior discussed in a separate section.)

The two categories, attending and deviant behavior, were described as follows:

1. *Deviant behavior*

   a. Being out of seat without permission or engaging in a permitted activity for a prolonged period of time

   b. Physical contact with or disturbing others

   c. Making audible noise

   d. Turning in one's seat (90 degrees or more)

   e. Vocalizing or answering without permission (swearing, etc.)

   f. Isolation (placement in time-out)

   g. Other behaviors not described above

2. *Attending behavior*

   a. Attending (eye contact with the task or teacher for not less than fifteen out of twenty seconds)

   b. Irrelevant activity (activity not related to assigned task)

   c. Daydreaming (more than five out of twenty seconds)

Behavior observations are recorded each twenty seconds for a fifteen-minute period of time. A ten-second rest period is also recommended after a twenty-second interval to ensure proper recording of behavior. Behavior is recorded by its occurrence (rather than its duration). In other words, this type of behavior observation is a frequency count.

The experimenters recommend that as many samples as possible be taken on various occasions to ensure a valid measure of the child's behavior, and that observers do not interact with the children. Interaction tends to make the observation less accurate since children would not be responding in their typical manner and observers would be less able to concentrate.

Werry and Quay mention certain cautions that it is desirable to note. First, deviant behavior can only be defined in reference to a particular classroom. Classrooms vary in the amount of teacher permissiveness and control. Hence, certain types of behavior will be exhibited much more frequently in some classrooms than in others. Second, accurate observation requires that the observer be close enough to the child to see what he or she is doing and, if possible, hear what the child verbalizes. Third, observation should be done under "typical conditions," not when a child may be receiving excessive individual attention. Fourth, though the amount of time a behavior is being observed is specified (twenty-second intervals for fifteen-minute total), it should not be considered as absolute. As previously stated, observational methods can be modified to fit each situation.

It is obvious from our rather brief synopsis of Werry and Quay's observational methods that the system has much to offer. Observational and/or behavioral categories are carefully defined, and the resulting observations should give an excellent picture of the identified pupil behaviors.

Teacher Behavior

It is important to observe teacher behavior because it has obvious reinforcing effects on the classroom behavior of students. Madsen, Becker, and Thomas (1968) devised an excellent system for observing and recording teacher behavior. Teacher behavior was classified according to the following categories:

1. *Teacher approval following appropriate child behavior*

   a. Contact: any type of observable physical signs of affection (a pat on the back, an embrace, etc.)

   b. Praise: any type of positive verbal comment regarding appropriate social and academic behavior

   c. Facial attention: nonverbal expressions of approval to a child (smiling)

2. *Teacher approval for inappropriate child behavior* (three categories defined above)

   a. Contact

   b. Praise

   c. Facial attention

3. *Teacher disapproval following appropriate child actions*

   a. Holding the child: use of physical force to restrain the child (hitting, slapping, or putting the child in the hall)

   b. Criticism: expression of negative remarks to the child, regardless of voice intensity

   c. Threats: consequences that will occur later if certain actions are exhibited by the child

   d. Facial attention: frowning at a child

4. *Teacher disapproval following inappropriate child behavior* (four categories described above)

   a. Holding the child

   b. Criticism

   c. Threats

   d. Facial attention

5. *Time-out procedures*

   a. Turning off the lights and saying nothing

   b. Turning back until the class is silent

   c. Not speaking or responding until the students are quiet

   d. Not allowing outside recess

   e. Sending the child to the office

   f. Denying a privilege

6. *Academic recognition*

   a. Calling on a child for an answer

   b. Giving the child feedback for a response he made

The observation and recording system of Madsen, Becker, and Thomas is used to help teachers learn how their behavior reinforces appropriate or inappropriate student behavior. Behavior is recorded into a specific category, depending on the teacher's response to a child's behavior. At certain times, two observers may be used, in which case one observer records inappropriate behavior of the children, and the other observer records the teacher's response. If one observer is used, he or she first records the deviant child behavior and then records the teacher's response to it. Teacher behavior is usually observed once a week and recorded in twenty-minute time intervals.

Using this system, teacher response to students can be measured objectively. Moreover, teachers can be shown the type of behavior they exhibit in the classroom and whether their response promotes appropriate or inappropriate child behavior.

The Madsen, Becker, and Thomas system need not be limited to the behavior categories specified. Depending on the classroom situation, other behavior can be observed.

Another system to observe and record teacher behavior has been reported by Kaufman and O'Leary (1972). It is similar to the Madsen et al. system but unique enough to warrant presentation. Teacher behavior is observed for thirty minutes in each class period and classified according to eleven categories. The teacher's behavior is observed for twenty-second intervals, followed by a ten-second recording period. The eleven categories of teacher behavior are briefly described as follows:

1. *Reprimand to the class:* Making disapproving remarks to a small group or the whole class.

2. *Praise to the class:* Making positive comments to a small group of students or the entire class.

3. *Loud reprimand to individuals:* Negative verbal comments of disapproval made to an individual that can be heard by other members of the class.

4. *Soft reprimands to an individual:* Negative verbal comments of disapproval to an individual that cannot be heard by other class members.

5. *Loud praise to an individual:* Verbal comments of approval given to an individual that can be heard by other class members.

6. *Soft praise to an individual:* Positive verbal comments made to an individual that cannot be heard by other class members.

7. *Educational attention — close:* Providing a child aid with an academic task (answering a question, correcting a paper, etc.) within three feet — praise or disapproval not included in this category.

8. *Educational attention — far:* Aid is provided from a distance of three feet or more.

9. *Negative facial attention:* Frowning without an accompanying verbal reprimand.

10. *Touching a child:* Any physical contact with the child.

11. *Redirecting attention:* Diverting the child's disruptive or inappropriate behavior without commenting on the child's particular act.

The Madsen, Becker, and Thomas system is similar to the Kaufman and O'Leary system in that both specify teacher behaviors that are used to promote or inhibit certain student behavior. However, the Madsen et al. system identifies more teacher response categories and appears to describe more precisely the actual teacher behavior.

Teacher Influence on Study Behavior

A simple but efficient method for recording the effects of teacher attention on study behavior is presented by Hall, Lund, and Jackson (1968). They divided their record sheet into three rows. The first row was used to record either study or nonstudy behavior of the student. A child had to attend to his assigned task for at least five seconds of the ten-second interval in order for it to be called study behavior. The second row was used to record whether the teacher verbalized to the child. The third row was used to record when the teacher was within a three-foot distance of the child. All three of these behaviors were recorded each ten seconds for the individual child. In each of the three rows, either one of the two behaviors was recorded. In the first row, study or nonstudy behavior was symbolized by S or N, respectively. In the second row, if the teacher verbalized to the child, a T was placed in the row, and if she did not, it was left blank. The third row indicated whether the teacher was within three feet of the child. This was symbolized by placing a slash mark for proximity, or the space was left blank if she was further away.

Autistic Behavior

Autism is one of the most serious maladaptive behaviors in children. Experts differ in the description and causes of the disorder, but most agree that the condition seriously inhibits appropriate intellectual, language, and interpersonal behavior. Like other maladaptive behaviors, autism must be carefully observed before treatment measures are undertaken.

Lovaas, Koegel, Simmons, and Long (1973) have devised a set of observational categories that are useful in observing autistic children. Two types of measurements are used: (1) evaluation of the child's intellectual and social development using the Stanford-Binet Intelligence Scale and the Vineland Social Maturity Scale, and (2) direct observation of the deviant behavior. As our chief interest is the observation and recording of behavior, the discussion will be limited to these facets.

The behavior observed and recorded consists of five categories:

1. *Self-stimulation:* Stimulation of the body by rocking back and forth, moving arms up and down, sitting and rocking, scratching or tickling self, masturbating, repeated jumping or twirling, playing intensely with and spinning physical objects.

2. *Echolalic speech:* Meaningless and inappropriate repetition of the speech of others. It may be described in three ways:

   a. Delayed repetition of speech that is inappropriate in the present context or situation

   b. Frequent use of bizarre-sounding words

   c. Immediate repetition of speech expressed by another in a mechanical manner

3. *Appropriate speech:* Speech that is appropriate and meaningful in the present situation or context. It may involve recording words or sentences used by the child that are correct and convey meaning that is comprehended by others.

4. *Social nonverbal behavior:* This category of behavior is described in two ways:

   a. Communication of a demand to another by nonverbal gestures, such as taking an adult's hand or pulling him toward a toy

   b. Obeying the request of another by exhibiting the appropriate nonverbal response

5. *Appropriate play:* Using or interacting with objects and toys in a way that is age-appropriate. The behavior category consists of two types of play, defined on the basis of appropriateness and complexity. The first or lowest level of play involves relatively simple activity such as putting crayons in a box or pouring water into containers. The second level involves a number of more complex motor movements: building something with blocks, pulling a wagon with items in it from one place to another, or setting up bowling pins.

Lovaas and his colleagues often use expensive equipment for observation and recording, but a stopwatch may be used to note the amount of time a child engages in any of the five behavior categories defined above. For example, the observer might record the amount of appropriate play in which a child engages from 10:00 to 10:15 in the morning. The following day the observer might choose another behavior for a specific time period and move on to the remaining behaviors to be observed. When each behavior category has been observed several times, the baseline data is summarized and plotted on a graph.

Disruptive Adolescent Behavior

The methods used for observing and recording adolescent behavior are not substantially different from those used with younger children. They differ mainly in the behavior categories employed. A study by Kaufman and O'Leary (1972) provides a good illustration. They report a system they used to observe and record the disruptive behavior of adolescents in a psychiatric hospital.

Sixteen adolescents were observed in twenty-second intervals for an average of twenty minutes each class period. Several undergraduate students were used as observers. The nine observational categories used are described below:

1. *Out-of-chair:* Leaving seat without permission

2. *Modified out-of-chair:* Moving the chair while a part of the body remains in contact with it

3. *Touching other's property:* Touching the property of another without permission, including grabbing and destroying

4. *Vocalization:* Vocalizing an audible sound without permission

5. *Playing without permission:* Using the hands to play with an object in a way that interferes with learning

6. *Orienting:* Turning in the seat more than ninety degrees from a properly oriented position

7. *Noise:* Making any type of sound other than vocalization without permission

8. *Aggression:* Physically moving toward another person to make contact with him

9. *Time-off task:* Not attending to one's task for the entire twenty-second interval

The adolescents' behavior was observed by noting the occurrence of any of the nine behaviors during a twenty-second interval. However, even if a particular behavior occurred more than once during any twenty-second interval, it was recorded only once. To record the daily level of deviant behavior as described in the categories, the total number of disruptive behaviors recorded was divided by the total number of intervals observed.

The Kaufman and O'Leary system is relatively comprehensive and useful in observing disruptive behavior in regular or special classrooms. However, the system may require more than one observer, and one may wish to include other behavior categories.

Child and Parent Behavior at Home

It is sometimes desirable to observe behavior at home. Trained observers have even been used in the home. For example, Zeilberger, Sampen, and Sloane (1968) trained observers to record instances of physical aggression, yelling, bossing, and any instructions that the child received from his mother. These are respectively coded A, Y, B, or I. If a child obeyed his mother, the I was circled; if he didn't comply, it was left uncircled. The observers recorded whether or not each of the behaviors occurred in a twenty-second interval.

Some of the mother's behavior was also recorded. Included were any verbal and physical contacts with the child, physical closeness, and longer verbal contacts. A time-out procedure was employed in their study, so the number of time-outs and the minutes per time-out were also recorded. By observing both the mother and child, Zeilberger et al. were able to study and manipulate how the mother's attention might affect the child's behavior. Also, the time-out technique could be studied to determine its effectiveness.

Wahler (1969a) did a study similar to that of Zeilberger et al. (1968), but he added an interesting dimension to his observation. As in the study by Zeilberger et al., Wahler observed oppositional children and their parents. Children were observed for either cooperative or oppositional reaction to a parental request. Social approach behavior, whether verbal or physical or toward one or both parents, was also observed, but only if it was child initiated. Parental behavior was recorded when parents attended either verbally or physically to a behavior of the child.

Parental instruction, defined as any requests or commands made by either or both of the parents, was the second class of behavior recorded for parents. All behavior was recorded each ten seconds, and every observation session lasted for forty minutes. Time-out procedures and the use of differential reinforcement were taught to parents, and observations were conducted during their training, which was concluded when parents properly administered time-outs (within ten seconds after the child exhibited oppositional behavior) and correctly used differential attention. Observations of both parent and child behavior were recorded throughout the study. However, Wahler was also interested in assessing the extent of parental reinforcement and determining whether these new techniques affected the parents' reinforcing value. He used a test by Gewirtz and Baer (1958), administered

by having the child drop a marble in either of two holes. When the preferred and nonpreferred holes are determined for the child, parents are asked to reinforce, through approval, the dropping of marbles in the nonpreferred hole. This is done by the parents for ten minutes, and a score based on the percentage of marbles dropped in the nonpreferred hole by the child is computed. This test was administered four times — (1) during the initial baseline period, (2) during the use of time-out and differential attention, (3) during the second baseline period, and (4) during the reinstatement of time-out and differential attention — and seemed to be highly effective in demonstrating the effects of parental reinforcement during the use of time-out and differential reinforcement.

Total Class Observation

Frequency-count and time-interval methods are also used to observe total class behavior. We will discuss two studies that present relatively complex methods for observing and recording class behavior and then discuss a few simpler methods.

Bushell, Wrobell, and Michaelis (1968) were interested in observing and recording three types of child behavior in a preschool class. The children were observed to determine (1) what they were attending to, (2) to whom they talked, and (3) what they did with their hands. Observation was divided into five-minute periods. At the beginning of each five-minute period, the observer looked at the first child on the list, noted the child's behavior, and then observed the next child on the list. Each child was observed just long enough to record his or her behavior before moving to the next child. Consequently, the behavior of as many children as possible was observed and recorded during each five-minute interval.

The three types of behavior were later classified into two categories, study and nonstudy behavior, and a study behavior score was determined for each child. The score was expressed as a ratio—the amount of time observed each day, divided by the number of study behaviors. The individual scores were summed each day to obtain a total class score.

Another method used to record the behavior of a total class that was larger than the one in the study reported above was discussed by Thomas, Becker, and Armstrong (1968). They did a study of teacher behavior and disruptive classroom behavior. They randomly selected ten children to observe each day. These children were observed for two minutes each. Every minute was broken down into ten-second intervals. The observers recorded classes of behavior which occurred in an interval. In other words, a given class of behavior could be rated only once during a ten-second interval for a particular child.

Five types of disruptive behavior and one of appropriate behavior were listed. The first of the five disruptive behaviors concerned gross motor behavior, such as getting up out of the seat, rocking in the chair, etc. The second class of behavior was noise making. The third class focused on verbalizations, such as calling out or talking to others. The fourth disruptive classification was orienting behaviors, including turning one's head or body toward objects or another child for more than four seconds unless the turn was more than ninety degrees. The last disruptive behavior classification was termed aggression. This class included behavior such as hitting, shoving, poking others, destroying property, or annoying others.

Relevant behavior was defined as doing the assigned task, looking at the teacher when she was speaking, raising a hand, answering questions when called on, etc. For behavior to be considered relevant, it had to occur for the entire ten-second interval.

When a response occurred that was not in either of the two main categories, it was defined as *Other Task*. No class of behavior could be rated more than once during a ten-second interval. That is, if a child talked out twice during the interval, his or her behavior was recorded only once. However, a child could be rated in more than one class of disruptive behavior. An overall level of disruptive behavior was the percentage of intervals in which one or more disruptive behaviors occurred; if a child was observed for ten intervals and seven of them involved disruptive behavior, disruptive behaviors occurred 70 percent of the time.

Time-interval observation and frequency counts may be employed using simpler procedures. For example, if a teacher wishes to determine the amount of time the class takes to quiet down after recess or how long the class requires to line up and remain quiet before going to lunch, a time-observation method is appropriate. The teacher just requests the children to behave in a specific way and starts timing with a stopwatch; the time interval required for the children to comply with the request is recorded. This procedure might be continued for three days to get a baseline measurement. A behavior modification procedure might then be implemented, and the time-observation procedure utilized again for three days. After six days, the total times for the two three-day observation periods are compared, and the effects of the behavior modification procedure can be determined.

A frequency count may be employed with almost equal ease. First, specify the behaviors to observe, limiting the number to two. Decide on symbols to record each behavior. For example, an *x* might be used for one and an *o* for the other. Compose a class list with each child's name typed in a column on the left side, so that the symbols can be placed to the right of each child's name. Decide on the length of time for the observation period (say, fifteen minutes, three times a day, for three days). When observation is begun, simply place an *x* or *o* behind each student's name as he exhibits either behavior. After three days of observation and recording, sum the frequency of the two behaviors. Implement the behavior modification procedure, record the two behaviors for three more days, compute a sum, and compare with the baseline.

Still another method that the classroom teacher can use when observing the total class is termed the "freeze" approach. Though only applicable in certain situations, sometimes this observational method will help to change behavior. Essentially, the approach requires the students in the classroom to stop and stay still when the teacher yells "Freeze." To illustrate the method, let us suppose that a teacher is bothered by the fact that students do not come right into the room and sit down at their desks. She notices that many walk around the room for quite a while before being seated. The teacher then instructs her students that when she yells "Freeze," they are to stop and maintain a statuelike position. Once the students are still, the teacher then places a mark by the name of each student seated.

This observational method can be used in the recording of other types of behavior, such as not doing assignments, talking to one's peers without permission, not being in line, etc. Methods for changing such behaviors are discussed in a later chapter.

Plotting Recorded Data

Baseline and treatment data are usually reported in graphic form to determine the effects of intervention. Although such data may be analyzed statistically, in applied situations the effects of intervention are typically depicted in graphic form. A *graph* consists of a vertical axis, or ordinate, and a horizontal axis, or abscissa. The vertical axis usually represents a measure of the target behavior (often referred to as the dependent variable) and the horizontal axis depicts the sequence of experimental manipulations or treatments (independent variable) expressed in units of time. Hence, a graph is used to convey pictorially the influence of treatment on the target behavior.

Figure 7 is a line graph that illustrates how observational and treatment data are portrayed

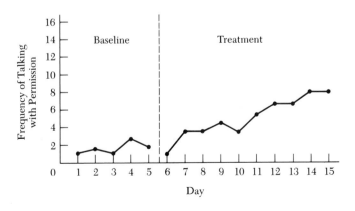

Figure 7 Increase in Talking with Permission Resulting from Social Reinforcement (all data are hypothetical)

in graphic form. The target behavior (talking with permission) is expressed in terms of frequency on the vertical axis, and baseline observations and treatment sessions are depicted in days on the horizontal axis. A broken vertical line has been drawn to separate the baseline and treatment phases. Inspection of the figure shows that social reinforcement of the target behavior appeared to have a positive effect. After ten days of treatment, talking with permission increased from a baseline high of three to a treatment high of eight on the ninth and tenth days. If treatment were continued for a longer period of time, and an intermittent reinforcement schedule were used, talking with permission might ultimately stabilize at a higher level.

Figure 7 also illustrates the two phases that are an inherent part of the AB treatment design. That is, a measure of the target behavior is obtained in phase A, and changes in the target behavior during treatment are reflected in phase B. If a positive change in the target behavior occurs after treatment is implemented, it is assumed that intervention was effective.[4]

It is often desirable to show the effects of intervention on more than one behavior. For example, in the case of the student in Figure 7, wouldn't it be desirable to determine whether both talking with permission and talking without permission are affected by the systematic reinforcement of only one of these behaviors? Indeed, from a teacher's point of view a decrease in talking without permission may be as important as an increase in talking with permission. We can probably assume that there will be a correlated decrease in talking without permission when the opposite behavior is reinforced, but we cannot be certain until we observe, record, and plot the behavior.

These two behaviors have been plotted in Figure 8. Note that talking with permission is designated by a solid line and talking without permission is designated with a broken line to distinguish the two behaviors. Inspection of the two lines shows that there is a general tendency for talking without permission to decrease as talking with permission increases. This is often true when one behavior is being reinforced and

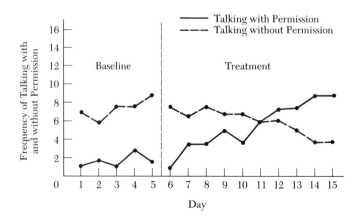

Figure 8   The Effects of Treatment on Talking Behavior (all data are hypothetical)

---

[4]The AB treatment or research design along with other methods of assessing treatment effects will be discussed in a subsequent section of this chapter.

the opposite and/or incompatible behavior is not receiving any specific treatment. However, it is also important to note from Figure 8 that on the fifteenth day, talking without permission still has a frequency of four. If we want to decrease this behavior even more, we might implement a response-cost condition (say, loss of one minute of recess each time the student talks without permission) to further decrease the inappropriate talking behavior.

As Figure 8 shows, it is relatively easy to graph the frequency of more than one behavior when the behaviors are expressed in comparable units and the measures are reliable. However, there are occasions when one may want to compare performance measures that are expressed in nonuniform units. For example, one may want to compare the number of tasks completed or the number of spelling words spelled correctly over a period of several days. If the assigned tasks are of unequal length or difficulty, a simple frequency count of the number of completed tasks is not likely to give an accurate picture of the student's response over time. To avoid these problems, the performance measures can be converted to equal units (e.g., responses per minute, percent of responses correct, etc.) or graphed in a way to show assignment length and responses that are correct and incorrect (Sulzer-Azaroff and Mayer, 1977).

Figure 9 illustrates how nonuniform data can be plotted on a *bar* or *line graph*. Graph A shows the number of words spelled correctly in relation to words assigned and words incorrectly spelled. By plotting the data in this form, one is able to get a more complete and accurate picture of a student's spelling progress than by the use of a frequency measure alone.

In Graph B the same student's performance in spelling has been converted to percentages. By so doing, performance measures are comparable across several days because the percentage of words correctly spelled expresses a relationship between number of words assigned and the

number of words spelled correctly. Hence, length of assignment is taken into account, as well as the number of words spelled correctly, and student progress can be accurately assessed.

The methods of plotting observational data that we have described in this section do not exhaust all the ways in which change in performance and/or behavior can be graphed. However, the methods we have described are the major ones and should provide the reader with the basic tools for plotting observational data collected in applied situations. A more sophisticated discussion of graphing data is contained in Pennypacker, Koenig, and Lindsley (1972) and is recommended to the reader.

Evaluating Treatment Effects

The evaluation of treatment effects should be an integral part of every change program. If the results of intervention are not evaluated, it is impossible to determine whether specific interventions are beneficial in promoting the change objectives. Indeed, therapeutic practitioners now recognize that change efforts may be "for better or for worse," and it is incumbent on the practitioner to ensure that the assistance provided is beneficial to the client (Carkhuff, 1969).

Intensive Experimental Designs

The central problem that a practitioner faces in determining the value of the intervention he or she uses is to attempt to establish a causal relationship between treatment and the target behavior of the client. In other words, when a practitioner uses X intervention, how can its effects on client behavior be evaluated? Behavioral psychologists have been in the forefront in devising evaluative methodology especially useful in assessing client change. The research methodology to which we refer has been variously labeled as "multiple-baseline methods," "single-subject designs," and the "intensive experimental design." These evaluative methods are especially designed to quantify changes in individual clients and share the assumption that individual change is a continuous process. To evaluate client change accurately, a series of observations of client behavior must be made. A single observation at a particular moment in time reveals what is happening at that moment, but it may not reveal the exact degree or direction in which the client is changing (Anton, 1978).

At the simplest level, variables that influence specific behaviors of a client may be determined by making continuous observations of two types of events: particular client behavior, and events that precede, occur with, or follow

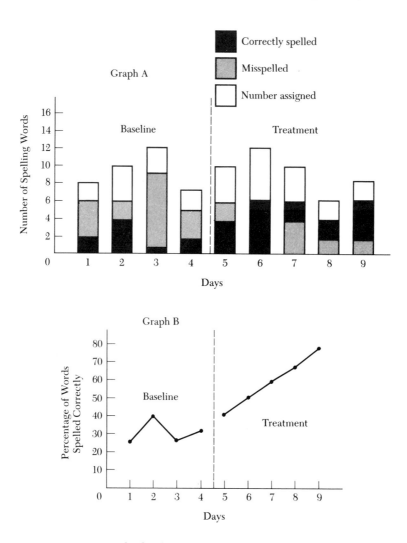

Figure 9   Two Methods of Graphing Nonuniform Data

that behavior. If specific events appear to covary with particular client behavior, there is some reason to believe that they are associated in some important way. These observed relationships can be further defined or specified by using an AB research design.

The AB Design

As we noted earlier, the AB design requires that a series of baseline observations (A phase) of the target behavior be made for a period of time and these observations be compared with observations of the target behavior during treatment (B phase). The A phase is used as a control phase and helps the practitioner to determine what happens to the target behavior when no systematic treatment is being used (Hershen and Barlow, 1976). If an appropriate change in the target behavior occurs during treatment (B phase), then there is some reason to believe that treatment has a positive influence on the target behavior.

Even though we are able to demonstrate positive treatment effects using the AB design, we cannot be certain that these changes are entirely the result of treatment. Other events occurring in the life of the client may have influenced the observed change. For example, the client may have had a favorite uncle or aunt visiting the family during the treatment period, and these interactions may have positively influenced the target behavior (Hershen and Barlow, 1976). Therefore, to further rule out the role of such extraneous variables, we must add other elements to our evaluative methodology.

The ABAB Design

An additional step that can be taken to give us more confidence that our intervention may be responsible for observed client behavior is to use the ABAB, or reversal, design. The major objective of the ABAB design is to establish a functional relationship between the target behavior and the treatment procedures. That is, if the practitioner can demonstrate that beneficial changes occur in the target behavior during treatment, but such changes are absent when treatment is temporarily terminated, the treatment is likely to be responsible for changes in client behavior (Baer, Wolf, and Risley, 1968; Anton, 1978).

When the ABAB design is used to evaluate treatment effects, certain events follow in a particular sequence. First, baseline observations are made of the target behavior (phase A_1). Second, treatment is given for a specific period of time (phase B_1). Third, treatment is temporarily removed or terminated (phase A_2), but the target behavior is continuously observed. During this phase the target behavior of the client often returns to a rate or type that is characteristic of the original baseline. Fourth, treatment is reinstated to determine whether the target behavior reflects the changes observed in phase B_1. If the target behavior changes in a positive direction during the first treatment phase (B_1), returns to a rate or form that is similar to the first baseline phase (A_1) during the second baseline phase (A_2), and then changes in a positive direction again in the second treatment phase (B_2), the treatment is probably responsible for the behavior change.

While the ABAB design is one of the most useful designs for establishing a causal relationship between treatment and the changes in the target behavior, there are certain conditions that limit its utility. For example, it may be difficult, if not impossible, to reverse the effects of treatment resulting from the B phase. If a client has learned a new skill in the first treatment phase, he or she may continue to use it. It may be positively valued by the client and act to change the responses of others to the client; both of these conditions may serve to perpetuate the newly learned skill (Kazdin, 1973).

A third reason why the ABAB design has some limitations in its utility is that in some cases it may be unethical to terminate treatment temporarily when the client is making beneficial changes. For example, if treatment has decreased or eliminated severe acting-out behavior in a child, a teacher or parent may be most reluctant to terminate treatment temporarily to demonstrate the power of the intervention. A teacher or parent may fear that once the treatment has been temporarily terminated, the acting-out behavior may not be brought under control in the second treatment phase.

Some of the objections we have raised regarding the ABAB design can be dealt with by making some slight variations in it. For example, when some form of reinforcement is used as the treatment procedure, during the second baseline phase (A_2), *reinforcement can be administered noncontingently rather than removing the reinforcement altogether.*[5] The client and others in his environment are not likely to object, and if the target behavior shows a rate or form similar to the first baseline period, this is excellent evidence of the value of the treatment (contingent reinforcement) on the target behavior.

A second variation of the ABAB design is to apply the treatment to behaviors other than the target behavior during the second baseline period (A_2). For example, suppose you are attempting to increase the academic performance of a nine-year-old fourth grader. Improvement in arithmetic and reading performance are identified as the specific objectives of treatment. A token reinforcement system is identified as the modification or treatment procedure. When the second baseline period is introduced, token reinforcement is temporarily terminated for arithmetic, and reading remains the same or deteriorates, there is some reason to believe that token reinforcement is an effective intervention procedure (Sulzer-Azaroff and Mayer, 1977).

Given the modifications in the ABAB design we have described, it is apparent that this design has considerable utility in evaluating treatment effects. Of course, the idiosyncrasies of the treatment situation, the circumstances or nature of the client's target behavior, may not warrant the use of this design. When these conditions exist, there are other procedures that can be used to evaluate treatments effects.

Multiple-Baseline Designs

Some useful alternatives to the ABAB design are multiple-baseline designs. There are three basic types of multiple-baseline designs: (1) across behaviors, (2) across situations, and (3) across individuals. These designs apply an intervention program to a selected subsample of behaviors, situations, or individuals, but all target behaviors, situations, or individuals are observed at the same time (Gambrill, 1977). Let's consider the essentials of each design.

Across Behaviors   When the multiple-baseline across behaviors design is used, baseline measures are taken simultaneously on two or more behaviors of the same person in the same situation. Treatment is applied to one behavior at a time, but repeated observations are made of all target behaviors. When the behavior receiving treatment has increased or changed in a positive direction and the other observed but untreated behaviors reflect no change, the second target behavior becomes the next object of treatment. Similarly, when this behavior has changed appropriately and the other untreated behaviors have not, the next target behavior is treated. This process continues until all target behaviors have been subjected to treatment (Baer, Wolf, and Risley, 1968; Gambrill, 1977).

---

[5] When noncontingent reinforcement is used, receipt of reinforcement is *not* dependent on the appropriate execution of the target response.

An example should clarify the use of this type of design. Suppose that you would like to determine the relative effectiveness of social reinforcement (praise) in changing the inappropriate behavior of a third-grade student. Observation of the student has revealed that he tends to be a "dreamer" and that he is not actively participating in class. These behaviors are stated operationally, and a five-day baseline observational period is begun. On the sixth day, treatment is initiated by praising attention-to-task behavior. The other two target behaviors, making verbal contributions to class discussions and offering assistance, receive no reinforcement but continue to be observed.

On the fifteenth day, observational data indicates that attention-to-task behavior has increased by 80 percent. The other two target behaviors are occurring at a rate similar to baseline. Therefore, social reinforcement of participation in class discussions is initiated. Social reinforcement of attention to task and class participation continues until the thirty-fifth day. At this point, class participation has increased 75 percent over baseline. You have good evidence that social reinforcement is likely responsible for increases in the target behavior. The two behaviors are relatively independent of each other (a condition essential for the use of this design), so you have additional confidence in the belief that treatment, rather than generalization effects or extraneous variables, is promoting the change.

Across Situations When this design is used, the same behavior is monitored in two or more situations, but the treatment is implemented in one situation at a time (Hershen and Barlow, 1976; Gambrill, 1977). For example, let's assume that you want to reduce a child's tendency to curse. He has been observed cursing in reading, arithmetic, and social studies classes. The program is begun in the usual way by taking a baseline. After five days of baseline measurement of cursing in each of the three classes,

treatment is initiated in reading class by reducing the student's recess time by one minute each time he curses. In ten days it is noted that cursing approximates the baseline measurement in arithmetic and social studies classes, but cursing has decreased by 85 percent in reading class. Treatment appears to be reducing the frequency of cursing in reading class, but treatment effects are not generalizing to other classes. Therefore, treatment is subsequently introduced in arithmetic class. When a substantial decrease in cursing is noted in arithmetic class, treatment is initiated in social studies. If a substantial decrease in cursing is also observed in social studies, there is reason to believe that the response-cost procedure is an effective treatment.

One of the more important contributions of this type of design is that it enables the teacher or practitioner to analyze the relationship between the stimulus properties of the environment (e.g., the type or amount of reinforcement operating) and the client's behavior. Indeed, if it can be demonstrated that the target behavior of the client changes in each situation after treatment is implemented, the changes in the client's behavior are probably a function of the treatment condition and not some mysterious personality trait (Anton, 1978).

An example of a multiple-baseline across situations design is contained in a study by Hall, Cristler, Cranston, and Tucker (1970). They were interested in decreasing the number of students who came late to class. A baseline rate was obtained for students coming to class late from recesses in the morning, at noon, and in the afternoon. After recording baseline data for fourteen days, the experimenters put the names of the children who arrived on time from noon recess on a chart hanging in the classroom. No experimental treatment was used for the morning and afternoon recess. Analysis of the data indicated that the experimental procedure decreased the number of children who came in late from the noon recess. However, the number of children who came in late from the morning and afternoon recesses remained the same. On the twenty-second day of observation, students were required to be on time from both morning and afternoon recesses before their names were placed on the chart. A reduction in the number of students coming to class late from both recesses was noted. On the twenty-eighth day, the children had to arrive on time from all three recess periods before their names were placed on the chart. With the extension of the treatment to the third time period, a reduction in the number of children arriving late from the three recesses was also noted.

Across Individuals When the multiple-baseline across individuals design is used, the same behavior of several individuals in the same situation is the object of observation and treatment. First, a baseline for the specified target behavior is taken for all persons who will receive treatment. Second, one person is given treatment while the target behavior of the remaining clients is observed. Third, when the target behavior of the treated client changes substantially, or has stabilized, treatment is applied to the same target behavior of the second client. A similar procedure is used until the treatment has been applied to the same target behavior of each client (Gambrill, 1977). If there are positive changes in the target behavior of all clients, there is good reason to believe that the treatment is responsible for the change.

The Simultaneous Treatment Design

There are occasions when the teacher or practitioner may want to bring about a change in client behavior but is uncertain which of several treatment procedures to use. One way to make this type of decision is to use the simultaneous treatment design (Hershen and Barlow, 1976; Gambrill, 1977).

For purposes of illustration, let's assume that you want to determine which of two treatment methods is most effective in changing the off-task behavior of a student. Informal observations of the student reveal that he wastes time playing with things in his desk, talking with his neighbors, and daydreaming. The student appears to respond positively to approval and greatly enjoys recess and after-lunch playtime. Recognizing that approval and playtime are reinforcing, two different treatment strategies are formulated. In condition A, social reinforcement will be administered for on-task behavior, and off-task behavior will be ignored. In the B treatment condition, the student will receive one minute of private talking time with the teacher for each fifteen minutes of on-task behavior. Also, one minute of recess time will be deducted for each fifteen minutes of off-task behavior.

The program is implemented by taking a baseline for five days. On the sixth day, treatment A is given from 9:00 to 12:00 in the morning, and treatment B is employed from 1:00 to 4:00 in the afternoon. The target behavior is monitored continuously, and both treatments are continued for five days. After five days of treatment, analysis of the observational data reveals that under treatment condition B on-task and off-task behavior have both changed in a more positive direction than is true of treatment A. Also, under treatment B the change in the target behavior has practical and/or social significance. That is, other students in the class are commenting that the client is "goofing off" and interfering with their work in the morning, but such comments are rare in the afternoon. The client is also completing more work in the afternoon than was true at baseline.

Since treatment B appears to be more effective than treatment A, treatment B is now implemented for the entire day. Treatment B is continued until the treatment objectives are realized. Thus, by using this design, one need not guess which one of two or more treatments is most effective. The observational data collected on the target behavior will clearly show it.

Sequential Treatment Designs

This design has some degree of kinship to the simultaneous treatment design in that both are used to determine the relative effectiveness of different interventions or a combination of interventions on client behavior. When the A-BC-B-BC form of the sequential treatment design is used, a baseline measurement of the target behavior is initially taken (A phase). A combined treatment (BC) is then initiated for a short period of time. When the observational data of this phase has been analyzed, one component of the treatment is temporarily terminated (the C component of the BC treatment strategy). The second treatment phase continues until a clear indication of treatment component B can be assessed. The combined treatment (BC) is subsequently reintroduced and continued until its effects can be properly evaluated. Thus, by analyzing changes in the target behavior in each treatment phase, the relative contribution of each component of the combined treatment strategy can be accurately assessed (Gambrill, 1977).

To illustrate, suppose we wanted to determine the relative contribution of feedback and token reinforcement on the amount and correctness of arithmetic assignments completed by a fifth-grade boy. Baseline measurements are taken (A phase), and the combined treatment (BC), feedback plus token reinforcement, is implemented. The feedback portion of the treatment consists of correcting each arithmetic assignment and specifying the problems done correctly and incorrectly. The token reinforcement treatment component requires that one token be given for each completed arithmetic assign-

ment. The tokens can be exchanged for a variety of privileges at school. The combined treatment condition (BC) is operative for five days. At the end of the five day treatment period, the number of completed arithmetic assignments has increased from 20 percent at baseline to 80 percent. The number of problems done correctly has changed from a 30 percent baseline rate to 70 percent. Treatment component C, token reinforcement, is temporarily terminated. At the end of seven days the percentage of correctly done problems is 60 percent. The percentage of arithmetic assignments completed has decreased from 80 to 40 percent.

The data suggest that the feedback condition (component B) appears to have some influence in promoting correctness of the arithmetic problems done but seems to contribute little to the number of assignments completed. Token reinforcement appears to influence the number of arithmetic problems completed. Therefore, if we want to promote correctness and the number of arithmetic problems completed, the combined treatment should be continued. The combined treatment is implemented once again and continued until the changed objectives are achieved.

Summary

1. Systematic observation and recording of behavior is essential to determine the frequency, intensity, or duration of the target behavior before, during, and after treatment and to determine treatment effects.

2. The behavior to be changed must be stated in terms that permit accurate observation and evaluation. Well-stated change objectives have three essential characteristics: (a) the target behavior is stated in observable or measurable terms, (b) the performance standards by which the target behavior will be judged should be stated precisely, and (c) the conditions under which the target behavior will be exhibited should be clearly identified.

3. Six basic steps are involved in the process of observing and recording behavior. After the target behavior is operationally defined, one must (a) select the setting in which the behavior is to be observed, (b) decide on a method for recording observed behavior, (c) determine the type of observation and the length of time the behavior will be observed, (d) take baseline measurements, (e) graph the recorded behavioral data, and (f) continue observation and recording until the effects of the behavior modification procedures are determined.

4. Behavior can be observed and evaluated in two ways. First, the permanent products resulting from a person's activity can be observed and evaluated. Second, the actual responses a person performs, or the events in which one engages, can be observed and measured. Permanent products can be assessed by the number of products produced or by preestablished standards of quality. Actual responses or transitory behavioral events can be measured using frequency counts and time-sampling methods.

5. A frequency count is a measurement of the number of times a person performs a discrete response or produces a product.

6. Two types of time-sampling methods are commonly employed to observe and measure behavior: partial-interval time sampling and whole-interval time sampling. When whole-interval time sampling is used, the target behavior must occur throughout the specified time period. Partial-interval time sampling is employed to observe behavior that persists for a period of time.

7. The behavioral data that are recorded during baseline, during and after treatment, are typically plotted in graphic form to show the effects of intervention. These data are usually plotted on a line or bar graph. Although both line and bar graphs are commonly used to plot behavioral data, the decision to use one or the other should be determined by the clarity and ease with which relationships among variables can be illustrated. When more than two variables are being plotted, line graphs are usually preferred.

8. Systematic evaluation of treatment should be a central ingredient in every behavior change program. Evaluation of treatment enables the practitioner to determine whether specific interventions are beneficial in promoting change objectives and also encourages practitioners to be accountable.

The primary problem in evaluating the effects of intervention is to establish a causal relationship between treatment and changes in the target behavior of the client. The single-subject, or intensive experimental design is probably the most useful in making this determination. Some of the more commonly used intensive experimental designs are the AB, ABAB, multiple-baseline, simultaneous treatment, and sequential treatment designs. The simultaneous treatment design enables the change agent to determine specific treatment effects by using different treatment procedures simultaneously to modify the same behavior in different situations. The sequential treatment design allows for the assessment of treatment effects by starting with a combination of treatments and systematically withdrawing or adding treatment components in a sequential time series.

Chapter Five

The Process of Behavior Change: Formulation and Implementation of Strategies

The process of formulating and implementing behavior change strategies involves three basic steps. First, the problem behavior is defined and carefully analyzed. Second, the behavior change goals are specified. Third, procedures for modifying the problem behavior are formulated and implemented. In this chapter, each step will be discussed, and behavior change strategies will be evaluated. The chapter concludes with a case study that illustrates each step in the behavior change process.

Definition and Analysis of Problem Behavior

The definition and analysis of a child's problem(s) begin with the stated complaint or difficulty identified by the referral agent. For example, a parent or teacher may indicate that a child is excessively aggressive or describe another child as very withdrawn; still other children are referred for assistance because they exhibit deficiencies in academic skills. Occasionally, a parent seeks help for a child because "he does not appear happy." The problems are varied and each appears in a unique matrix of circumstances.

The referral agent is encouraged to state the problem (as he or she conceives it) in as complete detail as possible. Then, the problem behavior and the circumstances in which it occurs should be delineated more specifically. The psychologist considers a number of questions. Is the child's behavior considered a problem by only one person or by a number of people in the child's family and school environment? Is the identified behavior a *real* problem or primarily a reflection of the referral agent's idiosyncratic or unreasonable expectations? Is the identified child client the *primary* or *secondary* client? How often is the identified problem behavior expressed and how severe is it? If the problem behavior continues, will it be detrimental to the child's development or other people? Investigations into these questions are essential for several reasons. It is difficult to formulate appropriate change strategies until the treatment goals are operationally stated, the basis for the problem is understood, and the primary client is identified. For example, we cannot modify a "low self-concept" until we identify specifically the ways that the client sees himself inadequate and reinforce behavior that will enable the client to successfully cope with the inadequacy. Similarly, it is neither efficient nor desirable to focus treatment exclusively on a child when the significant people in his life continue to reinforce the problem behavior. A child's behavior is largely influenced by the significant adults in his life, and they also must be actively involved in the treatment process. We are not suggesting that an all-out search for the "causes" of the child's behavior be undertaken, but it is necessary to identify the variables that appear to maintain it.

Once the problem behavior(s) has been clearly specified, it is desirable to determine *when, where,* and *with whom* the problem behavior is exhibited. First, if the central problem is excessive defiance or aggression, is it exhibited in the classroom, with one or both parents, or with peers? Second, in exactly what circumstances or situations does the aggression appear? Does the child become aggressive only when he loses in competitive situations, or is it a more pervasive coping style? What appears to incite his aggression in each situation in which it is manifest, and what seems to maintain or reinforce it?

By making this type of systematic analysis of the problem behavior or set of behaviors, we are able to make a determination of the stimuli or events that may be evoking it as well as to analyze the extent to which past and present expectations made of the child are realistic. Also, once the problem parameters have been established by systematic interview, careful observation of the child's problem behavior in the appropriate circumstances helps us to determine the reinforcing contingencies. If the frequency and intensity of the problem behavior are noted, we have some idea of its severity.

Systematic delineation, by interview and observation, of the situations in which the problem behavior is expressed, and with whom, tends to indicate *what* and *who* are maintaining the behavior. Once we have made these determinations, we are able to decide who the most significant client is. Obviously, if the child's problem behavior is exhibited in a variety of situations, a number of people may be considered as significant clients.

Presumably, if a child exhibits identical or similar behavior in a variety of situations, the behavior is being reinforced by people in those situations. That is, the assumption is made that if a child's behavior is learned (or maintained by constant reinforcement), then under appropriate learning conditions it may be unlearned. This appears to be true in the great majority of cases. However, there are some children whose problem behavior has physical or organic determinants. It may not be exclusively the result of the reinforcing conditions existing in a particular situation. These conditions must be identified and considered in behavior analysis and behavior change. For example, a chronically ill child may not be a productive learner regardless of the reinforcing contingencies. Similarly, a child who has a physically caused hearing deficiency tends to have difficulty making progress in learning activities that require adequate auditory reception. The presence and extent to which these deficiencies affect the problematic behavior must be evaluated before change or corrective measures can be arranged. For these as well as other reasons, a developmental and social history may be very helpful in problem analysis.

The Developmental and Social History

A developmental and social history identifies health status, physical deficiencies, chronic disease, and sensory deficiencies, and presents a picture of a child's developmental pattern. A comprehensive history should reveal areas of arrested development and the extent to which cognition (intellectual development) and social and emotional behavior are appropriate and/or adaptive. Since most behavioral disturbances are manifest in three general areas of functioning—cognition, social behavior, and affects or feelings—systematic inquiry into these areas provides an overall assessment of the adequacy of a child's coping efforts. Consequently, it is possible to spot developmental deficiencies before they become problematic and to formulate preventive as well as corrective strategies.

A developmental history also reveals the reinforcement history of the problem behavior, the extent to which the problem behavior may be resistant to change, and the parents' reinforcement style. We are immediately alerted to the disciplinary practices of the parents—the extent to which positive and negative reinforcement are used—and the relative success of these practices. The relative reinforcement properties of significant adults in the child's life may be determined and utilized in formulating change tactics.

There are other elements of the child's development that are important to consider in securing a history. It is important to identify the child's strengths (abilities, special talents, and achievements) as well as situations that are excessively frustrating to him. When a child's strengths are known, they may be used to increase the extent to which he is positively reinforced and the amount of positive feedback he receives. Knowledge of the situations that are frustrating to the child makes it possible to program the child's activities so that the undesirable behavior is reduced in frequency. For example, if a child is readily provoked to temper tantrums by competitive situations, it may be desirable to decrease the number in which he participates until more systematic change strategies can be used to alter the temper tantrums.

A good developmental and social history also should reveal stimuli, events, and conditions that may serve as potential reinforcers. We say *potential* reinforcers because, as we noted in Chapter 2, a reinforcer is a stimulus that increases the probability of a response. It is not possible to determine whether or not a stimulus is reinforcing until it is operative. Stimuli or events that are likely to have such potential may be revealed by inquiring about the activities or things a child selects when free choice is possi-

ble. The child's verbalizations about the things he likes, as well as the kinds of things that he does in his free time, provide additional clues. It is also possible to determine stimuli that may be reinforcing by directly administering to the child the questionnaires in Appendix A.

Although stimuli (tangible objects, candy, etc.) may have potential reinforcement property, *events* also do. It is important to determine them. That is, does the child like going to the store, circus, zoo, or movies, taking a note to the office, talking to the coach, or sitting in the front seat with Dad on a trip to the store? Potential reinforcing events are endless in number. Once they have been discovered, they have considerable capacity to promote the behavior considered desirable. If parents (and other significant adults) are not aware of them, it may be suggested to them that they keep a list of events that they personally observe the child pursuing freely and enthusiastically.

The specific type of information that is obtained in a developmental and social history is outlined in Form III in Appendix A. This form identifies areas about which one inquires and states specific questions that are helpful in securing useful information.

If the diagnostic information that is secured is comprehensive, a complete picture of the child and his or her problems is likely to emerge. That is, areas of successes and failures, competencies and deficiencies, relationships and coping styles, and areas of conflict tend to be revealed. If the additional step of observing the child interacting with significant adults is also taken, we are ready to formulate the treatment priorities.

Specification of Behavior-Change Goals

A careful analysis of the developmental and social history should identify high-conflict areas or intense problem behaviors that occur frequently. Extremely disruptive or injurious behaviors have the highest treatment priorities; intervention strategies are implemented immediately to promote desirable change in them. For example, if a child is about to be expelled from school because of excessive defiance of authority, it is important to deal promptly and effectively with this behavior.

A properly conducted study of a child client usually reveals a number of problem behaviors in which change may be desirable. And, as we have noted, the more provocative, aggressive, and socially alienating behaviors may be identified as immediate and short-term change goals, while others of lesser severity may receive more concerted attention later. Suppose, for example, that a parent is very upset by an eight-year-old child's thumb sucking. Because the behavior distresses the parents and prompts considerable ridicule by the child's peers, it is identified as an immediate treatment goal. However, thumb sucking is often only one of several dependent behaviors exhibited by a child. Termination of the thumb sucking may be the first-priority goal, but change of the other dependent behaviors may be desirable long-term goals. Once the thumb sucking has been terminated, the other dependent behaviors may subsequently — and sometimes concurrently — become the appropriate treatment targets.

The decision of which behavior change goals have the highest priorities must be based on the unique variables operating in each case. Moreover, the behaviors in which change is desired must be specified behaviorally. For instance, it is not useful to state as a behavior change goal "to help a child feel better about himself" or "to develop a more positive self-image." If a goal is stated in these terms, we are still left with the question, "Exactly how, and in what ways, do we wish the child to feel better or change his self-image?" It is relatively rare to

find a child who feels *totally* bad about himself. Rather, his "bad" feelings are anchored to specific referents. He may feel bad about himself because he is too small or too fat, inept at playing baseball, or because he performs poorly in mathematics. (Likewise, he may feel "good" about himself because he is popular with his peers, an excellent swimmer, or admired for his knowledge of automobiles.) Hence, to improve the child's self-image, we must first identify the areas of felt inadequacy, state them behaviorally, and select behavior modification procedures that enhance his ability to perform in the areas of felt inadequacy. At the same time, we would increase the reinforcement he receives from others by providing additional opportunities for him to exhibit his skills. If significant others make demands for performance beyond his ability, a reduction in these demands may also be beneficial. When modification procedures are appropriately implemented, his self-evaluation will likely change.

Formulation and Implementation of Change Strategies

When short- and long-term behavior change goals have been properly identified, change strategies must be formulated. This not only involves the determination of methods by which change may be promoted but also *how* and *with whom* these methods will be implemented. That is, will the child, parent, or parents and/or teacher be involved individually or jointly? These decisions are generally made during the problem-analysis stage, but they are further refined at this time. We will consider problems of implementation first and conclude with a discussion of stratagems for change.

Identifying the significant individuals who maintain the problem behavior does not necessarily mean they will be active participants in the change process for many reasons. An individual may not wish to recognize his responsibility for producing a child's problem behavior because it means he has failed. Or the individual may have little insight into his effect on a child and tend to attribute the problem to inappropriate causes. For instance, he may attribute the problem to vague hereditary causes, the child's lack of proper effort, or "willpower."

These types of objections and/or attitudes must be carefully assessed and, if possible, appropriately worked through with the individuals involved. There is no single procedure that is always successful. The authors have found two approaches, used individually or in combination, that are helpful. First, when therapeutic and/or change procedures are initiated with the child, the significantly involved adults are given the role of observers of the child's behavior. Frequent conferences are held with the significant adults to discuss their observations of the child's behavior. If conferences with these adults are scheduled frequently enough and the counselor or psychologist handles them skillfully, communication barriers are broken down, trust begins to develop, and the adults begin to take a more active role. Since the involved adults are not "blamed" for the child's problems and are in an advantageous position to observe changes beginning to take place in the child, additional cooperation becomes likely.

A second procedure that has proven useful is simply to invite the significantly involved adults to agree to a moratorium of the typical methods or ways of relating to the child that have been used in the past. They are asked to cease using the practices and imposing the expectations that they characteristically do for a specified period of time (usually a week or two weeks). They are told that such a practice has been found effective in helping many children. If their acceptance can be secured, the counselor or psychologist specifies exactly how the child's behavior will be handled in each of the high-conflict areas. The involved adults are asked to keep a record of the child's behavior (particularly in the problem areas), and the behavior is discussed with the psychologist in the conferences. Having the adults keep records of the child's behavior (and their reaction to it) is useful for determining whether or not they are performing their roles adequately and for helping the psychologist to make needed adjustments. Also, the adults may discover how their behavior is ineffective and maintains the child's behavior. By the time the moratorium has ended, the significant people are usually positively involved. If the procedures have proved effective, the child's behavior may have begun to change. The behavior changes may provide additional incentive or reinforcement for the adults' efforts. Thus, it is possible to consider a more comprehensive treatment plan.

As we have noted before, the type of total treatment plan that is implemented is dependent on the problem analysis, on who the significant clients are, and on the extent to which they can be involved as the *object* of change or the *agent* of change. At this point, it is desirable to consider change methods (or therapy) with the significant clients who can be appropriately engaged. The problem dimensions are clearly discussed, the form of intervention is specified, and the roles of each person are clearly delineated. For example, the type of therapy (individual or group) and the kind of therapy (play, family, or behavior) is discussed with the client or clients. If the client is a child, this may simply involve discussing generally his feelings about coming for assistance, appointment arrangements, and the type of things in which he will be involved. When parents or teachers are involved, roles, responsibilities, and appointments are carefully discussed. It is particularly important to provide adequate opportunity for the clients to raise questions and to express their attitudes and feelings regarding the procedures and treatment process. The clients' doubts, as well as any unrealistic expectations they may have of "cure," must be recognized and properly clarified. It is also critical during the initial stages (and throughout the entire treatment process) to keep records of the child's behavior. With this information, adjustments in procedures can be made and proper assistance can be provided to the adult clients to help them perform their roles effectively.

Strategies for Promoting Behavior Change

The previous discussion and analysis has identified some of the major steps that must be taken before change strategies can be implemented. The task of formulating specific strategies to change problem behavior is the final and most crucial step. Of course, strategies or therapeutic interventions are always based on the analysis of the client's problems, the variables operating to maintain problem behavior, and the use of principles that will promote the desired behavior. It is not possible to provide a procedure or strategy that exactly fits every client. It is possible, however, to provide, in general, paradigms or stratagems that illustrate how principles and procedures may be applied to a variety of nonadaptive behavior.

The stratagems that we will give represent learning or behavior change principles in combinations that are in some ways unique. Because they illustrate how stratagems can be formulated and applied in clinical situations, the thoughtful practitioner may find them useful as models which may be adapted to a variety of school and clinical uses.

The parameters of each stratagem are briefly described and are summarized in chart form. Each stratagem has three essential components:

(1) basic steps, (2) procedures for implementing, and (3) special considerations and cautions. The basic information is contained in each chart, and the written commentary for each stratagem is limited to the essential theoretical elements and the facets of its application. Each chart is read by starting with the first basic step at the left, and moving to the right; procedures for implementing and special cautions are noted at each step. When each of the elements in the first step is appropriately conceptualized and carried out, the steps are followed in order.

Stratagem 1: Extinction and Positive Reinforcement

The process of favorably altering nonadaptive behavior essentially involves two basic elements: (1) unlearning (or reducing in strength) the nonadaptive behavior; and (2) learning adaptive behavior. Although these two may not be entirely separate or occur independently, both must be achieved.

For a great number of problem behaviors, the basic operant procedures (see Chapter 1) are useful. That is, by systematic reinforcement of the desirable behavior, changes are often achieved. Similarly, the use of extinction (termination of all reinforcement for the nonadaptive behavior) may effectively eliminate some undesirable behavior. However, when these two procedures are used separately, more time may be required to achieve the desired result. Also, when extinction procedures are used in isolation, the nonadaptive behavior may increase in strength for a short time. Consequently, the change agent may become frustrated or disappointed and may give up or "just happen" to reinforce the nonadaptive behavior. For these reasons, it is desirable to use procedures that effectively combine useful change principles.

In Table 3 extinction and positive reinforcement are combined so that nonadaptive behavior may be eliminated and desirable behavior promoted simultaneously. Since each of the basic steps, procedures for implementation, and special considerations are specified, extensive comment is unnecessary. If the basic steps and procedures are followed, the strategies can usually be carried out effectively. Problems that typically arise are identified in the third column and should be carefully considered.

Attention may be profitably directed to a few of the elements that are crucial in its application. In using the stratagem, it is important to identify initially the *behavior to be eliminated* and *the desirable behavior to be promoted.* Specification of these behaviors is followed by systematic observation and recording of the behavior to obtain a baseline rate. Behavior observation and recording is continued throughout the treatment period to determine the extent to which procedures are effective as well as to make necessary adjustments. Once the behaviors to be eliminated and changed have been specified, extinction and positive reinforcement are used simultaneously. The novice may ex-

Table 3   Stratagem 1: Extinction and Positive Reinforcement

Basic Steps	Procedures for Implementing	Specific Considerations and Cautions
1a. Obtain baseline rate of behavior to be eliminated and/or changed.	1a. Observe child in appropriate situations.	1. State the *overt* behavior desirable to eliminate and/or change.
1b. Identify exactly the behavior to be eliminated and/or changed.	1b. Write down the exact behavior it is desirable to eliminate and/or change.	
2. Terminate all reinforcement for undesirable behavior.	2. Withdraw all positive and negative reinforcement coming from all sources (parents, teachers, and peers). a. Use time-out when necessary. *Example:* "You are having difficulty with (behavior) today. Please go to the time-out room."	2. Do not unintentionally reward the behavior (ignore undesirable behavior and do not criticize). a. Use time-out in a matter-of-fact, non-hostile way. Use it as soon as undesirable behavior is exhibited.

(continued)

perience difficulty at this stage because *all* reinforcement of the undesirable behavior is not terminated, reinforcers of the desirable behavior are not in fact reinforcing, or an inappropriate schedule of reinforcement is used. If the problem or undesirable behavior is well entrenched, use of time-out may be needed for a period of time, whenever the problem behavior occurs. If used properly, time-out effectively terminates all reinforcement that may be operat-

ing in the situation to sustain the problem behavior. When the desirable behavior has attained sufficient strength, a change to a variable schedule is advisable in order to make the adaptive behavior resistant to extinction.

The length of time the procedures are used is, of course, dependent on the variables operating in each case, their effects on the child, and the extent of their success. Behavior changes are typically noted within a period of two weeks. As

Table 3   (continued)

Basic Steps	Procedures for Implementing	Specific Considerations and Cautions
3. Modify the environment to decrease the possibility that undesirable behavior will be evoked.	3. Avoid placing the child in a situation in which undesirable behavior is a natural response. *Example:* If you are extinguishing aggression, do not place child in competitive situations.	3. Remember that undesirable behavior may increase in strength for a while.
4. Reinforce the opposite and desirable behavior with a continuous schedule. a. Reinforce approximations of desired behavior if not present in behavior repertoire.	4. Set up situations when desirable behavior is likely to occur. *Example:* Have aggressive child sit with teacher during reading (assembly) and reinforce for non-aggression.	4. Be certain that rewards used are reinforcing. If in doubt, begin with primary reinforcement.
5. Change reinforcement schedule when undesirable behavior decreases in strength and desirable behavior increases in frequency.	5. Reinforce every fourth, ninth, fourteenth, etc., desirable response. a. Provide bonus reinforcements occasionally.	5. Do not change to a variable ratio or interval schedule until appropriate behavior has the desired frequency.

the child's behavior begins to change, the significant adults begin to respond more positively to the child and the new behavior begins to be self-reinforcing. That is, the child obtains satisfaction — reinforcement — for exhibiting the desirable rather than the undesirable behavior.

Though the stratagem is not appropriate to behavior that is not under voluntary control or cannot be performed by the child, the use of extinction and reinforcement simultaneously is, as subsequent chapters will show, applicable to a wide range of behavior that *is* under voluntary control.

Stratagem 2: Modeling and Positive Reinforcement

The theoretical discussion of modeling (Chapter 2) suggested that observational learning might effectively promote behavior not already in a person's behavior repertoire, as well as change nonadaptive behavior. If reinforcement is given to the model for performing certain behaviors, or the learner is reinforced for imitative or matching responses, learning is even more efficiently promoted. Learning can be further enhanced if these two procedures are combined with successive approximations to promote the desired behavior. The modeling and positive reinforcement stratagem combines these three important ingredients. Although this stratagem is more complex and difficult to use than stratagem 1, it is a powerful behavior change method.

This stratagem is especially useful when a response (or behavior) does not exist in the client's repertoire, fear or anxiety inhibits the desirable behavior, or it is difficult to promote the desirable behavior because the problem behavior is extremely resistant to extinction. It is also effective in promoting a wide range of new behavior.

The essential elements of the modeling and reinforcement stratagem are presented in Table 4. It is important to note that the behavior to be promoted — or changed — must be operationally stated, and the successive approximations to the terminal behavior must be clearly specified before the procedures are initiated. Once this has been done, the procedures are initiated by modeling or demonstrating the first approximation that can and will be performed by the child. Each successive response approximation is modeled by the child and immediately reinforced with stimuli of known reinforcement property. In any one session, a single approximation and matching response may be performed several times with appropriate reinforcement (see Chapter 9). Each response approximation is increased to sufficient strength. However, care must be exercised to make certain that the beginning approximations are not excessively reinforced. As the child makes progress in imitating (matching) the successive approximations, the earlier responses need not be modeled, and the child may not be required to perform them. At the beginning of each session, new approximations are introduced as the child demonstrates his capacity to perform those at earlier points in the hierarchy. However, if at the beginning of any session the child is unable to readily perform previous approximations in the response hierarchy, it may be necessary to backtrack to earlier approximations.

As the child performs those responses that approximate the desired behavior, a change from a continuous to a variable reinforcement schedule is introduced. Also, if a primary reinforcer has been used previously, it may be desirable to change to tokens or points that can be exchanged for toys or reinforcing events. If the sessions have been conducted in the psychologist's or counselor's office, it is necessary to instigate procedures that will help the child generalize the terminal behavior to situations in which he must ultimately perform them. Consequently, the modeling and reinforcement procedures are performed in the presence of the people who compose the natural environment to which the behavior should

Table 4 Stratagem 2: Modeling and Positive Reinforcement

Basic Steps	Procedures for Implementing	Specific Considerations and Cautions
1a. Obtain baseline rate of behavior to be changed. 1b. Identify the exact behavior to be changed.	1a. Observe and record behavior to be changed. 1b. Write down the behavior that it is desirable to promote.	1. Behavior must be stated in operational terms.
2. Identify the successive approximations of the behavior to be modeled beginning with the least difficult or anxiety provoking.	2. Model (demonstrate) to child the first behavior approximation in the hierarchy.	2. Be certain that child can perform the behavior at each step. a. If anxiety associated with the behavior is too great, you must start with an approximation that can be performed.
3. Use continuous reinforcement for each execution of the modeled response(s).	3. Identify a variety of reinforcers, beginning with a primary reinforcer. a. Reinforce the first and each successively modeled response.	3. Avoid satiation by overuse of a specific reinforcer.

4. Sequential modeling of each response in the hierarchy.	4. Model or demonstrate each response in the hierarchy.
	   a. Reinforce the successful performance of each approximation.
		4. Limit the number of modeled approximations to a few each session.
		   a. Increase each modeled approximation to appropriate strength before proceeding to new approximations.

(continued)

generalize. When this procedure has been carried out for a period of time, a new reinforcing agent (teacher or parent) may become the contingency manager. Finally, the new contingency manager reinforces the desirable behavior in the natural setting until it is well entrenched in the child's behavior repertoire.

The modeling and positive reinforcement stratagem is illustrated in the case of Ray discussed in Chapter 1. The reader may wish to re-

Table 4   (continued)

Basic Steps	Procedures for Implementing	Specific Considerations and Cautions
5. Change schedule of reinforcement to variable ratio.	5. If approximations have increased to appropriate strength, reinforce every third, seventh, etc. modeled approximation. a. Utilize tokens or points as reinforcers and set exact time to be exchanged for toys, etc. b. Provide a bonus reinforcement occasionally.	5. Allow child to exchange tokens or points immediately in early sessions. a. Not more than two sessions should pass without exchange being made.
6. Structure situation so that behavior generalizes to appropriate situations outside of treatment.	6. Reinforce child in the presence of those to whom the behavior is to generalize (parents, teachers, and peers).	6–7. Make certain that behavior has acquired sufficient strength before beginning the generalization process and using other reinforcing agents. a. Reinforce the new contingency managers.
7. Switch reinforcement to people in the situations in which child's behavior will be performed.	7. Instruct people in natural situation how to reinforce and have them reinforce child in the presence of therapist.	
8. Maintain records of behavior in which change is desired.	8. Carefully evaluate the effects on behavior change.	8. If change is not taking place at any point, analyze difficulties, return to an earlier step, and increase the strength of that approximation before moving on.

view the case to see how specific steps in the stratagem are implemented.

Stratagem 3: Role Shift and Positive Reinforcement

The psychological practitioner is often asked to deal with child problems that adults find so persistently frustrating they are unable to take effective action. The significant adults may feel that in spite of their repeated attempts to change the child's behavior, the conflict continues unabated. The child's behavior may not be seriously disruptive or injurious, but it is continually distressing to the adults around him. The child may be stubborn, passively resistant, or extremely dependent, or may exhibit a variety of other behaviors that create conflict in home and school. When faced with a problem of this type, the role-shift and positive-reinforcement strategy may produce the desired effects.

The theoretical rationale for this strategy is based on role theory. According to the theory, each of us enacts in everyday life a number of different roles consistent with our position and status in groups to which we belong. In enacting these roles, we assume behaviors and attitudes that are consistent with them. As we perform these roles, other people with whom we interact perform reciprocal or complementary roles. For instance, if you thank someone for something he has done for you, his reply (behavior) to your expression of appreciation is likely to be "You are welcome." His reply complements your role behavior.

If others do not perform roles that are complementary to or consistent with the ones we enact, we experience role conflict and/or disturbed interpersonal relations. Similarly, if our attitudes and actions are not consistent with role expectations, we experience anxiety, and role conflict ensues. Consequently, there is some

pressure to change our behavior (role enactments) in ways consistent with the social role expectations and demands (Sarbin, 1964; Blackham, 1969).

When a person assumes a new or different role — that is, when a role shift is introduced — the behavior and expectations of others change, and the person tends to alter his behavior to meet the new role demands. Hence, the introduction of a role shift modifies the type of interaction that takes place between the person assuming the new role and others responding to it. For example, consider the situation of a teenage girl who is excessively critical in most of the interactions she has with her mother. And the more critical the teenager is of her mother, the more hostile and restrictive the mother is with her daughter. Now, suppose you have persuaded your teenage client to make a role shift from being mother-critical to compliment-giver for a weekend trial. If the teenager performs her compliment-giver role adequately, there is likely to be a dramatic change in the conflict. Once the mother begins to reciprocally adapt to the teenager's new role behavior, additional shifts are promoted in the teenager, and conflict tends to decrease markedly (Keirsey, 1965).

It can be seen, then, that the introduction of a role shift by one person necessitates an adjustment in the behavior of the other. The old ways of behaving are simply no longer effective. When a mother changes her role behavior in conflict situations with her child, a new response is elicited from the child. As he begins to perform a new and more desirable response, reinforcement of the new behavior tends to increase in frequency. If the mother continues to perform the new role prescription and also reinforces the desired child behavior, she promotes behavior change.

The essentials of the role-shift and positive-reinforcement stratagem are presented in Table 5. Before the procedures can be initiated, the conflict situations and the roles (behaviors) that the significant adults perform in those situations must be identified. Their actions and verbalizations are carefully identified, for each of these elements has significant reinforcement value, either positive or negative. Once such identification of behavior has been made, the adult is instructed to perform specific role prescriptions in the conflict situations.

Let us illustrate by another example. Suppose a mother has the habit of constantly nagging her son each morning to get ready for school. The more mother nags, the more Johnny resists. To help deal with this situation, she is instructed to perform a different role. She is told to request only once that he get ready for school. She is instructed not to nag, criticize, or punish. If Johnny does not carry out the demand within ten minutes, she quietly goes to his room and indicates that she will help him get dressed. Johnny is allowed to assume as much of the responsibility as he wishes, and mother begins to reinforce these efforts. On each successive

Table 5   Stratagem 3: Role Shift and Positive Reinforcement

Basic Steps	Procedures for Implementing	Specific Considerations and Cautions
1. Identify specific role conflict situations.	1. Ask parent (teacher) to describe high conflict situations and identify the role each person assumes in the conflict.	1. Identify the exact behavior and verbalization expressed by each party in the conflict.
2. Select the most highly conflicted situations and introduce role shifts for the significant adults.	2. Prescribe role shifts parent or teacher will perform where conflict is most intense (where parent or teacher is most upset and child is receiving most punishment or negative reinforcement). *Example:* If mother is a nagger, prescribe role in which mother gives one command and then acts to get child to complete desired behavior.	2. By concentrating on areas of high conflict and prescribing appropriate role shifts, much of the negative reinforcement the child is receiving is terminated.

(continued)

Table 5 Role Shift and Positive Reinforcement (continued)

Basic Steps	Procedures for Implementing	Specific Considerations and Cautions
3. Instruct significant adult(s) on new roles to be performed.	3. Specify actions and type of verbalizations in the role prescriptions parent or teacher will perform in conflict situations. a. Indicate to parent or teacher that you wish to try this "new procedure" for two weeks. b. Have significant adult make anecdotal record of all conflict situations involving child and himself during trial period.	3. For successful results, all actions and typical verbalizations in the new role must be specified for the involved adults. a. Anecdotal records of adult actions and verbalizations help involved adults and therapist determine to what extent role behavior is appropriate.
4. Specify with significant adult(s) the desirable child behavior in the conflict situations and set up reinforcement system.	4. Have parents state the exact behavior desired in each conflict situation. a. Identify potential reinforcers. b. Instruct parent (teacher) how they are to be administered in each situation.	4. Supervise the administration of reinforcement.
5. Evaluate effectiveness of role enactments and use of reinforcement.	5. Have significant adult(s) review their own and the child's behavior in each conflict situation in weekly sessions with therapist. a. Make necessary adjustments in adult role behavior as need arises.	5. Make certain that the involved adult(s) keep records of their own and child's behavior in the conflict situation. a. This procedure helps the adults become aware of the effects of their behavior on the child.

morning, the same procedure is followed, with reinforcement being given for each preparatory gesture. When Johnny has gotten dressed by himself, a bonus reinforcement (or reinforcing event) is given. When independent getting-dressed behavior has increased to reasonable frequency, tokens or points may be given, and the reinforcement schedule may be changed.

It is apparent from the example that several things may be operative when role shift and positive reinforcement are used. The mother's behavior becomes more predictable, the child's old resistance and delay tactics are inappropriate, and he gets reinforced for behaving differently. Since the mother's verbal behavior is no longer likely to evoke negative counterreactions, Johnny's minirebellion is brought to a halt.

This stratagem cannot be successful unless parents cooperate and are willing to follow the specified role prescriptions. To promote parent cooperation, it is often helpful to encourage them to try the procedure for a specified period of time. If they are distressed about the child's behavior, they would probably try any reasonable plan for a short period of time. They might be reminded that previous methods of handling the problem situation have proved unsuccessful, so little can be lost and something might be gained.

Once a trial period has been agreed on, the role behaviors are carefully specified in each high-conflict situation. The role prescriptions are carefully discussed until the individuals involved feel that they can perform the roles. The child behaviors that successively approximate the desired terminal behavior are identified and the adult is instructed in appropriate reinforcement procedures. During the trial period, the involved adult is requested to maintain records of both his behavior and the child's behavior in each of the conflict situations. In each of the sessions with the psychologist or counselor (which are initially very frequent), the records,

interactions, and feelings of all parties in the conflict situations are reviewed in detail. Such a procedure helps the parents to adequately maintain the role prescriptions and reinforcements. In each session, adjustments in role and reinforcement are made as needed. If the involved adults are given adequate assistance in performing their role prescriptions and properly reinforcing the child, dramatic changes in child behavior can be achieved. One of the authors, for example, was able to dramatically reverse in two weeks the behavior of a child who was about to be withdrawn from the second of two schools, each of which he had attended for less than six months.

Stratagem 4: Behavior Contract, Positive Reinforcement, and Withdrawal of Reinforcement

A behavior contract is an agreement between two or more parties to behave in certain prescribed ways in situations denoted by the terms. As such, it defines expectations, demands, and responsibilities that must be carried out and the consequences of infractions. The role of each person is clearly specified, so that there is no question about whom any default should be attributed to. Because the behavior contract as outlined in Table 6 is definitive, interaction among the parties is highly predictable, and each person is therefore encouraged to assume his responsibilities. The specificity of the terms makes people face up to "the games they play" and prevents the conscious use of defensive posturing, such as readily invoked excuses. Since the interaction among parties is clearly structured, a sense of security and safety appears to be an important by-product of the stratagem.

The addition of positive reinforcement and withdrawal of reinforcement to a behavior contract further specifies the rewards and withdrawals that depend upon the behavior of the child client. Consequently, as Keirsey (1965, 1969) has indicated, clients who tend to be impulsive, excessively manipulative, or lacking in adequate behavioral controls may be helped considerably.

Table 6 Stratagem 4: Behavior Contract, Positive Reinforcement, and Withdrawal of Reinforcement

Basic Steps	Procedures for Implementing	Specific Considerations and Cautions
1. Identify exactly the behavior to be eliminated and the behavior to be promoted.	1. Write down the behavior to be changed.	1. Specify each behavior in terms of its overt expression.
2. Hold initial conference with those involved in child's problems. a. Discuss problem with child.	2. Introduce contract idea to involved adults, indicating it will help child learn control. a. Indicate to child that you wish to help him control his behavior. Suggest that a method can be devised to help him get things he wants and to get people off his back.	2. Emphasize to each involved person that other approaches have not yielded success. Now it is time to take dramatic intervention procedures.
3. Devise behavior contract for presentation to all involved people. a. Contract specifies behavior to be eliminated and desirable behavior to be reinforced. b. Begin with the reinforcement of successive approximations of desired behavior if problem behavior is highly resistant to extinction.	3. Hold group staging conference with involved people (child, parent, teacher, etc.) indicating exact contract terms. a. Contract specifies consequence when child exhibits desirable and undesirable behavior. b. Reinforcements (which are varied) and withdrawal of reinforcement are clearly specified for all behavior.	3. Specify clearly the role of each person and how all phases of contract will be handled. a. Contract cannot be withdrawn for behavior the child exhibits that is not identified in contract. 1. i.e., reinforcement cannot be withdrawn for misbehavior not specified in contract.

(continued)

Prerequisite to the implementation of this stratagem is a careful definition of the child's problem behaviors, the situations in which they are expressed, and the willingness of the involved adults to try the procedure. The adults' motivation is usually enhanced when they rec-

Table 6 (continued)

Basic Steps	Procedures for Implementing	Specific Considerations and Cautions
	c. Points may be used for reinforcement and withdrawal of reinforcement. Child is able to exchange points for free time, toys, etc., any time he has sufficient number. d. Make certain all involved people understand and accept contract. e. All involved people sign and receive copy of contract.	b. Reinforcers for which points are exchanged *must be reinforcing.*
4. Supervise roles and administration of procedures.	4. Program is initiated the day following the staging conference. a. Check frequently with involved people to ensure that terms are carried out.	4. Do not change schedule until behavior desired is being performed with high frequency.
5. Modify reinforcement schedule as appropriate.	5. When behavior has increased in strength change reinforcement schedule so that desirable behavior will not extinguish. a. Increase number of points required to get toy or reinforcing events.	5. Check to make certain that reinforcement and withdrawal of reinforcement are properly administered.

ognize and accept the fact that other methods have not been successful in helping the child and that more effective intervention strategies are now necessary. Each involved adult (teacher, principal, parent, etc.) is interviewed individually, the dimensions of the child's problems are discussed, and the probabilities for success of the procedures are carefully explained. If there is some initial resistance to the procedure, it is usually helpful to persuade the adults to try it for a limited period of time (one to two weeks). With adult concurrence, the child client is interviewed, and his difficulties are discussed honestly without criticism or disapproval. It is suggested to him that a method can be devised that will "get adults off his back" and give him more opportunity to assume responsibility for his own behavior. After his acceptance, a group staging conference is held among all involved, to describe, explain, and discuss the terms of the contract previously drawn up by the psychologist or counselor.

As is true of any situation in which reinforcement is being used, the reinforcing stimuli or events must be carefully selected and varied to avoid satiation. In the initial stages, reinforcement is liberally administered (continuous ratio) until the desirable behavior is being performed frequently. Also, care must be exercised to ensure that positive reinforcement surpasses the reinforcement that is withdrawn for undesirable behavior. To enhance the ease with which reinforcement is administered, tokens or points can be given for the performance of the desirable behavior and removed for the undesirable behavior as specified in the contract. However, if tokens or points are used, the opportunities to exchange them for reinforcing stimuli or events must be frequent. At the appropriate stage and in consultation with all parties — especially the child — a change is made to a variable schedule to increase the durability of the desirable behavior.

Throughout the period of the contract, the procedures must be adhered to rigidly. Each of the major people involved must be carefully supervised to ensure that the terms are carried out. And even though the child may exhibit undesirable behavior not specified in the contract, such behavior has no influence on the terms of the contract. That is, reinforcement cannot be withdrawn that is specified in the contract. Such behavior is separate from the contract and must be handled independently and judiciously. Of course, the contract can be changed if adjustments need to be made to promote the desirable behavior effectively. However, these modifications must be jointly agreed upon by all parties, written into the old or new contract, and signed by all parties.

The utility of this strategy is illustrated by a case reported by Blackham (1977). A twelve-year-old learning disabled boy was referred by his teacher for his inappropriate academic performance. He rarely completed daily assignments, spent a great deal of time daydreaming, and generally appeared unhappy. Intelligence test data indicated that he had sufficient ability to do the work assigned to him, but he appeared unmotivated and disinterested in school work.

An interview with the boy confirmed his lack of interest in schoolwork. He seemed excessively dependent on others for direction and expressed few positive feelings for his teacher. He related that his father had died several years earlier, and he appeared to miss him. And while he expressed positive feelings for his mother, it was clear that his relationship with her was not without conflict. His mother appeared to dominate him and often became upset with him when he failed to perform chores and other requests made of him. He appeared to have adopted a strategy of passive resistance, never openly rebelling but procrastinating or "forgetting" to do things his mother frequently requested him to do.

To identify reinforcing stimuli and events, a reinforcement survey was administered to him. Several potential reinforcing stimuli and activities were identified: bike riding, free time, playing with his best friend, playing checkers or Monopoly, going to drag races, shooting baskets, spending time with the coach, doing errands for the teacher, watching athletic events, and obtaining ice-cream treats. When these potential reinforcing stimuli and events had been identified, the boy was asked if he would like to earn privileges he enjoyed by devoting somewhat greater effort to completing his schoolwork. In discussing the matter he indicated that he felt he needed something to provide an incentive for doing his schoolwork. As a matter of fact, he indicated that when he had not been allowed to watch a school athletic contest on a previous Friday for incomplete work, he had been motivated to devote more time to school the following week.

It was proposed to the boy that a new program be initiated that would enable him to participate more frequently in things he enjoyed doing while, at the same time, reducing the disapproval he received from his mother and teacher for his poor schoolwork. The boy agreed to try the new plan, and a contract was subsequently formulated. In essence, the contract stated that when Tom (the child client) completed all school assignments each day and exhibited proper student behavior (specified in behavioral terms) in the classroom and on the playground, every third day he would earn thirty minutes of free time to participate in one of the following events: (1) shoot baskets on the court with a male counselor; (2) play a commercial game (such as checkers); (3) perform errands for the teacher during the school day; or (4) go to the drive-in for ice cream. When he completed his daily work for five consecutive days, he would be permitted to engage in a special event on the weekend with his mother. However, if he

did not have all schoolwork done for the week by Friday at 1:30, he would not be allowed to watch the weekly athletic event at school. The teacher agreed to send daily notes home to the mother to inform her of Tom's progress, and the teacher, the mother, and Tom all signed the contract.

The effect of the contract on Tom's completion of assignments was immediate. By the end of the first week, all school assignments were completed, he was productively working in class, and he earned all privileges specified in the contract. Follow-up with the teacher several weeks later indicated that Tom was completing work regularly and his social behavior continued to be appropriate.

A Case Illustration

To illustrate the process of formulating and implementing behavior change strategies, we will present the case of R. R., an adolescent boy who was referred to us for psychological evaluation because of his severe academic and behavior problems. We will first present an overview of the boy's problems, including data obtained from the client, the parents, the school, and the psychological evaluation, and then analyze the case data according to the conceptual scheme outlined in this chapter.

R. R. was fourteen years of age and the oldest of three boys. At the time of referral his difficulties were so serious that he was in danger of being permanently expelled from school. In the initial interview the parents indicated concern about R. R.'s poor academic performance but were obviously most concerned about his behavior. The parents described him as extremely resistant and stubborn, unable to "get along with others," or "take failure." They were apprehensive about his secretiveness, lying, stealing, and temper tantrums and feared that his physically abusive behavior toward his brothers might lead to their being seriously hurt.

The school's report of R. R.'s difficulties was similar to the parents', although the school saw the problems as much more serious. At school he needed constant prodding to complete anything, and he was suspected of a variety of antisocial acts even though he was rarely seen executing them. However, he was observed defacing school furniture, pulling plaster off the classroom wall, and throwing rocks on the playground. Also, he was the leader of a small group of defiant and belligerent boys. When something was broken or missing at school, there was general consensus that somehow R. R. was involved. He was a constant source of classroom disruption and was frequently reprimanded for his noncooperative or defiant behavior.

The developmental and social history indicated that R. R.'s difficulties had existed for some time, although the parents apparently did not view them as unusual until he entered public school. He was toilet trained at about eleven months, walked at about the same time, and first talked at approximately two years of age. No sensory deficiencies were noted, but R. R. had had allergies and asthma since he was three years old. The parents noted that he had always been restless, easily frustrated, and tended to overreact to failure. Temper tantrums were apparent during the preschool years and occurred more frequently as he got older. When frustrated, he would either behave aggressively or become sullen and refuse to talk with anyone.

It was difficult to reconstruct the child-rearing practices and parent-child relationships, because the parents were exceedingly vague about them. From their descriptions and other data, they might be termed "emotionally distant." There were few indications that the family enjoyed doing things together or sharing experiences. Both parents seemed sincere in the care and concern for their children, but they did not translate their feelings into frequent demonstrations of praise, cuddling, or approval. Both parents appeared reserved or even withdrawn and did not seem to talk much with each other, the children, or others outside the home. The mother presented a picture of herself as somewhat controlling and overprotective of the children; the father seemed aloof and quite willing to relegate to his wife the upbringing of R. R. and their other children. Both parents indicated they had tried a variety of disciplinary measures and had not found one that worked effectively with R. R. Apparently, they had searched haphazardly for methods to achieve the desired results. They often used physical punishment to induce the desired behavior in R. R. but had abandoned it because such treatment appeared to exacerbate his inappropriate behavior.

Psychological evaluation indicated R. R. had a normal to bright normal level of intelligence. Perceptual-motor tests and neurological examination (done earlier) did not reveal significant perceptual-motor handicaps or neurological dysfunctioning. Diagnostic tests placed him at an independent reading level of 5.0 and 5.9 in reading. Although some deficiencies in phonic skills were noted, they were not major. Personality assessment tended to confirm the developmental and social history. R. R. appeared to be a secretive, socially alienated boy who fantasied the performance of a variety of antisocial acts about which he felt little guilt. He viewed people suspiciously. He seemed to resent his mother, whom he construed as unloving and controlling; he viewed his father more positively but thought he was rather inaccessible.

In addition to the evaluation procedures, R. R. was observed for five days in a special diagnostic classroom. Although baseline academic and behavioral data were not systematically recorded, the teacher reported strikingly different behavior from that described by the school. During the first day, when the typical reinforcement contingencies approximated the public school's, he appeared cooperative and task oriented. He did what was expected of him and exhibited no unusual disruptive or antisocial behavior. During the following four days, when a point reinforcement system was used to promote appropriate academic and social behavior, he behaved in both areas quite appropriately. However, he did become more resistant and manipulative.

Besides points, we were interested in discovering other potentially reinforcing stimuli and events. They were identified by talking with the client and his parents and by administering a reinforcing events inventory. The identified potential reinforcers were as follows: bike riding, photography, art, assisting the physical education teacher, playing checkers, and helping his father at work. The last reinforcing event, working with his father, appeared to be the most potent.

The general overview of our client and his background was now complete. However, before we give a detailed analysis of his problems, we should mention that he was seen and offered assistance by a neurologist, and on two separate occasions was studied by clinical psychologists. The parents described the assistance received as of little benefit to them or their son.

Identified Problem Behavior

The first step in analyzing the case material is to identify the client's problems and state them in behavioral terms. The results of this type of analysis are listed below:

1. Hitting, kicking, or shoving others; criticizing, cursing, or arguing with others (inappropriate physical or verbal behavior)

2. Writing or carving on furniture and walls, or pulling plaster off classroom walls (damaging school property)

3. Taking others' possessions or property (stealing)

4. Failure to carry out parent and teacher requests (defiance of authority)

5. Difficulty in attending and listening to the teacher, obeying classroom rules, staying in seat, and completing assigned work (inappropriate student behavior)

6. Arguing, yelling, screaming, or door-slamming when an ongoing activity is interrupted or when a request is not granted (temper tantrum)

7. Insufficient studying and noncompletion of school assignments (failing schoolwork)

8. Falsifying events or experiences and making excuses (lying)

9. Asthmatic attacks and allergic reactions

10. Reacting to failure by hitting, cursing, or refusing to talk with anyone (poor frustration tolerance)

11. Throwing rocks at people or property (antisocial behavior)

The summary statements in parentheses were placed there purposely for you to note the contrast between a problem stated behaviorally and a common description of problem behavior. Observe that when a problem is stated behaviorally, nothing is left to imagination or individual interpretation; the behavioral statement *describes the actual behavior* that is inappropriate. We know *what* behavior we wish to change and the *type* of change we wish to effect. After the problems are stated behaviorally, the opposite behaviors are the appropriate behavior change goals.

Analysis of the Problem Behavior

Once we have properly identified the client's problems and stated them behaviorally, it is desirable to determine their severity. In Chapter 1 we noted that the severity of a client's problems can be determined on the basis of frequency, the extent to which the behavior is hurtful to the child or the environment, and the extent they impede the client's adaptation and healthy development. Using these criteria, the relative severity of the problems is indicated by the order in which they are listed on page 119. You will note that the problem behaviors that are hurtful, destructive, and bring R. R. in conflict with others have highest priority. His difficulties with school subjects were important but not as critical as the antisocial behavior. School personnel were most understanding and tolerant of his academic difficulties but were upset by his antisocial behavior. To avoid expulsion from school, immediate change in his more provocative behavior was highly desirable. Hence, the first five problems listed can be considered the most severe. Ordinarily, these problem behaviors would be the first objects of therapeutic "attack." However, because some of the other problem behaviors (failing schoolwork, lying, rock throwing) were almost as serious, they too required rather immediate therapeutic attention.

The formulation of effective change strategies depends on the analysis of variables producing or maintaining the inappropriate behavior. If behavior is a function of its consequences, we can assume that the client's problem behavior was maintained by inappropriate reinforcement. Analysis of the data revealed a number of plausible hypotheses. First, the mother, who had the primary child-rearing responsibilities, did not define limits clearly nor enforce them consistently. The same client behavior was, at different times, variously punished or ignored. Consequences for unde-

sirable behavior were not always enforced, and the client learned that provocative behavior got what he wanted; the client's temper tantrums and stubborn and resistant behaviors were established and maintained in the same way. Second, the parents did not use positive reinforcement frequently or appropriately. Social or verbal reinforcement was dispensed so infrequently that desirable behavior was simply not maintained. When R. R.'s undesirable behavior began to escalate, the parents increased punishment. It is probable that the excessive punishment initiated R. R.'s secretiveness and falsehoods, which are often successful in avoiding punishment and are, therefore, negatively reinforcing. The parents' use of excessive punishment also served as a model which the client appeared to imitate. For example, when the client behaved aggressively at school or was physically abusive toward his younger brothers, he may have been modeling his parents. Third, his academic endeavors were not sufficiently reinforced. His socially undesirable behavior at school was probably an attempt to get thrown out—a convenient way to avoid an aversive situation.

Analysis of the variables that appeared to produce and maintain the problem behaviors led to three basic considerations:

1. A behavior modification plan was necessary to immediately and effectively control the more serious antisocial behavior to prevent the client's expulsion from school and possible detention by juvenile authorities.

2. Several of the client's antisocial behaviors were exhibited at home and school. Hence, a total behavior modification plan was necessary to control the reinforcing contingencies in both situations. Because the client frequently exhibited inappropriate behavior in the classroom, a systematic reinforcement system had to be devised for the classroom.

3. Because the client's parents, teacher, and school principal were the primary agents of change, behavior modification procedures had to be consistently applied to problem behavior at home and school.

Implementation of Change Procedures

After all the variables were analyzed, it appeared that a *behavior contract* was the most effective procedure for modifying the client's problem behavior. A behavior contract carefully prescribes the consequences for the problem and desirable behavior and clearly specifies the roles and behavior of all parties to the contract. Because it is formulated in detail, nothing is left to individual interpretation, and consistent response to the problem and desired behavior can be secured. If any party to the contract does not follow the contractual responsibilities, breaches are relatively easy to identify. Also, if the contract's behavior change strategies are inappropriate, the ineffective procedures can be readily identified.

The behavior contract in Figure 10 is self-explanatory, but it may be helpful to highlight some of the learning principles embodied in it. Positive reinforcement in the form of material rewards, points, and reinforcing events was used to promote desirable behavior. Time-out was used to decrease the frequency of undesirable behavior both at home and school. Bonus reinforcements (opportunity to work with his father and a special activity on the weekend) were also used to increase the desirable behavior. Points were paired with material reinforcers and reinforcing events to make them conditioned reinforcers; material reinforcers were phased out as soon as possible because points were easier to use in a classroom setting. Also, because points could be exchanged for a variety of reinforcing events, we avoided the problem of satiation that often accompanies the exclusive use of one or two reinforcers.

Because it was necessary to enforce firm and consistent limits on all expressions of undesirable social behavior, the use of time-out at home and school was absolutely essential. The use of *response cost* would have been appropriate if the client's desirable behavior was occurring at a more frequent rate. We feared that the withdrawal of points or privileges would deter the reestablishment of appropriate behavior (i.e., points or privileges would have been withdrawn so frequently, the client would have had little incentive to behave desirably).

Several activities preceded the implementation of the behavior contract. Our analysis of the problem behavior was explained to the parents and school personnel in separate interviews. In subsequent conferences with the parents and the school psychologist, the behavior contract was presented, and all individuals promised their cooperation. The school psychologist presented the behavior contract to the client and secured his agreement to it. The parents, client, and school personnel signed the contract and it was immediately implemented. One of the authors worked with the school psychologist to devise a more detailed classroom reinforcement system.

When the behavior modification program was put into operation, the consultants, school psychologist, and parents maintained frequent contact. For the first three days, R. R. exhibited model behavior. On the fourth day, his classroom behavior was quite disruptive, he was placed in time-out twice, and he completed few classroom assignments. Analysis of the classroom reinforcement system and the client's response to it indicated a need for change. Also, it appeared that the behavioral requirements in the contract were difficult for the client to perform and needed alteration. Two basic changes were instituted. First, the teacher was asked to reduce academic expectations so that the client could more easily obtain reinforcement. Because other problem students had a disruptive

CONTRACT

This contract has been formulated for the purpose of helping R. R. learn more desirable student and social behavior. To help R. R. achieve the objectives stated herein, the following terms and procedures will be used:

To help R. R. learn appropriate student behavior (staying in seat, working on classroom assignments, following teacher instructions, and observing classroom rules), he will be given rewards:

    a. For exhibiting the appropriate student behavior, a material reward and points will be given which may be exchanged for time to be with or help the Physical Education teacher.

    b. For exhibiting the appropriate student and social behavior described above for three consecutive days, R. R. will be given the opportunity to work with his father during the afternoon or after school for a minimum period of one hour on the third day and every third day thereafter.

    c. If R. R. has five consecutive days of good student and social behavior (as described above), he will be permitted a special activity on the weekend. This arrangement will continue every time R. R. exhibits five days of desirable student and social behavior.

Certain privileges will be withdrawn when R. R. exhibits undesirable behavior.

UNDESIRABLE BEHAVIOR

    a. Breaking equipment or school property
    b. Taking or destroying possessions of other students
    c. Breaking school pencils, tearing plaster off the wall
    d. Writing or carving on desks
    e. Refusing to comply with classroom rules

When R. R. exhibits any of these behaviors, he will be required to go immediately to the time-out room near the principal's office and remain there until R. R. determines that he can exhibit proper social and student behavior.

A second infraction of proper social or student behavior in any one day requires that R. R. be taken home for the remainder of the day. He will not be permitted to participate in any enjoyable activity for the remainder of that day.

Changes may be made in this contract as deemed desirable by all parties involved.

We, the undersigned, agree to these terms.

_____   _____
(Student)   (Teacher)

_____   _____
(Parents)   (Psychologist or Principal)

Figure 10   A Behavior Contract

influence on the classroom, she was advised to use a kitchen timer to administer bonus reinforcement. The kitchen timer was set for various time intervals. When it sounded, all students who had exhibited appropriate student and social behavior were reinforced. Second, the contract was changed so that R. R. could earn the opportunity to work with his father each afternoon if his student and social behavior were appropriate during the day.

We continued to encourage the parents (by telephone) to adhere rigidly to the terms of the contract and to positively reinforce all desirable behavior at home. Frequent telephone contact was also maintained with the school psychologist to discuss any problems that were occurring at school or home. The school psychologist carried out any modifications of parent response or problem-handling.

Three difficult weeks followed the initiation of the behavior contract. Some days, R. R. was noncooperative, aggressive, and disruptive and had to be placed in time-out or taken home. On other days, his student and social behavior were quite appropriate, and he earned the opportunity to work with his father in the afternoon.[1] Despite the inconsistent reports from school, he was making progress. He completed more classroom assignments and exhibited more socially appropriate behavior at school and home. He appeared less frequently in the time-out room and was more cooperative at home: School personnel had reservations about the behavior modification plan, but they continued to work energetically to fulfill its requirements.

By the fourth week, pronounced if not dramatic change was observed in the client. School personnel began to talk about the obvious improvement. The day-to-day crisis calls to the school psychologist dropped off noticeably.

[1] Records of the client's daily behavior were not kept by the school so the exact fluctuations cannot be reported.

The client's behavior and response to school improved enough to justify his attendance for the remainder of the year.

The school psychologist reported that the client experienced no difficulties during the following summer. The parents were extremely happy about R. R.'s progress and felt certain that he would experience little difficulty with high school in the fall. School personnel were somewhat more realistic and recommended that the client be placed in a class for emotionally handicapped students. They wanted to ensure that the client's gains be maintained and feared that a regular high school program would be too much for him. However, the parents did not accept the school's recommendation. Within a month after he entered high school, the client began to manifest some difficulties. He was placed in a special class for emotionally handicapped students and has continued to make progress since that time.

The case of R. R. was chosen for illustrative purposes because it shows the possibilities with a client when circumstances are less than ideal. The parents were disenchanted with their previous professional assistance and were not easily engaged in the change process. Although the client's problems had reached a crisis point, it was impossible to place him in an individualized and ongoing treatment situation. Because variables influencing the client's behavior were not under our direct control, we could not use precise experimental procedures, i.e., continuous observation and recording of the client's behavior. Yet, even under these conditions, relatively serious academic and behavioral problems reversed.

No doubt the reader is still wondering, "Was the client cured?" We may answer that the nonadaptive and/or inappropriate behavior of the client was reduced in frequency, and more adaptive behavior was increased. If the client continues to receive positive reinforcement for socially desirable and adaptive behavior, a self-reinforcement system will probably be internalized that will help perpetuate appropriate behavior and elicit more desirable consequences in the natural environment.

Summary

1. The behavior change process involves three essential steps: (a) problem definition and analysis, (b) specification of behavior change goals, and (c) formulation and implementation of procedures that appropriately modify the problem behavior.

2. The problem(s) identified by the client and/or referral agent is defined and analyzed in terms of the variables that maintain it; when, where, and with whom the problem is exhibited; and its general severity. Each problem is stated in behavioral terms to observe its frequency and to specify appropriate behavior change goals.

3. A developmental and social history is obtained to (a) define and analyze the client's problems, (b) identify who and what reinforcing events maintain the problem behavior, (c) identify potential reinforcers to promote behavior change, and (d) specify treatment priorities.

4. Problem behavior that creates intense interpersonal conflict or is destructive or injurious to others should be the object of immediate therapeutic attack. Other, less serious problem behavior becomes the object of therapeutic modification at a later time.

5. Behavior modification strategies produce more potent effects when they are combined to increase or decrease specific behavior. Many strategies and combinations are possible. Four stratagems are:

a. *Extinction and positive reinforcement:* The stratagem alters behavior by simultaneously decreasing undesirable behavior and increasing desirable behavior.

b. *Modeling and positive reinforcement:* The procedure promotes behavior that does not exist in the client's repertoire, decreases fearful or avoidant behavior, and enhances the frequency or strength of infrequently performed behavior.

c. *Role shift and positive reinforcement:* In this procedure an individual is reinforced for performing a behavior or role that is different or opposite to behavior that leads to undesirable consequences. Although the role shift is promoted by deliberate reinforcement of it, the client's role shift leads others to exhibit behavior that complements the new role and tends to facilitate the performance of it.

d. *Behavior contract, positive reinforcement, and withdrawal of reinforcement:* This procedure produces its effects by (1) specifying the response-consequence relationships for desirable and undesirable behavior and (2) encouraging individuals who maintain the client's behavior to utilize positive and negative consequences consistently. It is effective with clients who are impulsive, aggressive, or exhibit other self-control difficulties.

Chapter Six

Modification of Behavior in the Regular Classroom

In this chapter the focus of our attention will be on the management of behavior in the regular classroom. We will discuss general principles of classroom management and types of classroom reinforcement systems and illustrate how behavior modification procedures can be used by providing examples of a preschool-kindergarten class, an elementary school class, and a junior high school class.

Principles and Procedures of Classroom Management

The creation of a stimulating and productive learning experience is a rare achievement. Teachers recognize effective learning by student response, but they may find it difficult to conceptualize or describe exactly how it is created. It is not surprising, as even experts disagree on the ingredients that promote learning. However, evidence suggests that at least seven ingredients are related to effective learning and classroom management (Becker, Thomas, and Carnine, 1971; Dollar, 1972). The seven ingredients are stated in procedural steps to make them easier to understand and utilize.

Specify in Positive Terms the Desired Classroom Behavior Students should know the rules and standards of classroom behavior, for if they are not specified, students will "test its limits" until they discover what is and is not acceptable. To avoid this kind of confusion, the teacher should specify the appropriate behavior in *positive* terms. For example, a positive, precise rule might be expressed thusly: "Ask permission to talk by raising your hand." The statement leaves no question in the student's mind of how to gain permission to talk.

Individualize Learning Tasks So Every Student Can Succeed Much nontask or disruptive classroom behavior is often a result of uninteresting or too difficult learning activities. Most learning activities can be broken down into units that successively approximate the learning objective. Although this procedure requires considerable preparation, it avoids a great deal of disruptive classroom behavior.

Specify Consequences for Both Desirable and Undesirable Behavior If behavior is a function of its consequences, then appropriate behavior is maintained by employing *both* positive and negative consequences. However, desirable behavior cannot be achieved if negative consequences are used more frequently than positive ones. A good general rule is to positively reinforce appropriate behavior and ignore (and thus extinguish) the deviant behavior that is not in-

jurious or destructive. If the inappropriate behavior does not decrease in a reasonable period
of time, implement the negative consequence
immediately and consistently each time the inappropriate behavior occurs.

The teacher should have clearly in mind the
positive and negative consequences to be used.
It is a good idea to list positive reinforcers
(material reinforcers, reinforcing events, etc.)
and the specific negative consequences (response cost, time-out, etc.) for each student.

**Determine When and How Reinforcement Will
Be Administered** To increase the desired behavior most rapidly, the teacher should reinforce
the target behavior every time it occurs. Although material reinforcers and reinforcing
events may be used initially, praise should be
paired with them from the very beginning. The
reinforcement property of praise can be established and used in the future to maintain the
desirable behavior.

Some behaviors may be more difficult to
promote than others. It is appropriate to increase the magnitude of reinforcement (giving
more points or bonus reinforcement) for performance of these behaviors. Also, to increase
the desired behavior relate the student's performance of a desirable behavior to the rules.
For example, "I certainly like the way Susy listens during oral-reading period," is much more
effective in promoting listening behavior than
focusing on nonlistening behavior.

Most teachers find token systems the easiest
systematic reinforcement procedures to use in
the classroom. They give the students individual
cards identifying desirable social and academic
behavior. Then, they enter points or check
marks on the cards for task completion and performance of socially appropriate behavior.
Points may be exchanged for certain back-up
reinforcers based on their values. When the system is first formulated, points are exchanged for

back-up reinforcers rather frequently. For
example, during the first week the exchange
may occur daily or every other day. Gradually,
the exchange period is extended to every three
or five days. Back-up reinforcers are changed
periodically to ensure that they have the desirable effect. Students may be permitted to
accumulate a certain number of points, but
excessive accumulation of points should be
discouraged. Generally, desirable behavior
decreases when students "hoard" their points
and do not exchange them regularly for back-
up reinforcers.

Once the point system has promoted the
target behavior to an appropriate level, it is desirable to devise an "honor system." Students
who have demonstrated that they can complete
the assigned work and exhibit proper social behavior are taken off the point system, given offi-
cial honor status, and are permitted free access
to a wide range of privileges. Honor status continues as long as the students perform proper
academic and social behavior. If they do not, the
teacher returns them to the point system and
requires them to regain the honor status.

**Develop an Individual and Group Reinforce-
ment System** An individual reinforcement system promotes desirable individual social and
academic behavior and greatly facilitates classroom management. A group reinforcement system can also provide dividends by promoting
both individual and group goals. For example, a
class can be divided into teams with team points
given for almost any desirable behavior. If the
teacher wishes to promote cooperative behavior, he can give team points when students provide academic assistance or emotional support
to another team member. When a team earns a
certain number of points, they may "buy" a special event.

The teacher may also devise a class reinforcement system. Each time a student earns

points for desirable academic and social behavior, group points are won. When the entire class has earned a sufficient number of group points, it participates in a special reinforcing event. Dollar (1972) reports a group reinforcement system in which the class is awarded a star when all students behave appropriately for a period of time. However, if the class behaves inappropriately, the teacher gets a star. At the end of the week, teacher and class stars are totaled. If the students have more stars than the teacher (or a specified number), the class is awarded a special reinforcing event.

Model the Behavior Students Should Emulate Children imitate models that are prestigious, warm, and control power resources. If the teacher's behavior style is consistently reinforcing, students are likely to reflect it in their response to other students. However, if teachers tend to be punitive, sarcastic, and critical, students will tend to reflect the same type of behavior toward each other. Students cannot be expected to exhibit behavior not modeled by the teacher.

Develop Your Reinforcement Properties as a Teacher When teachers meet their students on the first day of school, their ability to promote desirable academic and social behavior is largely unknown. The students who have had "positive experiences" with previous teachers have learned that appropriate behavior is rewarded by teacher approval. Others, because of previous consistent success in learning, have acquired a self-reinforcing system (intrinsically motivated to learn). So, at first, both groups will exhibit appropriate academic and social behavior. However, other students who have not found teachers or learning particularly reinforcing will launch their protests early. Their behavior is likely to be resistant or disruptive.

Regardless of each student's generalized expectations and behavior patterns, appropriate behavior must be maintained and inappropriate behavior must be extinguished. To do both, the teacher must establish and maintain a reinforcement property, which is acquired just like any other stimulus object. Teacher responses must be paired with potent reinforcers or satisfy a learner need. When a teacher administers a primary reinforcer, bandages a cut knee, or listens sympathetically to a fearful child, he is building a reinforcement property. Such acts enhance his "influence quotient" and allow him to promote the behavior essential to desirable learning and personal development. Once a positive reinforcement property is established, the teacher must continue to perform the actions that maintain it. Like friendship, a reinforcement property must be constantly renewed.

As the following discussion will show, these seven basic principles occur repeatedly in classrooms designed according to behavior modification principles. In the next section, we will discuss in detail specific types of classroom reinforcement systems.

Types of Classroom Reinforcement Systems

Four types of reinforcement systems are used in schools: token, social, primary, and contingency management. The basic steps or procedures that are used in each system are the same, but each has advantages and disadvantages.

Token Reinforcement Systems

Token reinforcement systems have three basic characteristics. First, the behaviors to be reinforced are clearly specified. Second, a procedure is devised to administer a potentially re-inforcing stimulus (a token) when the target behavior is performed. Third, a set of rules is stated to regulate the exchange of tokens for reinforcing stimuli and events (O'Leary and Drabman, 1971).

A *token* is a tangible item given for the performance of a specified target behavior. It has no intrinsic value but acquires value when it can be exchanged for a material reinforcer or reinforcing event. A variety of items may be used as tokens: chips, stars, school money, stamps, points, check marks, etc. Depending on the situation, some types of tokens are more useful than others.

A token system has several advantages (Vernon, 1972):

1.   Satiation is avoided because tokens can be exchanged for a wide range of material reinforcers and reinforcing events. Children will work for them indefinitely if the back-up reinforcers include appealing activities and items.

2.   Tokens will often promote the target behavior when children are unresponsive to social reinforcement. Some difficult, disruptive, or unreachable children tend to respond very positively to a token system when other more traditional approaches fail.

3.   Tokens are easily administered, and the number of tokens given can be adjusted to the time and energy required to perform the target behavior.

4.   Because tokens are administered immediately after the target behavior is performed, the target behavior is effectively and exclusively promoted.

5.   Token-reinforcement systems make children sensitive to the response-consequence relationship. When children learn that all behavior has consequences, self-control is likely to be enhanced.

However, despite the advantages of token systems, they must be thoughtfully formulated and implemented. Phillips, Phillips, Fixsen, and Wolf (1973), O'Leary and Drabman (1971), O'Leary, Poulos, and Devine (1972), and Vernon (1972) have suggested the following important guidelines:

1.   The target behaviors that will earn tokens must be clearly specified and written on a chart or blackboard. If both individual and group token systems are used, the individual target behaviors should be posted on the student's desk. The rules governing individual and group contingencies should be reviewed frequently with the students.

2.   The student must be able to perform the target behaviors for which tokens will be given.

3.   The back-up reinforcers for which tokens are exchanged must be appealing to the students and should not be available outside the token system.

4.   The number of tokens earned must be consistent with the difficulty or effort required to perform the behavior. For example, if a student has great difficulty controlling his aggression, reinforcement for nonaggressive behavior must be sufficient to provide a potent incentive for proper behavior.

5.   If possible, the teacher should keep a record of tokens earned by each child (and the group, when a group system is used). Student incentive is often enhanced when the number of tokens earned is recorded on a chart displayed for the entire class to see.

6. If response cost (token fines) is also used, the exact conditions under which tokens will be earned or lost should be clearly designated to the student(s). When tokens are given or taken away, the teacher should relate the action to the student behavior involved. (The teacher's statement should be to the point, and arguments regarding token loss should be avoided at all costs.)

7. Usually, token exchange for the back-up reinforcer should occur at the end of the school day. If the material reinforcer (a toy or game) is given to a student during the school day, he is likely to play with it and distract other students from appropriate task behavior. When a student has earned enough tokens to exchange them for a tangible reinforcer, simply indicate to the child that his name tag will be placed on it so he can secure it at the end of the day.

8. Extend token reinforcement so that the target behavior will be encouraged in a wide range of situations (classroom, physical education, playground). Desirable behavior is not likely to generalize to nonreinforced settings.

9. Devise the token system so that a student competes with himself rather than other students, i.e., on the basis of desirable improvements in his own performance and behavior.

10. Always combine praise with tokens so that social reinforcement can ultimately be used to maintain desirable academic and social behavior.

11. A well-devised token system should gradually withdraw material reinforcers (candy, toys, trinkets, etc.) and rely on reinforcing activities and events. Ultimately, social reinforcement and reinforcing events should maintain the desired behavior.

12. The token system should be simple, functional, and not distract from learning. Tangible tokens (chips, stamps) can be traded or stolen and disrupt the reinforcement system. In school situations, check mark tokens are easiest to use. Each student is issued a card with his name on it. As he earns points or check marks, they are recorded on the card and initialled by the teacher. If the car is taken by another student, he cannot use it to obtain back-up reinforcers.

The increase of token reinforcement systems in schools indicates their utility. Although there may be some initial problems, few systems work perfectly the first time. After a system is initiated, certain changes are expected from time to time, and students should be informed of this fact from the outset.

Social Reinforcement

Most teachers know that attention, approval, and praise are powerful tools in promoting desirable academic and social behavior, and most humanistically oriented theories agree. Behavioral theories concur with the importance of social reinforcement but they also point out the crucial significance of *when* it is given.

Effective use of teacher attention to promote behavior has been demonstrated with elementary school children (Hall, Lund, and Jackson, 1968) and with high school students (McAllister, Stachowiak, Baer, and Conderman, 1969). These studies show that as verbal approval of desirable behavior increases, the frequency of that behavior also increases. On the other hand, if teacher attention to deviant behavior increases, an increase results in that deviant behavior.

Social reinforcement has obvious advantages:

1. Social reinforcement is more natural than tokens and primary reinforcers. Hence, parents and other potential critics of school practice are likely to be more positive about the procedure.

2. Attention, approval, and praise are easier to administer than tokens, material, and primary reinforcers. Less time is involved and no record-keeping is required.

3. Social reinforcement has no economic cost.

4. Social reinforcement can be used with any age group.

Like other systems, reliance on social reinforcement *alone* has certain disadvantages:

1. Not all children or adolescents respond positively to approval or praise. The reinforcement property appears to be learned from the simultaneous pairing of these verbal statements with primary reinforcers.

2. Not all teachers are capable of communicating genuinely positive social reinforcement to their students. Teachers who lack the ability experience difficulties promoting appropriate behavior in "normal" children and seem to have excessive difficulty with more deviant ones.

3. At certain developmental periods like adolescence, adult approval and praise may not have very potent reinforcement effects. With some adolescents (and with many delinquents), peer approval is far more important than adult approval. Some youngsters even provoke reprimands from adults to gain status with peers.

However, despite these limitations, social reinforcement is usually an effective way to promote appropriate behavior. With a new group of youngsters, it is probably unwise to utilize social reinforcement alone; primary reinforcers, material reinforcers, or reinforcing events should be used with it. As appropriate behavior increases to an acceptable operant level, the other reinforcement may be faded out.

Primary Reinforcement

Primary reinforcement is often used to promote a wide range of behavior. Because primary reinforcers satisfy a biologically based need, they are a highly reliable form of reinforcement. Appetite can be enhanced even further by inducing mild deprivation; that is, imposing a delay before reinforcers are consumed. For example, one of the authors promoted a target behavior in a child by using salted peanuts to reinforce it. The salted peanuts induced a craving for liquid, which was later used to promote a second target behavior.

Although primary reinforcement is generally reliable in promoting desired behavior, it has disadvantages:

1. Satiation occurs rapidly if the same primary reinforcer is used repeatedly. Popcorn may work well for three or four consecutive days but may lose its reinforcement property after that time.

2. Parents often complain about the use of sweets as a reinforcer, because they contribute to tooth decay and dental bills.

3. Repeated use of primary reinforcers can be expensive if the class is larger than five or ten children.

4. School critics often regard candy and other material reinforcers as undesirable forms of motivation.

Primary reinforcement, after initial stages, is rarely used alone. Once the target behavior reaches a steady rate, primary reinforcement is paired with secondary reinforcers to maintain its potency.

A study by Stone (1970) illustrates the use of primary reinforcement with seven boys afflicted with cerebral palsy. The boys exhibited a variety of inappropriate behaviors, including running around the room, standing up, talking out loud, inappropriate rocking, and short attention span. To change the inappropriate behavior, the following procedure was used. The teacher set an alarm clock to ring at five-minute intervals and told the students they were to remain quietly in their seats until the alarm rang a second time. The students who exhibited the appropriate behavior would receive a cookie. The students who did not sit quietly until the second ring were not reprimanded, but they did not receive a cookie. When this procedure was in operation for awhile, the time period between rings was extended to fifteen minutes. Each child was given a behavior chart that listed appropriate academic and classroom behavior. To encourage desirable behavior during the fifteen-minute interval, the teacher used social reinforcement; at the end of the fifteen-minute interval, the teacher reviewed the behavior chart and complimented each child who exhibited the desired behavior. For every task completed and each desirable behavior exhibited, the child received a cookie. Initially, the children were permitted to eat the cookies but were later encouraged to place the earned cookies on a tray and take them home. Eventually, the task period was extended to thirty minutes. Red check marks were used to reinforce the appropriate academic and classroom behavior. Each red check mark was exchangeable for one cookie.

Stone reports that the program worked very well for about two-and-a-half months. At that point, the children became restless and began to exhibit more inappropriate behavior. Obviously, they were satiated with cookies, and the reinforcement value was lost. If the primary reinforcer had been changed weekly, or if other tangible reinforcers had been used (toys, trinkets, etc.), the reinforcement effects on the desired behavior probably would have continued.

Contingency Management

The Premack Principle states that a low-probability behavior can be increased in frequency when its execution is followed by an opportunity to engage in a high-probability behavior. For example, if a student rarely completes arithmetic assignments but enjoys and frequently reads mystery stories, the low-probability behavior (completing arithmetic assignments) can be increased by providing the opportunity to read mystery stories after each completed arithmetic assignment.

Type I Contingency management can be employed in the classroom in two ways. With type I, when the student completes an assigned task, he is immediately given a specific amount of free time to engage in a reinforcing activity. The time allowed to complete the assignment is not specified; it may vary from fifteen minutes to an hour. However, when the assignment is completed, the student is allowed the opportunity to participate in a reinforcing activity for a definite time period.

Type II With type II contingency management, individually graded assignments must be completed within a specific time period. For example, suppose the school day is divided into fifty-minute time periods. At the start of the first fifty-minute period, all students begin an individualized assignment calculated to take thirty-five minutes to complete. If all students complete the assignment in thirty-five minutes, they are granted fifteen minutes free time to participate in a reinforcing event. However, if a student does not complete the assigned work within fifty minutes, he does not receive free time to participate in a reinforcing activity during this period or at a later time. If the assignment was too difficult to complete in that time, adjustments are made in the following day's assignment. If a student fails to complete an assignment of which he is capable because he does not devote himself to it, his response "costs" him the free time to participate in a reinforcing event.

Apparently, type II is easier to manage and is likely to elicit more predictable performances from the students. Because type II involves response cost, procrastination and irrelevant task behavior is likely to be reduced. However, type II requires careful preplanning to ensure that each student can complete the assignment within the specified time period.

Certain procedures should be observed when using either type of contingency management:

1. A separate reinforcing events (RE) area should be arranged, containing a wide variety of appealing toys, games, and activities. Items like a phonograph and records, a tape recorder, science kits, and various commercial toys and games should be included.

2. RE area rules should be clearly specified. For example, each child should select an RE when he enters the area, and once the selection is made, he should not be allowed to change it. If he tires of the activity, he is asked to return to his seat and wait until he has again earned free time to participate in another RE.

3. With young elementary school children, it is helpful to designate areas (by marking off an area on a table or floor with masking tape) for playing with certain toys or games. If he does not play within the designated area, he is asked to return to his seat.

4. Periodically, certain toys or games should be withdrawn from the RE area and replaced with others. At a later time, the withdrawn items may be returned. This procedure avoids satiation and preserves the reinforcing effects of the activities.

5. To avoid expense to the teacher and to introduce novel items from time to time, the teacher might ask parents to allow their child to bring an interesting toy or game for the RE area. These items should not be highly priced, because they may be damaged or worn out.

Contingency management has other advantages besides promoting desirable behavior:

1. Because the RE items are not consumable or taken home, little expense is involved once the system is initially set up.

2. Contingency management is a more "natural" approach than primary reinforcement or tokens. School critics are less likely to object because the "payoff" is simply the opportunity to participate in an activity.

3. RE's are varied and appealing to youngsters; satiation is not likely to be a problem.

Contingency management is not without disadvantages:

1. The teacher has some initial expense if the school will not purchase the items for the RE area.

2. Lessons must be carefully planned, and RE activities require constant supervision.

3. The room must have ample space so it can be divided into a study area and an RE area.

4. Depending on the type of contingency management used (especially type I), timekeeping in the RE area may require considerable effort. Also, teacher time is required to correct each child's assignment.

5. Students in the RE area may distract other students who are doing assigned work.

As one considers the advantages and disadvantages of contingency management, it is obvious that much can be gained by using it. After all, the teacher must deal with many of the listed disadvantages in any classroom.

Illustrative Behavior Modification Programs in the Regular Classroom

The three behavior modification programs that are discussed below illustrate how various reinforcement systems can be used in the regular classroom.

A Preschool-Kindergarten Class

Mrs. Lang is the teacher of a preschool-kindergarten class consisting of four- and five-year-olds. She uses a variety of behavioral methods including primary reinforcement, token and social reinforcement and contingency management. On rare occasions, mild forms of punishment are used to reduce the frequency of certain inappropriate behavior.

Before children arrive for the first day of school, Mrs. Lang begins to formulate a behavior management system. One or two weeks before school begins, she arranges interviews with the parents of each child and secures a social and developmental history and a list of stimuli and events that appear to have potential reinforcement value. By the opening day of school, she is acquainted with each parent and the behavior and developmental milestones of each child and has devised the basic outline of her behavior management program.

Beginning with the first day of school, a reinforcement system is implemented. As soon as children walk into the room, she greets them with a friendly "hello" and asks each child to be seated. When each child takes his or her seat, Mrs. Lang thanks them for sitting in their chairs and provides a primary reinforcer. She has found that it is important to pair primary and social reinforcement immediately. Popcorn, pretzels, pieces of fruit, and peanuts seem to work well as primary reinforcers.

Some children have difficulty separating from their mothers on the first day of school. To avoid problems, Mrs. Lang reassures the mothers that their children will quickly overcome their initial fear when the parents leave. Hence, parents are asked to leave and children are immediately involved in an interesting activity. If a child cries after the mother departs, the crying is ignored. As soon as the child stops crying, the teacher or the teacher aide immediately gives the child some type of positive attention. Social and primary reinforcement are used frequently during the day to encourage group participation and compliance to simple rules.

On the third day of school, a token reinforcement system is introduced. The token consists of a happy face mounted on a laminated card. As each child exhibits a desired behavior, he or she is reinforced with a primary reinforcer and a token. The primary and token reinforcers are paired so that the token will acquire appropriate reinforcement property. Each token a child earns can be exchanged for five minutes time in a special play area. The play area consists of a variety of selected items such as finger paint, clay, miniature toy people, art materials, and a doll house. Children are asked to exchange their tokens for playtime as they are earned.

By the middle of the week, the token system is modified. Three small, plain, nonred happy face cards can be exchanged for a larger red happy face token card. As each child receives a small, nonred, happy face, the child's name is written on it. When a larger red happy face token is earned, it can be exchanged for a tangible or material reinforcer. The tangible reinforcers are attached to the bulletin board at the front of the classroom out of reach of the children. The tangible reinforcers are changed periodically to avoid satiation effects.

Beginning with the third week, the children are required to complete two tasks or engage in two appropriate behaviors before a small, nonred happy face token is earned. Later in the week, a third task or behavior is required to earn a nonred happy face token. Also, at this point, children are given the option of exchanging the tokens for reinforcing items or events or saving them to be used at a later time. The use of free time in the special play area is also structured differently. When children exchange tokens for free time, a timer with the child's name on it is set for five minutes. When the timer goes off, the child is required to return to his or her seat and to engage in the ongoing classroom activity.

Mrs. Lang has found that these behavioral procedures work effectively with most children. However, there are some children whose behavior is so disruptive that a time-out procedure has to be used. A small part of the classroom has been sectioned off as a time-out area. Plywood has been used as a screen to separate this area from the rest of the classroom. Children who fight, yell, or have temper tantrums are temporarily placed in the time-out area. As soon as the child is placed in time-out, he or she is told that a timer will be started. The timer is set for two minutes, and if the child remains quiet during the two-minute period, he or she is permitted to rejoin the other children. If the child continues to exhibit inappropriate behavior after

the timer is started, it is reset for two minutes. The child remains in time-out until he or she has been quiet for the full two minutes. No one is permitted to give the child attention while he or she is in time-out.

Mrs. Lang has learned that it is unwise to bargain with children regarding the tokens they have earned. Tokens are given immediately after a task is completed or an appropriate behavior is exhibited. If a child asks for a token that is unearned, the request is refused.

Tangible reinforcers and reinforcing events are changed periodically. For example, after children have been in school for several weeks, tokens may be exchanged for various privileges. A token may be used to purchase the opportunity to be first to line up for recess, pass out papers, play a game with the teacher, or other similar types of activities. On some occasions, Mrs. Lang has a surprise field trip such as going to the zoo, the airport, or a TV station as a reinforcing event.

Token reinforcement is used to modify individual problem behavior as well as to promote specific task and behavior goals of all the children. Timmy, for example, gets extra tokens when he is able to wait for his turn during a group game. Sally gets extra tokens when she returns from the playground without shoving or pushing anyone. Harriet gets a token when she goes to twelve o'clock without crying. Jack receives tokens for interacting with his peers rather than isolating himself from the other children.

Mrs. Lang has found that it is important to explain her system to parents during the first parent-teacher conference and to invite their cooperation in using similar behavioral procedures at home. While she does not encourage the use of tokens at home, she teaches parents to use contingency management to encourage the target behaviors that are being promoted at school. She recognizes that behavior learned at school may not generalize to the home environment unless the target behavior is reinforced in both situations.

An Elementary School Class

There are a number of ways in which behavior modification procedures can be used in a regular elementary school classroom. One interesting approach was reported by Biciling, Shipman, Milligan, and Pipin (1971). Their study is of particular interest because the classroom consisted of forty-one "normal" third graders who attended a regular classroom in a typical elementary school.

A token system was developed to enhance academic and social behavior. It was possible for each child to earn fifteen points a day: six points for completing assigned work, six points for correct work, and three points for exhibiting appropriate social behavior. When a pupil earned 300 points, he was eligible to become a member of the Good Citizenship Council. If a student earned fifteen points per day every day, it would take him twenty days to achieve membership in the council. The council ruled on matters relevant to certain activities in the classroom, and all council members, including the teacher, had one vote. Council membership was maintained by earning a minimum of twelve points each day. If a student on the council exhibited socially inappropriate behavior, his membership could be revoked. Lost council membership had to be regained by earning an additional 300 points.

Students who became council members could enjoy many freedoms or privileges. For example, council members were permitted to leave their seats and go to the bathroom, get a drink of water whenever desired, do assigned work in a special place in the room, serve as monitors, attend council meetings, be eligible to elect the citizen of the week, month, or year, and participate in a ten-minute "talk time."

This token reinforcement system was simple but potentially effective. With a few creative strokes, the overall design could be extended to include more reinforcing events or privileges. By extending the democratic decision-making process further, the children could learn valuable lessons in self-government and self-management.

Although the authors do not report specific data regarding the maintenance of desired academic and classroom behavior, it apparently was effective. With a few creative strokes, the token reinforcement system might be phased out. For example, "honor status" might be bestowed on students who maintained continuous council membership for two or three months. When such status was achieved, free access to a variety of privileges could be given. As students demonstrated they could handle this increased freedom, greater (if not complete) responsibility for managing their own academic and social behavior could ultimately be given to them.

Mr. Campbell, a fifth-grade teacher, has combined some of the procedures described by Biciling et al. with other methods to devise his behavior modification system. Students are introduced to the system on the first day of school. Mr. Campbell explains to the students that he wants to operate the classroom so that everyone has a productive and satisfying year. One way to encourage this is to be clear about what is expected, to enforce proper rules of behavior, and to provide incentives for learning. Positive consequences are used to encourage proper academic and social behavior, and mild penalties are used for inappropriate behavior.

Students are shown a 20" × 30" piece of white cardboard, hung on the wall in the front of the room. The white cardboard contains the following rules:

1. Raise your hand to get permission to talk.

2. Remain in your seat until you are granted permission to leave it.

3. Face the front of the room.

4. Be quiet while working on an assignment or when the teacher is speaking.

5. Obey all school rules when you are in the halls, on the playground, in the cafeteria, and in the auditorium.

The students are told that failure to comply to the rules will lead to certain consequences. The consequences that are used depend on the type and severity of the infraction. For example, when students procrastinate or engage in non-task behavior, they may be asked to make up wasted time. That is, the number of minutes wasted is multiplied by two, and the resulting number is the amount of time made up. The time is made up after school or, in some cases, on Saturday morning. If a student exhibits serious disruptive behavior, the parents may be called and asked to take the student home for the remainder of the day.

To avoid placing an undue emphasis on negative consequences, Mr. Campbell emphasizes what can be obtained for appropriate student behavior. He explains that bogus money, or Campbell dollars, can be earned for appropriate academic and social behavior. The bogus money is printed in one, five, and ten dollar denominations. Each of the denominations has a picture of Mr. Campbell on it. The one-dollar denomination pictures Mr. Campbell sitting at his desk; the five-dollar bill pictures him reading a book; and the ten-dollar bill pictures Mr. Campbell and his dog.

During the first week of school, Campbell dollars are dispensed about every twenty minutes to those students who are exhibiting proper academic and social behavior. Near the end of each day, the Campbell dollars can be exchanged for candy bars, bags of popcorn, potato chips, raisins, ice cream, and fruit juice. The items are priced according to their value, although each item costs the student one hundred times its retail value. For example, a candy bar

costs ten dollars. The prices are set at these values to make it economically feasible to operate the system.

Beginning with the second week and continuing through the third week, the teacher opens the "Campbell General Store." The store contains water guns, comic books, and other carnival type items that are sold at even higher prices. The prices are set sufficiently high so that students will have to save their dollars for four or five days to purchase a store item. Starting with the third week, reinforcement is administered on a thirty-minute time interval. The students are informed that they must spend all of their money during the week because a new system will be implemented the following week.

On the fourth week, a different color of Campbell dollar is used. A new system is implemented. Students are shown a large cardboard with two hundred squares that are numbered consecutively from 1 to 200. Each number corresponds to a prize or a special event. For example, behind five of the numbers is a statement that permits a student to chew gum for any two days of his or her choice. One of the numbers is exchangeable for a rock record. The drawing of other numbers enables the student to get an autographed picture of Mr. Campbell, posters of famous singing groups, comics, art supplies, etc. To obtain the tangible reinforcers or the reinforcing events, students are required to purchase a number (from 1 to 200). They may choose any unselected number for a sum of twenty-five dollars.

The new Campbell dollars are now administered on a forty-minute interval schedule. As before, the dollars are used to reinforce appropriate academic and social behavior. The system is continued until the end of the fifth week. At this time the students are again informed that they must spend all of their dollars during the fifth week, since new currency will be issued on the sixth week.

Beginning with the sixth week of school, a different colored Campbell dollar is issued. Students are told that the new currency will be used for two weeks. Campbell dollars are used to reinforce desired behavior on a forty-five-minute schedule. The dollars are used to purchase hot dogs, hamburgers, potato chips, and soft drinks. A meal item (a hot dog for example) must be purchased before a snack item (pop). The Campbell dollars are exchanged for food items on Friday. Each Friday Mr. Campbell brings his outdoor grill and cooks the hamburgers and hot dogs.

During the eighth and ninth week of school, a slightly different system is initiated. Campbell dollars are used to purchase opportunities to throw darts at air-filled balloons on Friday of the ninth week. Fifteen dollars is charged for each throw. When a balloon is deflated with a dart, a student is awarded a prize or privilege that is written on a slip of paper inside the balloon. The privileges students are able to get are varied and more numerous than the prizes. For example, students may obtain privileges to be first to line up for an event, take notes to the office, pass out playground equipment, or serve as captain of the team during a game.

From the tenth week until the end of school, Mr. Campbell issues new Campbell dollars for periods lasting two, three, or four weeks. When he has exhausted all the primary colors for each new issue of currency, he starts with the original color and changes the pictures on each denomination. The interval reinforcement schedule is gradually extended so that students are reinforced for appropriate behavior every hour. However, to make certain that students are unable to predict when reinforcement will be received, he occasionally varies the schedule from fifteen minutes to sixty minutes. The average time interval is approximately an hour.

Table 7 shows the procedures Mr. Campbell used for the remainder of the school year. In addition to the reinforcement procedures specified in Table 7, Mr. Campbell occasionally sent "happy telegrams" to the parents of children who were doing good work or showed improvement. Quiet music was also played when students were behaving appropriately. However, the music was turned off when the class was too noisy. It was turned back on when the class was quiet again.

To encourage peer interaction, Mr. Campbell used the bogus money to reinforce cooperation, sharing, and helping behaviors. For example, he often used "courtesy awards" to promote considerateness on the part of the students.

Mr. Campbell's system incorporates a number of features that are important in a classroom behavior modification system. First, to promote desired academic and social behavior, both primary and social reinforcers are used. As the target behavior increases in frequency, primary reinforcers are used less often as back-up reinforcers; greater emphasis is placed on social and activity reinforcers. Second, after the target behavior is occurring with high frequency, variable-interval reinforcement is used. This type of schedule makes it difficult for students to predict when reinforcement will occur. Also, interval schedules are much easier to use than ratio schedules. Third, the material reinforcers and reinforcing events are changed periodically to avoid satiation. Classroom behavior modification systems often fail because this principle is not followed. Fourth, Mr. Campbell's system incorporates novelty and surprise. By using reinforcing events that have an element of mystery, as well as relying on games of chance, the interest and motivation of the students remain high. Fifth, reliance is placed on positive reinforcement rather than punishment. However, negative consequences are used to deal with more disruptive or chronically inappropriate behavior. Such behavior is rarely modified by the use of positive reinforcement alone. Finally, Mr. Campbell's sys-

Table 7 The Behavior Modification Procedures Mr. Campbell Used from the Tenth Week Until the End of the School Year

Time Period by Weeks	Form of Reinforcement	Reinforcement Schedule	Type of Back-up Reinforcer or Event	Response-Cost Procedure
10–11	Campbell dollars and social reinforcement	Variable interval with a mean of fifty minutes	Mystery trip purchased with $20.00 on Friday of the 11th week.	Response-cost procedures were relatively standard for most of the remaining weeks. Loss of recess time was used for minor infractions; time-out was used for more severe infractions and systematic exclusion for serious behavioral problems.
12–13	Campbell dollars and social reinforcement	Variable interval	Dollars used to purchase free time to play commercial games for twenty minutes at a time.	
14–15	Campbell dollars and social reinforcement	Variable interval	Same as weeks 12 and 13. New games are introduced.	
16–18	Campbell dollars and social reinforcement	Variable interval	Purchase opportunity to enter three different contests. Winner gets the opportunity to go to lunch with Mr. Campbell.	
19–20	Campbell dollars	Variable interval	Opportunity to see a movie each Friday for $20.00; purchase popcorn and candy.	Same as indicated in weeks 10–11.
21–23	Group contingency used. When all students exhibited proper student behavior, ten points given to class each hour.	Fixed interval based on behavior of all students	Sixty class points purchased one hour of time for field-day events on Friday of 23rd week. Five hours had to be purchased for event to take place.	

(continued)

Table 7 (continued)

Time Period by Weeks	Form of Reinforcement	Reinforcement Schedule	Type of Back-up Reinforcer or Event	Response-Cost Procedure
24–25	Campbell dollars and social reinforcement	Variable interval	Opportunity to purchase reinforcing events. Student earning the most dollars during the week received "Student of the Week" award.	
26–28	Campbell dollars and social reinforcement	Variable interval	Purchase trip to local miniature golf course; parents pay golf fees and PTA donated money.	Failure to earn enough dollars led to loss of trip.
29–32	Campbell dollars and social reinforcement	Variable interval	Free time to put on a videotaped puppet show; purchase food or other special events.	Same as previously.
33–34	Campbell dollars and social reinforcement	Variable interval	Fifteen dollars purchased one opportunity to take an item from the "grab bag."	
Final two weeks	Students evaluated own behavior and performance and awarded themselves dollars.	Fixed interval	Purchased special privileges and events.	

tem has as an ultimate goal the promotion of self-management in each student.

While the features we have discussed are important in the success of Mr. Campbell's system, there is one other important element. The behavior modification system is explained to parents earlier in the year to enlist their cooperation and support. If parents do not understand or support the program, it is relatively easy for them to sabotage it. They may, for example, misinterpret reinforcement as a form of bribery and convey their disapproval of it to their children. Also, since a supply of material reinforcers and reinforcing toys and games are required, part of the expense of the program can be decreased if parents are willing to make contributions of food, games, and other materials.

A Junior High School Class

Ms. Shaw, a junior high English teacher, developed her behavior modification system in response to the need to change a variety of student behaviors that were interfering with student progress. In one of her English classes students were often tardy, did not complete or hand in assignments regularly, talked inappropriately, left needed books at home, and occasionally fell asleep. In attempting to deal with the problems, she tried some of the usual remedies. Notes describing student behavior were sent home to parents, conferences were held with the parents, and some students were sent to the principal. However, none of these actions appeared to offer a permanent solution.

With the help of the school psychologist, Ms. Shaw began to devise a behavior modification program for her fifth-period English class. She identified the target behavior as getting to class before the bell rings, completing all class assignments before the period ends, and completing and handing in all homework assignments at a prearranged time. Ms. Shaw as-

sumed that the promotion of these behaviors would help to decrease other inappropriate, nontask-oriented behaviors. She obtained a baseline measurement of the target behaviors and then began to identify potential reinforcers. These were identified by observing the free choice activities of the students and by having them complete a questionnaire consisting of a variety of privileges and activities.

Ms. Shaw wanted to make her behavior modification program an integral part of the class. Therefore, she explained to the students that the class would be operated like the economy in an imaginary country called Tater. In Tater everyone worked and received compensation in the form of Tater dollars. As in the land of Tater, the students could earn Tater money by being in class on time and by completing and handing in class and homework assignments. Tater dollars could be exchanged for various food items, privileges, and reinforcing events. Tater dollars were earned according to the following plan:

In the room before the bell rings	$1.00
In the proper seat before the bell rings	2.00
Completing an "A" paper (grammatically correct)	5.00
Completing an "A" paper (good content)	5.00
Handing in a paper graded "B"	4.00
Handing in a paper graded "C"	3.00
Handing in a paper graded "D"	2.00
Completing any assignment	1.00

Test grades (A = $5.00, B = $4.00, C = $3.00, D = $2.00)

At the end of each class period students were allowed to deposit the money they earned in the class bank. Bankbooks were issued, and accurate records were kept of deposits and withdrawals. Each deposit and withdrawal was initialed by the teacher to avoid unethical manipulation of the bank account.

Students were told that they could bank their money for a maximum of three weeks. However, if they wanted to spend their money during the intervening period, two students would act as merchants and would sell food items from the store at various times. At the beginning of the third week, Ms. Shaw announced to the class that all Tater dollars must be spent by the end of the week because a new system would be introduced on the fourth week.

The system Ms. Shaw used for the remainder of the school year is summarized in Table 8. As Table 8 shows, the behavior modification system was changed in several interesting ways.

Table 8   The Behavior Modification Procedures Ms. Shaw Used from the Fourth Week Until the End of the School Year

Time Period by Weeks	Form of Reinforcement	Reinforcement Schedule	Type of Back-up Reinforcer or Event	Response-Cost Procedure
4–6	Tater dollars and social reinforcement	Fixed ratio	Tacos, tortillas, corn chips, & popcorn; the Mexican food donated by parents.	None
7–9	Tater dollars and social reinforcement	Fixed ratio	Time purchased to play chess, checkers, cards, listen to popular music, or to rest on pillows. $1.00 = 1 minute of free time.	One-dollar fines for disruptive behavior. This became a continuing response cost procedure from here on.
10–12	Tater dollars and social reinforcement	Fixed ratio	Money exchanged for time to see comedy movies each Friday; popcorn & pop.	

(continued)

Table 8 (continued)

Time Period by Weeks	Form of Reinforcement	Reinforcement Schedule	Type of Back-up Reinforcer or Event	Response-Cost Procedure
13–15	Tater dollars and social reinforcement	Fixed ratio	Money used to buy raffle tickets; on third Friday three tickets were drawn and owners each won a prize.	
16–18	Tater dollars and social reinforcement	Fixed ratio	An auction was held on the third Friday; items like canned fruit, juice, brushes. combs, and old magazines were auctioned to highest bidders.	Same as weeks 7–9.
19–21	Tater dollars and social reinforcement	Fixed ratio	Money was used to buy a trip to local TV station; pop and food items.	Students who had inadequate funds to purchase trip stayed at school.
22–27	Tater dollars and social reinforcement	Fixed ratio	Those used previously that students voted as most popular.	
28–30	Tater dollars and social reinforcement	Fixed ratio	Money used to play TV electronic games; competitive games between students.	
31–33	Tater dollars and social reinforcement	Fixed ratio	Those used previously that students voted as most popular.	
34–36	Reinforcing activities	Fixed ratio	Opportunity to participate in a reinforcing activity when work completed.	

First, for each three-week period a different issue of Tater dollar was used and reinforcement was changed to avoid satiation. Second, since positive reinforcement of target behaviors did not succeed in eliminating some types of disruptive behavior, a fine system was imposed during the seventh week and continued for the remainder of the year. Third, Ms. Shaw integrated the behavior modification system with the instructional program by having students write themes related to the forms of reinforcement being used. For example, when Mexican food was used as reinforcement, students were asked to write themes on various phases of Mexican life. Fourth, for several weeks Ms. Shaw used previous reinforcers that students voted as most appealing and/or desirable.

Ms. Shaw found her behavior modification system greatly enhanced student learning and classroom management. However, it did require considerable thought and work. It was not always easy to obtain the reinforcers that were needed to provide variety. Fortunately, the students' parents appreciated her efforts, and local merchants occasionally made donations of damaged goods. Ms. Shaw was pleased with the overall success of the program and looked forward to implementing a similar program in other classes the following year.

Farber and Mayer (1972) developed a behavior modification program similar to that of Ms. Shaw. They studied seventeen girls and boys in a high school English class. All students lived in an innercity environment, were predominately Mexican-American, and exhibited a variety of inappropriate behaviors in the classroom. The experimenters identified eleven target behaviors:

1. Arriving to class on time
2. Starting assigned work
3. Reading
4. Writing in the assignment books
5. Using a dictionary
6. Taking part in group discussions
7. Taking responsibility within a group
8. Asking questions that relate to classwork
9. Following directions
10. Handing in assignments
11. Handing in assignments on time

To promote the desired target behaviors, both individual and group reinforcement procedures were used. At the beginning of each class period, the teacher praised the class for displaying appropriate behavior. The teacher identified a student who had exhibited appropriate academic and social behavior the preceding day and offered a tangible reinforcer such as a school decal, movie ticket, or similar item. In the fifty-minute class period, the teacher reinforced the desired behavior during two five-minute time intervals. During the first interval (near the beginning of the class), the teacher walked around the room and praised the students who exhibited appropriate task and social behavior. Students who did not exhibit appropriate behavior were ignored. During the second interval (the last five minutes of class), the teacher again praised the appropriately behaving students.

Specific individual and group privileges had to be earned by the students, and the means to earn them were communicated to the class orally and in writing. For example, a student could earn an unlimited hall pass for a week if all assignments had been turned in the previous week. To facilitate the desired group behavior, a "thermometer" was drawn on the blackboard showing the number of students who had turned in their assignments. Students who had earned the hall pass were also listed on the blackboard.

Thus, social and material reinforcement were used to promote the desired target behaviors on an individual and group basis. To extinguish inappropriate or deviant behavior, ignoring was used. These procedures proved effective. The average percentage of assignments completed increased significantly after the reinforcement contingencies were implemented. School attendance increased and academic grades improved.

Farber and Mayer's study, as well as the three illustrative behavior modification programs we have presented in this chapter, should alert the reader to the kinds of behavioral procedures that can be used to enhance student development in the regular classroom. Indeed, the potential application of behavior modification procedures in the regular classroom are limited only by the desire, sophistication, and ingenuity of the user.

Summary

1. Effective classroom management is predicated on seven major elements: (a) specification of desirable learning and behavioral objectives, (b) individualization of learning tasks, (c) specification of consequences for desirable and undesirable behavior, (d) reinforcement procedures that effectively promote the desired behavior, (e) utilization of both individual and group reinforcement systems, (f) appropriate modeling of desirable behavior, and (g) the establishment and maintenance of teacher reinforcement property.

2. Four types of reinforcement systems have been used in the classroom: token, social, primary, and contingency management systems. Primary reinforcement is often used initially to shape the desired behavior or when the reinforcement property of other stimuli and events are unknown. Social reinforcement is effective with many students but is often paired with other types of reinforcement to establish or maintain its reinforcement property. Token reinforcement has demonstrated utility in promoting a wide range of behavior when a number of back-up reinforcers are made an integral part of the procedure. A token reinforcement system is probably the easiest to use of the four reinforcement systems. Contingency management is not only effective in promoting desirable target behavior but is often seen as more "natural," because reinforcing events are considered less artificial than other types of reinforcement. Contingency management may require greater amounts of time to administer because of the record-keeping involved. However, many of these chores can be reduced to a minimum when type II contingency management is used.

3. Many classroom modification systems fail because the user is not thoroughly conversant with the basic principles and procedures. To demonstrate the use and applicability of these principles and procedures, three illustrative classroom behavior modification programs were presented in detail. Careful study of these systems should help regular classroom teachers to devise and implement effective programs.

Chapter Seven

Behavior Modification with Special Groups

In this chapter we will discuss the applications of behavior modification procedures with special groups of children and youths. The special groups to which we refer consist of individuals whose social, emotional, and/or intellectual development is delayed, arrested, maladaptive, or atypical in other ways. Because of their problems, these individuals require more than a normal amount of care, instruction, and psychological assistance. A variety of terms have been used to describe these atypical developmental patterns. Perhaps the most commonly used diagnostic labels are learning disabled, mentally retarded, emotionally handicapped, delinquent, behaviorally disordered, or disturbed.

To mitigate or correct these handicaps, a variety of programs have been developed. In the following pages we will describe some of these programs and illustrate how behavior modification procedures can help to promote program goals.

The Disabled Learner

Children who have difficulty learning have long been of interest and concern to educators. However, it was not until the mid-sixties that authorities recognized that among this group there is a special type of child with normal or higher intelligence who has marked difficulties with certain types of learning tasks. As the condition was recognized as a distinct entity, descriptions of the disabled learner began to emerge. For example, some noted that these children have marked attentional and concentration difficulties, while others observed rather obvious perceptual-motor problems. Still others commented on the excessive difficulty these children have in the acquisition of reading and writing skills. The cluster of symptoms did not fit into a coherent syndrome, and causal variables appeared even more obscure. Did the child have a neuropsychological deficit of unknown origin? Had genes conspired to produce an impaired neurological structure? Had the child suffered an injury to the brain resulting in impairment to the central nervous system? Was there a metabolic disorder that impaired certain psychological functions? All of these factors have been postulated as causal, but to date research has failed to identify which, if any, of these variables act to produce the learning disability (Wallace and McLoughlin, 1975).

Recognizing the need to define the condition clearly, the National Advisory Committee on Handicapped Children offered the following definition of a learning disability (1968, p. 4):

Children with special learning disabilities exhibit a disorder in one or more of the basic psychological processes involved in understanding or in using spoken or written languages. These may be manifested in disorders of listening, thinking, talking, reading, writing, spelling or arithmetic. They include conditions which have been referred to as perceptual handicaps, brain injury, minimal brain dysfunction, dyslexia, developmental aphasia, etc. They do not include learning problems which are due primarily to mental retardation, emotional disturbance, or environmental disadvantage.

The above definition helped to clarify some of the confusion that surrounded the learning disability concept and provided some general guidelines for identifying the condition. The criteria alluded to in the definition, along with others, are generally used in diagnosing a learning disability. For specificity and clarity, let us state them briefly. First, the disabled learner manifests a discrepancy between expected and actual achievement. That is, while the disabled learner has normal or higher intelligence, there is a difference of one or more years between the expected and actual achievement in one or more academic areas. Second, the underachievement is usually manifested by marked difficulties in listening, thinking, reading, writing, and/or arithmetic. One area may be more affected than another, or more than one area may be involved. Third, while the learning disabled child may exhibit deficiencies in functioning characteristic of other disorders, he or she is not *primarily* impaired by visual, hearing, or motor handicaps, environmental disadvantage, or emotional disturbance (Wallace and McLoughlin, 1975).

Proper identification and thorough evaluation of the child's disability is an essential step in placement and program planning. Although assessment practices may vary, an individual intelligence test is usually given to determine intellectual level, and various informal and standardized tests are used to ascertain the child's acquired skills in each primary academic area.

When a deficiency is found in a particular area or psychological function, additional testing and/or analysis may be done to determine the extent and exact type of disability. Also, since the child may have difficulties in processing information, further analysis is usually performed to specify the processing difficulty. That is, one wants to determine whether the child has greatest difficulty in receiving, expressing, or processing (associating or integrating) information. Finally, an attempt is made to explain why the child is not learning. This information not only helps to determine whether a child has a learning disability but is essential for planning an instructional program (Lerner, 1976).

Programs for the Disabled Learner

A number of programs and placement facilities exist for the education of children with learning disabilities. Perhaps the most common of these are the special day school, special classes in a public school, the itinerant teacher, and the resource teacher.

Special day schools are usually privately owned and have facilities and programs that are designed to meet the needs of learning disabled children. Enrolled children usually attend school for a full day and receive instruction oriented to their specific disabilities. When their learning disabilities have been adequately modified, they are returned to the public school (Lerner, 1976).

Learning disability classes in the public schools are considered by many to be one of the more viable options for educating the disabled learner. The public school LD class tends to be less expensive and enables the child to remain in a more familiar social environment. The LD class is usually self-contained and consists of six to ten children. The instructional program is individualized, and the LD teacher assumes primary instructional responsibility. Ancillary services (psychological, speech therapy, etc.) are usually provided, and attempts are made to integrate the LD child in activities outside the classroom (Lerner, 1976).

The itinerant teacher is often used to work with children whose particular handicaps are not serious enough to be placed in a special class. Usually, an itinerant teacher provides instructional services to several schools and may work with a number of children at each school served. Children are tutored outside the classroom, individually or in small groups. Instructional sessions generally last from thirty minutes to an hour and may be held daily or several times during the week. Except for these special tutorial sessions, the child's regular classroom teacher assumes the primary responsibility for instruction (Lerner, 1976).

The use of a resource teacher is probably the most common arrangement in current use for dealing with the special instructional needs of the disabled learner. The resource teacher is well trained in the diagnosis, formulation, and implementation of an individualized instructional program. Besides teaching LD children on a regularly scheduled basis for short instructional periods each day, the resource teacher may serve as a consultant to regular classroom teachers in adapting their programs to the needs of the LD child. The resource teacher may also be given responsibilities for conducting in-service training of the regular teaching staff, serve as a liaison person to other school specialists, and devise a system for the continuing evaluation of LD children (Lerner, 1976).

The Use of Behavior Modification with Disabled Learners

Behavioral principles and procedures have been used in two basic ways to work with the disabled learner: (1) by specifying and analyzing the learning tasks and (2) by arranging the learning environment to promote the acquisition of the skills or desired learning outcomes. Let us consider what each process entails.

The specification and systematic analysis of the learning task essentially involves four elements: (1) a clear specification of the task(s) the child is to learn, (2) identification of the sequential steps in the learning task, (3) determination of the behaviors the child must perform to learn the task, and (4) using a method of presentation that will facilitate learning of the specified task (Bateman, 1967; Johnson, 1967).

The specification of the tasks to be learned is, of course, related to the particular disabilities uncovered during the evaluation process, the present skill levels, and based on that information, the statement of the target learning objectives in behavioral terms. Once the tasks to be learned are described behaviorally, each task must be divided into its component parts. For example, suppose you want to teach a child to print his name. The learning task might be broken down into the following units:

1. Recognition by sight of each of three letters in his name (P-A-T)

2. Holding a pencil in the correct position in his dominant hand

3. Drawing a straight vertical line between two lines on ruled writing paper

4. Drawing a semicircle between two (smaller lines) on ruled paper

5. Drawing a straight vertical line between two ruled lines connected to a semicircle (P)

6. Drawing two angled straight lines to form a triangle, connected at midpoint with a straight horizontal line (A)

7. Drawing a straight vertical line between two ruled lines connected at the top with a straight horizontal line (T)

8. Drawing the letters P-A-T between two ruled lines in proper sequence from left to right

9. Drawing or writing the letters P-A-T between two ruled lines, written in proper sequence and in legible form

As the above example illustrates, the division of a task into its component parts shows clearly what has to be learned to acquire a specific skill. Also, since the task is broken down into sequential units, a teacher has some guidelines for the type of instructional activities that can be used to promote learning.

The determination of the responses a child must perform to learn a task requires an analysis of the response modalities involved in the task to be learned. For example, in the previous example, visual perception, auditory discrimination, visual sequencing, memory, and motor coordination are all involved in learning the task. If a child does not have adequate abilities in each of these areas, he or she may not be able to learn the task. Hence, the child will have to be helped, through focused instruction, to acquire the deficient ability or skill before the task can be learned.

Finally, one needs to decide how the task (or task units) can be presented to facilitate efficient learning. In other words, given the learner's abilities and deficiencies, will the child respond best to a visual, auditory, or multisensory approach? Should the learning task be introduced using guided practice? Or, will the child need only occasional prompts with periodic feedback? Once a mode of presentation is decided on, the instructional activity is tried out. If the child experiences success, the instructional activity and the method of presentation are continued. If difficulty is experienced, an analysis is made to determine why. The learning steps may be too difficult, the instructional sequence may need to be altered, or a different form of presentation may need to be tried. Once the difficulty is located, the appropriate instructional modification is made, and instruction continues until the child demonstrates the desired mastery.

Arranging the Learning Environment   In addition to the factors we discussed in the specification and analysis of learning tasks, there are four other ways to structure the environment to promote desired learning. First, the physical environment can be arranged to reduce the distractions that interfere with learning. The reduction of distracting stimuli can be accomplished in several ways. The room can be divided by using partitions or screens, the floor can be carpeted, and the windows can be made of translucent glass. With some students who are highly distractable, directions and instructions for assignments can be presented through earphones from recorded tapes. The seating can be arranged so that classmates cannot readily reach or touch each other while seated. Study carrels can be used that shut out distracting stimuli. Objects that tend to be seductive (games, playground equipment, etc.) can be kept out of sight (Barsch, 1968).

A second way that the learning environment can be structured is to control the amount of work that is given or the time that is required to complete it. Disabled learners are easily distracted when work demands appear too great. This type of frustration can be avoided by assigning tasks in small units. For example, a one-page assignment that can be completed in a short time is much better than a multiple-page assignment that requires a long period of sustained work. Or, a more difficult assignment can be broken down into smaller units so that the task can be completed in five or ten minutes. Appealing task activities can be scheduled at periodic intervals to reinforce the performance of tasks that are difficult or less interesting.

A third way to facilitate learning is to control the difficulty level of assigned tasks. Disabled learners have difficulty concentrating and maintaining on-task behavior. If assigned tasks are too difficult, LD children may become frustrated, require excessive teacher help, and find distracting activities to consume their time. Such difficulties can be avoided by doing a task analysis and sequentially grading the learning activities, or by using commercially developed and sequentially graded instructional materials. For example, Valett (1969) has specified fifty-three operationally defined tasks divided into six learning areas: gross motor development, sensorimotor integration, language development, conceptual skills, perceptual-motor development, and social skills. He describes learning activities and instructional materials that can be used to promote these skills. Bush and Giles (1969) have also compiled a variety of psycholinguistic learning activities that are useful with disabled learners.

The fourth way to promote learning is to arrange systematically the reinforcement contingencies. We have discussed these principles and procedures at length in earlier chapters. Therefore, to avoid repetition we will present two studies to show how behavior modification may be employed to promote efficient learning.

McKenzie, Clark, Wolf, Kothera, and Benson (1968) designed a token reinforcement system to increase the academic performance of ten learning disabled elementary school children. They wanted to promote performance in five academic areas: reading, spelling, arithmetic, penmanship, and English composition. The children were given weekly assignments in each area, and the teacher aide recorded the number of responses completed and done correctly and the child's grade.

The teacher used a variety of reinforcers. The children were able to earn recess if assignments were completed for the prior week; a free-time activity if work was completed before the period ended; classroom-helper jobs for pupils who were working or had made recent improvements; eating lunch with other children if classwork was completed before lunch time; teacher attention for appropriate work behavior; and weekly grade cards that parents were asked to sign. Weekly grades were A, B, C, or incomplete if assigned work was not complete. Parents were encouraged to praise A and B grades.

A unique feature of the motivational system was that of having the parents pay their children for the grades they obtained. The payment each child received was based on his weekly allowance as well as his academic performance. The total amount of money that could be received by each child varied from $0.70 to $3.50. The suggested method was to divide the total possible allowance by 7 (music, physical education, and five academic subjects) and give the child this amount for every A. Half of the amount given for an A was given for a B, and one-tenth the amount for a C (for example: A=50¢, B=25¢, and C=5¢). When an incomplete appeared on the child's report card, the amount that could be received for an A was subtracted. If, however, a debt was incurred because of the incompletes, he was permitted to do household chores to pay off the debt.

Parents were encouraged to allow their children to spend as much of the money they earned as possible. The children, who were expected to purchase items and activities they valued without parental assistance, were not permitted to earn money other than that received for their academic performance. These measures were employed to ensure the reinforcing value of the money to the children.

The children were eventually returned to the regular classroom. However, the system was altered by including penalties for grades of D and F. The results showed that performance increased from 68 percent during the baseline period to 86 percent. Both reading and arithmetic attending behavior increased significantly, and all pupils except one enhanced their academic performance. It is apparent from these results that the described system may have considerable utility in a public school setting. The token reinforcement system can be administered with sufficient ease by the teacher, and the system is not costly since the parents provide the monetary reinforcement.

The McKenzie et al. study illustrates how systematic reinforcement procedures increase academic performance. However, since the above study did not use contingencies to deal with nontask or disruptive social behavior of disabled learners, a study by Medlund and Stachnik (1972) is of interest. They did not work with disabled learners, but the procedures that were used are quite applicable. Medlund and Stachnik wanted to evaluate the utility of a "Good Behavior Game" in modifying the out-of-seat, talking-out, and disruptive behavior of two groups of fourteen students in a fifth-grade reading class. All of the students were in the same class, but it was divided into two groups by positioning half of the seats to face in opposite directions.

The study consisted of six phases and three different treatment conditions. The six phases were as follows: first baseline, games, second baseline, rules, rules plus lights, and games. A five-day baseline was first taken, and the games condition was then introduced. The teacher explained to the groups that they were going to play a game which each group should try to win. The conditions and rules of the game were as follows:

1. Both teams would be able to win by meeting certain rules and behavior standards.

2. Special privileges would be given to the winning team or teams.

3. Whenever a team broke one of the rules (behaved inappropriately), the team would receive a mark against them.

4. A team could win if they received five or fewer marks each day.

5. A winning team would be entitled to three minutes of extra morning recess.

6. When a team received less than twenty marks for a week, they could have extra activity on the following Monday afternoon.

7. If a team member received four or more marks in one day and prevented the team from winning, the group was permitted to exclude that person from the game for that day. The next day the offender would be placed behind a screen in the room to study alone.

8. A green and a red light were mounted on the wall in front of each group. The students were told that a shining green light indicated "all is well." A shining red light conveyed the message that "someone had made an error and the team should be careful." (The red light was turned on when a team member exhibited an inappropriate behavior; it remained on for thirty seconds after the infraction.)

The first game phase was continued for ten sessions and was immediately followed by the second phase. In the second phase (rules), the teacher repeated the rules each morning. To involve the students, the rules were divided into three categories, and students were asked to give examples appropriate to each category. At the end of the class each day students were simply informed whether they had earned extra recess time. This phase lasted for ten sessions.

The third phase consisted of a twenty-session baseline period. The students were simply told that there would be no more extra recess or free time.

Rules were reinstated in the fourth phase. As before, the teacher repeated the rules each day and invited students to give examples. This phase continued for five sessions.

The fifth phase consisted of ten sessions in which both rules and lights were used. The rules were repeated each day and the lights were used to indicate proper or improper rule behavior to the teams. No additional recess or extra time was given.

In the sixth phase the Good Behavior Game was reinstated for a period of five days. The same conditions were in operation as in phase two.

As might be expected, analysis of the data revealed that the Good Behavior Game phases were most effective in reducing the frequency of inappropriate behavior. The game condition reduced the target behaviors by 99 percent for group 1 and by 97 percent for group 2. The amount of reading material both groups covered increased by 25 percent under the game condition. Both the rules and the rules and lights conditions proved useful in reducing the target behaviors, but the latter condition was the more potent of the two.

The Mentally Retarded

Mental retardation is a condition of arrested development manifested primarily by "subaverage general intellectual functioning" and deficits in adaptive behavior (Grossman, 1973). The condition may result from a number of factors including hereditary variables, chromosomal abnormalities, biochemical and metabolic disorders, diseases of the mother during pregnancy, toxic agents such as carbon monoxide or lead poisoning, birth injuries, and sociocultural factors (Goldenson, 1970). Early diagnosis of the condition is important, and determination of etiology may play a significant role in subsequent treatment and education.

Once the condition has been diagnosed and proper medical treatment is given to cases involving biochemical or metabolic factors, the subsequent opportunities for development and education are determined largely by the care received from the parents and the severity of the intellectual deficit. Four categories of retardation are commonly used to indicate severity of impairment (Coleman, 1976):

Mild	I.Q. between 52 and 68
Moderate	I.Q. between 36 and 51
Severe	I.Q. between 20 and 35
Profound	I.Q. below 20

Individuals who are mildly retarded are by far the most frequent of the four categories. These people are considered "educable" and are capable of intellectual development comparable to a normal child of eight to eleven years of age. With early diagnosis, supportive parents, and special education assistance, a large percentage of these people can master simple academic and occupational tasks, make reasonable social adjustments, and become self-supporting (Coleman, 1976).

Moderately retarded individuals are generally considered "trainable" and can develop intellectual capacities comparable to a normal child of four to seven years of age. With parental guidance and appropriate training opportunities, the moderately retarded can assume some self-care responsibilities and become economically useful in a closely supervised environment (Coleman, 1976).

The severely retarded person is very retarded in the development of most functions. Speech and motor development is severely impaired, and motor and sensory handicaps are often present. Although most severely retarded persons can learn some rudimentary personal hygiene and self-help skills, they require supervision and care all of their lives (Coleman, 1976).

As the label "profoundly retarded" implies, individuals so classified have serious deficiencies in adaptive behavior and are able to learn only the simplest tasks. Various anomalies such as physical deformities, central nervous system impairments, and mutism and deafness are not uncommon. These individuals usually require custodial care all of their lives (Coleman, 1976).

Fortunately, many public schools have established special class programs for elementary and junior and senior high school persons who are classified as mildly or moderately retarded. The mildly retarded are considered educable and are typically placed in special classes that emphasize practical reading, writing, and arithmetic skills, desirable self-care and social adjustment skills, and later, the development of occupational skills that may provide for partial economic support. Moderately retarded individuals are usually placed in trainable mentally retarded special education classes that emphasize self-care and social adjustment. Intellectual limitations usually preclude the acquisition of academic skills (Erickson, 1978).

Retarded persons in the other two classifications are often placed in institutions when their families can no longer assume the burden of their care. Institutional programs for the retarded vary widely in terms of quality. These institutions are often understaffed, and legislative appropriations may be insufficient to rectify the existing inadequacies (Erickson, 1978).

Illustrative Behavior Modification Programs and Procedures

Behavioral procedures are now used extensively in many school and institutional settings to promote or modify a variety of behaviors of retarded persons. To illustrate the utility of these procedures, we will describe a special class and an institutional program for the retarded.

Birnbrauer, Wolf, Kidder, and Tague (1965) designed an experimental classroom to work with seventeen mentally retarded students ranging in I.Q. from 50 to 72. The classroom was designed so that the students would spend part of the time in the experimental classroom and the remainder of the day in other activities such as arts and crafts. With these program arrangements, only six students were in the experimental classroom at any one time. Each student was given individualized assignments in reading, writing, and arithmetic; no group instruction was given. Each day the student's assignments were planned on the basis of his performance the previous day. Changes in the nature or complexity of the student's assignment were based on his error score for each completed assignment (i.e., if there was a 10 percent increase or decrease in his error score, a change in assignment level was made the following day). Assignments varied from five to forty-five minutes. As assignments were completed, each student was immediately given the results.

The experimenters designed the class to determine the relative effects of praise and tokens on the academic and social behavior of the children. In one experimental condition praise was used. In the second experimental condition tokens and praise were used. Under both conditions, ignoring and time-out were employed to deal with disruptive behavior. If a student engaged in minor disruptive behavior such as talking out loud or responding inappropriately, his behavior was ignored. If the behavior was more serious (refusing to do assignments, destroying property, fighting), time-out was used. Students who were placed in time-out were asked to remain for ten minutes. If proper behavior was not exhibited at the end of that time, the door to the time-out area was closed and the student remained in time-out for an additional ten minutes.

The token system had several features. Each pupil was given a folder which contained three sheets of paper divided into squares. The value of each sheet varied according to the number of squares. When students performed the desired target behaviors, check marks were placed in the squares. If the student finished his work each day, he was able to exchange the check marks for back-up reinforcers such as gum, balloons, pencils, and other tangible items. The maximum monetary value of the check marks a student could earn in a single day was two cents (or a maximum of $7.00 for the entire year).

A student received a check mark for each correct task unit on an assignment. Ten additional check marks were awarded if an assignment was completed without error. Students were also given check marks for doing additional work or for unusually appropriate social behavior.

The differential effects of praise and token reinforcement on the behavior of mentally retarded students were compared. When tokens were withdrawn and praise was the only reinforcement operating, five students appeared relatively unaffected, ten students showed an increased number of errors on assigned work, and four became serious discipline problems. Obviously, the combination of token reinforcement and teacher praise has a more potent effect on academic and social behavior than praise alone.

Perline and Levinsky (1968) also used a token system to modify inappropriate behavior in four severely retarded children ranging in age from eight to ten. Five behaviors were identified as the object of modification: (1) aggression toward peers, (2) taking property belonging to others, (3) aggressive behavior toward the teacher, (4) getting up from a chair, and (5) throwing objects.

Two experimental conditions were established for approximately ten days each. In the first experimental condition, two children received tokens for cooperative social behavior and lost tokens for inappropriate behavior. Deviant or inappropriate behavior also resulted in time-out. The second experimental condition with the two other students was identical to the first except that time-out was not used.

The results indicate a substantial decrease in all five inappropriate behaviors in both groups; no differences could be discerned between the two experimental conditions. That is, token reinforcement, response cost, and time-out were not more effective than just token reinforcement and response cost in decreasing the inappropriate behavior.

Like token reinforcement, contingency management has demonstrated utility in promoting desired learning and social behavior in mentally retarded children. For example, Daley (1969) employed contingency management with five mentally retarded youngsters who ranged from eight to eleven years. The children were difficult to motivate and displayed a variety of inappropriate behaviors in the school situation.

The five children were extensively observed to identify high-probability behaviors. These observations led to the identification of twenty-two such behaviors. Each behavior was illustrated by a drawing of children engaged in it. The drawings were referred to as an RE menu.

The contingency management program was introduced to the children by asking them to name the activity depicted in the RE menu. They were told that they could engage in the depicted activities when they completed assigned work. On completion of the first lesson, the RE menu was shown to each child. The child selected an RE and was allowed to engage in it for four minutes. Then, the child was returned to his seat and another lesson was begun.

The experimental sessions lasted sixty minutes. Initially, each student earned an RE after working at an assigned task for five minutes. By the eleventh session, each student was required to work thirty minutes. Work periods were gradually extended by successively increasing the time required to do the task.

The results show that the contingency management procedures were quite effective. At the end of fifteen sixty-minute sessions, the children were reevaluated on the Utah Verbal Language Developmental Scale. The reported range of improvement was from 2 years 0 months to 2 years 6 months, a very impressive result considering the length of actual instruction time.

A rather comprehensive institutional program for the retarded is described by Lent (1968). The Minosa Cottage Project is a school for mentally retarded females ranging in I.Q. from 25 to 55. The basic purpose of the project is to help the residents eventually return to regular community life, or in the case of the severely retarded, to make an easier transition to other institutions. The program focuses on four major training areas: personal appearance, occupational skills, social behavior, and functional academic areas.

The personal, social, and academic objectives are promoted by a token economy system. The tokens may be exchanged for a wide variety of tangible items (food, cosmetics, candy) and privileges (movies, dances). Primary reinforcement initially promotes the desired behavior but is gradually replaced with tokens. The girls learn the value of tokens by exchanging them for back-up reinforcers as soon as they are earned. (Coins are used as tokens with the younger girls.) The tokens may be exchanged for items at the school store or for special privileges. When the girls go on a "shopping spree," they are required to exhibit behavior typical of any person shopping in a real store. They are required to dress properly and to name the items they wish to purchase. If they are unable to name these items, they must repeat the name after the storekeeper has mentioned it and ask for the object using a complete sentence.

A more complex token system similar to banking is used for the older female residents. Tokens assume the form of marks on a card. The points on one side of the card may be redeemed for money; the points on the other side may be exchanged for privileges. One day a week is designated as banking day. On banking day, the points on the monetary side may be exchanged for actual cash, or the money may be saved in the bank. (To approximate the real-life setting to which the girls would eventually return when they left the cottage, the tokens were equivalent to the amount of money an unskilled laborer could ordinarily earn.) At this same time, points earned for privileges are recorded to be used at some future time. The older female residents do not spend the money at the school store but at stores in town if they earn enough privilege points.

A response-cost procedure is also used. When an older female resident refuses to do a chore or exhibits inappropriate behavior, a token fine is levied.

The training program at Minosa Cottage is a rather comprehensive one. Few aspects of personal hygiene and domestic skills are left to chance; the residents are taught various cleanliness habits and proper ways of sitting and walking. They are taught housekeeping skills and are systematically reinforced for learning appropriate social-relationship skills. Rudimentary but essential training in the "tool" subjects is also taught. For example, the residents are taught to tell time and are given basic instruction in vocabulary development, reading, and arithmetic.

The methods of instruction and reinforcement used to promote the terminal objectives of the program are most interesting. For example, to teach proper matching of colors, patterns, and styles of clothing, a movie is made of the girls in their typical attire and then shown to a girl. She is asked whether the various articles of clothing match and fit properly. The girl is shown colored cards and samples of material and is asked to match them. When she correctly matches the color card with the appropriate clothing sample, she is given a token. Depending on the ability of a particular girl, various clothing combinations are taught. A more intelligent girl may be taught to properly match combinations of checks and plaids. At the conclusion of this training phase, another movie is made and shown to the girl to evaluate the effects of instruction. The girls make significantly fewer errors in proper dress than is true before training is begun. A local beautician teaches other elements of personal grooming including proper hair care. Successful applications of the techniques are reinforced with tokens. When the girls attain a reasonable criterion level, tokens are faded out and praise and Polaroid pictures are used as reinforcers to maintain proper hair care behavior.

Walking instruction is important because the mentally retarded are often identified by their walking style. A girl is taught to focus on a certain spot on the wall twenty feet away while walking toward it. After this skill is learned, the girls are taught to walk toward the instructor and maintain visual contact with him. Each girl is also taught to hold the chin in a proper position. For example, if the chin is held too low, the instructor may raise it or an audio signal is used to convey that information. In the final stages of walking instruction, the girls are taught to walk toward a mirror twenty feet away and use the mirror reflections to make postural adjustments. Additional cues are given by auditory signals.

Leisure-time activities are also utilized to teach the girls physical and social skills. At school dances, girls are taught good posture. When asked to dance, the girls are instructed on what to say and to express appreciation to the partner when the dance has ended. Points earned for proper dance behavior may be exchanged to attend a party.

Lessons in homemaking and domestic skills are also given. The girls are taught how to sew, take care of the cottage, read prices on items in a store, recognize the contents of canned food, and distinguish similar products in cans that are labeled differently. For instance, they are taught to identify canned tomatoes even though the can label varies with the trade name.

Behavior modification procedures are also used to deal with the girls' special problems. For example, one girl had a habit of putting various objects such as beads in her ears. To remove these objects necessitated a trip to a hospital and the assistance of a nurse or physician. The special attention she received on these occasions appeared to reinforce the undesirable behavior, so a procedure was implemented to decrease the reinforcement. When the girl arrived at the hospital, she was told that the hospital staff was too busy to see her; if she wished aid, she would have to return the following day. The next day she was required to wait before the physician attended to her, and when she was finally seen by the physician, he did not talk to her. After the physician cared for her immediate needs, she was placed in a recovery room for two weeks. During that time her physical needs were cared for, but she had minimum contact with the staff. The modification procedures were apparently effective. In the next eight months the girl returned to the hospital only once.

The Minosa Cottage Demonstration Project uses behavior modification procedures comprehensively and rather ingeniously. However, as Lent (1968) points out, questions are often raised about the program. Won't the girls become dependent on the token system? Won't their personal hygiene habits deteriorate if they are not reinforced? Isn't the program expensive? These inquiries are answered by indicating that learned behavior will be maintained by natural reinforcers operating in the environment (praise and the natural consequences that usually follow the performance of any desirable behavior). The program does cost approximately $35,000 more than programs in other institutional or hospital settings. However, as Lent suggests, the training enables the girls to be largely self-supporting, saving the taxpayers approximately $100,000 a year. Even if that were not true, it is difficult to place a dollar value on the acquisition of self-sufficiency and self-respect in any human being.

The Juvenile Delinquent

In the most literal sense, a juvenile delinquent may be defined as a person below the statutory age limit who has committed an unlawful act. The act or acts committed may or may not be unlawful for adults and may vary from state to state (Erickson, 1978). The incidence of juvenile crimes has increased at an alarming rate for several years. Coleman (1976) has reported that "Between 1968 and 1975, arrests of persons under 18 years of age for serious crimes increased more than 100 percent—some four times faster than the increase in the population for this age group" (pp. 386–387).

A variety of factors have been postulated as causal in the development of delinquent behavior. The etiologic variables that are most often mentioned include chromosomal irregularities (an extra Y chromosome in males), abnormal brain wave patterns, deficiencies in the capacity of the delinquent to experience anxiety, poor school performance, unfavorable economic conditions, social and family disorganization, and inadequate or inappropriate child-rearing practices leading to antisocial or maladaptive behavior patterns. While any one of these factors may make a disproportionate contribution to delinquent behavior in specific cases, the search for simple causes has been largely abandoned. The most popular view today is that delinquent behavior has multiple causes; and, contemporary research has increasingly focused on environmental and psychological factors as being basic in unraveling the etiology (Coleman, 1976; Erickson, 1978).

A number of treatment approaches have been used in working with delinquents. Perhaps the most common of these are placing the delinquent on probation under the supervision of a probation officer and the parents, individual psychotherapy, placement in a group home for delinquents, and institutionalization. Although probation and individual psychotherapy may be useful in selected cases, neither approach has been successful with large numbers of cases (Erickson, 1978). However, as we will discuss in the following section, the use of behavior modification procedures in special classes and other group settings has been more effective.

Illustrative Behavior Modification Programs and Procedures

Kaufman and O'Leary (1972) devised a special classroom for sixteen maladapted adolescents in a psychiatric ward. Two classrooms were set up and eight adolescents were placed in each classroom. To promote the desired behavior, positive reinforcement was used in one class and response cost in the other. The classes met for forty-five minutes a day, four days a week. The forty-five-minute classes were divided into three fifteen-minute periods.

In the positive reinforcement class, an adolescent could earn up to ten tokens for each fifteen-minute period. In the response-cost class, each adolescent was given ten tokens for each fifteen-minute period and could retain the tokens as long as his behavior conformed to the rules. However, if his behavior violated the rules, he could lose up to ten tokens each period. In both classes, depending on the behavior exhibited, each adolescent could earn a total of thirty tokens. (Each token had an established value of one cent; thus, the student's potential earnings each day were thirty cents.)

The first day of class, the students were taken to the "store," where they examined various items purchasable with earned tokens. Items ranged in value from $0.01 to $4.00. If a student earned the maximum number and wished to exchange the tokens for back-up reinforcers, he was able to purchase a thirty-cent item in the store.

Tokens were distributed or withdrawn in intervals of fifteen minutes. The end of each interval was signaled by a kitchen timer. When the timer went off in the positive reinforcement classroom, the teacher told the students what rules they had appropriately followed and the number of tokens earned. In the response-cost classroom, the teacher informed each student what rules he had broken and the tokens he had lost.

To analyze the effects of reinforcement and response-cost procedures, the classrooms were experimentally manipulated in several ways. First, tokens were terminated in both classrooms for a period of time. With this change, the behavior of the students quickly reverted to its previous baseline level. Second, positive reinforcement and response cost were reintroduced. However, in the positive reinforcement class, response cost was implemented instead, and the response-cost class was changed to positive reinforcement. Third, each student rated his own behavior (self-evaluation), and tokens were awarded (or lost) on the basis of that rating. In the positive reinforcement class, students decided how many tokens they would earn; in the response-cost class, students determined how many tokens they would lose.

Analysis of the data revealed that both positive reinforcement and response cost greatly decreased the amount of maladaptive or disruptive behavior. However, positive reinforcement was more effective than response cost, although the difference was not statistically significant. When the reinforcement procedures were switched, both procedures brought marked reduction in the disruptive and deviant behavior. Apparently, positive reinforcement and response cost worked equally well to reduce deviant behavior in both classrooms. Also, both procedures produced significant gains in reading achievement.

The use of student self-evaluation to determine tokens earned or lost also functioned to keep deviant behavior at a low level. Deviant behavior during this condition was not significantly different from positive reinforcement and response-cost conditions.

Behavior modification procedures have also proved useful in working with delinquents in group homes. An excellent example of a home-styled program for delinquent boys is Achievement Place (Phillips, Phillips, Fixsen, and Wolf, 1973). Residents are boys twelve to sixteen years of age who have been placed there by the court. They are average or above average in intelligence but are academically retarded by three or four years. The home is operated by two "professional parent-teachers."

The major goals of Achievement Place are to teach the boys academic, social, behavioral, self-help, and prevocational skills that will help them adjust more adequately to the home and community environment. Goals are promoted by a home-wide token economy system. Tokens are given for the performance of certain specified tasks and can be exchanged for certain privileges and desired objects. The privileges include use of television, telephone, radio, record players, and tools; snacks; allowance "bonds" which can be used to buy clothes; and other special privileges.

When a boy first arrives at the home, he is given a tour of the premises and introduced to the token economy system. Each boy is given a point card to record his behavior and points earned or lost. Initially, points earned for the performance of specific tasks are exchanged for back-up reinforcers each day. As soon as points acquire a reinforcement property, the points are exchanged for privileges on a weekly basis. When a boy is performing the desired target behaviors at a reasonable rate, the point system is faded out and a merit system is introduced. The merit status gives a boy free access to all privileges and is the final preparatory stage before returning home. If a boy is returned home prematurely and experiences problems, he may have to go back to Achievement Place for a short period to overcome the difficulty.

Each day at Achievement Place is characterized by a standard routine. First, the boys take care of personal hygienic needs and clean bedrooms and bathrooms. The performance of these tasks is supervised by a manager who administers points for properly completed tasks and levies fines for tasks incompleted or poorly done. After breakfast, the boys pick up their daily report cards and go to public school. Their teachers give daily reports on the cards regarding their school performance and behavior. The teachers return the cards to the home each day and points are given or taken away depending on teacher evaluation of school performance.

A family conference is held each evening to discuss activities of the day, evaluate performance, and consider the addition or alteration of existing rules and violations of rules. Consequences for rule violations are considered and implemented. After the conference, the boys and the houseparents may discuss highlights of the day or listen to records or watch television. Before retiring, the boys calculate the number of points earned during the day.

Achievement Place typifies in many ways behavior modification programs that are presently operating in home-styled or institutional settings. However, its program evaluation techniques are unique. After leaving Achievement Place, measures of the boys' school attendance, contacts with the police and the court, and recidivism are extensively analyzed.

These types of data have also been collected for comparable delinquent youths who were committed to the Kansas Boys' School and thirteen other delinquent youths placed on probationary status. The data for each group were collected one year after release from treatment, detention, or institutionalization. The Boys' School and Achievement Place youths had very similar records in terms of their contacts with the law before and during treatment.

Comparisons made of the three groups after release indicate that the Boys' School youths had more frequent police contacts than the Achievement Place boys. Boys on probationary status had a smaller number of contacts with the police *before* detention and treatment but a greater number *after* treatment than the Achievement Place boys. Two years after detention and treatment, 54 percent of the probation youth and 53 percent of the Boys' School youth committed delinquent acts resulting in institutionalization. Only 19 percent of the Achievement Place youth were institutionalized after release.

School attendance comparisons also indicate the beneficial effects of Achievement Place on the boys' subsequent behavior. Three semesters after treatment, 90 percent of the Achievement Place youth were attending school. Only 9 percent of the Boys' School youth and 37 percent of the probation youth were still in school. Comparison of school grades after treatment favor the Achievement Place youth, although the difference is not significant.

The reported statistics on Achievement Place show quite clearly the beneficial effects of the behavior modification program. The results are even more impressive when costs are considered. The per-bed cost of Achievement Place is approximately one-fourth the cost of building a state institution for boys. In a home-styled behavior modification program, the boys receive more individual care and maintain contact with parents, friends, and the home community.

The success of Achievement Place spurred other, similar home-styled treatment programs, but they were not as successful as Achievement Place. Comparative analysis of Achievement Place and an attempted replication revealed that the programs were outwardly the same. However, careful analysis indicated three crucial differences between the programs. First, the two programs differed in interaction, instruction, and feedback. At Achievement Place, instructions were given in a positive manner, and when the boys behaved deviantly, feedback was straightforward and positive rather than punitive. Second, at Achievement Place social skills were taught and reinforced so that the boys' behavior brought a positive response from others. Third, the Achievement Place boys learned about and participated in self-government. They learned how to criticize in a positive way and to negotiate in the decision-making process. Thus, token programs that do not include a positive, warm human dimension will not thrive.

A final example of the use of behavioral principles in working with delinquents is contained in Cohen and Filipczak's (1971) report of the Case II Project at the National Training School in Washington, D.C. The main purpose of the project was to establish appropriate educational behavior in delinquent boys who exhibited a wide range of antisocial behavior.

The Case II Project was modeled after a "student research employee" concept. Students were able to earn points for the mastery of academic work, part-time work in the dining room and kitchen, clerical, janitorial, and maintenance work, and for exemplary social behavior. Students were not required to perform academic tasks; however, if they did not, they were unable to earn points. Each point was worth one-hundreth of a cent ($0.0001) and could be used to buy items from a catalog, special privileges, or reinforcing events. For example, students were able to exchange points for soft drinks, milk, potato chips, Polaroid snapshots, smoke breaks, rental of a private room, private tutoring, and so on.

A brief description of a typical day provides a glimpse of the overall program format. Students would get out of bed between 6:00 and 8:00 A.M. Breakfast was served at specific times for particular age groups. The cafeteria closed at 8:15, and all boys could have free entrance to the lounge. Classwork started at 8:30, and students typically spent the remainder of the morning in various study programs. At 11:45, there was a fifteen-minute free-time period. Lunch was served at 12:00, and students were permitted entry to the lounge without charge from 12:00 to 1:30. The afternoon schedule was similar to the morning, consisting mainly of study activities. At 3:00, the lounge was opened, but to be admitted a student was charged 100 points per hour. The evening meal was served between 5:00 and 5:20. Students were free to choose their own activities from 6:00 to 10:00. The store was opened at 6:00, and students were able to exchange points for things they wished to purchase. Other activities were also available to students. For example, they could go to the library, watch TV, participate in supervised study or gym activities, or perform an elected part-time job. Lights were turned out at 10:00, and students were expected to have taken care of personal needs and chores by that time.

As the description indicates, the Case II Project was essentially a token reinforcement program. However, boys were not coerced to participate in it. They had considerable freedom to make choices affecting their daily activities. However, since most things at the institution had to be purchased, there was considerable incentive to participate in the school program.

The results of the Case II Project were quite impressive. Statistically significant changes in I.Q. occurred, and there were substantial changes in academic achievement, number of hours of study, and points earned. Analysis of the recidivism rate showed that it was much lower than that reported prior to the initiation of the Case II Project.

It is apparent from this study, as well as the outcome data on Achievement Place, that token reinforcement programs can be highly effective in modifying inappropriate educational and social behavior of delinquent youths.

The Emotionally Handicapped

An emotionally handicapped child or adolescent is a person whose social and emotional problems are sufficiently severe to make it difficult or impossible for the individual to adapt to the academic or behavioral demands of a regular classroom. Although there is no common agreement regarding the specific behaviors included in this category, temper outbursts, aggressive acting out, and disruptive, distractive, and socially withdrawn behavior are often mentioned. Thus, the label "emotionally handicapped" refers to a variety of inappropriate or maladaptive behaviors that do not appear to have a clearly defined or common etiology.

Illustrative Classroom Designs

Special education classes for the emotionally handicapped are now rather common in public schools. These classes are often self-contained and are limited to a maximum of ten students. The programs are usually highly structured, and behavior modification is an integral part of the class program.

Mattos, Mattson, Walker, and Buckley (1969) have provided a good description of a class for emotionally handicapped children. The class consisted of fourth, fifth, and sixth grade students who exhibited a variety of behavior that interfered with desirable academic performance. They were hyperactive, abusive toward their peers and the teacher, distractive, and defiant with such high frequency that they attended to academic tasks less than 50 percent of the time.

A token system was devised, and points were given for appropriate academic and social behavior. The children attended the special class in the morning and returned to their regular classes in the afternoon. Academic performance was reinforced by giving points for working on assigned tasks (interval reinforcement) and completing assigned tasks (ratio reinforcement). The work assigned to each child was consistent with his achievement level. Earned points were recorded on a student work card and were exchanged for free time. Each point was worth one minute of free time and could be used to engage in various activities such as model building, playing with cars, and working at different craft activities.

Kitchen timers were used to signal the end of academic work periods and free time activities. To receive points children were required to clean up and be in their seats within five minutes after the signal.

Initially, tokens were given for very small amounts of academic work. For example, a child was reinforced for being prepared to learn or even beginning an assignment. Gradually, both appropriate academic and social behavior was shaped. As the performance of the children improved, they were required to complete longer assignments to receive reinforcement.

A group reinforcement procedure was also used. To earn group points, all members of the class had to exhibit the appropriate academic and social behavior from 11:00 to 11:30 A.M. each day. A large-faced, electric, interval timer, set for a specific number of minutes, was used. The clock was started and continued running as long as children were engaged in task-oriented activity. If children engaged in behavior incompatible with academic work, the clock was stopped and reset. If children engaged in task-oriented behavior through the preset time interval, they received group points. When the clock reached zero, points were given and entered on a graph which could be seen by all children. Group points were exchanged for field trips.

Time-out and exclusion from school were used to deal with various types of socially inappropriate behavior. Less serious deviant behaviors (talking, wandering around the room, throwing objects) were handled by placement in time-out. Behaviors such as leaving the classroom without permission, fighting, and defying the teacher led to suspension from school for a minimum of one day. When this action was taken, the suspended child was required to complete assignments at home and was not permitted to return to school until the work was satisfactorily completed.

The authors report five experimental phases that were conducted with this group and a second group. The object was to determine the combinations of positive reinforcement and aversive control measures that were most effective in promoting identified target behavior. (As we have described the behavior modification techniques used with each group, we will not report the detailed treatments used in each phase.) Analysis of treatment effects in the five experimental phases was based on task-oriented behavior. Baseline measurements indicated that the children displayed task-oriented behavior less than 50 percent of the time. During and after specific treatment phases, task-oriented behavior varied from 51 to 84 percent. In the last treatment phase, task-oriented behavior was maintained at 84 percent, and the children were returned to the regular classroom. A follow-up conducted two weeks after the children were placed in the regular classroom revealed that task-oriented behavior was being maintained at 77 percent.

In consulting with and designing EH classrooms for public and private schools, the authors have found that a combined token reinforcement and levels system is often effective in promoting desirable academic and social behavior. In this type of system, points are earned for the performance of target academic and social behavior, and the reinforcement available is determined by the points and level attained. In broad outline, a combined token reinforcement and levels system takes the following form:

Level 1:   The Lowest Level

   a.   The student remains in the EH class all day.

   b.   Earned points may be used to purchase food or material reinforcers. A small number of points are needed (e.g., 60 percent of the total number that can be earned).

Level 2

   a.   The student remains in the EH class most of the day but can attend special activities in a regular classroom such as a movie, guest speaker, etc.

   b.   Earned points can be exchanged for food or material reinforcers, or certain free-time activities. A larger number of points are needed for this level.

Level 3

   a.   The student may spend lunch and recess with students from regular classrooms. Also, one hour a day can be spent in an ancillary class such as art, music, or physical education.

   b.   Earned points may be exchanged for food or material reinforcers, any classroom privilege, or several different special activities or events.

Level 4

   a.   The student spends the morning in the regular class and the afternoon in the EH classroom.

b. The student evaluates his or her performance and behavior and decides the points earned. The teacher has the right to adjust the points if the student has been too generous in his or her evaluation. Earned points may be exchanged for all reinforcers and privileges described at Level 3. The student may also receive privileges as bonuses from time to time.

Level 5: The Highest Level

a. The student spends the entire day in a regular classroom. However, academic and social behavior in the regular classroom must be maintained at an acceptable level. This level is ordinarily attained after a student has performed for a minimum of three weeks at Level 4.

b. If the student's behavior and academic performance are acceptable in the regular class, the student is awarded 90 percent of the total points that can possibly be earned. These points may be spent on any food or material reinforcers available in the EH classroom and on special privileges at school and home (e.g., early dismissal from school, a trip to a local amusement park, etc.).

As the reader may have noted, the system described above has three important elements: (1) reinforcement and/or privileges are increased as a student progresses through the levels; (2) a student is ultimately given responsibility for evaluating his or her performance and behavior; and (3) a gradual transition is made to the regular classroom.

The EH class should also contain other features. First, a portion of the classroom should be set up as a reinforcement area where students can engage in appealing academic projects, read magazines, play commercial games, build models, etc. Time to engage in these activities should be purchased from points earned for desirable academic and social behavior. Second, some arrangement has to be made to deal with disruptive student behavior. Some teachers have found that a system of point fines for inappropriate behavior works reasonably well. However, in most EH classrooms there are usually one or more students who exhibit behaviors that can be more adequately dealt with by using time-out. Hence, some arrangement for a time-out area should be made. Third, it is usually wise to have parents ready to take a child home on those occasions when a student's acting-out behavior cannot be controlled with the use of nonpunitive methods. Finally, it is usually desirable to help parents implement a behavior management system at home that is similar to or consistent with the behavior modification system used at school. Differential treatment at home and school makes it difficult for treatment effects achieved at school to transfer to the home.

The Psychotic Child

Childhood psychosis is one of the most severe behavior disorders a child can develop. It may occur anytime after birth and, unless properly treated, can severely handicap a child for life. Fortunately, the incidence is relatively low (less than 1 percent in the child population), although the condition occurs nearly three times as often in boys as girls (Erickson, 1978).

Two separate disorders are ordinarily referred to when childhood psychosis is discussed: childhood schizophrenia and autism. However, there is some overlapping of symptoms, and some authorities believe that it is impossible to clearly distinguish one from the other. For instance, Coleman (1976) suggests that the differences between childhood schizophrenia and autism are imperceptible, with the time of onset being the chief distinguishing factor. The schizophrenic child appears to evidence a period of normal development before the schizophrenic symptoms appear. On the other hand, the autistic child tends to manifest symptoms of the disorder during the first year of life. Therefore, in the face of this apparent lack of consensus regarding the differential diagnosis of these two conditions, our discussion will be limited to the autistic child.

Besides the obvious tendency of the autistic child to withdraw from social contact and interaction, several other symptoms are characteristic of the disorder. Lovaas and Newsom (1976) have described the autistic child in the following terms:

1. *Sensory deficits:* The autistic child appears not to attend to people or things in the environment. Although he or she may seem to be blind or deaf, these sensory capacities appear to be normal.

2. *Deficits in affect:* The autistic child seems indifferent to the attention and affection expressed by others. The child does not laugh, smile, or exhibit sadness or depression in an appropriate way.

3. *Repetitious self-stimulation:* The autistic child engages in the same behavior over and over again. For example, the child may rock back and forth, repeatedly hum a specific tune, or turn in circles.

4. *Tantrums and self-destructive behavior:* The autistic child may engage in "self-mutilating" behavior such as pulling his own hair, banging his head against a wall, or scratching his face. Autistic children have been known to engage in aggressive or violent acts toward parents,

tear and destroy things, or refuse to go to sleep at night.

5. *Psychotic speech and echolalia:* Many autistic children are mute. They make sounds or even hum but often do not talk. Children who do not talk often exhibit echolalic speech. That is, they simply repeat the remark that another person has addressed to them.

6. *Behavioral deficiencies:* Autistic children have limited self-help skills and need excessive care from others. They often do not perceive or show an awareness of danger. For example, they may walk out into a busy street, lean over the ledge of a high building, etc.

A moment's reflection regarding the autistic symptoms we have described will suggest that this disorder is a profound handicap. Yet, present theorizing and research has generated little that is useful in understanding the etiology or the course of the disorder. To provide a flavor of the theorizing, let us note the views of two prominent theorists. Ferster (1961) has suggested that autistic symptomotology can be explained on the basis of the child's learning history. The behavior the autistic child exhibits is essentially the result of unplanned or accidental reinforcement contingencies and is maintained by similar contingencies operating in the child's present environment. Rimland (1964) has postulated a constitutional basis for the disorder. He believes that the reticular formation of the brain stem has been damaged. This neurological damage leads to an impairment in the capacity of the autistic child to relate new stimuli to remembered experience. As a result, autistic children are deficient in their ability to synthesize or integrate sensations as a whole. Thus, they tend to perceive the world as vague, unpatterned, and often overwhelming.

Given the present state of research, an adequate statement regarding etiology cannot be made. However, as Ross (1974) has indicated, Rimland's theorizing fits the facts reasonably well; and acceptance is growing for the notion that organic brain dysfunction may play an important role in the disorder.

Although the specification of causal variables is usually prerequisite to the formulation of definitive and effective treatment procedures, some useful methods have been developed for working with autistic children. Bettelheim's (1967) work is well known, and more recently, Lovaas (1973) has demonstrated that behavioral procedures hold considerable promise. In the following section we will describe a behaviorally oriented class for autistic children.

Illustrative Behavior Modification Programs and Procedures

One of the most comprehensive descriptions we have seen of a class for autistic children is contained in Donnellan-Walsh (1976)[1] and Donnellan-Walsh, Gossage, Lavigna, Schuler, and Traphagen (1976). The two manuals contain almost everything one needs to know about setting up and implementing a class for autistic children. Since their description is both comprehensive and detailed, we will simply try to capture some of the main program features.

The first step in setting up a class for autistic children is to determine what children will be admitted to the class. Donnellan-Walsh et al. suggest that eligibility be determined by the manifestation of any one or more of the following behaviors: (1) inability to use oral language to communicate, (2) a history of being unable to

interact or relate to other people, (3) preoccupation with or inappropriate use of objects, (4) an intense need to maintain sameness, (5) a striking resistance to controls, and (6) unusual motor behavior or motility patterns. If a child meets eligibility criteria, admissibility to a class is made only after comprehensive medical, psychological, educational, and speech evaluations are done.

The class usually consists of six children, a teacher, and a minimum of one teacher aide. An attempt is made to place children in the class who are functioning on a similar level. The children attend the class for 240 minutes each day. The physical features of the class are similar to facilities used for the trainable mentally retarded. Floors should be carpeted to reduce the noise level, toilet facilities should be adjacent to the classroom, and cooking facilities should be available. A time-out room should be readily accessible to deal with the more disruptive behavior of the children.

The recommended curriculum consists of five major areas: (1) behavioral management and socialization, (2) communication skills, (3) cognition, (4) motor development, and (5) self-help and independent living skills. These areas are listed below with examples of learning objectives in each category.

1. *Behavioral management and socialization.* The basic instructional objectives in these areas are to:

    a. Decrease off-task behaviors such as indulging in tantrums, self-stimulation, etc.

    b. Increase appropriate behaviors such as learning necessary classroom behaviors, working in a group, and interacting with others

2. *Communication skills.* Autistic children have severe limitations in their ability to communicate. They need to learn:

---

[1] The administrator's manual of this work also describes guidelines and standards that are used in California for these classes.

a. Expressive language such as nonverbal and verbal imitation, sign imitation, etc.

b. Receptive language such as following simple commands, labeling, etc.

3. *Cognition.* Autistic children have excessive difficulty in processing information and need to learn:

a. Preacademic skills such as matching to classification, sequencing, spatial relations, etc.

b. Academic skills (at later stages) such as number concepts, reading, computation, etc.

4. *Motor development.* Autistic children have severe deficiencies in gross motor and fine motor coordination. Instructional objectives include:

a. Acquisition of gross motor behaviors such as body awareness, development of game skills (kicking, throwing, etc.), and some group game skills (kickball)

b. Acquisition of fine motor behaviors such as grasping and releasing, manipulation of objects, and prewriting and writing skills

5. *Self-help and independent living skills.* The basic instructional objectives in this area involve:

a. Self-help skills such as toileting, feeding, and dressing

b. Independent living skills such as household activities and prevocational and vocational skills

These overall curriculum goals are further refined, adjusted, and individualized to the needs of each child on the basis of information obtained through the preadmission evaluation, parent input, and ongoing teacher observation.

The most immediate objective for the class is to establish those behaviors that are most basic to learning. However, since most of these children exhibit a variety of behaviors that interfere with learning, these inappropriate behaviors must be eliminated first. Hence, much of the teacher's effort is initially directed to the elimination of self-mutilation, screaming, tantrums, meaningless verbalizations, and ritualistic behavior. The behavior modification procedures that are used to eliminate these behaviors are reinforcement of incompatible behavior, extinction, response cost, time-out, and other forms of punishment. All these procedures are now well known to the reader and need no further discussion.

At the same time the teacher is working to eliminate the inappropriate autistic behaviors, his or her efforts are also directed to the promotion of basic classroom behaviors. Perhaps the most important of these are appropriate sitting and on-task behaviors, eye-to-eye contact, following simple directions, and specific self-help behaviors. The procedure that is used to promote these behaviors is called the *discrete trial format.* It involves five major elements: (1) an S^D or verbal instruction, (2) a prompt, (3) a response, (4) a consequence, and (5) an intertrial interval. Let us illustrate each component by using an example.

Suppose you want to teach a child to sit down on a chair in response to a verbal command. The first step in the process is to present an appropriate S^D, or discriminative stimulus. Secure the child's attention, and then say, "Doug, please sit down" (*discriminative stimulus*). As soon as you have made the verbal request, *prompt* the behavior requested by moving the child to his chair and gently pushing him down until he is seated. The prompt is used to ensure that the correct response is performed. When the child executes the correct *response* (e.g., sitting in chair with feet on the floor and facing toward the front of the room), a *positive consequence* is administered immediately. In the initial stages of learning a new behavior, it is usually desirable to reinforce the correct response by providing immediate verbal reinforcement ("Good sitting") and follow it with food. The *intertrial interval* is the time period of three to five seconds that immediately follows the administration of the consequence. It is used to record the child's response and to provide a definite beginning and end for each learning trial. Each of these steps is repeated until the child's response meets a predetermined criterion level. However, the prompt is gradually faded until the verbal instruction is all that is necessary to instigate the response.

Once the teacher has succeeded in eliminating interfering or inappropriate behaviors and the children have learned basic classroom behaviors, the teacher proceeds to concentrate on other elements of the curriculum. A substantial amount of time is spent on helping children work in a group, acquire independent working skills and, of course, acquire a usable communication system. The system that is taught to the children may be verbal, sign language, or both. Each phase of the instructional program is carefully outlined and sequenced, behavioral methods are integrated into it, and child progress is constantly evaluated and graphed. Mastery of each basic task, concept, or skill is prerequisite to moving to the next component in the instructional program.

A final and indispensable part of the program is parent involvement and training. Initially, a group meeting is held with all parents and staff. Program objectives and structure are discussed, and parent involvement is requested. Parent involvement is encouraged in four ways. First, two teacher visits to the child's home are made at the beginning of the program. Teacher observations are made of parent-child interaction, and parents are asked to identify problem

areas they believe should be the object of modification. Parents are also asked to identify learning goals that should be a part of the instructional program. Second, observations of the child's classroom behavior are recorded in logs that are sent to parents regularly. The log describes child progress, problems, and things that parents might do to enhance the child's development or adjustment. Third, parents may be involved as volunteers, teaching their own or other children in the classroom. Fourth, parents are asked to participate in a parent training workshop. The workshop has three important goals: (1) to achieve greater control over the child's inappropriate behavior, (2) to establish and maintain appropriate behavior, and (3) to accelerate the learning of self-help and communication skills. In the workshop parents are taught general principles of behavior modification including (1) how to select target behaviors of the child to modify, (2) charting of behavior change, (3) methods to increase and decrease behavior, (4) the discrete trial format, and (5) implementation and monitoring of the behavior change program at home.

The Donnellan-Walsh et al. program is, as we have indicated, well conceived, comprehensive, and clearly outlined. Although evaluation data on the effectiveness of the program are not reported in the two manuals, the care with which it has been designed suggests that it is not likely to have many competitors. If one is designing a school program for autistic children, this one can serve as an excellent model.

Comprehensive and detailed descriptions of classroom programs for autistic children are difficult to find, and thorough evaluations of them are even more scarce. Those that are available suggest that well-planned, behaviorally oriented programs are effective. Needels and Jamison (1976) reported the first-year results of the Los Angeles County Autism Project. This project consisted of three experimental programs that included twenty children ranging in age from two to nine. Curriculum and change objectives were similar to the program described by Donnellan-Walsh et al., and behavioral procedures were an integral part of the program.

Of the twenty children in the program, nineteen made measurable gains in mental age. Nine children gained a minimum of one developmental month for every month in the class. Eleven of the children gained less than one month per each month of class attendance, but their measured I.Q.'s placed them in the severely retarded range. Only eleven of the twenty children attended classes for the entire academic year. Therefore, considering the length of school attendance and measured intelligence of the children, the program was obviously effective.

Lovaas and Newsom (1976) summarized the results of a number of behaviorally oriented treatment procedures and classroom programs for psychotic children. They concluded that educational programs can be set up for psychotic children that approximate those for less disturbed children. When teaching personnel are properly trained in the use of behavioral procedures, a variety of appropriate behaviors such as eye contact, affectional responses, and receptive and expressive language can be established. However, individual modification of grossly inappropriate behavior must be achieved first, and group instruction must be delayed until basic classroom behaviors have been learned. Classroom treatment effects can be maintained if parents are properly trained and continue to use behavioral procedures at home.

Summary

1. In this chapter we described the use of behavior modification with youths who are learning disabled, mentally retarded, emotionally handicapped, delinquent, or psychotic. Although the symptoms and etiology of each handicap may vary, behavior modification procedures are useful in promoting desired change in each.

2. Disabled learners are individuals with normal or higher intelligence who manifest a disorder in one or more of the psychological processes that affect listening, thinking, reading, writing, or arithmetic. Behavioral principles and procedures have been used in two primary ways to modify the difficulties of disabled learners. First, task analysis has been used to (a) specify clearly the learning task, (b) specify the sequential steps in the tasks to be learned, (c) determine the responses to be learned, and (d) devise methods of presentation that will facilitate learning. Second, behavioral principles have been used to arrange the learning environment so that stimulus-response-consequence relationships are programmed in an effective way.

3. Mental retardation is a condition of arrested intellectual development with associated deficits in adaptive behavior. The degree of retardation largely determines the extent to which the retarded person is educable and can be trained to be self-sufficient. Behavioral procedures have been used extensively in schools and institutions to educate or train these persons to lead more productive lives. Token reinforcement and contingency management procedures have demonstrated utility in promoting desirable educational and behavioral goals.

4. A juvenile delinquent is a person below the statutory age who commits acts that are unlawful. The behavior is believed to have multiple causes, although environmental and psychological factors may be primary. While a variety of individual and group treatment approaches have been used to modify the maladaptive patterns, the use of program-wide behavior modification procedures have been found to be efficacious in group homes and institutions.

5. An emotionally handicapped child is a person whose social and emotional problems are

sufficiently disabling to make it difficult for the individual to adapt to the demands of the regular classroom. Special education classes using token reinforcement and contingency management systems have been effective in altering these maladaptive behavior patterns.

6. Childhood psychosis is a severe behavior disorder that may occur anytime after birth. It is characterized by severe impairments in cognition and affect and adaptive behavior. While a variety of constitutional, biochemical, and learning variables have been postulated as basic to the etiology, research has not clearly delineated the contributions of each. Behavioral procedures have demonstrated effectiveness in altering many of the bizarre, self-destructive, and/or inappropriate behaviors of these children. More recently, behaviorally oriented special class programs have been shown to modify both behavioral and learning deficits. However, the extent to which these changes are maintained and transfer to the environment appears to be related to the proper utilization of behavior modification procedures in the home.

Chapter Eight

The Management and Modification of Classroom Problems

Teachers ask for assistance with a variety of problems children exhibit in the classroom. Although the problems may vary in type and severity from one classroom to another, behavior modification procedures have demonstrated utility in dealing with most of them. To illustrate the efficacy of these procedures in altering classroom problems, we will discuss intervention strategies that have been used with twenty of them.

Inattention

Some normal children and many academically disabled children have considerable difficulty attending to learning tasks. Because the ability to attend to and concentrate on learning tasks is a prerequisite for successful learning, deficits in this ability must be modified.

A relatively simple procedure for increasing task attention is a token reinforcement system. The child who exhibits the difficulty is given a work-record card. Assignments are given that are appropriate in length and difficulty. As each task is completed, he is given points that are recorded on the card. When the child accumulates a specified number of points, he is permitted to exchange the points for tangible reinforcers or reinforcing events. Initially, to develop the reinforcement property of points, time should be set aside each day to exchange the points for back-up reinforcers. As the child's task attention increases, the exchange period is changed from every day to every second or third day. The success of this procedure can be further enhanced by periodically giving bonus points when the child exhibits periods of good task attention.

Wolf, Giles, and Hall (1968) used a token reinforcement system for low-achieving fifth- and sixth-grade children in a poverty area. The reinforcement system used was similar to saving stamps given in stores. Every child was given a folder that had different colored pages, each color representing a different reward. For example, one of the pages was for a weekly field trip, another was for money and items available in the "store," another was for long-range goals that might take several weeks, and another page was for daily snacks. When the child completed an assignment, he was given points by the teacher, who marked the squares. The teacher determined the number of points obtained for completing an assignment. In addition, bonus points were given for grades. Using these procedures, Wolf, Giles, and Hall were able to attain significant changes in pupil achievement. Though the classroom they dealt with had a small number of students and teacher aides, the method might be adapted to a regular class setting. Also, in many communities part-time volunteer aides from various women's social clubs can be used.

O'Leary and Becker (1967) worked with seventeen nine-year-old children described as emotionally disturbed. They used a token reinforcement system. The tokens were ratings placed in a small booklet on each child's desk. The children were told that they could receive from one to ten tokens, depending upon the extent to which they followed directions. The points or ratings they obtained could be exchanged for reinforcers that were available in the back of the room. The reinforcers were small prizes such as candy, comics, etc. Using these procedures, the teachers were able to significantly decrease the amount of deviant behavior in the classroom.

Token reinforcement systems do not, of course, have to be limited to just elementary-school-aged children (Broden, Hall, Dunlap, and Clark, 1970; Nolen, Kunzelmann, and Haring, 1967). The system does, however, have to be modified. What the points earn is one of the crucial factors for success in the junior high or high school program. Elementary-school-aged children generally respond more favorably to trinkets, while older children usually choose an activity or special privileges. We will discuss choosing potential reinforcers later in the chapter.

Token systems are not the only way to help a child increase his attention to task. Hall, Lund, and Jackson (1968) demonstrated how teacher behavior could affect a child's attention. They had an observer sit in the classroom and hold up a small piece of colored paper when a particular child was attending to his task. This was done to help teachers discern when study behavior was occurring. The signal was presented in such a manner that the pupil was unaware of it. Upon this signal, the teacher would verbally reinforce the child's attention, or ignore the child when he was not attending.

Hall, Lund, and Jackson (1968) state that the teachers did not have to pay more attention to the pupils than before the study started. It was the type of attention that the pupils received that made the change. The teachers who were involved in their study were initially unfamiliar with reinforcement principles. Yet, through in-class supervision, they were able to learn and carry out an effective procedure to increase attention to a task.

In the regular classroom, secondary reinforcement (praise) might be used most effectively with pupils who have milder difficulties in paying attention. It is the opinion of the present writers, however, that students with severe problems need tangible reinforcers such as toys, candy, or time-activity privileges paired with secondary reinforcers. Both methods should be discussed with teachers, and they should be helped to decide whether the use of check marks or social reinforcement (social approval) is most useful in their situations. If the teacher wishes, he can experiment with one of these first and shift to the other later.

Refusal to Complete Assigned Work

Another problem similar to inattention is refusal to complete assigned work. The problem is a relatively frequent one and causes teachers a great deal of concern. To deal with this problem, contingency management has demonstrated utility.

Addison and Homme (1966) have used contingency management to promote appropriate academic and social behavior; their procedure is simple but ingenious. The child is given an assignment at an appropriate level of difficulty. When the assignment is satisfactorily completed, the child may choose one of several activities pictured on a reinforcement menu and engage in it for a specified period of time. Because the reinforcement menu contains a number of activities that children enjoy, opportunity to engage in one after completion of an assigned task increases the probability of the child doing schoolwork subsequently.

In a regular classroom, it may be difficult to handle a contingency management approach if limits are not set on the time a child has to complete an assignment. Unless limits are set, the time taken by each child may vary from fifteen to sixty minutes. Because children are permitted to engage in a selected reinforcing event on task completion, children will likely be involved in reinforcing activities constantly. Such activity not only requires a good deal of timekeeping but may be distracting to other children working on assignments. If each child's assignment is individualized and a limit is set for its completion, a certain period can be set aside for participation in reinforcing events. All students will be finishing assignments at the same time and will be engaging in reinforcing events at the same time. Hence, some students will not be engaging in studying while others are engaging in reinforcing events. This type of scheduling reduces distraction in the classroom and avoids a great deal of student procrastination on assignments.

Daley, Holt, and Vajanasoontorn (1966) found the reinforcement menu to be highly effective with mentally retarded girls. When arithmetic was paired with one of the choices on the reinforcement menu, they found a great increase in the number of arithmetic assignments that were completed. Also, because it was paired with a reinforcement event, arithmetic came to be a pleasurable activity for many children. Daley et al. discovered that the girls began to select arithmetic as one of their choices on the reinforcement menu for completing a reading assignment.

Addison and Homme (1966) have indicated that this method can be effectively used with many age ranges, and that it has been used successfully with high school dropouts as well as grade school children with academic problems. It has also been used in psychiatric wards and with Anglo and Indian preschool children.

The menu approach, they indicated, tends to create some conflicts for the child, since he may desire to do more than one of the activities. There is a way to reduce this conflict of choice. When the child chooses one activity, he can be told that he may choose another activity next time. Addison and Homme (1966) also recommended that for variations in the reinforcement menu approach, a special activity can be employed. Viewing cartoons, field trips, messy but fun activities, or even a party might be used. Since it is a "special" activity that is presented infrequently, it is easier to manage and has the motivational appeal of a rare event.

Although contingency management has often been used on an individual basis, it also has some important group applications. Long and Williams (1973) compared the effects of group and individual contingencies in promoting appropriate academic and classroom behavior with inner-city junior high school students. The individual contingency condition allowed students to earn points that could be exchanged for free time. However, before students could engage in free-time activities they were required to earn twelve out of a possible sixteen points. Points were earned in several ways. First, two points were earned by being in class on time and bringing the appropriate study materials. Second, students could earn two points for appropriate sitting and study behavior during each of three variable intervals. A kitchen timer was set to go off three times at varying intervals during the class period. If a student was exhibiting proper sitting and study behavior when the timer sounded, he or she was awarded two points on each occasion. Fourth, assignments completed during the class period earned four points. Students kept a record of the points they earned, but the points had to be verified by the teacher before the student was permitted to engage in free-time activities.

Under the group contingency condition, points were awarded to the class for conformity to specific rules. The class as a group was able to earn a total of eighteen minutes of free time during a class period. However, each time any student violated a rule, one minute of free time was deducted from the class total. Near the end of the class period earned free time was calculated and students were given that amount of time to play games, talk with friends, read magazines, or work on other assignments.

An analysis of treatment effects indicated that group reinforcement was slightly more effective than the individual contingency condition. However, both individual and group reinforcement contingencies produced substantially higher levels of appropriate behavior than was present at baseline. Apparently, individual and group contingencies may be used to promote appropriate task completion and classroom behavior.

Deficiencies in Academic Work

Deficiencies in academic work can be improved with many different procedures. Zimmerman and Zimmerman (1962) wished to increase the number of words a child spelled accurately and employed the following procedure. A child was given a ten-word spelling quiz. When the test was scored, the child was directed to go to the blackboard and spell each word on the spelling test. Each time the child misspelled a word, the teacher simply did not respond to the child's performance. When the child had spelled all ten words correctly, the teacher praised him, gave him an A, and asked him to help her color Easter baskets. The procedure proved effective.

There was a successive decrease in the time required to spell each word correctly and a consistent decrease in the number of negative comments the child made regarding his spelling ability. On subsequent occasions, this method was continued by the teacher with a great improvement in the academic performance of the child.

Similar methods can be used with an entire class to improve the accuracy of assigned work. Lovitt, Guppy, and Blattner (1969) used contingency management to increase spelling accuracy with thirty-two fourth graders. Before their experimental procedures, spelling lessons were assigned each Monday, and the words were presented each day of the week in some form for study. Each Friday, the class was given a spelling test on the assigned words.

During the experimental period, pupils were given a test on Tuesday, Wednesday, Thursday, and Friday of each week. If a pupil obtained a 100-percent score on any test (Tuesday through Thursday), he was not required to take the test on the remaining days of the week. During the time that other pupils were taking the spelling test, the successful pupil could participate in any other school-related activity at his desk that he wished. After ten weeks of this procedure, another was added. In addition to the free-time activity that was earned for a 100-percent accuracy score, the pupils were told that if all pupils received a 100-percent score on any day, the whole class could listen to the radio for fifteen minutes.

The results showed that prior to the experimental treatment, the median number of perfect papers each week was 12.0. During the free-time contingency condition, the median number of perfect papers rose to 25.5. When the group contingency condition (listening to the radio) was included, the median number of perfect papers increased to 30.0. The last phase (listening to the radio for total class performance) was recorded for a three-week period. Although it was effective, the class was never allowed this opportunity because all pupils did not obtain a perfect score on any one day.

Although the Lovitt, Guppy, and Blattner method was obviously effective, even better results might have been achieved if the radio-listening reinforcement contingency had been set at a lower level; total class performance might have been further improved if reinforcement had been given for total class improvement rather than requiring a 100-percent score for all, and might have improved even more if both the radio listening and the free-time activity were used simultaneously.

Williams, Long, and Yoakley (1972) used behavior modification procedures with advantaged high school students. They compared the relative effects of behavior contracts and behavior proclamations in promoting identified target behaviors in academically superior students. Two experimental conditions were established. In the first, behavioral contracts were written that identified rewards and penalties for desirable and undesirable behavior, the means by which grades would be assigned, how classroom procedures would be conducted, and the pledges made by the students and teacher. The students had an active role in formulating the contracts. In the "proclamation" condition, the procedures were formulated entirely by the teacher without student participation. The students were informed of the plan and requested to comply. The specific elements of the proclamation plan were very similar to behavioral contracts.

The results indicated that both the behavior contract and proclamation approaches were superior to the standard classroom procedures used during the baseline period. However, the behavior contract proved slightly more effective than the proclamation approach in promoting the desired target behaviors. Because the basic elements of both procedures were very similar, it appears advantageous to involve advantaged students in the design of classroom management.

Forgetting Assignments and Study Materials

One of the most exasperating but common problems teachers encounter is the student who forgets assignments and other study materials. Compared with many other classroom problems it is not serious, but it is annoying. Students may deliberately provoke a teacher by pretending they have forgotten an assignment when, in fact, they have not completed it or done it at all. It is difficult for the teacher to prove that the student is being untruthful or manipulating the teacher for his own purposes; yet, if the behavior is permitted, it becomes strengthened because the student successfully escapes a class requirement.

This problem can be quickly altered with positive reinforcement and response cost. A point system can be set up that reinforces bringing completed assignments and study materials to school and imposes fines for not doing it. The teacher can prepare a chart that indicates the items to be brought to school each day and post it on the classroom board. Five points might be given for bringing a pencil, ten for a notebook, fifteen for a textbook, and twenty for a completed homework assignment. Fines may also be imposed (usually of the same magnitude) when such materials are not brought to class. Points are exchanged for a variety of back-up reinforcers.

Another novel approach used by a teacher whom one of the authors observed is a variation of the television program, "Let's Make a Deal." The procedure is very simple. On the first day and on an intermittent basis thereafter, five student names are picked out of a hat or box. These students are asked to produce two items written on the wall chart. The listed items on the wall chart are things like completed assignments, books, pencils, etc. If the children can produce the specific items, they are immediately reinforced with candy, gum, or a special privilege; if they cannot, fines are imposed.

Young children and high school students enjoy playing the game, and it is effective in promoting the desired behavior. The teacher must remember to have all students' names in the box for each drawing, or the students whose names were picked most recently may regress to their old habits. Because the law of averages will eventually lead to every student's name being chosen periodically, the procedure has a beneficial motivational effect on the whole group.

A third procedure that can be used to deal with the problem is overcorrection. For example, suppose as a teacher you have several students who constantly forget to bring assignments and study materials to class. Call the parents of the forgetful students and indicate that you would like to secure their cooperation in initiating a procedure that will teach the students to bring their assignments and study materials to class. Indicate that the next time one of the students forgets an assignment or study materials, he or she will be asked to return home. When the student arrives the parent is instructed to permit him or her to return only half of the assignment and/or study material that has been forgotten. When the child arrives at school, he or she is instructed to return home and get the remaining half of the assignment and/or study materials. However, before the child returns to school after the second trip, the parent is asked to sign a note indicating that the child has, in fact, made two trips. Requiring the child to make two trips rather than one overcorrects the forgetfulness and quickly instigates the desired behavior.

Obviously, this procedure would not be appropriate if the child does not live within walking distance of the school. However, if the parent is willing to cooperate, the overcorrection procedure could be used by having the parent drive the child part of the way to school on each of the two trips.

Tardiness

Lateness is a rather frequent problem among high school students, for many find events outside class highly reinforcing, and some like to "bend" school rules as a means of demonstrating their independence or power to resist adult authority.

One simple approach to reducing tardiness is to take from a student's free time the amount of time he or she is late for class. Suppose, for example, that a student is five minutes late for his first class at nine o'clock each morning. The teacher can terminate his tardiness by informing the student that he will be required to stay five minutes extra in his first period class. Because class breaks are highly reinforcing times for most adolescents, he will probably find that tardiness is much too costly to continue.

For most instances, the above procedure should handle the problem. However, excessive lateness (more than ten or fifteen minutes) may be impossible to deduct from break time. In this case, the student can be required to double the time he must make up for his lateness; that is, his release from school at the end of the day is delayed by that amount.

Another method for dealing with tardiness is to reward promptness with tokens. For example, the teacher might give students ten points for being in class on time and deduct one point for each late minute. Earned tokens may be used to "purchase" special privileges.

Group contingencies may also be effective in dealing with the tardiness problem. For instance, if all students enter the room before the bell rings, the class may be allowed to keep a radio on while they are doing assigned work or talk to friends for the last ten minutes of the class.

A group token system may also be used. Each day all students arrive on time, one class point is given. When a certain number of class points have been earned (five or ten), the whole class participates in a reinforcing event. The last period on Friday might be devoted to democratically determining the activity, or the teacher may simply declare that their promptness will be rewarded by no weekend homework assignments.

Out-of-Seat Behavior

Children who roam aimlessly about the room or leave their seats without permission cannot be considered serious behavior problems. Such behavior becomes problematic, however, when a number of students do it, for it is disruptive to the working students and detracts from the learning of the offenders.

A technique one teacher used to deal with this problem involved taking a chair away from a student whenever he was out of his seat more than twice a day. Once the chair was removed, the student was required to earn the privilege of having a chair by exhibiting appropriate academic and classroom behavior. That is, the student had to stand by his desk, complete an assignment, and conform to all classroom rules at the same time.

Gallagher, Sulzbacher, and Shores (1967) discuss a procedure they used to deal with out-of-seat behavior in a classroom of emotionally disturbed elementary school children. Students were informed that they would be granted a twenty-four-minute Coke break at the end of the day if they did not leave their seats without permission. The teacher posted a chart which displayed two-minute intervals ranging from 24 to 0. The chart also listed each student's name with a different colored chalk. The students were told that each time one left his seat without

permission, two minutes would be deducted from the class's Coke break. When a student left his seat without permission, the appropriately colored check mark was placed in one of the squares, and two minutes were deducted from the break. With this procedure, the students knew who was responsible for the lost break time.

Baseline data indicated that students left their seats without permission 69.5 times per day. After modification procedures were initiated, the rate decreased to 1.0 times per day. Thus, out-of-seat behavior was reduced dramatically, and other disruptive behavior generally declined.

Wolf, Hanley, King, Lachowicz, and Giles (1970) utilized a similar procedure in working with underachieving boys from low-income families. They were interested in determining the effects of a "timer game" on the nontask behavior of the children. The procedure involved setting a timer that rang at various time intervals ranging from one to forty minutes. When the timer rang, every student who was in his seat earned five points. Although students were receiving points for other target behaviors, the use of the timer and positive reinforcement for appropriate seating behavior proved effective with most students.

One student, however, was not positively affected by the procedure, so an additional method was used. The child was told that she would be able to earn extra points during the timer game. A piece of paper was placed on the wall by her name and the numbers 10, 20, 30, 40, and 50 were marked on the paper. The child was told she would begin with fifty points but would lose ten points on each occasion the timer rang and she was out of her seat. After this procedure had been in operation for a period of time, a second experimental procedure was introduced. She was informed that the rules would be changed slightly. She would not only earn points for herself but also for students sitting next to her; at the end of the timer game, the points she had left would be divided between herself and these other students.

The individual point system decreased the incidence of out-of-seat behavior in the girl, but a further decrease was achieved by the use of the timer and the sharing of points earned with peers. Apparently, peer approval and pressure were powerful incentives for modifying the girl's out-of-seat behavior.

Masturbation

It is not uncommon for a counselor or school psychologist to have a child referred for masturbation. Although boys are more often referred than girls, teachers appear to express greater concern when girls engage in masturbatory activity. Apparently, teachers view masturbation in boys as less objectionable.

Masturbation is not likely to be extinguished by ignoring it; the act is self-reinforcing. Thus, if the behavior is to be decreased or eliminated, more decisive intervention methods must be used. One of the authors eliminated masturbation in a third-grade boy by using positive reinforcement and response cost. The boy was told that a certain procedure would help him stop the undesirable behavior. (The class was informed that a system would be implemented to help him exhibit better student behavior.) The child was reinforced with check marks for each fifteen-minute interval he was able to keep his hands on top of the desk. However, every time the boy placed his hands under the desk, the teacher removed a check mark from his card. When his card was filled, he was permitted to select a small toy. The procedure proved effective in eliminating classroom masturbation.

The same type of procedure was employed with a girl who stimulated herself by rubbing the edge of a chair. The child was simply rein-

forced for sitting back in her chair so that she could not engage in self-stimulation. Points were withdrawn every time she engaged in the inappropriate behavior. The procedure proved effective and the masturbation ceased.

Wagner (1968a) utilized behavior modification procedures to treat compulsive masturbation in an eleven-year-old girl. The girl was reported to masturbate four or five times in the morning and six or seven times in the afternoon by rocking back and forth in a chair and rubbing herself on the edge of the desk and, occasionally, using both hands and a foot to engage in the masturbatory behavior.

The teacher was instructed to give the child special attention by patting her on the head and making positive comments when she was not masturbating. When the child was able to refrain from self-stimulation for an hour in the morning, she was permitted the opportunity to engage in a reinforcing activity. Because masturbation was more frequently exhibited in the afternoon, the child was reinforced for each half-hour afternoon period she did not engage in the undesirable behavior. If the child was able to go a whole day without masturbating, a note was sent home to her parents commending her behavior. On the receipt of the note, the parents further reinforced the desired behavior by buying a record for the child, taking her bowling, or allowing her to stay overnight with her grandmother. The teacher also used an aversive behavior method by calling the child's name out loud when she was observed masturbating.

As the child reduced the frequency of masturbation, the contingencies were changed. To have a note sent home to her parents, the child was required to go two consecutive days without masturbation. As further progress was made, reinforcement intervals were extended even further.

The results indicated that by the tenth day the child's masturbation decreased to a few times in the afternoon, and consistently decreased throughout the year. A follow-up seven weeks after the beginning of the next school year indicated that the girl had ceased masturbation in the classroom.

Obscene Behavior

There are children in every classroom who verbalize obscene words or engage in obscene gestures. It is not a serious problem, but it annoys teachers and often detracts from learning.

Sulzbacher and Hauser (1968) report a simple but effective procedure that reduced the frequency of obscene gestures exhibited by a special class of fourteen mentally retarded boys. The boys were informed that they would receive a ten-minute recess at the end of the day. The class would lose one minute of recess, however, each time a student verbalized or exhibited an obscenity. The procedure proved effective. Expression of obscenity decreased from a baseline rate of 16 per day to 2.11 during the experimental period.

In addition to Sulzbacher and Hauser's methods, time-out and positive reinforcement procedures can be used. For example, when a child makes an obscene comment or gesture, the teacher can place him in time-out for ten minutes. The procedure continues until the behavior decreases or extinguishes. If a time-out room is not available, the teacher can tell the offending student that he has exhibited an inappropriate student behavior and ask him to sit in a nonstudent chair in the back of the room for a specified period of time. He should be instructed to face the wall so that he cannot see other students and be reinforced by their attention. The procedure can be repeated each time the inappropriate behavior occurs. The assignments missed while he is in the nonstudent chair must be made up at a later time.

Another variation with more positive features is to give the offending individual five points for each hour he does not engage in obscene language or gestures. The accumulated points will be used for a total-class reinforcing event. To purchase the reinforcing event for the class, he must accumulate 100 points. Because the class will want to participate in the event, they are not likely to reinforce his obscene behavior, and his status will likely be elevated in the eyes of his peers.

Negative practice may also be used to reduce the frequency of obscene behavior. When this procedure is used, the student is required to stay after school and continue the obscene gestures in private. In the presence of an adult, the student would be asked to repeat the inappropriate gesture for fifteen minutes. If the student stops before the fifteen minutes are up, he or she would be required to start over and continue for fifteen minutes of uninterrupted practice. The prompting or guidance of the negative practice should be handled in a matter-of-fact way, and care should be exercised to ensure that the student receives no reinforcement when the behavior is being performed.

Profane Language

Profane language may not appear to be a particularly important problem, for almost everyone curses once in a while. However, because teachers are charged with the responsibility of teaching "proper" social as well as academic behavior, profanity is not something to be encouraged. Indeed, if profane expressions are permitted in the classroom, parents are likely to register their firm disapproval to the teacher.

The most common method used to eliminate profane language is simply ignoring it. Ignoring the behavior is not likely to be effective with the more frequent offenders, however, because profanity often gets reinforced by peer attention.

One of the authors has used a simple procedure to reduce cursing. The teacher is instructed to place a tape recorder on the offender's desk. The child is told that if he continues to swear, a tape recording will be made and sent home to his parents. This simple procedure usually terminates the swearing behavior quickly, but if it does not, an additional step may be taken. Inform the youngster that unless the profane language ceases immediately, he will be taken to the office and be required to phone his mother to describe the language he has been using in the classroom.

Burchard and Barrera (1972) experimentally tested several procedures to reduce profane language in a group of institutionalized, mentally retarded adolescents. The eleven boys resided in a training unit that was operated on a token economy system. Small aluminum discs were given when appropriate target behaviors were performed. The tokens could be exchanged for different items in the store or special privileges.

To modify six of the boys' undesirable behavior, four experimental conditions were established: (1) no time-out, but loss of thirty tokens for any incident of swearing; (2) five minutes in time-out; (3) no time-out, but loss of five tokens; and (4) thirty minutes in time-out, but no token loss. These conditions were presented in random order, and the experimental conditions were used with each of the boys at different times.

The results indicated that, for four boys, the higher response-cost conditions (1 and 4) were most effective in reducing the undesirable behavior, and the difference between them was insignificant. For one boy, the more severe form of response cost did not reduce the frequency of swearing, but a milder form (reduction of token fine or time-out) did produce the desired effects.

The study clearly shows that response cost is an effective procedure for decreasing or eliminating swearing in mentally retarded children. Although token fines and time-out appear equally effective, token fines are somewhat easier to use — especially if the offending subject physically resists placement in time-out. Also, because the magnitude of response cost required to produce the desirable change differs from person to person, it is probably wise to start with a moderate token fine. If it does not work, a larger fine will likely produce the desired effects.

Chronic Misbehavior

The classroom problems discussed up to this point are not generally considered serious even though it is desirable to modify them. Chronic misbehavior is quite another matter, for it is disruptive and hurtful to others and to the child.

A procedure that is often effective with chronic misbehavers is time-out. Placement in time-out terminates the reinforcement the child receives in the classroom and prevents any "contagious" effects on other students. When time-out is used, the child is taken to an empty room as soon as the undesirable behavior occurs, and he remains there for ten minutes. If his undesirable behavior continues, he is required to remain in time-out until it has ceased. Similarly, if the child is returned to the classroom after ten minutes and begins to exhibit undesirable behavior again, he is immediately dispatched to the time-out room for another ten minutes.

To be effective the time-out procedure must be employed so that it does not further incite the misbehavior. The teacher should not scold, demean, or ridicule but rather inform the child his behavior is "out of control." Time-out provides the offender the opportunity to reconstitute himself so that he can exhibit more adaptive behavior in the classroom. The time-out room should be free of reinforcing objects, neither pleasant nor unpleasant, and should not be referred to as, for example, "The place where the disturbed kids are placed."

The time-out procedure is effective with most misbehavers, especially when the classroom is a reinforcing place. With some children, however, additional measures may be necessary. Keirsey (1969) has described a method that appears effective with more seriously disturbed children. It is called "systematic exclusion." It essentially involves a contract, since it requires an agreement between all parties to perform predetermined roles. The teacher agrees to give the child a signal to leave the room at the first instance of his misbehavior. The child agrees to be responsible for himself and to go home for the rest of the day when the teacher signals him to do so. The principal ensures that the daily suspension is carried out, and will use physical force if necessary. The parents cooperate by not scolding the child or even asking him the reason for his exclusion.

Keirsey (1965) indicates that this method works well with kindergarten-age children as well as seniors in high school. It is a particularly effective system with impulsive children, because they are able to predict the consequences of their behavior. Predictability allows the child to feel more security, and, as Keirsey further points out, it simplifies the environment for them.

The authors have utilized this approach and have found it effective. However, we disagree with Keirsey's (1969) view that being sent home should be made pleasurable. When we have used this method, it has been recommended to the parents that the child be placed in a room with low reinforcement value. The child's own room is not a desirable place. The child should remain in the room with no reinforcement property until the time he normally comes home from school. Thus, being sent home does not reinforce the misbehavior.

Another method for handling less intense misbehaving can be performed in the classroom. There have been some studies (Hall, Panyan, Rabon, and Broden, 1968; Ward and Baker, 1968; Hall, Lund, and Jackson, 1968; Thomas, Becker, and Armstrong, 1968; and Madsen, Becker, and Thomas, 1968) that have shown that if teachers ignore inappropriate behavior of students and show approval for appropriate behavior, they can reduce disruptive behavior in the classroom. However, as Madsen et al. (1968) point out, the task is a difficult one. When some teachers have to ignore inappropriate behavior of their students, they become upset because the classroom at first becomes worse. Madsen et al. suggest that a training program be instituted to help teachers tolerate the periods of misbehavior of their pupils, and help them realize how they affect the behavior of their pupils.

An ideal approach for working with disruptive children is to teach them self-control. Drabman, Spitalnik, and O'Leary (1973) attempted to do this with eight disruptive nine- and ten-year-old boys that were placed in a university laboratory school class. The class met five times a week for one hour each day.

The study lasted for fifty-eight days and was divided into eight phases: baseline, token reinforcement, matching, four separate fading phases, and self-evaluation. The baseline phase was used to record the frequency of a variety of behaviors such as moving one's chair, playing, making noise, turning around in the chair, and the performance of aggressive acts. In the token reinforcement phase students were awarded points for appropriate behavior that could be exchanged for prizes. During the matching phase, students were asked to rate their own behavior and to attempt to match their ratings with those of the teacher. For example, when students rated themselves within one point of the teacher's rating, they were awarded the number of points they had given themselves. If student and teacher ratings were the same, an additional bonus point was given. However, if students rated themselves more than one point above or below the teacher's ratings, they received no points.

In the first fading phase, the students were divided into two groups. The students were told that the teacher would flip a coin every fifteen minutes to select one of the groups for special treatment. The group that was selected by the coin toss were given the "privilege" of receiving bonus points when their ratings matched teacher ratings. The unselected group received the points they had awarded themselves.

The second fading phase was similar to the first—with one major exception. All students' names were placed in a jar, and two names were selected every fifteen minutes. When student ratings matched teacher ratings, the students were praised. If there was a mismatch, the teacher simply ignored it.

The third fading phase was similar to the second except that only one student's name was drawn from a jar. In the fourth fading phase, a coin was tossed every fifteen minutes to determine whether a student's name would be drawn from the jar.

The last twelve days of the study consisted entirely of student self-evaluation. During this final phase, students rated their own behavior. Points were awarded to each student based on his self-rating. The teacher simply praised those students who awarded themselves a fair number of points.

The results indicate that the treatment was effective. Disruptive behavior decreased during the token phase, increased slightly during the matching phase, but decreased substantially during the first fading phase. Disruptive behavior during fading phases two, three, and four was similar to the first fading phase. There was a slight increase in disruptive behavior during the self-evaluation phase. Apparently, token rein-

forcement procedures can be used successfully to promote self-control in children who are disruptive.

Deficiencies in Verbalization

Compared to the chronically misbehaving child discussed above, children who are reticent or who lack verbal fluency may appear to be a minor problem. But if such a child is to learn, he or she is, of course, just as much in need of help.

One of the authors worked with Mexican-American and Yaqui Indian children who were very reluctant to verbalize in the classroom. The class was divided into rows, and a chart depicting the seating arrangement was drawn on the board. Each seat or chair was indicated by a box. Because there were thirty children in the class, the chart contained five rows with six boxes in each row. Check marks could be earned by participating in class discussions. The students were told that they would be awarded a piece of candy or gum if everyone in their row earned at least two check marks. The students were then urged to discuss their assigned work; questions were asked to encourage further verbalization. Each time a student responded orally, a check mark was placed in his box. As this process continued, and most children in a row had two check marks in their box, they began to urge students who had not yet verbalized to speak. When the last member of a row finally spoke, the contribution was often greeted with loud applause. It was not long before the whole class was engaged in lively discussion.

Hart and Risley (1968) attempted to teach disadvantaged preschool children the use of descriptive adjectives in their speech. They found that the traditional methods were ineffective in changing the infrequent use of descriptive adjectives during free play. The traditional methods involved direct teaching of adjectives and providing social interaction with peers and teacher praise when a child used descriptive adjectives. It was decided to focus on increasing color-noun combinations of words. Teachers were instructed to withhold materials the children usually used until they asked for them by using a color to describe the materials. During the first three days the method was employed, teachers prompted the children to use both the name of the object wanted and the color. After the third day, a child had to use both the name of the object and the color without being helped by the teacher. The results showed a significant increase in the color-noun combinations during free play.

With basically the same type of approach, Reynolds and Risley (1968) made teacher attention and allowing a four-year-old disadvantaged child to use materials contingent upon verbalizations. When the child requested the use of materials, the teacher would question her and require further verbalizations. The child had to respond to at least one question before receiving the materials. This combination (teacher attention and materials) proved effective in increasing the child's spontaneous verbalizations. Prior to treatment, the child rarely talked. If attention and materials were given when the child did not verbalize, her talking decreased to its former level. Reinstatement of the contingency quickly increased the talking to its previous high level. When the content of the child's verbalizations was analyzed, the increase was found to be only in terms of repeating requests for materials, but little increase in other types of verbalizations to the teacher or to other children. Reynolds and Risley, however, were optimistic, believing that this procedure could be further used to require the child to exhibit different types of speech contingent upon teacher attention and materials.

A common approach to developing verbal fluency in children is role playing. This procedure can be used effectively to enhance verbalizations in situations that are not responded to as aversive stimuli. Since classrooms are frequently seen as hostile by nonverbal youngsters, it may be best to introduce role playing in a more neutral setting such as on the playground, in the gymnasium, or in the counselor's office. Once children are engaged in role playing, the activity can be transferred to the classroom.

Shaftel and Shaftel (1967) list various steps to follow when role playing is used in a class setting. The first step is getting the group "warmed up." To achieve this, the teacher may wish to read a problem story to the children. Containing elements of human relations, the problem story provides a structured situation that readily initiates the group into role playing. When this has been accomplished, the second step, selecting the participants for role playing, is taken. Children should volunteer rather than be assigned to roles. Ideally, children should perform roles with which they can identify. In the third step, the teacher should have the role players develop a very brief plan of their proposed role playing. When these steps have been completed, the teacher prepares the audience to be participating observers. The teacher may direct the children to ask themselves questions, such as whether they think the actors would really behave that way in a similar situation and whether the roles are true to life. When certain pupils have difficulty listening, the teacher may ask each one of them to observe a particular player or to think of the consequences of the actions. The fifth step involves the actual role-playing situation. The sixth step is a discussion and evaluation. According to Shaftel and Shaftel, at the close of an enactment, discussion usually is quite fast, since most students are quite enthusiastic. At this point the teacher may wish to introduce another step—further role playing. That is, he or she may allow the role players to play their roles over again, changing their interpretations in the light of some of the comments made by their peers. The final step is sharing experiences and general discussion.

It is during the sixth step of discussion and evaluation and the eighth step of sharing experiences that the teacher must be careful to reinforce children for comments they make. At first, the teacher should reinforce by extending recognition and approval of any type of comment that is made by the children. She may smile, nod her head, and perhaps say something like "That is interesting," or "I am glad you said that." After children are able to verbalize, the teacher may want to reinforce more meaningful verbal statements. It should be remembered that the teacher must be instructed by the psychologist or counselor to approximate successively more meaningful comments by the students.

When difficulty in speaking is limited to only a few members of the class, role playing may still be an effective method. Instead of involving the whole class, individuals can be worked with after class. Hosford (1969) worked with a sixth-grade girl who experienced great anxiety when talking before her classmates. The child was seen by a counselor once a week for six weeks. At that time she was requested to role play giving a report in class. Each session involved a greater degree of report-giving behavior. For example, in the first session, the girl practiced getting up out of her seat and going to the front of the room. She also read a short paragraph aloud from her seat. Each week the child gave a longer report.

The classroom teacher worked with the counselor to increase the amount of talking the child did in class. The child was assigned to a social studies committee that had to give oral presentations every week. The child was told by the teacher to participate only when she was able to do so without any tension. The child gradually participated to a greater degree and was reinforced by both the teacher and her peers. By the end of the school year the child was able to speak in front of not only her own class but other classes as well. It was also reported that she began to volunteer to give oral reports to the class.

Inappropriate Talking

Although some children are reluctant to talk, other children talk not only excessively but often without permission. As this type of inappropriate talking increases, the ongoing learning activity is disrupted.

Hunter (1967) has discussed a method for dealing with excessive or inappropriate talking. The child is told that his talking is inappropriate and that each time he talks, a tally will be placed on the board. This type of response-cost procedure generally decreases the incidence of inappropriate talking, and the opposite behavior (listening) may then be positively reinforced. The child can be praised for not talking, a note can be sent home commending his behavior, or he may be allowed to go home first at dismissal time.

Barrish, Saunders, and Wolf (1969) employed a group contingency method to reduce inappropriate talking and out-of-seat behavior in a fourth-grade class. The class was told that they would play a game during their math period. The teacher divided the class into two groups based upon rows and seats. Children were told that one or both teams could either win or lose. The team(s) that won would obtain special privileges. The privileges were wearing a victory tag, obtaining a star by one's name, being first to line up for lunch, and thirty minutes of free time at the end of the day.

The class was told that the way they could earn the privileges would be to have team members avoid talking out or being out of their seats. Every time one of these rules was violated, the team got a check mark. To win, the team needed the fewest check marks. However, both teams could win if they had no more than five marks each.

The results showed a sharp decrease in talking-out and out-of-seat behaviors during the math class. The experimenters then decided to apply the game method during reading and discontinue it temporarily during math. This procedure resulted in a decrease in the talking-out and out-of-seat behaviors during reading but a recovery of former levels during math. The game was then applied during both math and reading. These two periods were combined and treated as one long period. Disruptive behavior remained at its low level during reading and declined to its former low level during math.

Barrish et al. (1969) report a problem that arose when these methods were employed. Two students announced to the class that they would not go along with the rules. The teacher simply excluded their names from the teams and kept a separate score. If during the free-time activity either child refused to work, he was kept after school.

Sometimes a behavior that a teacher wishes to modify can be used as a reinforcer to change the behavior itself. A good example of this is talking out in class. To implement the procedure the class is informed that they will be able to earn time to talk at the end of the class period if they restrain the tendency to talk out during the remainder of the class period. The numbers 1 through 15 are written on the board to signify the potential number of minutes of talking time. Then, each time a student talks inappropriately the largest number is erased, reducing the talking time by one minute. For each succeeding occurrence of talking, the largest number is consistently erased. At the end of the class period the largest number remaining on the board sig-

nifies the number of minutes of talking time the students will receive. Although the procedure is simple, it is often effective in reducing the frequency of inappropriate talking.

Disruptive Noise

Observations of public school classrooms reveal highly variable noise levels. In some classrooms, noise is a result of interested and busy learners and usually a sign that something productive is happening. Other classrooms, however, have so intense a noise level that learning is disrupted, and various degrees of confusion prevail. The students may be talking excessively, banging books, tapping pencils, or participating in activities with reckless abandon. In these classrooms, steps must be taken to reduce the disruptive noise.

Disruptive classroom noise can be reduced by using a token system, group contingencies, and response cost. The students can be informed that for every five minutes they work quietly on assigned work, a check mark will be placed in a box on the blackboard. However, if the noise level becomes too high during any five-minute period, an X will be placed in the box. When three boxes are filled with check marks, the class earns the opportunity to listen to the radio. On the other hand, when X's appear in three boxes, the class loses one minute of lunch time. Also, when the noise level becomes too high, the radio is turned off until the noise level decreases appropriately.

The proposed system has several advantages. It is easily implemented and designed with both positive and negative consequences. A group contingency provides an incentive for students to monitor their own and peers' behavior. The teacher does not have to constantly issue warnings or threats or use other, more punitive tactics. However, it is important to be aware of the fact that some parents may object to the use of this method. Parents may feel it is inappropriate for peers to monitor each other's behavior.

Hyperactivity

In a typical elementary school, 3 percent of the children are likely to be severely hyperactive (Grimley, 1976). Such children are likely to be easily distracted, unable to concentrate, unpredictable, irritable, impulsive, prone to have temper tantrums, and perform poorly in school (Treegoob and Walker, 1976). While primary causal variables have not yet been precisely identified, some authorities have noted certain developmental and historical findings associated with hyperactivity. For example, during pregnancy mothers of hyperactive children are more prone to experience vaginal bleeding and preeclampsia (swelling, high blood pressure, and protein in the urine). The birth weight of hyperactive children is more frequently below normal. Hyperactive children also have more frequent histories of respiratory distress, colic, delayed language development, brain malfunction, and brain injury (Safer and Allen, 1976).

Both medical and behavior modification procedures have proved useful in altering the behavior of hyperactive children. For instance, Safer and Allen (1976) have indicated that "stimulant medication is the most commonly used and the single most effective treatment for hyperactive behavior" (p. 47). Indeed, medications such as Ritalin, Dexadrine, and Cylert produce immediate and marked changes in hyperactive behavior. Although indications for use of these drugs are not always clear, present data suggest that the more neurologically deviant the child, or the more excessive the hyperactive reaction, the better the clinical response is likely to be (Safer and Allen, 1976).

While it is apparent that stimulant medications have a beneficial effect with many hyper-

active children, some side effects may occur. During the first and second weeks of use, approximately 15 percent of the children experience headaches, moodiness, stomachaches, suppression of appetite, and nausea. And, if stimulant medications are used over a long period of time (particularly dextroamphetamines), some suppression of the growth rate may occur. However, this effect is reversed when a child is taken off the medication (Safer and Allen, 1976).

As we noted, behavior modification procedures have also been used to alter the behavior of hyperactive children. Indeed, most of the principles and procedures we discussed for decreasing and increasing behavior in earlier sections are applicable to the hyperactive child. For example, Sachs (1973) used a specially designed time-out room to deal with the inappropriate behavior of a ten-year-old hyperactive boy. The time-out room was devoid of any type of visual, tactile, or auditory stimulation and contained a microphone that had a voice-operated relay. The hyperactive boy was told that whenever he exhibited certain behaviors he would be placed in time-out for five minutes of silence. If the boy made any noise while in time-out, his stay was extended until he remained quiet for five minutes. Although relatively simple, the procedure proved effective in decreasing the boy's inappropriate behavior.

The authors have found that hyperactive children usually respond best in a highly structured program. Academic and behavioral standards must be clearly specified, and both positive and negative consequences must be used consistently for appropriate and inappropriate behavior. Academic tasks should be carefully graded and within the performance abilities of the child.

Perhaps one of the more exciting forms of treatment being used with hyperactive children is self-instructional training. Several people have been involved in developing these methods, but Douglas's (1972) approach will be used to illustrate. Children are introduced to self-instructional training by being informed that their typical approach to dealing with problems (or learning tasks) creates difficulties for them. They are likely to be more successful if they learn better methods. Second, the child is impressed with the desirability of saying out loud—before a task is begun—what the task involves and how one goes about completing it. Third, the therapist models appropriate problem-solving steps by verbalizing the strategies and goals aloud. If the therapist is modeling putting a puzzle together, she might verbalize how she is arranging the pieces according to color, since these pieces are likely to go together. If a maze is being used to demonstrate, the therapist might emphasize the need to stop and think at choice points before moving on. Fourth, when the therapist has modeled each of the essential problem-solving elements, the child is asked to imitate by verbalizing each of the steps in the process. Or, the therapist may ask the child to instruct her on each of the problem-solving elements. As the child successfully verbalizes and performs each of the approximate steps, he is reinforced for his performance.

Finally, once the child has verbalized each of the important problem-solving elements, he is encouraged to use self-instructional or thinking responses as he moves through the problem-solving or task completion process. These procedures appear to hold great promise and appear to be efficacious in modifying the performance and impulsiveness of hyperactive children (Meichenbaum, 1977).

Inappropriate Imitations

Almost every classroom has a student who performs various kinds of imitations. In the middle of a math lesson, he may suddenly break into an imitation of a roadrunner or a screeching car. Of course, educators do not wish to stifle student creativity, but math lessons are hardly the place for screeching car imitations.

Inappropriate vocal imitations may be modified by using the principle of negative practice. The "impressionist" is taken to a private room and required to make the inappropriate imitations for fifteen minutes. If the student stops his imitations, he is given a firm request to continue for the full fifteen minutes.

At first, the child might respond to this procedure quite positively, but after five or ten minutes the novelty wears off and the act becomes aversive. And, because the child receives neither adult nor peer approval for his performance, the constant repetition tends to extinguish the undesirable response.

Response cost can also be used. A cup with ten tokens is placed before the child. For each inappropriate imitation, one token is taken from the cup. At a certain time, the remaining tokens are counted, and an equal number of check marks are placed on a card. When the card is filled with check marks, he is permitted the opportunity to exchange them for a tangible reinforcer or special privilege. As the child begins to reduce his inappropriate imitations, the "price" of the tangible reinforcer or special event is increased. Rather than giving him ten tokens for each half-hour period, the student is given ten tokens for an hour period. Because the longer time interval provides greater opportunity to lose tokens, the child has to exercise greater self-control to get the same number of tokens he earned earlier. By gradually extending the time period, the inappropriate behavior can be reduced. Eventually, the token system can be eliminated, and the desirable behavior can be maintained with social reinforcement.

Peer Reinforcement of Undesirable Behavior

Some of students' undesirable behavior is maintained by peer reinforcement. Inappropriate behavior such as clowning are both elicited by classmates and reinforced deliberately by them when it occurs. To control the undesirable behavior, all reinforcement maintaining the behavior must be terminated.

The reinforcing effects of peer attention and approval can be controlled by positive reinforcement and response cost. Carlson et al. (1968) wanted to modify a child's severe temper tantrums. It was observed that the child was receiving a good deal of attention from the school staff. Thus, the staff members were instructed to use firmer methods with the child, such as placing her at her desk and holding her there when the tantrums occurred. Attempts were also made to ignore the tantrums. When the child engaged in tantrum behavior, however, the other children looked at her, thereby reinforcing the behavior.

A simple method was devised to handle this problem. A primary reinforcer was used with other class members. Children were given a candy treat when they did not turn around to watch the girl who was exhibiting the deviant behavior. If a class member did attend to the deviant behavior, negative reinforcement was used by removing the candy placed at the side of each child's desk. Candy was also given intermittently to the children in the classroom so that they would not provoke the girl to have tantrums. In addition to the candy treat, the children in the classroom were allowed to have a class party when the child who had temper tantrums exhibited four half-days of nontantrum behavior. At this time, the child who had exhibited the deviant behavior distributed the candy to the rest of the class, and thus her peer acceptance was increased.

Patterson (1965b) believes that the more a behavior is valued by peers, the more that behavior is likely to elicit reinforcement. However, this can be used in a constructive manner. Children depend upon peers to get their reinforcement, and increasing peer pressure can cause a child to change his behavior. Patterson used a technique similar to Carlson's et al. with a hyperactive child. To assist this child in improving his behavior, he told the other children in the class that the subject was having trouble learning and sitting still; they were made part of the experiment to teach the child more appropriate behavior. They were told that the hyperactive child would earn a piece of candy from time to time, and when he accumulated enough candy it would be divided up among the class. To help the hyperactive child earn candy, other class members were asked not to pay attention to him.

Another procedure for decreasing the effects of peer reinforcement in sustaining deviant behavior was mentioned earlier. Discussing the time-out procedure, Sulzer, Mayer, and Cody (1968) stated that this method removed the opportunity for a student to receive essential reinforcement from his peers. The time-out procedure can be further extended: When peers reinforce the undesirable behavior of each other, both the offender and the child who reinforces the offending behavior should be placed in a time-out room. In this way, children learn to ignore deviant behavior in their peers.

If a check mark system is being used in a classroom, as discussed earlier, points can be given to the children who do not reinforce deviant behavior in their peers. For example, when a child turns to talk to another child and the second child does not respond, the second child should be given check marks for exhibiting good pupil behavior. In the same manner, pupils who ignore a peer who is exhibiting deviant behavior can also be rewarded with bonus check marks.

Dickinson (1967) has also suggested a method to change the manner in which a child seeks reinforcement from his peers. When a child exhibits appropriate behavior for a designated period of time, he is permitted, if he so desires, to tell jokes in front of the class. It can be seen how obtaining reinforcement for joke-telling behavior might decrease the need for seeking reinforcement of deviant behavior. Also, since being able to tell jokes is contingent upon exhibiting appropriate behavior, the probability of appropriate behavior occurring tends to increase.

Students can be taught to reinforce appropriate rather than inappropriate behavior of their classmates. Solomon and Wahler (1973) worked with a sixth grade to reduce disruptive classroom behavior. They used five popular students as "therapists" who were trained to give or withhold their attention in interacting with their disruptive peers. That is, when their peers were disruptive, they were instructed not to attend to them; when peer behavior was appropriate, they reinforced it by attending to it. As a result, changes occurred in the student therapists as well as the behavior of their disruptive peers. However, it is interesting to note that no changes occurred in the teacher's response to the disruptive students or in the way other students responded to their disruptive peers.

The methods we have discussed show that the teacher can have control over the extent and manner in which children receive reinforcement from their peers. Counselors and psychologists can help teachers increase the number of situations in which children can produce positive effects on each other. However, it is not implied that a teacher can eliminate the total effects of peer influence on deviant behavior, but rather that he or she can greatly decrease the number of times the deviant behavior will occur.

Social Isolation and Withdrawal

Every classroom contains some children who are shy, withdrawn, and socially isolated. Frequently, because they are quiet and do not "cause trouble," no active attempts are made to promote more adaptive behavior in these children. Socially withdrawn or isolated children often experience anxiety and personal distress, however, and it is desirable to help them to become more active social participants.

Sulzer, Mayer, and Cody (1968) have shown that shy or withdrawn behavior can be modified using appropriate modeling procedures. The withdrawn child is seated near a peer model who frequently receives positive reinforcement for his behavior. As the teacher reinforces the peer model, she is careful to emphasize the desirable behavior exhibited by the model. For example, she might say, "I certainly like the way John helps other people when they have a problem." Reinforcing peers for exemplary behavior tends to elicit imitative responses in the withdrawn child.

O'Connor (1969) has demonstrated that film-mediated models are also effective in promoting socially desirable behavior. He presented a twenty-three-minute film of children interacting in a nursery school. Its eleven scenes showed the child model gradually engaging in more social interaction followed by reinforcing consequences. The film had the predicted effect on the observers. The preschool children who viewed the film increased their social interaction. A control group that did not view the film showed no change in its interaction patterns.

Barclay (1967) has shown that social acceptance of socially rejected children can be increased by planned intervention. In his study, Barclay asked the classroom teacher to appoint the low-status children in the classroom as monitors in the hall and to have them perform errands. Teachers were further instructed to reward the low-status children for appropriate behavior and for displaying any interest in learning. Procedures were also designed in which low-status children could participate with pupils in their class as equals or superiors. Attempts were made to break up cliques in the classroom. Activities were designed that required mutual cooperation for success and were as unthreatening to the low-status children as possible. Barclay used role playing in which low-status children played the hero roles and a spelling game in which popular and unpopular children worked together to spell words correctly and obtain rewards of candy. Although his results were not significant on all of the criteria, they did demonstrate the significant utility of his methods in changing the sociometric status of children.

One of the authors used student aides and token reinforcement to alter the behavior of a socially withdrawn fifth grader. Initially, the therapist invited the client to his office and asked him if he wanted to be more involved in the play activities of his peers. The boy recognized that he spent much of the recess and playtime alone and felt that he would like to have more children with whom to play. With his concurrence, the following plan was implemented. One point was given to the client for each five minutes of play with his peers. To increase his athletic abilities and participation in sports, two points were given for each five minutes he practiced throwing or hitting a baseball or throwing or kicking a football during recess or playtime at school. Up to ten bonus points could be earned each day for talking or actively participating in group learning activities in the classroom. When he had earned a sufficient number of points (fifty), the points were exchanged for a giant candy bar.

Three of the more popular boys in the client's classroom were used as student aides. It was explained to them that the therapist wanted their help in encouraging the client to develop better play, sport, and social interaction skills. The client's token reinforcement system was explained to them, and they were asked to perform two basic functions: (1) encourage certain specified behaviors in the client and (2) determine the number of points the client earned each day according to the rating system previously described. It was also explained to the student aides that when the child client earned enough points to exchange them for a prize, they would also receive the same or a similar prize.

Although all three boys were initially enthusiastic, only two of them followed through consistently. When the client accumulated fifty points, he and the student aides were each awarded a giant candy bar. At this point it was explained to the student aides that the therapist wanted the client to become better acquainted with other classmates. Consequently, one would be eliminated from the aide position. The aides' names were placed in a hat, a name was drawn, and that person was eliminated from the group. Another popular boy was added to the student aide group. At this point it was explained to the client and the student aides that seventy-five points had to be earned by the child client for all of them to receive a reward.

Over a two-month period several changes were made in the reinforcement schedule and the back-up reinforcers. New student aides were added periodically. The results were not dramatic, but the token system and student aides greatly increased the client's peer interaction, play, and sport skills.

Disorderly Behavior in the Cafeteria

At most public schools, the school cafeteria is the busiest place on campus during the luncheon recess. Large numbers of students eat or are backed up in lines waiting to secure their food. The lunch break offers some respite from the more concentrated and structured morning activities, and many students use it to participate in many behaviors the classroom does not permit. Various degrees of noise, rowdiness, and disorder often prevail. Because this behavior is generally undesirable, teachers and administrators are usually most willing to prevent or control it.

Although many procedures might be employed to handle disruptive behavior in the cafeteria, a method employed by Sherman (1973) has several advantages. The experimenter developed a procedure to modify the cafeteria behavior of one hundred first and second graders in an elementary school. As in most school cafeterias at lunch time, the children engaged in a variety of undesirable behaviors. They were noisy, ran around excessively, and often left the cafeteria in a mess. Five objectives were formulated: (1) reduce talking to normal conversational levels; (2) limit out-of-seat behavior to those students who have to go to the restroom, return their trays, or dispose of their garbage; (3) require each child to clean up the immediate area around him; (4) require each child to leave the cafeteria quietly after lunch and not return; and (5) keep one rather than two teachers on duty.

To improve the cafeteria behavior of the students, a class competition system was devised. The students were told that their behavior in the cafeteria would be judged on criteria similar to the objectives stated above. After lunch each day, the five classes involved in the study were notified which class had won the competition for that day. The winning class received a star that was posted on the class chart in the cafeteria. Also, the class that exhibited the best cafeteria behavior was awarded a plaque that was hung on the outside of the classroom door. Each month, the class with the most stars was awarded a special prize.

To promote the desirable cafeteria behavior further, teachers on duty were encouraged to attend to and commend the behavior of those students who were behaving appropriately. Inappropriate or deviant cafeteria behavior was ignored. And, because group reinforcement was used, on-duty teachers were asked to commend the entire class when they exhibited appropriate behavior.

The procedures proved effective. Behavior improved immediately after the system was implemented. Students enjoyed the competition and often used peer pressure to reduce inappropriate behavior in their more disruptive classmates. There were occasions, however, when the students regressed to more disruptive behavior. These periods seemed to occur when the weather did not permit the children to go out for recess or some of the classes were not winning the competition and stopped working for the group rewards.

Another approach that might be utilized is to divide the class into groups of three. Each child in the group becomes a monitor of the other two children's cafeteria behavior. In other words, every one of the three children is observed by the other two children as well as being a monitor for the peers in his triangle. To make the technique operable, a few simple rules have to be explained by the teacher. First, the teacher should tell the class that they can earn up to four points for exhibiting good cafeteria behavior. Each child is told that he begins with a total of four points. When a child's behavior is too noisy he is informed by one of the monitors, and one point is lost. On each subsequent occasion, a point is deducted for noisy behavior. Moreover, if a pupil hits another or throws food, all four points are eliminated. Similarly, being reprimanded by a teacher for excessive talking might result in a loss of two points. When a total of twenty points has been accumulated by a pupil, he should be able to exchange the points for an activity privilege, inexpensive trinket, or even a dessert. After this procedure has been in operation for two weeks, the teacher can gradually increase the number of points required to obtain the trinket or activity privilege. To ensure some success, as soon as the pupils return to the classroom, the teacher should have them write on a piece of paper the names of the two pupils for whom they were monitors and rate them according to the points they feel these two pupils deserve. Furthermore, the pupil should rate himself as to how many points he feels he has earned in the cafeteria. If two monitors disagree, an average of the two marks should be taken. By following the latter procedure, pupils learn to discern when their behavior is inappropriate. Also, the use of pupil monitors in small groups is a way to help pupils learn responsibility.

For extreme behavior deviations in the cafeteria, a time-out procedure may be used. To make this procedure operative, individual tables or desks need to be brought into the cafeteria. They should be placed at the corner of each wall, and, if necessary, one in the middle of each wall. Children who become disruptive after appropriate warning are moved to one of these tables and isolated from the rest of their peers for a ten-minute period. A second infraction of the rules might result in a two- or three-day suspension from being able to eat in the cafeteria. These students might be forced to eat in a classroom so that it is not possible to talk to other children. If, in addition, recess is made contingent on proper cafeteria behavior, the disruptive behavior may further decrease. It is important that these rules be adhered to consistently. If they are not, the child's disruptive cafeteria behavior may be reinforced on an intermittent schedule.

Response cost may also be used in combination with positive reinforcement to deal with inappropriate cafeteria behavior. For instance, each class might be given a certain number of points (e.g., ten) at the beginning of each week. Each class is permitted to keep the points if class members exhibit proper behavior in the cafeteria during the week. However, any time a student in a class exhibits an inappropriate be-

havior, a point is deducted from the class total. At the end of each week the class points that remain are posted on a bulletin board. The points are totaled for all classes each week, and those classes that acquire a total of 100 points in three weeks are given a special privilege. That is, each winning class might have a party, take an interesting field trip, or have the privilege of watching a comic movie. Such a system makes it possible for all classes to win, and the public display of accumulated point totals provides an element of competition as well as the possibility of public recognition for appropriate cafeteria behavior.

Classroom Integration of Minorities

School systems are now required to integrate minority-group children into schools they have not previously attended. To accommodate these youngsters, schools should do everything possible to help these children adapt to the new school environment.

Studies dealing with this issue are rare. A study done by Hauserman, Walen, and Behling (1973) at Towson State College in Baltimore, Maryland, utilized behavior modification procedures to encourage the integration of five first-grade black children in a predominantly white classroom. Specifically, the experimenters desired to increase the interaction between white and black children in the lunchroom and in a free-play setting.

During the first baseline observation period, the black children interacted with white children in the cafeteria at a level of 0.8 out of a possible score of 5.0. In the free-play period following lunch, interaction was 2.7. In the first, "prompting" phase, the teacher told the children that they were going to play a game that involved eating lunch with a "new friend." No mention was ever made of race or minority status. To prompt the desired behavior, all children's names were placed in pairs (each black child paired with a white child) and drawn from a hat. The pairs were encouraged to sit together at lunch time. Children received verbal approval and a "ticket" when they sat with their new friend. If the new friends continued to sit with each other for the entire lunch period, they were given a second ticket. After lunch, the tickets could be redeemed for candy, cookies, or pretzels.

During the experimental phase, teachers did not assign pairs but encouraged the children as a group to sit and interact with new friends. Children received reinforcement for this type of interaction.

The results showed that both the prompting and experimental phases greatly increased interaction between the black and white children. During the prompting phase, the interaction increased from 17 to 80 percent, although the increased interaction during lunch did not generalize to the free-play period after lunch. During the experimental phase, the mean interaction was 50 percent during the lunch period, and interaction between the black and white children did generalize to the free-play period.

A second baseline measurement was taken after reinforcement was terminated; interaction between white and black children decreased to 16 percent. This was not particularly surprising as the prompting phase lasted four days and the experimental phase only nine days. If the reinforcement procedures were continued longer and gradually faded out, black-white interaction may have continued at a higher level. The results suggest that when spontaneous interaction between minority and other children is systematically reinforced, it will likely generalize to nonreinforced situations. The study also suggests that in ethnically heterogeneous situations wider reinforcement of interactions may have more promise than changing attitudes to promote interactions.

Inappropriate School Bus Behavior

School officials often ask for assistance in altering the inappropriate behavior of students being transported to and from school. During these times many students are at their worst and exhibit behavior that may be disruptive, hurtful, or jeopardizing to the safety of themselves or other students. If these behaviors occur frequently, steps must be taken to modify them.

Axelrod (1977) did a study to determine whether behavioral procedures could be effective in reducing the out-of-seat school bus behavior of fifty students in grades one through eight. Observations of these students revealed a high frequency of shouting, standing on seats, running, and climbing while riding the school bus. Indeed, baseline measures of these inappropriate school bus behaviors indicated a frequency of thirty-four incidents during the first ten minutes of the bus ride home.

To modify the behavior, the students were divided into two groups. Students sitting on one side of the aisle were identified as group 1, and those sitting on the other side as group 2. The students were told that they could receive a candy treat if members of their group left their seats three or fewer times during the ride home. Each group could win, one could win, or neither could win, depending on the behavior of group members. At the end of the bus ride an eighth-grade student distributed candy to the group(s) that met the behavior criteria.

The use of this simple reinforcement procedure resulted in a significant decrease in out-of-seat behavior. Using a variable ratio schedule in the later phases, out-of-seat behavior was ultimately reduced to a mean of 1.8 inappropriate behaviors per day.

One of the authors used a procedure similar to Axelrod's to control disruptive school bus behavior. Bogus money was used instead of candy, and a response-cost procedure was also employed. Students were given two bogus dollars when they entered the school bus. They were told that they would be able to keep the money and exchange it for a reward later if they exhibited desirable school bus behavior. However, each time a student exhibited an inappropriate behavior, he or she was fined a dollar. If a student exhibited two inappropriate behaviors, a fine of two dollars was levied, and the student was not permitted to ride the school bus the next day. The bogus dollars students earned were exchanged for back-up reinforcers once each week.

The system was effective in reducing the frequency of inappropriate behavior. The operation of the system did require the use of an older student to monitor bus behavior and to handle the distribution and withdrawal of the bogus money.

Summary

1. A positive reinforcement system is usually all that is needed to modify most minor classroom problems. Although any of the reinforcement systems discussed may be used, token systems are functional and appealing to children and adolescents.

2. More serious individual learning or behavior problems usually require several simultaneous procedures; positive reinforcement alone is not likely to bring about the desired change. Rather, a system consisting of positive reinforcement, response cost (token fines), and time-out will tend to modify the deviant behavior much more rapidly than any one of the procedures used alone.

3. When classroom problems involve the whole group rather than a few individuals, a total classroom modification system composed of individual reinforcement systems and group contingencies should be implemented. Group contingencies reduce peer reinforcement for deviant behavior and encourage children to monitor their own and their classmates' behavior.

Chapter Nine

Therapeutic Intervention with Child and Adolescent Behavior Problems

In this chapter we will discuss intervention strategies to modify a variety of problem behaviors in children and adolescents. The specific problems often come to the attention of teachers, counselors, and psychologists. They vary in seriousness from a child's refusal to talk to adolescent drug abuse. The proposed interventions are based on the clinical and experimental literature as well as the authors' experience. Because some of the procedures and problems are complex, it is not assumed that by simply reading the material one will be able to utilize the intervention strategies. Hence, some of the procedures should not be used unless the reader has proper training and/or supervision.

Phobic Reactions

Fearful reactions are common in childhood. Certain fears seem to characterize certain ages and are reflections of normal developmental phenomena. For example, very young children often exhibit fearful reactions to loud noises, animals, strange persons, dark rooms, high places, and being left alone (Hurlock, 1964). Many of these fears are transitory and create no real problems. As children get older and recognize that these situations pose no real threat, the fearful reactions disappear.

Some fears persist, however, and greatly affect the child's everyday functioning; when they do, therapeutic intervention is desirable. Early use of conditioning procedures to modify fearful reactions was demonstrated by Jones (1924) many years ago. The child with whom she worked had a phobia of furry animals. Counterconditioning was accomplished by feeding the child near a caged rabbit—at first placed a considerable distance away but gradually brought nearer until the rabbit was placed on the table and later in the child's lap. Deconditioning of the child's fear of the rabbit generalized to other furry objects as well.

Lazarus (1960) used a method not greatly different from that of Jones. He treated an eight-year-old child who had a fear of moving vehicles. The fear, which persisted for two years, was apparently related to a car accident in which the child was involved. Therapy was initiated by talking to the child about motor vehicles other than cars. When the child volunteered any type of positive statement about other vehicles, he was casually offered a piece of chocolate. Lazarus then set up a series of "accidents" with toy cars. After each of the play accidents, the child was given a piece of chocolate. This type of activity continued for some time until Lazarus was able to encourage the child to sit with him in a stationary automobile. At this time, the accident in which the child had been involved was discussed. The child was once again provided with chocolates as the discussion continued. Soon afterward, the child was taken for short rides in the car. On the seventeenth therapy session, the child willingly went for a ride with a stranger and traveled approximately a mile and a half to a store at which the child bought chocolate. According to Lazarus, the child soon began to enjoy car rides without the inducement of chocolate.

It is, of course, not always possible to use the phobic object in a therapy session. If the phobic object is so aversive that the child will not go near it, or if it is highly impractical to deal with the actual phobic object, other methods have to be used.

Lazarus and Abramovitz (1962) attempted to eliminate children's phobias through the use of "emotive imagery." Although this method is similar to that used by Wolpe, his relaxation methods were not used. Their technique involved determining the nature and magnitude of the child's fears and arranging these in a hierarchy. The hierarchy ranged from each child's most to the least feared situations. The clinician then determined who the child's favorite television, movie, and fiction hero images were. When this had been done, the child was asked to close his eyes and to imagine some events which involved his favorite hero. Gradually, the clinician introduced into the story phobic items low in the hierarchy. As each item in the hierarchy was introduced, the child was instructed to raise his finger if he felt any discomfort. At this sign of discomfort, the phobic stimulus was withdrawn temporarily from the story, but later on, of course, was reintroduced. The method was continued until the most feared situation in the hierarchy was tolerated without stress.

Lazarus and Abramovitz (1962) used this method with nine phobic children ranging in age from seven to fourteen years. Seven chil-

dren were considered improved in an average of only 3.3 sessions. Follow-up results indicated that there were no symptom substitutions.

Ritter (1968) used a method of vicarious and contact desensitization in treating snake phobias. In this study, the actual phobic object was present during treatment. Both boys and girls, their ages ranging from five to eleven years, were used as subjects. To determine which children had snake phobias, a snake-avoidance test was used. There were two experimental conditions; in both, the children had two thirty-five-minute treatments. In the *vicarious* desensitization condition, the children who had snake phobias watched their peers and the experimenter pet and play with the snake. The *contact* desensitization treatment was similar to the above condition but also involved having the examiner move around the room making an effort to have children participate with him. The results showed that the contact group had significantly greater reductions in avoidance behavior than did the desensitization group. Both groups showed a significantly larger decrease in avoidance responses than did the control group. Ritter concluded that group contact desensitization is a very useful and inexpensive therapeutic method for eliminating children's phobias of animals.

The severity of the children's phobias in Ritter's study is questionable. The children obviously had some avoidance reactions to the snake. However, it was reported that only one child was afraid to enter the room when the snake was present. Children were also included in the study who were not afraid to briefly touch the snake but were fearful of holding it for five seconds. This leads to the conclusion that the intensity of the phobias was not too great. Perhaps this is why results were obtained in a total of 140 minutes, or two therapy sessions.

Silberman (1972) modified a five-year-old boy's phobic reactions to dogs using procedures similar to Ritter's. The boy's mother reported that he became hysterical when a dog was present. Although the mother could not specifically identify the reason for the child's fear of dogs, she did remember one incident in his history when he was nearly bitten. She had attempted to reassure her son that he need not fear dogs, but the fear continued unabated.

It was suggested that she no longer try to discourage the child's fear, but handle and pet a dog in her child's presence. The child was also told stories that depicted dogs as friendly, lovable creatures and then taken to a room containing small, inexpensive toys ranging in value from six to fifteen cents. The boy was asked to identify which toys he would like to have and told that he would have an opportunity to earn them. He was shown a card with boxes on it and awarded one check mark for listening to the previous stories; when the card was filled with check marks, he would be able to take one of the toys.

At this point, another procedure was implemented. The child was told that a small poodle would be brought into the room, and if he went near the dog he would receive a check mark. With some hesitation, the boy complied and was awarded a check mark. He was then asked to pet the dog, and once again he complied and received a check mark. The child was praised for his behavior. Finally, he was asked to hold the dog, and when he did, he was again praised and awarded a check mark. The small dog was taken from the room.

A second, much larger white dog was brought into the room on a leash. The dog's appearance created considerable fear in the child. He first began to cry and then jumped up on a table. Silberman and another counselor petted the dog for a few seconds. The boy was then shown the check-mark card and reminded of the toys he could earn when the card was filled. A ruler was placed on the floor, ten feet from the dog. The child was told that if he could go to the

ruler and count to three, he would receive another check mark. Courageously, the boy went to the ruler, counted to three and returned to safe territory. Gradually, the ruler was placed closer and closer to the dog, and the child was required to count to a higher number each time he advanced to the ruler. Using this successive approximation procedure and token reinforcement, the child was able to approach the dog. When this step was finally achieved, the therapist began to pet the dog, asked his subject to watch him, and then asked the child to imitate his actions. As he did, he was rewarded with check marks and praise. After forty-five minutes, the session was terminated for that day.

Three days later, the large white dog was once again brought into the room, and the child reacted with little observable fear. He walked up to the dog and began to pet her. The therapist was called out of the room, and the boy was asked to hold the leash. He did so without demonstrating any fear reactions to the dog; it appeared that the child had overcome his fear. However, to make certain, the large white dog was taken out of the room and a boxer was brought in. The child responded with some fear but less intensely than his original reaction to the white dog, and (although the procedures were conducted within a ten-minute period) the boy played nonfearfully with the boxer. Counterconditioning appeared complete. A follow-up interview with the mother eight months later showed that the boy's fear of dogs appeared permanently extinguished. The boy now plays happily with a dog his mother purchased shortly after treatment was concluded.

Wish, Hasazi, and Jurgela (1973) used a variety of procedures to treat an eleven-year-old boy who was intensely afraid of loud sounds. The fear began at age two when he was very frightened by a fireworks display. Over time, the fear generalized to a variety of loud sounds. When the child was in the presence of such stimuli, he would not only attempt to escape or avoid them but often developed a headache or became nauseous.

The treatment of the boy's phobic reactions involved several steps. First, a graded anxiety hierarchy was constructed consisting of sounds that induced various degrees of fear. For example, at the lower end of the hierarchy items like surf noises or the popping of a balloon or cork were included; at the higher end of the hierarchy sounds of thunderstorms and fireworks were included. Second, the boy was trained to relax using systematic relaxation procedures. Third, automated and self-administered counterconditioning procedures were used.

One of the child's favorite music albums was recorded on tape interspersed with items (sounds) from the anxiety hierarchy. Initially, items that induced minimal anxiety were included on the tape. Later, when the child had made appropriate progress, more intense fear-provoking items were included and the volume was increased during the practice sessions. The treatment essentially consisted of having the child listen to the tape three times a day. It was kept playing until he experienced anxiety. As soon as he began to feel tense or anxious, the tape was turned off and the child was instructed to practice relaxation exercises he had been taught by the therapist. Actually, the latter procedure was unnecessary because the child was able to tolerate the anxiety he experienced without turning the tape off.

The counterconditioning procedures proved very effective. In eight days of treatment, the boy appeared to have conquered his fear of loud sounds. Nine months later the child was asked to rate his fear in the presence of previously anxiety-provoking stimuli. His rating suggested that previous anxiety-provoking stimuli were no longer responded to with anxiety. Indeed, the boy was now able to attend fireworks displays and enjoy them.

School Phobia

The symptoms of school phobia are relatively standard. When the child thinks about school or approaches the school grounds, he is overcome with intense anxiety. The child may complain of a headache or nausea or display rapid breathing. He fears that something terrible is going to happen but can rarely verbalize what he actually fears. Reassurance that everything will be all right when he gets to school rarely helps him to deal with the anxiety that he experiences. Although many procedures have been used to deal with the problem, behavior modification methods have demonstrated effectiveness.

Patterson (1965a) worked with a first-grade child who was not only afraid to go to school but was afraid to go outside unless his parents accompanied him. Treatment was implemented using systematic reinforcement. During the first session, the child was given a chocolate drop for each thirty-second interval that he did not watch for his mother. Use of this reinforcement procedure enabled the mother to leave the room and sit outside the closed door after five minutes. The child and the experimenter engaged in doll play. The play was structured so that when the child replied that the boy doll was not afraid of being alone, he was praised and received a chocolate drop. The themes of the feared situations varied from the experimenter's office, going to school, physical injury, peer aggression, playing with other children, and so on, until all important situations were dealt with and appropriate behavior was reinforced. These procedures proved effective, and the child returned to school. The results were achieved in twenty-three twenty-minute sessions with the child, followed by highly structured ten-minute interviews with the parents. It required ten hours of staff time and twenty bags of chocolate drops.

Kennedy (1965) has suggested that school phobia occurs every year in about seventeen cases per thousand of school-age youngsters. He cited the work of Coolidge and the Judge Baker group who found two types of school phobia. The first type was a neurotic crisis, while the second type appeared to be chronic, occurring in families in which one or both parents had serious emotional problems.

Kennedy included in his study only type-one school phobias, involving fifty cases over an eight-year period. The treatment comprised several steps. First, as soon as the problem was identified, parents were encouraged to refer the phobic child on the second or third day after the problem occurred. Second, the parents were requested to handle the child's somatic complaint in a casual manner. Third, the child was forced to attend school and to stay in the classroom. The father was asked to take the child to school; the mother could visit the school if she wished, but could not stay. A structured interview with the parents was the fourth step; the parents were given instructions to follow and received support from the staff. The formula stressed to the parents was that they were not to discuss school attendance with the child, were to be firm, and were to compliment him when he stayed in school. The fifth step was brief counseling with the child after he was in school for a few hours. Interviews with the child used stories that had as their basis the need to go on in the face of fear. Last, a follow-up phone interview with the parents served as both a source for data gathering and prevention of further school phobias. The phone calls were scheduled two weeks after treatment, six weeks later, and then once a year. The results (based on self-report data and follow-up with the school principal) showed that there was no evidence of any recurrence of the phobia or of substitute symptoms in any of the fifty cases.

Kennedy's method basically required parents to ignore all somatic complaints relating to school avoidance and to reinforce through praise the child's staying in school. Kennedy's approach is also interesting in that behavior incompatible with attending school was not allowed to continue and therefore was not able to be reinforced.

Though both studies reported in this section obtained positive results, their differences should be noted by the reader. The child in Patterson's (1965a) study had a more intense school-phobic reaction than seemed to be true of the children in Kennedy's (1965) study. It will be recalled that the child Patterson dealt with was fearful of being without his parents even at home. In severe cases Patterson's elaborate procedures may be necessary, while for less involved cases Kennedy's methods may work more efficiently.

Children Who Will Not Talk

There are children who do not stay away from school as the school-phobic child does but will not verbally communicate with others at school. The child with this problem will talk at home but will not talk with peers or adults at school. Such a child is often found in kindergarten, but many times this problem behavior seems to remediate itself before first grade. Some children maintain their refusal to talk for many years. Despite this, however, they do appear to learn. Teachers report that they will respond to printed material and will occasionally answer "yes" or "no" by shaking their heads or pointing.

Though it is not known why children display this behavior, it is plausible that initially not talking is used either as a defensive mechanism or for manipulation. These children see school as aversive and frightening. By not communicating, they are able to reduce some of their anxiety in the school situation. However, although the anxiety tends to decrease after several months in school, the behavior still persists. It is possible that the behavior persists because both teachers and students tend to reinforce this not talking by giving attention to the child. Also, not talking activates many people to see if the child can be induced to talk, producing more attention for the child.

Two children who had a history of not talking at school were seen by one of the authors. As is typically true, teachers had tried a variety of approaches to stimulate talking. One teacher offered the child five dollars if he would talk to her; another offered the same child a big "all-day sucker"; still another placed the child in a room with his brother and friends, left the room and hoped that he would talk, but monitoring by intercom revealed that this procedure did not produce talking. None of these efforts worked; nor did the parents' threats of punishment.

By the use of appropriate learning-theory principles, both of these children were persuaded to talk with one of the authors during the first session. Since one of the children had not spoken at school for three-and-a-half years, this was notable progress. By the end of the fifth session, both children were talking occasionally to their teachers (who were present from the fourth session on). As a matter of fact, the method ultimately proved so effective that one of the teachers jokingly asked the author if he might reverse the procedures to "shut the child up."

Briefly, the procedures used were as follows. In the first session, both modeling and successive approximation principles were used. As the child entered the room, an empty cup was placed by him and a cup full of candies was placed by the clinician. First telling the child, "Watch me," the clinician moved his mouth in a specific way and asked the child to do the same thing. When the child complied, a candy was placed in his cup. The clinician then opened his mouth wide, and asked the child to do the same. Each time the child complied, he was given a piece of candy. Always modeling the response that the child was asked to imitate, the clinician

also asked the child to pretend to blow out a match and to imitate various sounds. Eventually, the various sounds composing the child's name were sounded out. When this was accomplished, the child's first name was enunciated. As soon as the child had successfully spoken his first name, the same procedures were used to get the child to speak his last name.

In the second session, the same principles used in the first session (modeling and successive approximation) were again employed. The empty cup was once again placed in front of the child, and he was requested to perform the same responses. This required only one-fourth the time it had taken in the first session. The remaining time was spent encouraging the child to imitate one-word responses such as "good," "yes," and "no," and then to repeat three-word sentences. Finally, he was encouraged to speak longer sentences. Although a fixed-ratio reinforcement schedule was used during these two sessions, praise was regularly paired with a candy reinforcer.

In the third session, successive approximation, secondary reinforcers, and variable-interval schedules were employed. When the child entered the room he was told, "Today we are going to do something a little different from what we have done before. I am going to let you earn check marks as well as candy. The check marks can be traded in later for a small toy. You will not always know anymore when you are going to receive the candy and check marks, but every time you receive a piece of candy, it will also count as one check mark. When this card [containing about eighty squares] gets filled, you can trade it in for one of these five trinkets that you see." The child was given his choice of the toy for which he wanted to work.

He was no longer asked only to imitate the word spoken by the clinician. He was first asked his name, then asked to tell his grade level, the name of his school, etc. Each response had to be spontaneous and not motivated by desire to be eligible for the reinforcement. In the beginning, reinforcement was continuous, being given for every alternate appropriate response. Ultimately, he was changed to a variable schedule. When approximately fifty check marks were earned, the session was terminated and the child was told that next time he would be able to complete the card.

In the fourth session, the child's teacher was present, sitting in the corner of the room. The clinician informed the child that he had only thirty spaces left to fill his card in order to get the toy. Since the teacher was present, it was considered advisable to start with the same procedures that were used in the first session. A continuous reinforcement schedule was used. That is, the child was reinforced for every response. After ten check marks and candies were earned, the teacher was requested to move to the table where the child and clinician were working. The clinician then told the child that now only the child's teacher would be able to record the check marks he earned. Many of the procedures employed in the second session were repeated. Just before the child approached his last ten check marks, he was told that the teacher would continue to give him the last ten check marks required to get his toy. In addition, he was asked to do things for her. The teacher, who had been instructed by the clinician before the session began, asked the child to do the things that were requested of him in the first session. As soon as the child acquired his last check mark, he was promptly given the toy he had chosen. A new card was taken out and the child was told that he could continue to earn check marks on the card. At this time, the child was told that the clinician was running out of candy. Consequently, the candy would be discontinued and only check marks would be given. The teacher continued to ask questions and reward the child by a continuous reinforcement schedule.

The fifth session took place after school in the child's classroom. It was hoped that the previous sessions' effects would generalize to the classroom, the teacher, and the child's peers. At the beginning of this session, the child was told how many check marks he had earned previously and was allowed to choose one of five toys. The teacher continued with the same procedures that she had used previously with the child. She attempted to get the child to respond to her without imitation. At this point, a variable-interval schedule was employed. The session was terminated before the child completed his card, the child being informed by the clinician that he would begin to earn check marks in the classroom from his teacher (he would be able to earn up to five in the morning and another five in the afternoon). In order to earn check marks in the classroom, he had to go to the teacher's desk and respond appropriately to her. When the teacher implemented these procedures in the classroom, she was advised not to require the child to respond when his classmates were observing him. However, it was essential to have his classmates present.

When the child had earned ten check marks, the clinician drew up a contract with the child at the end of the day. (The contract method was discussed in an earlier chapter and will be mentioned again in a later section of this chapter.) Basically, the approach required the child to sign his name to the following statement:

I, (name), will earn check marks when I act as a student. A student is one who answers questions when his teachers ask him and one who talks to the other students when they talk to him.

The teacher was advised that if the child responded only to her and not to his classmates, she was to keep him after school with one of his friends. She was to take out her check-mark card without telling the child what she was doing, but making it obvious enough for him to understand. The child received check marks for appropriate responses to questions asked in the presence of his friend. When this was achieved, the teacher had the child's friend ask him questions. As the nontalking child responded, check marks were given. The teacher was told that if difficulties still persisted in the classroom, a few children should be asked to stay after school, and the same procedure should be employed. The use of these procedures in the classroom, in the presence of the teacher and classmates, ensures that the greatest generalization effects will be achieved.

Another type of communication difficulty may be encountered: the child who is very resistant to making appropriate verbal responses. He responds to questions with a "yes" or "no," shrugs his shoulders, or says, "I don't know." A method that creates mild deprivation is applicable to a child like this.

One of the authors employed such a method with a child who resisted talking. During the initial session, the child was given salty peanuts and encouraged to eat them. He was told that he could have as many as he wanted. When the child became satiated with peanuts, he was told that he could earn some soda pop. He was instructed that he could earn twenty checks which could be exchanged for a soda pop. Essentially, to earn a soda pop the child was required to respond to questions to which a short answer was not acceptable. That is, a response of "yes" or "no" did not receive a check mark. However, questions were asked that did not create anxiety. For example, he was asked questions like, "What kinds of things do you like to do?" or "What do you do in your spare time?" Gradually, questions were asked that were more personal and relevant to the verbalizations being sought. He was reinforced for appropriate responses by receiving a check mark and praise. When twenty check marks had been earned, he immediately received a soda pop.

Since this method utilizes the creation of mild deprivation (salty peanuts make one thirsty), there may be some objection to its use. If this approach is not considered desirable, the check marks might be used to earn a small toy. At any rate, in the second session it is advisable to use check marks that can be exchanged for a toy. In later sessions, the reinforcement can be discontinued, and appropriate verbal response can be maintained with praise.

Excessive Worrying and Obsessional Thinking

Occasionally, teachers and psychologists encounter children who worry excessively. With some of these children worrying appears to be a way of life; practically everything they do has an element of apprehension associated with it. Other children tend to be obsessed with a thought or an intensely frightening experience that is difficult to dispel from their minds.

Campbell (1973) treated a twelve-year-old boy who had the unfortunate experience of witnessing the violent death of his sister. Subsequent to his sister's death he continued to recall and/or be obsessed with the terrifying experience. He began to perform poorly in school and had difficulty eating and sleeping.

The boy was treated using a thought-stopping procedure. First, the boy was asked to invoke a negative thought. When the negative thought was clearly in mind, the boy was instructed to count backward aloud, from ten to zero. When he reached zero, he was taught to imagine a very pleasant scene. Once the child had mastered this procedure, he was taught to repeat it with subvocal verbalizations.

The thought-stopping procedure was used for four weeks. Starting with the first week, there was a consistent decrease in the negative thoughts the child experienced. By the end of the fourth week, the child had learned to control and/or rid himself of obsessional thoughts. A follow-up conducted four years later indicated that the positive treatment effects continued and the boy was no longer troubled with obsessional thoughts. Subsequent to treatment, school performance improved and eating and sleeping were no longer problematic.

Systematic reinforcement is sometimes useful in decreasing some children's tendency to worry. This is true largely because worrying may be used to obtain reinforcement or to avoid appropriate task-oriented behavior. With such children a reinforcement procedure can be set up that rewards nonworrying behavior. For example, a child can be told that his tendency to worry not only makes him unhappy but greatly interferes with a number of things he can enjoy. It is explained to the child that the mind is like a TV with several channels. We can use a dial to change the channel and reprogram our thoughts. We are often able to control our thoughts if we make a conscious effort to do so.

A program is then set up which reinforces a child for decreasing the number of worries he reports. Also, to encourage problem solving rather than worrying, the child is told that he will be rewarded for any solution he has worked out that relates to the problem(s) he worries about. Such a procedure helps to decrease the child's unproductive rumination and encourages a more active mastery of events over which control is possible. Of course, it should be recognized that a child's worrying may be symptomatic of a more important problem. If such is the case, the main or high priority problem should be the first object of intervention. Resolution of the main problem may do much to reduce the child's worries.

Stuttering

Stuttering is a condition characterized by spasmodic blocking and repetition of initial sounds of words. In milder cases, stuttering may involve a few words that require great effort to articulate. In more severe cases, blocking occurs with most sounds and may be accompanied by grimacing and other body contortions. Stuttering rarely occurs when an individual is alone and most often appears in anxiety-provoking situations. These observations have led some authorities to conclude that stuttering appears to be reinforced by the anxiety-reduction that occurs when verbalizations are completed. Hence, learning theorists have suggested that stuttering may be reduced by making anxiety-reduction contingent on nonstuttering rather than stuttering (Browning, 1967).

Flanagan, Goldiamond, and Azrin (1958) demonstrated that the degree of stuttering can be increased or decreased. Using a noxious stimulus, they attempted two different experimental conditions. In the first, a noxious stimulus was presented and could only be terminated when stuttering occurred. In this experimental condition, the stuttering increased. In the second condition, the noxious stimulus was presented only when stuttering occurred; stuttering decreased.

The study suggests that certain elements in a child's environment can affect his speech difficulties. For example, Flanagan et al. indicate that the child's mother may become attentive when he is stuttering and thereby reinforce it. If the mother at first decides to ignore the child when he stutters, but later on, when the usual burst of stuttering occurs, she observes that the child's stuttering is increasing (this frequently happens during the onset of extinction), her anxiety tends to increase, which may cause her to again pay attention to the child. When she behaves in this way, she is reinforcing the child on a variable-interval schedule. Extinction is difficult to achieve.

Browning (1967) treated stuttering in a very practical way. Although the child with whom he worked was schizophrenic, his methods can easily be applied to "normal" children. Browning first had an assistant obtain a baseline rate of the percentage of words emitted that contained speech errors. After this baseline rate was obtained, he trained the child to relax with procedures similar to Wolpe's. The child was subsequently brought to his office for ten-minute daily sessions for a total of eight days. While the child was in his office, he was not permitted to speak; if he wanted to talk to the therapist, he was told that he would have to go into the hall. This prevented the development of an association between stuttering and the therapist's office. Relaxation training was used to instigate a counterresponse that could be used to reduce the anxiety that was associated with stuttering.

At this point, procedures were employed to help the child successively approximate normal speech. This phase lasted thirty-five days. At first, the child silently rehearsed each word before saying it aloud. Gradually, as the sessions progressed, the number of words used in a sentence was increased; then the number of sentences was increased. Up to this point, all words or sentences were preceded by a silent rehearsal. Eventually, spontaneous conversation was attempted. Correct speech was rewarded with marbles that could be traded in for toys; praise was paired with the marbles.

During each of the sessions, relaxation periods were followed by correct speech in order to associate anxiety reduction with errorless performance. At first, the therapist directed the child to engage in relaxation, but eventually the child himself initiated the relaxation response. To develop self-control of speech errors, the child was taught to stop speaking when speech errors might come about, relax, and then to successfully complete what he was about to say. Once the child was able to speak without errors, the training sessions were conducted in various settings so that the treatment effects would generalize.

Later stages involved the staff of the treatment center in which the child resided. The staff members were instructed not to respond to the child if he made a speech error, but as soon as the child repeated his statement correctly without stuttering, they were to praise him. However, at times it was also necessary for the staff to help the child discriminate when he was stuttering by turning their heads slightly. Sometimes they told him that he should try again to say what he was going to say. Because the staff acted as social reinforcers for the correct speech of the child, it was eventually no longer necessary for the child to see the therapist.

Browning (1967) indicates that his procedures can be used in a clinical setting or by parents to help the child extinguish his stuttering responses. What Browning claims to do is first to make the response of correct speech available to the child. He then creates greater conflict in the child for stuttering by not responding to him when he stutters and giving an appropriate response when he speaks correctly. This procedure changes the speaking contingencies. That is, stuttering, which was earlier reinforced because anxiety was reduced when the child was finished speaking, now can only be reduced when correct verbalization is completed. Browning wisely cautions that the approach can only be used if the child is able to speak correctly. If the child did not have correct speech available to him, this would, of course, result in increased anxiety and the method would be ineffective.

Martin, Kuhl, and Haroldson (1972) used a puppet and a novel time-out procedure to treat two child stutterers. The first child treated was three and a half years old and stuttered severely. During the first three twenty-minute sessions the child sat in front of a puppet stage and talked with a puppet. The female experimenter operated the puppet. In the fourth session each time the child stuttered the stage lights were turned off and the puppet remained silent until the lights came on. During the initial sessions (fourth through the sixteenth), the time-out procedure was used whenever the child stuttered for two seconds. Beginning with the seventeenth and continuing through the thirty-first, the time-out procedure was used anytime stuttering occurred. The last ten sessions were used as an extinction period and the time-out procedure was not used.

The treatment proved very effective. The stuttering was reduced to near zero during the last treatment session. The rate of stuttering remained low during the extinction period and the treatment effects generalized to situations outside the experimental room.

A four-and-a-half-year-old child was also treated using similar procedures. However, since this child had a less severe stuttering problem, he had approximately half the number of treatment sessions. The treatment proved equally positive for this child. There was a marked decrease in stuttering, and treatment effects generalized to both home and school. This study, as well as the others reported in this section, shows that systematic reinforcement and mild punishment can be useful in altering the frequency of stuttering.

Excessive Fantasy and Bizarre Talking

Everyone engages in daydreaming and fantasy. It is typically employed to gain momentary refuge from the demands of reality or to mobilize one's resources to solve problems. As such, fantasy is normal and may even help the person to better cope with day-to-day demands. However, when daydreaming or fantasy is excessive or is substituted for reality, it is nonproductive (Coleman, 1976).

Bijou (1966) has discussed the case of a four-year-old boy who exhibited excessive fantasy behavior. The procedures used to change the behavior were rather simple, but highly effective. First, a baseline record was kept on the child's fantasy for a nineteen-day period. During this time, the child was responded to in nursery school in the usual manner. That is, teachers participated in the child's fantasy play and restrained him only if it appeared that he might hurt other children; he received attention and understanding when it appeared desirable. The experimental period was begun on the twentieth day. The teachers were then instructed to attend to the child only when he engaged in appropriate play and not when he exhibited fantasy behavior. The result was a gradual decrease in the amount of fantasy behavior and an increase in appropriate play.

A method that combines both secondary reinforcement and modeling was used by one of the authors to treat a kindergarten child who expressed a good deal of bizarre talk—nonsense words, repetitive phrases, inappropriate singing, and verbalized sexual thoughts. After the third week of individual-play therapy sessions, another child, a few years older, was introduced. Prior to entering the sessions she was instructed to ignore all "silly" talk of the younger child and to listen when she was not talking "silly." The psychologist and the older child role played some typical verbalizations that the younger child might express in order to train and desensitize her to the comments that the younger child might make. In the subsequent play therapy sessions, the psychologist attended to the model for appropriate talk and would make comments like, "Caryn talks so nicely, I like to listen to Caryn talk, I can always understand what Caryn is talking about," etc. When the younger child talked appropriately, both the model and the psychologist would pay attention.

A basic approach in handling bizarre talk or fantasy behavior is to simply ignore the inappropriate behavior and attend to or reinforce the appropriate behavior. In the example above, modeling was also employed. Models can produce even better results if they are reinforced for appropriate talking.

In some instances, bizarre talk can be unknowingly increased. One of the authors saw this occur among a well-meaning group of psychology students working in a state hospital. A few of the students became very interested in a newly admitted child who exhibited a good deal of inappropriate talk. In an attempt to figure out the meaning behind the bizarre terms the child was using, the child received considerable attention. The child's bizarre talking rapidly increased. Apparently, the good intentions and the increased attention of the students acted to reinforce the bizarre talking.

Urination and Defecation Problems

Psychologists and counselors are often asked to assist youngsters who have various urination or defecation problems. Some parents seek help for mentally retarded children who have never been completely toilet trained. A greater number refer children who were once successfully trained but develop problems at a later time. Although psychological factors are often responsible for such relapses, a physician should evaluate the difficulty before psychological treatment is implemented.

Various apparatus have been used to modify urination and defecation problems. Lovibond (1963) has described equipment that may be used with enuresis, and Quarti and Renaud (1964) have discussed apparatus used with defecation problems. Results on this equipment are contradictory. Turner, Young, and Rachman (1970) concluded from their study of 115 children that conditioning apparatus often ended in high relapse rates. Other investigators, such as DeLeon and Mandell (1966), concluded that the bed-buzzer apparatus may be more effective with enuresis than other types of treatment.

In toilet training normal and retarded children, mechanical apparatus have been quite effective. Mahoney, Van Wagenen, and Meyerson (1971) demonstrated the use of auditory signals and systematic reinforcement in toilet training normal infants eighteen to twenty-one months of age and retarded children.

The apparatus consisted of a modified model of the signal-generator-urinal pants (Mark II Toilet Trainer) which activates an auditory signal when urination occurs. The signal-generator-urinal pants were connected to a miniature radio receiver which could be used to activate an auditory signal at any time. In addition, earphones were also attached to the apparatus and worn by both child and experimenter so each could hear the activated auditory signal.

To teach the subjects a chain of operant behaviors required for proper elimination (walking to the toilet, lowering the underclothes, sitting on or facing the toilet, urinating or defecating, and pulling up their clothes), the experimenter used auditory, physical, and verbal prompts. Toys were placed near the lavatory entrance, and the experimenter activated an auditory signal and instructed the child by saying, "Let's go potty." When all of the behaviors were performed with reasonable effectiveness, the verbal and physical prompts were faded out and only the auditory signal was used. Performance of the desired behaviors was reinforced with consumables and verbal praise. In the final phases, the experimenter-initiated auditory signals are faded out and only activated by the child's urination. Finally, when all operant steps have been appropriately learned and the child is responding correctly to physiological cues of a full bladder, the auditory signal is phased out completely.

The procedure appears highly effective. Of the eight children studied, seven were successfully toilet trained. The only exception was a profoundly retarded child.

More recently Mahoney (1978) has eliminated the use of the radio transmitter and receiver in his procedure. The signal generator has been miniaturized and named the "Potty Pager." This moisture sensor measures approximately $1\frac{1}{2}'' \times 2'' \times \frac{5}{8}''$ and weighs less than an ounce. The trainee wears the pager on his waistband. Leading from the device around the outside of his pants is a ¾-inch strip of clear, pressure-sensitive tape. Two thin layers of copper foil run the length of the tape. The foil in the tape is attached to contact points on the pager. The tape runs from the waistband in the back around the crotch to the waistband in the front. When the trainee wets the tape, a circuit is completed causing the pager to beep.

Systematic reinforcement without mechanical apparatus has also been effective in toilet training. For example, Madsen (1965) has shown the utility of positive reinforcement. Though the procedures he used were employed with a nineteen-month-old child, they can readily be used with older children experiencing elimination difficulties at school. Madsen's method required that a child be given a candy reward whenever successful elimination occurred. No pressure was placed on the child and she was permitted to leave the toilet when she desired. The child was told that she would be given candy when she eliminated in the toilet. Candy and praise were given for either urination or defecation. Once the child had eliminated in the toilet several days, she was encouraged to tell her parents when she had to eliminate. Eventually the child was reinforced only if she requested to be placed on the toilet.

This method can be adapted with children at school. However, as Madsen (1965) has pointed out, there must be a physiological readiness as a necessary condition for training. If this method is used at school, the child with the difficulty should be sent frequently to the nurse's office. Upon urination or defecation in the toilet, the child should be rewarded with candy. Since it is impractical in a school situation to entertain the child while he is sitting on the toilet, the child may be permitted to read comic books. Gradually, the frequency with which the child is requested to use the toilet is decreased. That is, at first he may be requested to go every half hour, then every forty-five minutes, etc., until the interval is appropriate. When these results have been achieved, the child can be told that he can decide when he wishes to go to the toilet. He should be rewarded every time he eliminates successfully in a toilet.

For working with more severe cases, Neale (1963) has suggested a similar procedure. He worked with children exhibiting encopresis, or involuntary defecation. In all of the cases the children were previously trained, but, as Neale postulates, anxiety had become associated for various reasons with the child's inability to defecate in a toilet. (Neale emphasizes the need for an accurate medical diagnosis to determine the presence of physiological causes before any techniques are applied. This practice is also very desirable in cases of enuresis.)

Since the children treated were in a residential treatment center, it was possible to take the children to the toilet after each meal and at bedtime. Some of the children were provided with candy and comic books to read while sitting on the toilet. These measures were used to inhibit anxiety reactions that had become associated with the toilet. To assist in the treatment of two cases, certain foods were given that provided additional bulk for the colon to work and to ensure that the stools would not be painful to pass. When each of the children successfully eliminated in the toilet, he was rewarded. Rewards consisted of either candy, stars in a book, pennies, etc. Reinforcements were changed when it was felt that the child was getting bored or satiated. Neale believed that the most powerful rewards the child obtained were approval from the nurse and the child's own knowledge of his improvement.

Once the child was no longer soiling, the four-times-a-day routine was abandoned and the child was instructed to eliminate whenever he felt the sensation or need to. When the child reported a successful result, he was reinforced. If the child soiled his pants, clean ones were provided without any comment. This was desirable because often the child who soils has received much punishment.

Sometimes medical treatment along with behavioral methods might be employed. Lal and Lindsley (1968) cite an example where both were used. They were concerned with reducing constipation in a three-year-old boy who as an infant had had severe diarrhea. After the diarrhea had been treated for about three months, the child became afflicted with constipation and was able to defecate only if a drug was administered. Under Lal and Lindsley's treatment, in order to elicit a bowel movement, a suppository prescribed by the child's physician was used, but was needed only once during the treatment. Once the child defecated, the behavioral procedures were employed by the child's mother; playing in the bathtub and parental praise were used as reinforcers. The mother was instructed to hug or praise the child if he defecated in the toilet and to leave the bathroom immediately if he did not defecate while sitting on the toilet. She reported that soon after the reward system was begun, the child would ask to be placed on the toilet. In the beginning the child spent about two hours on the toilet, but this was slowly reduced to fifteen minutes. Also, the use of the bath as an immediate reinforcer was phased out. The results, confirmed by a follow-up eight months later, showed that once the behavioral methods were begun, the child did not have constipation difficulties.

Still another treatment approach in dealing with a child's elimination difficulties was described by Peterson and London (1965). At the time the child, three years four months old, was referred, he had not defecated in a toilet for more than three months, and while he was defecating he would hide. Since the child experienced pain when defecating, not eliminating was negatively reinforced.

The treatment was conducted over an eight-day period. Two types of reinforcers were used. Popsicles were used as primary reinforcers and parent praise as secondary reinforcers.

During the first session, the therapist attempted to hypnotize the child but was unsuccessful. However, the therapist continued in a somewhat hypnotic fashion to deal with the child's problem. Lying the child on a couch and beginning to stroke his forehead, the therapist told the child that he knew he did not like to go to the "potty," but that his parents very much desired him to. The child was told that he would subsequently do it and feel good when he eliminated. Arriving home after the first session, the child went with his mother to the toilet and eliminated. Both the praise and the popsicles were given. In the second session, similar somewhat hypnotic suggestions were used. The parents were instructed not to make any comments about the sessions. For the next four days, the child successfully defecated in the toilet. In the final session, five days later, when the therapist congratulated the child on his success and asked him if it felt good when he went to the bathroom, the child answered affirmatively. Asked if he intended to go regularly and not have any more trouble, he again answered positively. These suggestions were repeated several times in a hypnotic fashion. In addition, the therapist lavished praise on the child for his good behavior and emphasized the happiness that characterized the child's home. One year after the treatment was terminated, follow-up revealed complete remission of symptoms.

All of these procedures for treatment of elimination problems focus on the positive rather than the negative behaviors. This focus is especially desirable with defecation and urination difficulties, because the child may have previously associated anxiety with the toilet. In most of the studies reported above, candy, stars in a book, popsicles, taking a bath, etc., were paired with praise. In severe cases, some physiological methods were employed (e.g., limiting the diet or the use of suppositories). Parents who were requested to implement the behavioral methods were able to do so. These methods seem to further show that elaborate equipment does not have to be used to obtain results. With parental cooperation and the skillful application of learning-theory principles, success can be achieved in many cases.

Timid and Unassertive Behavior

Unlike a child with any of the behaviors mentioned above, the shy, withdrawn child has been viewed by educators as having few serious difficulties. This was originally shown by Wickman (1928) when he reported a negative statistical correlation between the respective judgments of teachers and clinicians toward behavior problems. Since that time, however, educators have become more aware that withdrawn behavior can be a real handicap to a child (Schrupp and Gjerde, 1953). Consequently, when it appears in a classroom or in clinic situations, it is usually desirable to encourage more spontaneous, outgoing behavior.

Timidity and unassertiveness, like aggressiveness, are learned behaviors and can be modified like any other operant response. The situations in which a child is unassertive must be identified, the desired response must be clearly specified, and approximations of that response must be systematically reinforced.

Once the desired assertive response(s) has been clearly specified, prompting and role playing are used to encourage the performance of the assertive response. A situation in which the child has difficulty being assertive is first modeled by the therapist, and the child is asked to imitate the modeled response. As the child imitates the modeled behavior, the therapist verbally reinforces the correctly performed responses. The therapist also specifies aspects of the performance that need to be improved and gives suggestions that will help the child perform the behavior in an appropriate way. Each element of the situation is role played until the child has mastered all of the component verbal and nonverbal behaviors. When the child is able to perform the desired assertive behaviors in the accepting atmosphere of the therapist's office, the child is encouraged to try out the assertive behaviors in a real-life situation. Usually a situation is identified in which the newly acquired assertive skills are likely to meet with success. Subsequently, other situations in which the child experiences difficulty are modeled and role played until the assertive skills are mastered and can be transferred to the environment.

A study by Bower, Amatea, and Anderson (1976) illustrates how group assertive training is used to modify unassertive behavior in children. They selected nonassertive nine- and ten-year-old girls to participate in eleven group training sessions. In the first session, the children were introduced and the distinctions between passivity, aggressiveness, and assertiveness were defined. To illustrate the differences, each of the behaviors was role played by the group leader. In the second and third sessions, the girls were asked to complete a large chart that identified characteristics of the three types of response. The group members were also asked questions to elicit how they felt when they acted passively, aggressively, and assertively.

In the fourth session, group members role played—with the leader or another group member—a situation in which they had to act assertively. After the role playing, the leader asked questions that specified aspects of assertiveness (e.g., eye contact, tone of voice, gestures, and verbalizations) that were considered desirable to learn. The leader also reinforced aspects of the role playing that were performed well.

The fifth session was similar to the fourth. Group members role played, appropriate performances were reinforced, and feedback was provided to identify responses that needed to be changed. In addition, the role playing was videotaped and subsequently replayed for corrective feedback.

During the next four sessions the group members were asked to discuss specific situations in which they had difficulty being assertive. These situations were role played, and improved ways of responding were suggested. Group members were also encouraged to try out newly learned assertive skills in real-life situations. To ensure some degree of success, teachers and parents were contacted to inform them of the type of assertive behaviors group members would be practicing.

The final session was devoted to a review of what had occurred in the training sessions. The group members discussed what they had learned, consolidated their gains, and considered how newly learned skills might be used subsequently.

No statistical analysis is reported regarding outcomes, but teachers were asked to rate group members' assertiveness and the children were asked to rate their assertiveness. Both teacher and group member ratings indicated a decrease in passiveness and increased assertiveness.

Excessive Crying

Most of us know children who cry habitually in mildly frustrating or provocative situations. These children have learned to cry as a means of gaining attention, escaping situational demands, or manipulating others to "run interference" for

them. Crying for such purposes is obviously not adaptive and often alienates the child's peers. It is usually desirable to modify it.

Hart, Allen, Buell, Harris, and Wolf (1964) studied two boys in a preschool setting who cried excessively. Since they considered the crying to be operant in type, they used operant conditioning techniques (reinforcement and extinction) to reduce inappropriate crying. Teachers were instructed to ignore the child when inappropriate crying occurred and to utilize reinforcement each time he responded appropriately to a painful situation. Teacher attention and approval (secondary reinforcers) were employed. The results indicated that within five days after the treatment procedures were introduced, both children had a maximum of two crying incidents each day. Since the baseline rate (pretreatment crying) was approximately five to ten episodes per day, treatment appeared to be effective.

As is typical in many studies, the procedures were reversed. When they were reinstated, successive approximation was also employed. Teachers were told to gradually reinforce only verbal responses to painful situations rather than crying. Eventually, even verbal responses were differentially reinforced. That is, only certain types of verbal responses (those more socially acceptable) were reinforced. Only when the child responded in this predetermined appropriate verbal manner did the teacher use reinforcement. In both cases, crying was almost eliminated. However, in one of the cases, the teacher unknowingly reinforced the child on an intermittent basis for crying behavior when she thought it was eliminated. This resulted in the crying behavior being resistant to extinction, but it was eventually modified.

One of the authors has used a modified form of time-out to reduce the frequency of inappropriate crying. The child who cries excessively is simply informed that she may cry as much as she likes but it must be done in a "crying chair." The crying chair is placed in an isolated corner of the room away from the immediate notice of the teacher and other children. The child is told that she may return to the group when crying has ceased. If the child complains that she has a problem that she wants to talk about, the child is told that when the crying stops, time will be made available to discuss the problem. When the crying has terminated and the child has remained quiet for a brief period, she is asked to rejoin the group.

With adolescents, a slightly different approach may be used to deal with inappropriate crying. Instead of a time-out or crying chair arrangement, crying behavior is simply not reinforced. It is explained to the adolescent that it is very difficult to understand or communicate with them while they are crying; so, when they have regained their composure and have stopped crying, conversation will be resumed.

It goes without saying that these procedures should not be used indiscriminantly. When excessive crying is a manifestation of a more serious problem, careful analysis should proceed any intervention. Also, when excessive crying is an expression of real hurt or grief, it is often desirable to provide an opportunity to express it.

Inappropriate Sexual Behavior

Striking changes in attitudes regarding human sexuality have occurred within the last ten years. "Proper" sexual behavior has been redefined, and premarital sexual activity has greatly increased. Although these changes are most clearly reflected in young adult populations, they are also apparent in high school and adolescent age groups. Premarital pregnancy and venereal disease are no longer infrequent occurrences.

Many schools have developed sex education programs that are helpful in promoting appro-

priate heterosexual relationships and likely serve a very important preventative role. When these programs are not an integral part of the curriculum and adolescents are exhibiting inappropriate sexual behavior (either by word or action), encouraging these individuals to research and write papers on human sexual behavior may often prove corrective. For example, when adolescents systematically survey the incidence of unwanted pregnancies, the failure rates of adolescent marriages with unwanted pregnancies, or the effects of venereal disease, changes in behavior and attitudes can be effected.

Liberalized sex attitudes and increased sexual themes in the media appear to have heightened the interest of elementary school children. Teachers frequently request assistance from counselors and psychologists to modify their inappropriate "sex talk," sexual gestures, or simulated sexual activity. Several behavior modification procedures can be used to alter these behaviors. The authors have found that the use of positive reinforcement, response cost, and time-out procedures often prove effective. For example, when parents have been made aware of the problem, they inform the child that a system will be implemented to help him exhibit more appropriate social behavior. Appropriate and inappropriate social behavior are specified and the child is systematically reinforced for exhibiting nonsexual talk or behavior. Response cost (fines or time-out) is used to decrease the undesirable behavior. If such procedures are not effective, the child is asked to phone his mother or father and describe the undesirable behavior on its next occurrence. This latter procedure should be used cautiously, particularly if the child becomes excessively upset when making the phone call.

Silberman worked with a fourteen-year-old girl who participated in frequent sexual intercourse with teenage boys and exhibited many other problem behaviors. An interview with the girl revealed that she did not obtain sexual pleasure from the activity but did get a great deal of attention from boys. For example, at one party the girl reported involving herself in a game called "train," which consisted of successive sexual relationships with each boy at the party. The girl did not feel that the sexual activity was wrong because she had been "very careful." The girl apparently assumed that submitting herself to these activities enhanced her popularity and did not damage her reputation.

Because the girl was seen in a clinic setting and it was believed that her sexual behavior was motivated primarily by male approval, she was asked if she would like to receive honest adolescent feedback on her behavior. She agreed, and a small group of high school adolescents who attended different schools, but were receiving group counseling, were brought into the sessions. Prior parent consent was secured, and the adolescent boys were coached to express their reactions to the girl's sexual activity honestly but not hurtfully. At the first session, the girl was asked to discuss her sexual attitudes and values, which led her into a discussion of her sexual behavior. When she concluded, the other students were invited to respond. In essence, the high school seniors suggested that her sexual behavior probably brought her negative attention, that boys rarely cared about but simply used "free" girls for their own satisfaction. The seniors pointed out to her that these girls were the objects of jokes and were generally demeaned by both boys and girls. They also suggested ways toward more meaningful relationships with both male and female peers. The therapist asked them to discuss how sexual invitations from boys could be gracefully refused and encouraged the girl to discuss the situations or events that usually preceded her involvement in sexual behavior. Apparently, parties where alcohol and drugs were used frequently preceded the girl's sexual behavior.

After three sessions, the girl was asked to choose one of the group's female members who

she felt understood her problem and whom she would like to know better. The two girls were asked to meet three times a week. The fourteen-year-old was also asked to call the "new friend" when she felt an urge to involve herself in sexual activity. The older girl, who served as a counselor aide, talked with her frequently and always left a telephone number where she could be reached on weekends. This relationship continued for approximately a month. At this point the "counseling" relationship between the two girls was terminated with considerable change in the fourteen-year-old's problem behavior.

This case points out some important considerations. Honest, straight, nonmoralistic, constructive peer feedback can be very helpful in modifying the behavior of adolescents. With a little counselor-aide training, adolescents can play important therapeutic roles with peers, and the therapeutic effects are not one-sided; often as much positive change occurs in the counselor as in the counseled. Adolescents may have more potential reinforcement property for their peers than adults and may be quite effective in therapeutic situations.

The procedures used with the adolescent girl should be implemented cautiously. It is important to safeguard the confidentiality of the client and to secure proper consent from all parties involved.

Aggressive Behavior

Teachers are probably more concerned about aggressive behavior than any other form of behavior, because it disrupts ongoing classroom activities and often evokes counteraggression. If teachers allow aggressive acts to continue, they are likely to be modeled by others.

Those working with aggressive children have often assumed that the desirable therapeutic method is to encourage catharsis. That is, if a child releases some of his anger, he will have less need to be aggressive. There are some, however, who are beginning to question this view. For example, Nighswander and Mayer (1969) question the validity of catharsis in reducing aggressive behavior in elementary-school-age children and maintain that catharsis may increase aggressive behavior.

It is possible that if aggression increases when catharsis is permitted, it results from the fact that children have not been taught to discriminate when it is an appropriate response. Some children need help in being able to understand events that elicit anger. When they do, there tends to be a decrease in aggressive behavior (Mallick and McCandless, 1966).

Obviously, children need to learn when aggression is adaptive and when it leads to punishment or negative consequences. Bandura (1967) cited the work of Chittenden, who attempted to teach domineering and hyperaggressive preschool children alternative solutions to conflicts that they might encounter. The children observed various scenes in which dolls reacted to a frustrating situation. The dolls first expressed aggressive reactions and then they expressed cooperative reactions. The results of the aggressive actions which the dolls exhibited were unpleasant, while the cooperative reactions were shown to be rewarding. The children who observed the actions of the dolls showed a decrease in aggressive and domineering behavior as compared with a similar group of children who received no treatment.

Gittelman (1965) has used procedures with older children that produced results similar to those achieved by Chittenden with preschoolers. Gittelman asked the children he worked with to note situations in which aggressive behavior resulted in negative consequences. Situations invoking aggressive behavior were listed in an intensity hierarchy from mild to severe. Groups of children were formed, and each member acted out these situations beginning with the least severe and moving toward those

which provoked more intense anger. As each situation was role played, more effective ways of dealing with anger were learned.

In more severe cases of aggressive behavior, where self-control is minimal, various approaches have been attempted. Graziano and Kean (1968) taught psychotic children muscular relaxation with a resulting decrease in aggressive outbursts. When aggressive behavior is self-directed, positive reinforcement (Peterson and Peterson, 1968), time-out (Wolf, Risley, and Mees, 1964), and electric shock (Tate and Baroff, 1966; Lovaas, Freitag, Gold, and Kassorla, 1965) have been used to control the behavior.

The authors have successfully used a method to deal with aggressive behavior typically found in the schools. The approach is in part based upon the work of Keirsey (1965). The persons most involved with the child (parents, teacher, and counselor) identify one or two of the most severe behaviors that the child exhibits (i.e., hitting other children, throwing things, making loud noises, etc.). A frequency count is kept to determine the frequency of the behavior. A contract with the child regarding that behavior is drawn up. In it, the most reasonable time period that the child can control his behavior is stated. The behavior and time interval is listed on a written contract in the following manner:

I, Tommy Adams, agree that I will try not to get into fights or hit. When I do not hit or fight with other children for a half hour, I will receive one check mark. If I should happen to lose control and hit or fight, a check mark will be taken away. When I have received twelve check marks, I may choose a candy bar or small toy. However, if four or more check marks are taken away, I will give up watching television for that day.

The contract is signed by all parties involved (teacher, parents, child, and counselor). Note that the withdrawn privilege must be something that the child likes doing, and it should be withdrawn for a maximum time of one day. Both parents and the teacher must agree to give check marks according to the terms of the contract. All other behavior should be handled in the usual way, and should not interfere with the behavior or behaviors specified in the contract. That is, if the child receives points or checks for not hitting, they should not be removed because he was verbally aggressive, rude, uncooperative, etc. As the child is able to control his behavior for the stated period of time, the length of the interval should be increased.

One of the important values of this approach is that children receive recognition for desirable behavior. As soon as the child's behavior begins to improve, adults working with the child should use secondary reinforcement (praise) to further enhance the child's satisfaction in controlling himself. As a matter of fact, the authors occasionally find children who will indicate that they no longer need the check marks. They are able to control the behavior by themselves.

Response cost and time-out can also be used to reduce the frequency of aggressive behavior. One of the authors worked with a preschool child who hit, spit, or cursed approximately ten times each morning. The child's teachers observed that he wanted peer approval but had not learned the appropriate behavior to secure it. To reduce the frequency of these aggressive behaviors, a time-out chair was used. Each time the child exhibited one of the three behaviors, he was required to sit in the time-out chair for ten minutes. If he resisted, he was held firmly in the chair.

A response-cost procedure was also used. Each morning the child was given ten chips deposited in a plastic bottle. Each time he hit, spit, or cursed, he was placed in the time-out chair and one chip was withdrawn from the bottle. The chips remaining in the bottle were counted at the end of the morning, and a piece of candy was awarded for each chip. He was allowed to eat one piece of candy himself and to share the rest with other children he selected.

The child's aggressive behavior decreased dramatically. At the end of the morning, the child frequently had ten chips left in the bottle. Friendships with other children developed, and he learned behavior that enhanced his peer acceptability.

Response-cost procedures have similar applicability to adolescent behavior problems. For example, the teacher first specifies and takes a frequency count of the inappropriate behavior. The adolescent starts the day with a certain number of points, and each time an undesirable behavior occurs, one point is subtracted from the total. At the end of the day, the remaining points are exchanged for special privileges. If the adolescent's parents are willing to cooperate in the plan, the points are also exchanged for privileges at home, such as taking driving lessons, using the family car, staying out late on weekends, or using the telephone. This system not only decreases the adolescent's undesirable school behavior but may also decrease conflicts between parents and adolescents at home.

One of the more intriguing approaches to the treatment of anger and hostility is reported by Novaco (1975). He worked with thirty-four clients ranging in age from seventeen to forty-two who had serious problems controlling their anger. Some of the clients had assaulted others, destroyed property, and performed other highly aggressive acts.

In a group setting, each client was asked to describe the nature, duration, and severity of their problems managing anger. The clients were then asked to identify and/or determine the provocation that generated the anger and the kinds of thoughts and feelings that preceded or accompanied the anger. To help the clients relive the sequence of events leading to the experienced anger, the clients were asked to close their eyes and recount the provocations, thoughts, and feelings that occurred.

Once the clients were aware of the sequence of events that appeared to lead to anger, Novaco suggested to them that their anger was primarily a result of the thoughts and self-statements they uttered to themselves in provocative situations. That is, in a provocative situation the interpretation of it leads to self-statements that may overemphasize the degree of threat or the damage to self-esteem. These self-statements or attributions trigger the anger or the aggressive reaction. For example, the individual might say to himself, "He thinks I'm a pushover; I'll show him," or "Who the hell does he think he is; he can't do that to me!" Interpreting the provocation in this sort of way not only generates an emotional response but is likely to serve as a stimulus to act in an aggressive manner.

In addition to the educational procedures described above, the treatment procedures contained three other major features. First, clients were taught relaxation skills to enable them to identify and control emotional arousal. Second, the clients were given cognitive training that enabled them to (1) identify and/or specify anger-related self-statements, (2) make a situational analysis of situations provoking anger, and (3) arrange these situations in hierarchical order from least to most provocative. Third, the clients cognitively rehearsed more positive ways of coping with identified provocative situations. The clients not only learned more appropriate self-statements but were also taught to discriminate situations that in fact offered some potential threat.

Treatment effects were subsequently analyzed using client self-reports, daily diaries, and physiological measures obtained during simulated provocative laboratory exercises. Analysis of results revealed that the treatment was effective in modifying anger. Also, the combination of relaxation and self-instructions was much more effective than either one alone in learning to control or manage anger.

In a study not greatly dissimilar to the one reported above, Goodman and Mahoney (1975) demonstrated that modeling and self-instruction have considerable utility in decreasing aggression in children. Three aggressive and disruptive boys were subjected to a verbal taunting game. Each subject was stationed in the inner of two concentric circles while they were taunted by others. The taunters were instructed to make the subjects "lose their cool" in a two-minute period. The taunters were allowed to use any words or gestures they wanted that might cause the subjects to lose their temper. However, the taunters were required to stay in the outer circle and were not permitted to touch or spit on the subjects. Tokens were awarded if the taunters succeeded in getting the subjects angry.

The subjects were told that the other children were going to try to arouse their anger, but they would not be permitted to touch or spit on them. The subjects were also informed that they could respond to the taunts in any way they wanted as long as they stayed in the inner circle. If the subjects felt the need to terminate the taunts, they simply had to turn on a flashlight which served as a signal to stop.

Two modeling sessions with the subjects were conducted subsequently. The modeling procedure consisted of having the subjects view a video tape of a nine-year-old male being taunted but maintaining his composure by the use of covert coping self-statements. The following week the video tape was again presented to the subjects, and the thoughts and actions of the model were discussed with them. The covert self-statements were emphasized as desirable coping responses. Also, each subject was asked to repeat as many coping statements as was possible to recall. A week later another taunting session was held.

Analysis of treatment effects revealed that the subjects' coping responses increased when compared with baseline measures. Also, classroom nondisruptive behavior increased by approximately 30 percent. As this and the previous study show, the use of modeling and/or self-instruction, relaxation and behavioral rehearsal, or some combination thereof, may be very useful procedures in helping clients to deal more adaptively with anger and aggression.

Truancy and Absenteeism

Truancy and excessive absence are problems in most schools. When students do not attend school, they jeopardize their educational future and decrease the money schools are allotted on the basis of average daily attendance. Thus, many schools hire truant officers to encourage school attendance. However, many truant officers see their role as a "holding action," recognizing that causative factors are largely out of their control.

Truancy and absenteeism appear to have many causes. Some children are truant simply because they have not made desired academic progress; school becomes an aversive experience and nonattendance reduces the unpleasantness. Children from economically disadvantaged homes often do not receive adequate encouragement from parents to maintain regular attendance. Duties at home may simply have a higher priority than school attendance. Other students conform to a neighborhood or peer code that is more reinforcing than regular school attendance. To deal with this problem, schools should analyze the natural reinforcers present in the school environment and structure a token economy system that will make reinforcement more available to the truant youngsters.

On a small scale, the authors use the "triangle method" to encourage regular school attendance. We first identify the child or children with whom the absentee child typically comes to school. Each child who is frequently absent is placed with two other children with whom he is friends but who attend school regularly. The three children are told that they will work as a group and have a chance to earn toys, candy, and special privileges. It is explained that when all three of them are in school on any particular day, their group will earn three points. This means simply that the earning of points is dependent upon the absentee child's being in school. The behavior of the other members cannot earn points. Hence, the absentee is motivated to maintain his friendships by coming to school. Also, because he can earn points that can be exchanged for toys, his status is enhanced in the eyes of his peers. Of course, the absentee's school-attending behavior is further encouraged by the fact that the two other group members tend to use some persuasion in increasing his school attendance.

Modifying behavior by the use of peers has been done by Wolf and Risley (1967). They worked with a child under two conditions. In the first experimental condition, the child earned five points for decreasing her disruptive behavior. Under the second condition, the child earned only one point (one-fifth of the previous amount needed to obtain the reinforcement), and each of her peers also received a point for her improved social behavior.

The results showed that when peers are reinforced for improved behavior in another child, the child's behavior is more easily modified. Using peers in this manner puts pressure on the child when negative behavior occurs, but it results in secondary reinforcement when the desired behavior is exhibited.

With children who frequently miss school on specific days of the week, it may be desirable to add an innovation to this procedure. When these days are identified, the children are told that on those days a "bonus" may be earned. The bonus they will receive is a "free-time ticket." The free-time ticket will allow them to see cartoons or a humorous movie in the cafeteria or counselor's office. Additional bonus activities may be added as reinforcements. The children can be allowed to earn thirty minutes free time on the playground or to visit with the counselor. Opportunities to choose from many activities are most effective. This type of "reinforcing-events menu" can greatly enhance the desired behavior.

Fire Setting

Many normal children are fascinated with fire and enjoy bonfires, fireplaces, and lighting matches, but few carry this fascination to the point of starting fires indiscriminately. When this behavior appears, it should be altered immediately.

Holland (1969) has reported highly successful results in treating a seven-year-old boy. His treatment, interestingly enough, was performed by working with the parents. The first step was to suppress fire-setting behavior through punishment so that new behavior could be learned. An object (a baseball glove) was used that was prized by the child. The child was told by the father that if he set another fire, the glove would be permanently taken away from him. At the same time, procedures were implemented so that adaptive behavior might occur. The father told the child that if any matches or match covers were found, they were to be brought to him immediately. During that evening, the father deliberately placed an empty match packet on a table. Since the packet was empty, it was assumed that the child would comply with his father's request. When the child brought the packet to his father, he immediately received five cents and was told that he would be taken to a store and he could spend the money as he wished. It was hoped that because the child was given the freedom to spend the money in any way he wished, the value of money as a rein-

forcer would be increased. During that same evening and on subsequent evenings, the father placed packets containing matches around the house. The child promptly returned these to his father. The boy was reinforced each time that they were returned for a total of eight times. The value of the reinforcers varied from one cent to ten cents. It is interesting to note that during this time the father was instructed to tell the child that he should not expect money all of the time. This was done, of course, in order to place the child on a variable-ratio schedule. Match finding occurred with such frequency, it was clear that even matches and match covers found outside of the house were saved and given to the father during the evening.

Holland (1969) recognized that the child might, if he found matches outside the home when neither parent was there, have the opportunity to set fires. Therefore, a procedure was used to strengthen match-nonstriking behavior. About one week after the program was started, the child's father told him that if he wanted, he could strike a pack of matches while the father supervised. During this time, the father placed twenty pennies by the pack of matches. The child was told that for every match he did not strike he would receive one penny. Every time the child struck a match, a penny was removed. During the first trial, the child struck ten matches. During the second evening, the child earned seventeen pennies, and during the third trial, twenty pennies were received by the child, and thereafter the child would not strike matches. The father told the child that he would not know how much money he would receive or even if he would obtain any money if he did not strike a match. The reward varied from no money to ten cents. Secondary reinforcement (praise) was also paired with the monetary rewards.

The results showed that at the end of the fifth week, the child's fire-setting behavior was eliminated. Upon follow-up eight months later, the child's fire-setting behavior had not recurred. However, it should be noted that during this eight-month period, the father continued to use ratio reinforcement.

Holland's method combined both punishment (threat of taking away a highly valued object) and positive reinforcement (money and praise). We noted earlier that a combination of these two approaches (punishment and reinforcement) might be useful under certain conditions. Holland's study demonstrated the utility of this combination. In addition, the use of continuous reinforcement with a change to an intermittent schedule at a later time also helped to maintain the desirable behavior. Holland (1969) did not assume that teaching the child to return the matches he found would generalize to a decrease in his striking of matches. Consequently, the match-striking behavior was dealt with separately.

Name Calling

Like cursing, name calling occurs frequently in elementary and high school youth. The behavior is used not only to express anger but also to deride another person's different or unusual physical features (e.g., "fat," "skinny," "freckle face," etc.). Obviously, this kind of labeling hurts the child who is the brunt of it and annoys teachers and parents. The most common way of handling the problem is to reprimand the offending individuals. Although this method may reduce name calling in the reprimander's presence, it does little to reduce the behavior when the reprimander is not present. Because the response of the student who is called a name often acts to reinforce the name caller, modifying the behavior of the name callers may not be as effective as modifying a student's response to being negatively labelled.

One of the authors was asked to work with a moderately retarded child who was the frequent target of name calling. When he was called "fat," he would yell at his peers and on some occasions would take off his shoes and throw them at the offenders. If he was restrained by the teacher on these occasions, he would become so frustrated that he would hit his head with his hands.

Initially, to modify the child's response to the word "fat," he was encouraged to say the word. Every time he said "fat," he was given an M & M. When he was saying the word with high frequency, the contingencies were changed so that, to be reinforced, he had to say the word "fat" and laugh. Because the subject did not see very much that was laughable about saying the word "fat," successive approximations were used. Any utterance approximating a laugh was reinforced. When the boy was saying "fat" and laughing with high frequency, another procedure was added. A classmate who called the child "fat" was encouraged to do so in the therapist's presence. The subject was reinforced with M & M's each time he laughed after being called "fat" by his classmate. This procedure continued for ten minutes at which point the peer virtually became the dispenser of reinforcement. The logic of this procedure was to induce a response incompatible with anger, i.e., make it unlikely that the subject would get angry at the peer when the peer was reinforcing him.

Subsequently, other classmates were called in individually, asked to call the subject "fat," and dispense M & M's each time the subject laughed. After each session, the subject was encouraged to share some of the M & M's he had received with members of the class, a procedure that was utilized to enhance his peer status and thus reduce their name calling.

There was a dramatic decrease in the frequency of name calling. Moreover, the subject's violent reaction to the label fat decreased notably. Unfortunately, follow-up data are not available, for the child was transferred to a residential treatment setting soon after treatment measures were concluded.

Essentially the same procedures were used by a school counselor with a girl who responded negatively to the label "boy." The girl had an extremely short haircut, and her clothes were similar to boys' attire. In treating her, steps similar to those outlined above were completed in two sessions on two consecutive days. A third session was held one week later to help the subject learn (via reinforcement) other responses to teasing and to encourage her to dress in attire similar to her female peers. The subject's response was positive, and her reaction to teasing was no longer a problem.

Both case examples show that the identified procedures were effective. Teaching the child who is the target of name calling more adaptive behaviors appears more effective than attempting to control peer name calling or teasing.

Self-Injurious Behavior

Acts of self-injury do not occur often in children or adolescents. When they do occur, however, immediate intervention steps must be taken. In Chapter 3 we discussed the case of Sam, a nine-year-old psychotic boy who exhibited several self-injurious behaviors: He banged his head and punched his face and head with his hands. Because it was feared that he would blind himself, Tate and Baroff (1966) intervened immediately to eliminate the behavior. As Sam liked physical contact and disliked being left alone, initial treatment sessions consisted of twenty-minute walks around the hospital grounds holding hands with the therapists. When Sam hit himself, the therapists withdrew their hands and immediately stopped all conversation. Conversation and hand clasping were reinstated after a three-second interval. This

procedure greatly decreased the self-injurious behavior.

To further decrease the self-injurious behavior, a cattle prod administered an electric shock to Sam's right leg whenever he made self-injurious responses in his room. He was also reinforced with praise for noninjurious behavior. This procedure resulted in a complete cessation of the self-injurious behavior after 167 days.

Corte, Wolfe, and Locke (1971) compared the use of primary reinforcement and electric shock in reducing self-injurious behavior in four retarded adolescents. During the reinforcement condition, the retarded adolescents were rewarded with candy or food every fifteen seconds they engaged in noninjurious behavior. However, when the children engaged in self-injurious behavior, the experimenter walked to the opposite wall, remained there, and then walked back to the middle of the room. This action was timed to take thirty seconds, and an additional fifteen seconds elapsed before a child was given candy or food. Thus, a total of forty-five seconds would elapse between self-injurious acts and reinforcement. The procedure markedly reduced self-injurious behavior in one of two adolescents treated; the other child showed little change in his self-injurious behavior.

Two additional procedures were instituted. One method (which proved ineffective) involved isolating a child from all social stimulation in a room for one hour a day. The other method, response-contingent electric shock, greatly decreased the self-injurious behavior in all four retarded subjects. However, self-injurious behavior continued in other situations where adults were not present. To increase the generalization of noninjurious behavior to other settings, the subjects were secretly observed and electrically shocked every time self-injurious behavior occurred. Response-contingent shock, in a variety of situations, substantially reduced the self-injurious behavior in those settings.

Numes, Murphy, and Ruprect (1977) used a unique form of reinforcement and withdrawal of reinforcement to modify the self-injurious behavior of two adolescent retardates. The sixteen-year-old male subject was given a hand vibrator which he was allowed to hold as long as he did not engage in self-slapping behavior. However, as soon as the self-slapping behavior occurred, the vibrator was turned off. If the boy discontinued the self-slapping behavior for fifteen seconds, the vibrator was turned on again. This procedure was successful in reducing the inappropriate slapping behavior in the treatment situation and was subsequently employed in the classroom and at home.

A slightly different procedure was used to treat the twelve-year-old retarded girl. The girl was allowed to hold the turned-on vibrator as long as she did not slap herself and engaged in assembling a puzzle. In addition, each time the girl was observed to slap herself, she was instructed to put "hands down." Praise was also used to reinforce the nonslapping behavior. To extend the duration of the appropriate behavior, fifteen seconds of reinforcing vibrations were made contingent on sixty seconds of nonslapping behavior and puzzle assembling. Ultimately, the period of nonslapping behavior that was required to receive the reinforcing vibrations was extended to three minutes. The self-slapping behavior decreased considerably. The gains were maintained for several months, but the self-injurious behavior returned to near baseline level during a long absence from school.

Follow-up data on the sixteen-year-old retarded boy suggested that treatment effects were quite durable. The nonslapping behavior was apparently being maintained at a low level several months after treatment.

Based on the reported studies, self-injurious behavior can be substantially reduced by response-contingent shock, withdrawal of reinforcement, and positive reinforcement of the opposite or incompatible behavior. Although some punishment procedures may seem inhumane, where the potential for serious body injury is present, aversive procedures can have humane applications.

Nightmares

Individuals of all ages experience nightmares. They can provoke anxiety in anyone but are especially frightening to children. Although various theories have been formulated to explain them, nightmares often indicate a person's attempt to resolve inner conflicts and aversive experiences.

Clinical analysis of frightening dreams often reveal aversive stimuli in the child's environment. Most parents realize that "scary" movies or television programs may sometimes produce fear in a child. When these stimuli generate more fear than the child can handle, parents should restrict the child's viewing. Not all parents are aware of the relationship between such stimuli and the child's frightening dreams. A parent reported to one of the authors that a particular religious picture was frequently present in her child's frightening dreams. Removal of the picture from the child's environment greatly reduced the frequency of the frightening dreams. No doubt the child associated the picture with something he imagined or experienced as aversive. Removal of frightening stimuli from the child's environment is not a "cure" for nightmares, but it may help to reduce their incidence.

Effective parental handling of nightmares is also helpful in reducing their frequency. For example, when a child is awakened by a frightening dream, it is desirable to reassure but not overly reinforce the child at that time: "You're just having a dream. Try to go back to sleep. Everything will be all right." A bad dream may prompt a parent to be extremely sympathetic and reinforce the frequency with which a child reports having frightening dreams. Sleeping with the child for the remainder of the night often complicates the problem.

The authors have found that successive approximation, in a play-therapy medium, may desensitize the child. For example, if a child has frightening dreams involving witches, he is asked to draw (and be reinforced for drawing) a picture of a witch. The child would then be reinforced for verbalizing that he is not afraid in the presence of the picture. Later, the child is engaged in play with witch puppets and dolls. And still later, he may be asked to dress up in witch clothing. Finally, the child may be encouraged to role play scenes in which the witch's fearful power is completely overwhelmed by a smaller, less powerful opponent.

Frightening dreams are not uncommon in adolescents and adults, although they are usually transitory events and do not cause serious anxiety or distress. However, some dreams are traumatic, reoccur frequently, and lead some individuals to seek professional assistance. For example, Silverman and Geer (1968) worked with a nineteen-year-old graduate student who reported having frightening dreams twice a week for four years. In the dreams the client walked on a high bridge and feared she would fall through the wood slats. She also reported fear of heights without the presence of enclosures to support her. Case history information did not reveal other areas of disturbance or serious personality difficulties. However, the client did reveal that her brother had once frightened her on a bridge. The client was an honor student and appeared content and well adjusted in other areas.

Silverman and Geer used systematic desensitization to recondition the client. On the basis of the information secured from the client, a six-item anxiety hierarchy was developed. The items on the hierarchy ranged from approaching a long, high bridge by automobile to crossing a footpath at the side of the bridge on a windy day. The client was first trained in deep muscle relaxation and visualization of the nightmare's phobic elements. Then, she was systematically exposed through visualization to each item on the fear hierarchy while relaxed. The treatment consisted of seven sessions in four weeks.

During the first two weeks, four treatment sessions were conducted and four items on the hierarchy were worked through. The client reported a total of six nightmares. In the last two weeks, the subject was desensitized to the two remaining items on the hierarchy. During this two-week period, the client reported no nightmares. In fact, she reported two pleasant dreams that involved bridges. A final session was held in which the client crossed a bridge of formidable length while stopping several times to look at the water. A follow-up eighteen months later indicated no recurrence of the nightmares.

Silverman and Geer believe that desensitization can be effective with nightmares related to chronic fears. However, they cautiously state that more research is needed to determine whether desensitization can be used with dreams in which the manifest content is symbolic, i.e., not a result of aversive conditioning experiences but symbolizing a more basic inner conflict involving fear impulses.

Nervous Habits

Nervous habits such as tics, eye blinking, and nail biting occur in individuals of all ages, and they are initially learned to reduce tension but often continue long after the original anxiety-producing situation. Like other behaviors learned by negative reinforcement, they do not "naturally" disappear.

Costello (1963) effectively modified a twelve-year-old boy's persistent eye blinking by using negative practice. Initially, the boy was instructed to practice eye blinking for five minutes several times a day while observing himself in a mirror. Gradually, these eye-blinking sessions were increased to an hour, and a significant decrease in eye-blinking behavior occurred. At follow-up one year later, although the eye blinking was not completely eliminated, its incidence remained at a low level.

McNamara (1972) worked with college students who had long histories of nail biting. All subjects were assigned to one of six groups. Subjects in group I engaged in finger tapping every time they started to bite their nails. They were also asked to record the frequency of finger tapping. Group II subjects also engaged in finger tapping when they started to bite their nails, but they were not asked to make a frequency count. Subjects in group III engaged in finger tapping but were instructed to take frequency counts of nail biting. In group IV, subjects were told that any time their hands touched their lips, the hands should be immediately withdrawn. They were asked to record the frequency of this behavior. Subjects in group V had nail growth measured periodically. Subjects in group VI were encouraged to continue nail biting and to record the frequency of this behavior.

Treatment effectiveness was determined by increased nail growth during the four weeks of the study. Interestingly enough, the results showed that there were no significant differences among the groups. The males, however, showed significantly longer nail growth than females. Apparently, simply asking the subjects to record the frequency of the nervous habit, or making them more aware of it, increased their ability to exercise self-control.

Allen and Harris (1966) were interested in modifying a five-year-old's excessive scratching. The parents had used a variety of approaches (including ignoring and severe beatings) with no apparent success.

Many procedures were used to alter the scratching behavior. First, the child was rein-forced with gold stars and periodic primary reinforcement when she was able to go for short periods without scratching. The gold stars were traded several times a day for inexpensive trinkets. These procedures resulted in a slight but not significant decrease in scratching. Hence, another procedure was implemented. Because the girl liked buying clothes for her doll, she was told she could do so if she was able to go for a whole morning without scratching. However, she could not receive the doll clothes until the following morning; the clothes were placed on a high shelf within the child's view to increase incentive. When she went through a morning without scratching, they were given to her along with generous praise. Within six weeks a significant reduction in scratching occurred. The sores on the child's face healed, and both mother and child were pleased with the outcome.

Azrin and Nunn (1973) used a variety of procedures to treat twelve clients with various types of nervous habits. The clients ranged in age from five to sixty-four years of age. In all cases, the nervous habits had been present for three years or more.

The treatment consisted of several things. First, all clients were required to record the frequency of the nervous habit on a daily basis. After two weeks, recording was reduced to twice a week, and subsequently, twice a month. Second, clients were trained to help them become aware of the nervous habit. This involved (1) asking the client to describe and exhibit the habit, (2) teaching the client to detect the occurrence of the habit by pointing it out as it was exhibited, and (3) providing practice sessions to help the client note the earliest sign of the habit or movement.

The third step focused on teaching the client to make a competing response. For example, if a client had a nervous habit involving a backward head jerking movement, the client practiced pulling his chin in and down. Later, the client was asked to perform a similar competing response that was less obvious and more socially desirable. Clients that exhibited inappropriate thumb sucking, nail biting, or eyelash picking, were required to put their hands by their sides or tightly grasp an available object.

The fourth basic step consisted of making clients aware of places, persons, and situations in which the habit was likely to be exhibited. To heighten this awareness, clients were asked to describe how they performed the nervous habit in each situation.

Recognizing that poorly motivated clients are often unsuccessful in modifying their behavior, several methods were used to increase client motivation. First, the counselor helped the client assess the embarrassment and inconvenience associated with the habit. Second, when the client was able to control the habit in the treatment situation, significant others were asked to comment positively on the effort and improved appearance of the client. Third, the clients were encouraged to practice the exercises when the nervous habit was exhibited. With child clients, parents assisted by guiding the child through the corrective exercises.

Finally, to encourage generalization the counselor used symbolic rehearsal. Clients were asked to imagine situations producing the nervous habit and to imagine they detected the habit in an early stage and performed the competing response.

The results of treatment were impressive. The pretreatment incidence of the nervous habits for the clients ranged from twenty per day to eight thousand per day. After treatment, the habits decreased by a minimum of 90 percent for each client. Three weeks after treatment, ten of the twelve clients were free of the nervous habit. Seven months later a follow-up was done with seven clients. There was a reduction in habit frequency of 99 percent.

It is clear from the studies reviewed that behavioral procedures can effectively reduce a variety of nervous habits. Azrin and Nunn's pro-cedures are especially worth noting since there were a wide range of ages and nervous habits represented and significant results were achieved in a very few sessions.

Test and Performance Anxiety

In a society that places a high premium on achievement, it is not surprising that many students experience considerable anxiety when faced with a test. The anxious reactions of students during examinations is commonly observed by university, high school, and elementary teachers. Eysenck and Rachman (1965), for example, have estimated that 20 percent of all school children fear examinations. Most students are able to deal with the anxiety effectively, but for those who cannot, anxiety substantially affects their test performance.

Mann and Rosenthal (1965) worked with seventh-grade students who experienced test anxiety. Fifty seventh-grade students were ranked according to scores on a test-anxiety scale and randomly assigned to five experimental treatments: (1) direct desensitization on an individual basis; (2) vicarious desensitization on an individual basis; (3) direct group desensitization; (4) group vicarious desensitization (observing desensitization of another group); and (5) vicarious group desensitization (observing desensitization of a peer model). Twenty-one eighth-grade students were assigned to a control group.

Two basic procedures were used in the desensitization. First, all experimental subjects were trained in relaxation for two sessions. Second, a sixteen-item anxiety hierarchy was developed and presented to the individuals and groups involved in direct desensitization. In the group conditions, the items were presented so that the group's most anxious subject could resolve his anxiety before additional items were undertaken. When a subject indicated anxiety on any item, the therapist moved back to an item that was less anxiety provoking. During each session, no fewer than three, and not more than five, items were presented. Sessions were approximately fifty minutes long and, in all, eight sessions were used.

Analysis of the subjects' pretest and posttest scores on the test anxiety scale and the Gates McGinnitie Reading Tests indicated significant decreases in test anxiety and increases in reading skills for all experimental groups. No experimental treatment, however, was demonstrated to be superior to the others: Individual desensitization was no better than group desensitization, and direct desensitization was no more effective than vicarious desensitization. Also, some unanticipated and incidental results were found. One mother reported that her son could better control his asthma attacks. Other parents indicated that their children exhibited much less anxiety from dental examinations, piano recitals, and school attendance.

Kondas (1967) used procedures similar to those of Mann and Rosenthal to modify fear of performing before a group. Subjects consisted of elementary school children and university students in a psychology class. The elementary school children were referred by teachers and were subsequently given a fear survey schedule and a diagnostic interview.

The elementary school subjects were assigned to three experimental and one control group. Group I received relaxation (autogenic) training—breathing exercises and activities that relaxed various body parts. Children practiced these exercises at school and at home. Group II received five systematic desensitization sessions. Group III was presented the items on the anxiety hierarchy but did not receive any relaxation training. Group IV served as a control.

The treatment procedures used with the university students were similar. The university subjects were divided into three groups. Group I received autogenic training; group II, systematic desensitization: group III served as a control.

Analysis indicated that systematic desensitization was the most effective treatment for both the elementary school children and the college students. The autogenic training produced significant changes in the elementary school children but nonsignificant changes in the college students.

Deffenbacher and Kemper (1974) also used systematic desensitization to deal with twenty-eight test-anxious junior high school students. The subjects were placed in groups of two to five and met for an hour for six to eight weeks. With the exception of one or two unique features, the standard form of systematic desensitization was used. A twenty-item anxiety hierarchy was developed and relaxation training was given. However, in the second session, students were taught to imagine two pleasant or nonanxiety-provoking scenes. Also, abbreviated relaxation was used in each of the subsequent sessions before being exposed to the desensitization procedure. Each group then worked through the anxiety hierarchy until the most anxiety-provoking item no longer generated anxiety.

Changes in grade-point average were used to evaluate treatment effects. The results indicated significant change in grade-point averages for all subjects. The treatment appeared equally effective for both male and female subjects.

Systematic desensitization is a highly effective procedure for treating test-anxious clients. As the studies show, it is applicable to a wide range of subjects and is effective with both sexes.

Excessive Vomiting

On the surface, it would seem that vomiting is primarily the result of a physical etiologic agent and should be regarded as a physical rather than a psychological problem. Most cases of vomiting are physical, and medical assistance should be secured if the case appears problematic. The psychologist or counselor is occasionally asked to deal with a child's excessive vomiting when the family doctor can find no physical basis for the problem. In these cases, the child often utilizes vomiting as a means to manipulate others or as an inappropriate response to situational demands.

One of the authors and an elementary school counselor worked with a boy who vomited almost daily before going to school. Some mornings the child would vomit seven times before going to school. The counselor noted that vomiting did not occur during holidays or summer vacation. The boy vomited occasionally at school when substantial demands were made of him, but much less frequently than at home. When it occurred in school, the boy usually ran to the restroom. On his return, the teacher usually sent him to the nurse's office to lie down for a while. The teacher was able to decrease the frequency of vomiting at school by reducing the amount of schoolwork given to the child.

Interviews with the parents revealed that the child would usually get up in the morning feeling well and eat his breakfast, but as soon as one of them mentioned it was time for school, the child would run to the bathroom and vomit. When this behavior occurred, the parents' responses varied from ignoring or yelling to encouraging the child to lie down for a brief period.

The parents were instructed to tell the child to use plastic-lined paper sacks when he vomited rather than running to the bathroom. He was not permitted to delay going to school and was told to take a paper sack with him and vomit into it while riding to school. On arrival at school, the paper sack was thrown in the garbage.

After one week, the teacher had a conference with the boy and informed him that if he had to vomit, he would be required to wait until the morning, noon, or afternoon recess. If he vomited in the classroom, he would be required to get a mop and bucket and clean it up. The teacher was reluctant to try this procedure but ultimately conceded. Her cooperation was immediately and continuously reinforced. The child did not vomit in the classroom on a single occasion. In a short time, the child's vomiting was completely eliminated.

Kohlenberg (1970) used aversive conditioning to modify the excessive vomiting of a twenty-one-year-old severely retarded woman. The woman had vomited after every meal for three months. The problem had become so serious that loss of body weight and malnutrition seriously jeopardized the woman's life. Because it was noted that milk and orange juice created stomach tension, they were used to facilitate vomiting. As soon as the stomach tension appeared, the subject was electrically shocked for less than one second. This procedure was used in the treatment sessions for three days. In the second experimental phase, the woman was allowed to roam freely around the ward but was casually observed. If vomitus was present, the woman was confined to a chair and observed for one hour. When the stomach tension was observed, a shock was administered.

Twenty-five days after the experimental sessions were completed, sixty-four out of seventy-five meals were consumed without vomiting. In twenty-five days, the woman gained 10.5 pounds. The program continued for five months with a low frequency of vomiting and weight gain. After aversive conditioning was discontinued, however, the vomiting did reappear.

The experimenters conclude that aversive shock can effectively control vomiting, but periodic maintenance shock may be required to permanently extinguish it. Aversive shock should be used only when other approaches have failed and continual vomiting has extreme negative physical consequences for the patient.

Drug Abuse

Habitual use or abuse of some drugs may result in physical damage, marked personality change, and serious problems in adapting to the ordinary demands of everyday life. Drug use is difficult to modify because the drug's effects are inherently reinforcing. Anxiety is likely to be decreased, conflicts are temporarily avoided, and the induced drug state is often experienced as very pleasant.

Madsen and Madsen (1970) used a simple procedure to modify drug-taking behavior in a teenager. To motivate the teenager to become familiar with the literature on drug use and abuse, they positively reinforced him for writing a research paper on drug effects. He was paid five dollars for each completed page, although a limit was set on the paper's length. The parents were given the opportunity to censor pages if they were not consistent with certain predetermined criteria. This procedure was successful in terminating the adolescent's use of LSD, but he did not stop taking marijuana because of the conflicting evidence on the drug. Apparently, motivating adolescent drug users to become acquainted with the negative effects of drugs (without using lectures or sermons) can have a positive effect in reducing drug-taking behavior.

A second procedure used frequently by one of the authors is to have the adolescent drug user meet and become acquainted with a former user. The former user must have credibility in the eyes of the adolescent user so that the adolescent can identify with or model him. If the prospective model appears too "straight" or moralistic, identification or modeling does not take place. Young, "long-haired," college students who have been through the "drug scene" or are presently involved in a rehabilitation program have proven very helpful in modifying drug-taking behavior in junior and senior high school students.

Aversive conditioning has often been employed to treat drug users. When these procedures are used, actual or imagined punishment of drug taking is paired with stimuli that precede the drug-taking behavior. By so doing, the preceding stimuli (thoughts, for example) acquire the capacity to induce aversive or avoidance reactions (Gambrill, 1977).

Kolvin (1967) used covert sensitization to treat a fourteen-year-old boy who was "addicted" to petrol sniffing for seven years. Fear of heights and falling were identified as aversive images used in the counterconditioning. The subject was encouraged to relax and then visualize his engagement in petrol sniffing. When he had a clear image of the scene, the subject was asked to invoke the aversive imagery. This procedure was used for twenty half-hour sessions, five days a week. The treatment proved effective. Petrol sniffing was eliminated, and thirteen months later, a follow-up indicated that the subject had not returned to his former petrol-sniffing habits.

As we have noted, the use of certain drugs is inherently reinforcing and also allows the user to escape from the anxiety associated with skill or personality deficits. Hence, a single treatment procedure may not be effective with many drug users.

A good example of the use of multiple intervention procedures was reported by Boudin (1972). He treated a female graduate student who consumed sixty or seventy milligrams of amphetamines daily. Boudin combined self-administered aversive conditioning (via a portable shock apparatus) with a contingency contract and frequent therapy. The contingency contract required, among other things, that the client (1) submit a weekly schedule to the therapist, (2) call the therapist three times a day to discuss any "potentially dangerous" drug-taking situations, (3) give up all drugs readily accessible to her, (4) call the therapist anytime a crisis situation occurred, (5) carry with her a shock apparatus which she would use when she was aware of the urge to seek drugs, and (6) write out ten fifty-dollar checks which could be cashed by the therapist and sent to the Klu Klux Klan for any suspected client drug use. The therapist also used money drawn from a joint client-therapist bank account to reinforce specific client behaviors.

The treatment appeared effective. Shortly after treatment, the client spent a year abroad and apparently abstained from any drug use during that time. Although it is impossible to separate out the relative contribution of each intervention procedure Boudin used, the use of multiple procedures that are applicable to the unique problems and/or requirements of the client is well worth emulating.

Vocational Information Seeking

High school counselors spend much time encouraging vocational exploration and assisting students with their educational-vocational choices. Speakers are brought in to talk to students about various professions, career weeks are held, and interest and aptitude tests are administered. Some students, however, may not be avid seekers of the vocational information so vital to making wise career choices; procedures must be used to encourage such vocational information-seeking behavior.

Krumboltz and Thoresen (1964) used a simple but effective method. High school students who had difficulty making vocational decisions were randomly assigned to several groups. In one group, the counselor used verbal praise to encourage students to explore various career possibilities. A second group was praised for exploring career possibilities but also listened to tape-recorded interviews that depicted how other students had handled their career deci-

sions. The control groups received no specific treatment.

Analysis of the data indicated that the use of models and verbal reinforcement (experimental group II) proved to be the most effective treatment. Individual experimental treatments proved no more effective than group treatment. The model and reinforcement treatment appeared to be more effective for males than females — probably because the model was male.

Lafleur and Johnson (1972) conducted a study with 140 tenth- and eleventh-grade suburban high school students to increase vocational exploration and career planning. The treatment consisted of prepared material in booklet form containing stick figures engaged in specific tasks.

In the first experimental group, the subjects read the descriptions of the stick figure engaged in four specified tasks: (1) sending away for further vocational or educational information, (2) requesting an appointment with the school counselor, (3) attending a meeting in which a speaker discussed the need for career planning, and (4) using various materials in the library.

A second experimental group received a booklet very similar to the first group, except that the model was rewarded for the four tasks by receiving some very helpful career-planning information. The control group also received a booklet, but the information was taken out of the *Occupational Outlook Handbook*. In these booklets there were no stick figure models nor any specific mention of the desirability of career planning.

When the experimental treatments were completed, the booklets were collected, and the students received a "vocational-educational planning packet." The packet contained a postcard to send for further information, a form to request an appointment with the school counselor, and a form that could be used to attend a lecture-meeting discussing skills needed for career-planning. The students also received a form listing various career-exploration materials available in the library.

To determine the effectiveness of the treatments, six criterion measures were used: (1) number of postcards sent, (2) number of books or materials selected at the library, (3) number of requests to attend the lecture meeting, (4) number of requests for an appointment with the high school counselor, (5) knowledge gained by students, and (6) student ratings of interest in seeking career information.

The results indicated that both experimental groups differed significantly from the control group in (1) information-seeking activities, (2) scores obtained on the interest scale, and (3) acquisition of educational-vocational information. There were no statistically significant differences between the two experimental groups. This study, like the Krumboltz and Thoresen study, indicates career planning and vocational information seeking can be greatly enhanced using modeling and reinforcement. With a little ingenuity, several career-exploration activities can be facilitated with groups using these procedures.

Self-Control

Parents and teachers realize and a host of research studies support the fact that the development of self-control is a signal achievement. The ability to regulate one's behavior is associated with successful achievement, ability to plan, acceptance of social responsibility, and level of competence (Mischel, 1971).

If self-control is an important acquisition, it is appropriate to ask: What is it and how can it be enhanced? In popular parlance self-control is often viewed as the possession of a quality or ability called "willpower." Yet, if one asks how it originates, or the conditions under which it de-

velops, it is often viewed as an inexplicable trait or a "vaguely defined inner force" (Mahoney and Thoresen, 1974, p. 20). One either has it or doesn't have it.

For our purposes, self-control may be defined as a process by which an individual learns to regulate his or her behavior in a way that is situationally appropriate, maximally rewarding, and personally satisfying. Successful self-control involves three essential processes: (1) specification of the behavior that is the object of self-regulation, (2) identification of the cues that precede and the consequences that follow the targeted behavior, and (3) initiation of a plan that changes the antecedent cues and the consequences (Mahoney and Thoresen, 1974). When a self-management program is devised, these processes are divided into a series of steps or phases.

Williams and Long (1975) have divided the process of self-management into six steps: (1) selecting a goal; (2) observing the frequency (or amount) and the circumstances surrounding the targeted behavior; (3) altering the setting events in which the targeted behavior is to occur; (4) utilizing effective consequences; (5) focusing on or being aware of the reinforcing contingencies; and (6) utilizing coverant control. Let us describe each of these steps briefly.

Selecting a Goal

The selection of an appropriate goal is the crucial first step in formulating a self-management program. It involves at least four essential ingredients. First, the goal should be important and one that an individual is motivated to achieve. The behavior that is to be brought under control should be one that causes some discomfort or acts to produce consequences that are personally undesirable. Second, the goal should be stated in measurable behavioral terms. A precise specification of the goal not only helps to determine ways to promote it but also enables one to know when it has been achieved. Third, the goal should be relatively easy to attain. If the goal is set too high and excessive effort is required to achieve it, individual motivation is likely to wane. Fourth, the goal should be stated in terms of positive behaviors. While the reduction or elimination of a negative and/or inappropriate behavior may be a step forward in self-control, appropriate adaptation requires that an individual perform behaviors that are reinforcing to self and others. For example, a reduction in the devaluing comments one makes to oneself or others is a worthwhile change, but an increase in the praise and compliments one gives to oneself and others is a much more appropriate goal (Williams and Long, 1975).

Observing the Amount and Circumstances of Behavior

Once the goal of self-management has been stated in appropriate behavioral terms, the circumstances in which the behavior occurs and its frequency must be observed. There are two reasons why this is important. First, a baseline measure of the target behavior must be obtained before change strategies are implemented to determine their effectiveness. Second, it is important to observe and analyze the context in which the behavior occurs to determine the events that precede and follow the behavior. This analysis is crucial since self-control is intimately related to a person's awareness of the stimuli and events that precede and follow the behavior. Later, when strategies are devised to enhance self-control, these stimulus-response-consequence relationships will need to be changed (Mahoney and Thoresen, 1974; Williams and Long, 1975).

As we noted earlier, self-observation and recording can be done in several ways. If one desires a simple frequency count, wrist or golf counters can perform this chore very well. If response duration—such as the length of a temper tantrum—is the type of observation desired, a stopwatch is necessary to get an accurate measurement.

Besides getting measures of frequency or duration of the inappropriate response, a good self-management program requires the assessment of other factors. Such data can be obtained by recording on a piece of paper three types of events: (1) the situation, (2) the events or cues preceding the target behavior, and (3) the consequences that follow the target behavior. With this type of information, we can proceed to the next step.

Altering Setting Events

Applied behavior analysis reveals that many behaviors that individuals exhibit are often triggered by stimuli or events that precede their occurrence. Therefore, one important way to enhance self-control is to alter the situation or antecedent events that trigger the target behavior. For example, if we are attempting to enhance control over eating, smoking, drinking, or becoming angry, avoid those situations where these behavior excesses are likely to occur. Reduce the number of times that you eat at your favorite restaurant, the number of parties you attend, or the provocative situations that incite your anger. Of course, this is not the most elegant form of self-control, but it does reduce the presence of cues that are associated with the undesirable response (Mahoney and Thoresen, 1974; Williams and Long, 1975).

A closely related approach is to arrange the environment so that eliciting stimuli are not present. For example, if one tends to procrastinate when attempting to study, the environment can be arranged so that distracting cues are not present. That is, studying should be done in a place where temptation to engage in other be-havior (eating, watching TV, etc.) is not present. Similarly, if one tends to eat or smoke exces-sively, these behaviors should take place away from stimuli that elicit or reinforce its occur-rence. Finally, the environment can be *prear-ranged* so that the problematic response is less likely to occur. For example, one can limit the variety or quantity of food that is available to eat, the number of cigarettes or money carried to avoid excesses (Mahoney and Thoresen, 1974).

Utilizing Effective Consequences

If behavior is a function of its consequences, then the use of effective positive and negative consequences should help to promote self-control. There are several ways that an indi-vidual can arrange reinforcement for exhibiting desirable self-control responses. First, one can make a reinforcing event contingent on the per-formance of a specific behavior. For example, if an individual wants to increase his study behav-ior, after an hour of studying he can reinforce himself with a fifteen-minute Coke break, a ten-minute chat with a friend, a ten-minute swim in his pool. Second, an individual can ne-gotiate with a family member or friend to ad-minister a material or social reinforcer each time the target behavior is executed. Third, a token reinforcement system can be designed that specifies the behavior to be performed, the token to be received for the execution of the target response, and the back-up reinforc-ers that can be purchased with the tokens (Mahoney and Thoresen, 1974).

Although positive reinforcement is likely more useful than punishment in promoting self-control responses, punishment has its place. As Mahoney and Thoresen (1974) have sug-gested, a very useful strategy is to reinforce the desired self-control response and punish its

opposite. But, what procedures can be used to administer punishment? Several procedures have been used. First, and certainly not the most desirable, a portable shock apparatus has been used to decrease undesirable behavior ex-cesses. For example, McGuire and Vallance (1964) used self-administered shock to reduce the frequency of smoking, drinking, and deviant sexual behavior. Initially, the clients were shocked by the therapist each time they im-agined or engaged in the inappropriate behav-ior. Later, clients carried a portable shock ap-paratus and administered a shock each time the problem behavior occurred.

A second procedure that has been used is response cost. For example, before an indi-vidual begins a self-control program, he or she is asked to deposit a specific sum of money with a therapist, a friend, or a family member. The self-control program is devised, and each time the individual fails to reach a goal, or exhibits a specific number of undesirable responses, a por-tion of the deposited sum is sent to an organiza-tion that the person greatly dislikes.

A third form of punishment that has been used in self-control programs is aversive imag-ery. When this procedure is used, the individual imagines the performance of an inappropriate behavior and immediately invokes the aversive imagery. By so doing, the undesirable response begins to assume some of the aversive qualities and decreases in frequency (Davison, 1969).

Finally, a token system can be devised in which token loss or fines are self-imposed whenever the inappropriate behavior occurs. A token system that combines fines and positive reinforcement can be quite useful. Tokens can be awarded or subtracted immediately after the desirable or undesirable behavior occurs and it is relatively easy to administer. Such a system can provide a record of progress and helps to maintain motivation to continue in the self-control program.

Focusing on Contingencies

There is some research to suggest that the more aware one is of the operating contingencies, the more effective one is likely to be in learning self-control (Williams and Long, 1975). Hence, any procedure that is used to make one more aware of the consequences is likely to be an effective method. There are two basic ways in which this can be done. One procedure is to arrange the setting so that several requisite responses are made before the target response is executed. For example, if the behavior excess is overeating, the consumption of foods that require preparation is likely to reduce the amount eaten (Williams and Long, 1975).

Another procedure that has been found effective in reducing impulsive responding is to verbalize the operating contingencies before a response is made. That is, people who verbalize the positive or negative consequences of an act before it is performed appear to manifest better self-control. Once such a habit is established, an individual is more likely to deliberate about a response rather than behave impulsively (Blackwood, 1970; Williams and Long, 1975).

Utilizing Coverant Control

This final step, the use of coverant control procedures, may be unnecessary. However, some behaviors may be difficult to alter, and coverant control methods may add the element that is needed.

Coverant control therapy is a treatment procedure devised by Homme (1965) to increase or decrease certain thinking responses. He assumes that thinking is an operant response that is influenced by consequences that follow it. Also, since thinking responses are precursors of action, the inhibition of a thought is likely to decrease the probability of performing the behavior to which the thought refers. For example, suppose a person begins to think about food. As soon as one is aware of the thought, covert responses can be made to inhibit it. First, one immediately counters the thought with a second thought that is incompatible to it (e.g., "I'll feel terrible if I eat and gain weight."). Second, the thought emphasizing the negative consequences should be immediately followed by a thought that emphasizes the positive aspect of *not* performing the act (e.g., "I will be proud of myself for being able to control my eating."). Third, the sequence of negative-positive thoughts should be followed by a high-probability behavior that acts to reinforce the thoughts that precede it.

Another way to increase the frequency of overt or covert responses is to use covert reinforcement. You will recall from our discussion in Chapter 1 that covert reinforcement involves the use of a pleasant image to increase the frequency of a preceding thought or act. For example, suppose a person wished to increase the frequency of positive self-statements. This can be done by invoking a positive image immediately following the emission of a positive self-statement. If this process is continued over a period of time, it is likely that the individual will begin to think of himself in much more positive terms.

It should be clear from the processes and procedures we have discussed that self-control can be enhanced in a number of ways. Indeed, the writings on the subject are now abundant and are being applied with children. In the next section we will present some studies that illustrate what is being done.

Illustrative Studies

In a simple but effective study, Broden, Hall, and Mitts (1971) have demonstrated that self-recording of one's own behavior can greatly facilitate self-management. They were interested in increasing study behavior in one student and decreasing talking out in another. They recorded the first subject's study behavior in a history class for eight days. Following baseline observation, she was asked to record her own study behavior. The counselor first instructed her on the constituents of study and nonstudy behavior. She was then given a self-observation behavior sheet consisting of three rows, with ten boxes in each row. She was requested to place a "+" on the sheet when she noted she was studying and a "−" when not studying. The counselor and student met once a week to review her observation sheets, and the counselor praised her when the plusses exceeded the minuses. This procedure continued for thirteen days. From the fourteenth to the eighteenth day, a second baseline was taken and no observation sheets were given to the student to record her behavior. On the nineteenth day, the self-observation sheets were again given to the student, and she was asked to record her behavior as before and to meet with the counselor once a week. In their weekly sessions the counselor verbally reinforced her for improvement in study behavior. On the thirty-seventh day, observation sheets were not issued but the teacher continued to praise her for appropriate study behavior. On the forty-first day, teacher praise was discontinued.

Analysis of the data revealed that during the first baseline the student's study behavior was 30 percent. During the first self-observation and recording phase, the study's study behavior increased to 78 percent. During the second baseline when no experimental treatment was used, study behavior decreased to 27 percent. When the self-observation and recording procedures were again implemented, the student's study behavior increased to 80 percent. The addition of teacher praise to the self-observation and recording procedure increased study behavior to 88 percent. With the use of praise alone, the study behavior was 77 percent. During the

third baseline when both praise and self-observation were discontinued, there was a slight decline, but study behavior remained at a high level.

Broden et al. used a similar procedure with the second subject who talked excessively in class. Baseline observations recorded the frequency of talking-out behavior during two specific time periods. The student's behavior was recorded for twenty-five minutes before lunch and twenty minutes after lunch. In the first experimental phase, the student was asked to observe and record his talking-out behavior during the twenty-five minute period before lunch and to turn in his recording sheet during lunch time. In the second phase, the student recorded his talking-out behavior during the period following lunch. During the third phase, the student was asked to record his talking-out behavior before and after lunch. After this phase, a second baseline was done, and the experimental procedures were once again implemented. Contrary to procedures used with the first subject, reinforcement was not used.

The results indicate that for the first baseline observation, the student talked out 1.1 times per minute during the prelunch period and 1.6 times per minute during the postlunch period. After the self-recording procedures were introduced, the frequency of talking out was 0.3 times a minute during the prelunch period, but the postlunch period remained the same as the baseline measurement. When self-recording was implemented during the twenty-minute postlunch period, talking without permission decreased to 0.5 times per minute, but talking out increased in the prelunch period (when self-recording procedures were not used). When the self-observation and recording procedures were used in both periods, talking-out behavior decreased to 0.3 times per minute during the prelunch period and 1.0 times during the postlunch period. Talking-out behavior increased during the second baseline period but decreased after the treatment measures were implemented again. The decrease, however, was less than occurred after the treatment was first implemented.

The treatment procedures were obviously more effective with the first subject than with the second subject. The authors suggest three possible reasons: (1) The first subject voluntarily sought the counselor's help, (2) reinforcement was part of the treatment, and (3) it is probably easier to increase a desirable behavior than to decrease an undesirable behavior. In spite of the different levels of success, self-observation and recording of behavior enhanced self-control in both subjects.

Bolstead and Johnson (1972) utilized similar procedures to enhance self-control in disruptive first- and second-grade children. First- and second-grade teachers identified forty disruptive children, who were then randomly assigned to three experimental and one control group. Treatment measures were implemented for thirty minutes daily for eight weeks and were divided into four experimental phases.

1. The first experimental phase consisted of external regulation of the subjects' behavior by reinforcement. The subjects were told that their behavior would be evaluated according to three criteria: (a) when they exhibited fewer than five disruptive behaviors, they would receive eight points; (b) when they exhibited fewer than ten disruptive behaviors, they would receive four points; (c) if more than ten disruptive behaviors occurred, they would receive no points. Points could be exchanged for back-up reinforcers that differed in value. Subjects who acquired four points could choose an item from a box labelled "4" that contained objects worth seven cents or less. For eight points, the subjects could choose an item from the box labelled "8" with slightly more expensive prizes. They could also save their points and select a prize from a box that required twelve points. Earned prizes were kept in the counselor's office and were dispensed at the end of the day.

2. In the second experimental phase, two of the three experimental groups were trained in self-management procedures. The purpose of this phase was to train the subjects to evaluate their own behavior and dispense reinforcement to themselves based on their evaluation. The subjects were instructed to record on self-observation cards the incidence of three disruptive behaviors: (a) talking without permission, (b) hitting or annoying other children, and (c) leaving the desk without permission. After each self-observation period, the cards were checked with observers' ratings to determine accuracy. If the subject's card was within three disruptive behaviors of the observers' ratings, he received the number of points he received in the first experimental phase. If the subject's ratings were outside this range, however, he received two points less than he received during the first experimental condition.

3. In the third experimental phase, one of the three experimental groups received points according to their own ratings.

4. In the fourth experimental phase, treatment measures were terminated. The subjects were informed that prizes were no longer available for self-observation and recording.

Analysis of the data (as well as replication of the experiment in another school setting) indicated that the three experimental groups exhibited significantly less disruptive behavior than the control group. Although both external regulation with reinforcement and self-management procedures with reinforcement were effective in reducing disruptive behavior, *self-management with reinforcement proved more effective.* The experimental results show very clearly that young children can be taught to effectively monitor their own behavior, and when self-management is properly reinforced, young children can make significant strides in the acquisition of self-control.

Teaching Children to Modify Behavior of Others

Most people realize that children are able to influence the behavior of those with whom they interact. However, it is only recently that investigators have begun to study how children can be taught to influence the behavior of peers and adults in a planned way. For instance, Graubard, Rosenberg, and Miller (1971) taught six emotionally handicapped children to use extinction and social reinforcement with their peers. As a result of the training, the frequency of positive social contacts with their peers increased considerably.

In a similar type of study, Solomon and Wahler (1973) taught popular sixth-grade students behavioral methods to reduce disruptive behavior of five students in their class. The training succeeded in changing the way in which the disruptive students responded to the "student therapist," but did not alter the disruptive students' responses to other students in the class.

Sherman and Cormier (1974) did a study to determine whether two disruptive fifth-grade students could be taught to change the manner in which their teacher responded to them. To conceal the purpose of the study from the teacher, other students were selected but were not given specific training. In the experimental phase, the two disruptive students met with the investigators to discuss ways in which their behavior should be changed. Both students recog-

nized their behavior to be inappropriate, and agreed to try to change. The two students were asked to observe the way the teacher responded to them — especially when they behaved appropriately. However, since observation of the students' behavior in the classroom revealed relatively little change, tangible reinforcement was used to promote the desired behavior. In addition, the students were also informed that their classroom behavior would be observed and were subsequently given daily reports of these observations.

The experimental procedures proved to be effective. The disruptive behavior of the two students changed, and teacher response to the students was also altered. As the students exhibited more appropriate behavior, the teacher made fewer negative verbal comments and increased positive verbal responses. The teacher began to attend more to the students' appropriate behavior and developed a more positive attitude toward them as measured by the teacher's ranking of students in the class.

In a popularized article Gray, Graubard, and Rosenberg (1974) described their success in teaching problem students in junior high school to shape and/or alter the response of teachers. Similar to the other studies reported, they instructed junior high students to use behavior modification procedures. For example, students were taught to exhibit desirable behavior such as learning to smile appropriately, sit up straight, make proper eye contact, and use verbal reinforcement procedures such as "I really feel good when you talk to me nicely," and "I really want to learn when you take time to explain things to me." Although students initially felt awkward in using these new ways of responding, in time they became more comfortable and learned to use the new behavior more naturally.

It is apparent from these and other studies that behavior modification is a two way street. Teachers and students can be taught to modify positively the behavior of each other. The behavior changes that occur in one tend to promote complementary changes in the other. And, perhaps, when all members of a classroom or any other intact group learn to use their influence beneficially and humanely, the group may exhibit a more productive level of functioning.

Summary

1.   In this chapter we have discussed a variety of problem behaviors and procedures to modify them. Although the problem behaviors seem largely heterogeneous, there are some common elements. Many problem behaviors may be grouped into two major categories: (a) behaviors that are socially inappropriate or excessive and (b) maladaptive avoidance behaviors, i.e., behaviors that appear to be established by frightening or aversive experiences and are maintained because they reduce anxiety.

2.   Modification procedures used with socially inappropriate or excessive behaviors (e.g., crying, aggression, self-injurious behavior, bizarre talk, and fantasy) involve similar principles. The studies reviewed suggest that these problem behaviors can be effectively modified using response cost, withdrawal of reinforcement, time-out, and negative practice, accompanied by positive reinforcement of the appropriate adaptive behavior.

3.   Maladaptive avoidance behaviors (various phobic and withdrawal reactions) can be effectively modified with successive approximation and positive reinforcement, modeling, and systematic desensitization. Successive approximation and reinforcement reward the client for exposing himself to the anxiety-inducing situation to a tolerable degree. Because negative consequences do not follow this exposure, approach responses are reinforced. Systematic desensitization utilizes a similar principle but also induces a state of relaxation inherently antagonistic to anxiety. Hence, the anxiety-provoking potential of the phobic stimulus is greatly reduced, and extinction of the phobic response occurs. Observation of a model responding nonfearfully to the phobic stimulus and imitative performance of the model's responses likely produces feedback information that enables the client to reevaluate the threat potential of the phobic stimulus. The tendency to avoid the phobic stimulus is greatly reduced.

4.   Various forms of systematic desensitization have been used. The anxiety-provoking stimulus can be presented in imagination, vicariously, or by direct exposure with one or several clients simultaneously. Several studies show that group desensitization is usually as effective as individual desensitization and may be preferred because of its economy.

5.   Methods that enhance self-control are of particular interest because many behavior excesses reflect self-control deficits. Self-control is primarily a product of learning and may be enhanced like any other operant response. It involves a process in which (a) the desired self-control behavior is clearly specified, (b) the targeted behavior is observed and events preceding and following it are recorded, (c) the environment is altered to reduce the cues that trigger the inappropriate response, and (d) overt and covert consequences are administered to increase the desired self-control behavior and to reduce the opposite or incompatible behavior. Research studies suggest that individuals have much greater capacity for self-management than has previously been assumed. This area of research holds great promise, because it may move us closer to the ultimate therapeutic goal—complete individual choice and self-management.

Chapter Ten

Modification of Problem Behavior at Home

Parents influence the personality development of children in many ways. First, the hereditary endowment the child receives from each parent determines his potential for development. The child cannot transcend his genetic inheritance, but his learning environment can substantially determine his ultimate abilities. Second, the care and interaction patterns that parents use to meet the child's survival needs significantly influence how he learns, relates to others, and copes with the environment. Third, parental models, expectations, and child-rearing methods largely determine the child's behavior repertoire, goals, attitudes, and self-reinforcement system.

During the early years, parental influence is primary because the child is dependent on them for almost everything he needs. Parents control sanctions, restraints, resources, and reinforcers. As these elements of influence and power are meted out, the basic structure of the child's behavior repertoire is formed; the structure is changeable, depending on past history and present circumstances. The child learns behavior and can unlearn maladaptive behavior. Thus, parents continue to exert a powerful influence until complete independence is attained.

Methods of Analyzing Parent-Child Interaction and Conflict

Four methods have been used to analyze parent-child interaction and conflict: (1) obser-
vation of the identified client and family members in the home; (2) observation of the identified client and his parents in a clinic setting; (3) parent observation of the identified client and the family relationship at home; (4) personal interview with the parents and identified client.

Perhaps the most precise and useful method for analyzing parent-child interaction is the observation of family members at home, for variables (specific interaction between family members, areas of conflict, family member roles, reinforcement practices) that contribute to family conflict or problems can be observed directly. Because observation is done firsthand by the counselor or clinician, it is not subject to the distortions that often occur when parents report about family life. Once the observational data is recorded, it is difficult for parents to deny their actual behavior or interaction with the identified client.

The second method has many of the virtues of family observation at home. An office or clinic situation is created where the family is encouraged to interact as naturally as possible. For example, the counselor may invite the family into a play or activity room and observe (through a one-way window) their activities and interaction. Frequency counts can be kept of the identified client's undesirable behaviors and the operative reinforcement contingencies.

Although the third procedure, parent self-observation and observation of the client, has many advantages, it is more difficult to implement. Parents often need instruction to devise an observation schedule and record observed behavior. The observation schedule need not be complex, however, and the parents can be initiated by asking them to observe only one or two problem behaviors and their own reactions. If the parents are willing to cooperate, there are some immediate dividends. The child's problem behavior tends to decrease almost immediately, and the parents become more aware of their responses to the child. Unfortunately, it is difficult to get parents involved in this procedure, and sometimes they just "happen to forget" to do it.

The fourth method, a personal interview with the parents and child, often accompanies the methods but can be used alone. It is economical of time and easily employed.

Regardless of the methods used to collect information, certain data is essential before problem behavior and conflict can be modified. This type of information may be listed as follows:

1. Secure a history of the problem behavior and areas of conflict, how long they have been present, and the occasions when it is manifest. To secure this information, the counselor may have the parents select a particular day of the week and describe the family's activities and interactions.

2. State identified problem behaviors in behavioral terms so their frequency can be observed and measured. If this information is obtained by personal interview, encourage the parents to avoid vague descriptions of the problem behavior. Have them describe exactly the identified client's *words* and *actions*.

3. Identify the persons present when the problem behavior occurs and the reinforcement maintaining it.

4. Specify the responsibilities and roles each parent assumes. Based on this data, one

parent may be "set up" for more conflicting interaction with the identified client. For example, if the mother is assigned the role of "disciplinarian," she probably has more frequent conflict with the client and is more prone to use punishment. A change in parental roles and reinforcement practices may quickly bring the undesirable behavior under control.

5. Identify parent expectations and behavior requirements for the client to determine whether the expectations are realistic. This information can be obtained by asking the parents to indicate how they would like the client to behave and then comparing it to the client's playmates or classmates of similar age and background. The reasonableness of the parents' expectations is quickly revealed.

6. Identify the type and frequency of reinforcement and punishment the parents use in dealing with problem behavior. This step usually reveals the parent who has the more positive reinforcement property and who is likely to be the most effective change agent. It also reveals the reinforcement procedures that must be changed.

7. Inquire about and list reinforcing stimuli and events that are likely to change the client's problem behavior.

8. Observe and record the frequency of the problem behavior and note each area of parent-child conflict. Encourage the parents to make these observations so they are aware of the problem behavior's frequency and have some basis to judge the effectiveness of treatment procedures.

When the appropriate data have been obtained and analyzed, behavior modification procedures are implemented, although parents are not always willing to implement the behavior change procedures. They may minimize the frequency or severity of the child's difficulties or attribute the causes to the child's stubbornness, lack of "will power," or inadequate motivation to behave more acceptably. By so doing, they extricate themselves from involvement by denying the problems and their contribution to them.

Parental resistances can be handled in three ways. First, if the parents have not observed and recorded the child's behavior at home, encourage them to do it for three days. Indicate that it is a systematic way to determine the extent to which the child's behavior is problematic. Second, if they declare that they are unable to observe the child's behavior at home, ask them if you may do so for three evenings when all family members are present. The prospect of having someone else in the home to observe and record child behavior is likely to increase their incentive to do it themselves. Third, observe and record the child's behavior at school. If the child has problems at home, the probability is high that he exhibits problems at school. The problem behaviors exhibited at school are defined in behavioral terms, and six thirty-minute observations should be obtained at various times during the day. Observations should record whether the child's problem behavior is self-initiated or in response to someone else. Then, if the parents claim that the client is "victimized" or forced to misbehave because of the actions of someone else, the data will show the extent to which it is true.

The results of the behavioral observation are presented to the parents. These data are not presented in a threatening or coercive way; rather, the parents are asked to examine the frequency with which certain behavior is exhibited and in whose presence. They are encouraged to look for trends and relationships and draw their own conclusions. If the procedure is handled properly, parent resistance is reduced and they

are more willing to proceed with treatment measures.

Intervention Methods

A child's or adolescent's problem behavior can be changed using several different methods. Traditionally, three general approaches have been used: (1) the child is the object of direct therapeutic attack and the parents are worked with incidentally; (2) both parents and child are seen as major clients and are directly involved in the therapeutic process; and (3) parents are regarded as the major clients and are directly involved in therapy or training.

Our discussion in Chapter 9 showed that few child problems exist in isolation. The child's behavior is a function of the reinforcement contingencies that maintain it and these contingencies are usually controlled by adults in the child's environment. Thus, most counselors and psychologists recognize that the simultaneous involvement of the parents and the child is often desirable and sometimes necessary.

With the advent of learning-based therapeutic procedures, a variety of methods have been used to work with parents alone or with both parents and child to modify undesirable problem behavior. We will briefly list several of them and then illustrate their use with a variety of problem behaviors that occur frequently in the home.

1. *Instructing the parents to respond appropriately to the child client.* The therapist encourages the parents to respond to the child in a way that promotes desirable behavior and extinguishes undesirable behavior. Instructions to the parents are "tailor-made" to the child's difficulties. The parents are not taught the basic principles

and procedures of behavior modification, although the therapist instructs the parents to use procedures based on learning theory.

2. *Therapist modeling of appropriate response to the child client.* In the clinic setting, the parents observe a therapist interacting appropriately with the child client. While the therapist-model is interacting with the child, another therapist describes or explains the therapist-model's selective responses to promote or extinguish certain behaviors. Subsequently, the parents are asked to imitate the therapist-model by responding to the child client in a similar manner.

3. *Audio-monitoring of parent response to the child client in the clinic setting.* Parent and child are placed in a playroom, and the therapist observes the interaction through a one-way window. The parent has an "ear-bug" communication device to receive instructions from the therapist. The parent is instructed to ignore certain behaviors, reinforce appropriate behavior, etc. (Welsh, 1966).

4. *Observation and instruction of parents at home.* The therapist observes and analyzes the parents' interaction with the child client at home. The therapist identifies problem behaviors and instructs the parents to positively reinforce the desired behavior and also extinguish the undesirable behavior (Peine, 1969).

5. *Therapist-modeling, instruction in behavior modification procedures, and implementation of the program at home.* In the clinic setting, the therapist demonstrates responses that promote the desired behavior and eliminate the undesirable behavior. Parents are instructed in the use of specific behavior modification principles and procedures that are subsequently implemented in the home. Baseline measures are taken before the treatment program is initiated, and treatment and post-treatment effects are carefully evaluated. Observation and instruction of the parents at home continue until the parents are able to operate independently (Wetzel, Baker, Roney, and Martin, 1966; Risley, 1968).

6. *Group training of parents as therapists to their own children.* Parents are trained to perform therapeutic roles using a variety of procedures. Hanf (1969) developed a six-week training program for nineteen mothers to modify a variety of maternal behaviors. Mother-child interaction was analyzed using videotapes, and mothers were taught to analyze antecedent and consequent events. Appropriate maternal responses were taught using an ear-bug monitoring system, and a therapist modeled selective responding procedures while mothers observed the interaction. The mothers were also trained to use several procedures to help them become more "socially rewarding" in parent-child interactions. Although Hanf does not report specific data on the success of the program, her training program is most comprehensive. Also, because her program focuses on broad classes of maternal response rather than specific problems, her training methods may be preventative as well as corrective.

Berkowitz and Graziano (1972) describe a training program developed by Walder and his associates. The program consisted of fifteen weeks of training parents who had children with difficulties ranging from conduct disorders to autistic behavior. Parents were taught methods of behavior analysis and operant methods in modifying parent-child relationship problems. The training program had several interesting features.

(a) A contract was devised with each family specifying their involvement. (b) Weekly meetings were held with several families in which films, lectures, discussions, reading assignments, and homework were used. (c) Individual sessions between a family and therapist-consultant were conducted to apply the specific procedure to the identified problem. (d) Pre-test and post-test data using videotapes, personality tests, and parent reports of home behavior were used to evaluate treatment effects. (e) Contingencies to maintain appropriate parent behavior were also developed. A response-cost procedure was devised that resulted in a loss of tokens (check marks) when the parents did not complete certain assignments. Consultants visited the home weekly, and two families met together on a weekly basis.

The training program proved to be highly effective. The results indicated positive change on personality tests and videotape ratings. A follow-up conducted two years later indicated that the changes were maintained.

The six basic types of intervention methods do not exhaust all of the possibilities; others have used various combinations of the procedures we have discussed. One final intervention procedure is very useful in treating problem behavior in the home and will be discussed at some length below.

The Home Token Economy

The home token economy (HTE), like other token reinforcement systems, is used to alter child home behavior that parents consider problematic. Tokens in the form of points, chips, or tabs are used to promote the desired behavior,

and a response-cost system in the form of fines is used to reduce the frequency of undesirable behavior. Earned tokens are exchanged for material reinforcers or reinforcing events. The development of a home token economy may be divided into a series of steps:

1. An initial interview is held with the parents to analyze the nature of parent-child conflict and to identify behavior parents consider inappropriate or problematic. Parent-child interaction is carefully analyzed, and the parents' disciplinary and reinforcement practices are determined.

2. Undesirable and desirable behaviors are specified.

3. Material reinforcers and reinforcing events are identified that will serve to promote the desired behavior.

4. The therapist constructs a chart of the desirable behavior, undesirable behavior, and privileges (material reinforcers and reinforcing events). Point values for the desired behavior, fines for the undesirable behavior, and the point cost for each privilege are listed on the chart. For bookkeeping purposes, the chart also contains spaces for recording the points earned, fines levied, or privileges purchased by the child (or children) each day.

5. The system is explained to the parents. They are told that the home token economy is a way of promoting or altering a child's behavior by systematically regulating consequences for both desirable and undesirable behavior.

6. The parents observe and record the child's behavior for a period varying from three days to a week. On the chart, they tally

every occurrence of desirable and undesirable behavior exhibited by the child daily. It is also helpful to have the parents note the child's free-choice activities and the privileges the parents have granted him. These data are used to establish a baseline for the desirable and undesirable behavior and to check the potential value of the privileges that have been tentatively identified. If so indicated by the parents' data, the program is modified.

7. The program is explained and presented to the child. Reactions are solicited, and privileges that the child feels are highly desirable may be added to the program. It is explained to the child that the program will enable him to do or acquire things that he wants and will make home a more pleasant place for everybody concerned.

8. The parents implement the program and are encouraged to contact the therapist by phone during the week if problems arise that the parents cannot handle. The parents are asked to *not change the program without first consulting the therapist.* Initially, three or four weekly interviews are held with the parents to modify the program if necessary and to make certain that it is being carried out properly. The parents are requested to bring in the completed charts so the therapist can analyze the system's operation and have a continuous record of it. After the first month or so, parent interviews are held every two or three weeks. These interviews help the parents improve their general style of interacting with the child and to learn social reinforcement procedures that will ultimately be required to maintain the desired child behavior when the HTE is faded out.

To make a home token economy operable and effective, several important questions must be answered: What point values will be assigned to the desirable behaviors? What types of fines should be levied for the undesirable behaviors? How do you avoid the prospect of the child going in "debt" if the undesirable behavior occurs with high frequency? What happens if the parents "nag" the child to perform the desirable behavior? How can the parents be encouraged to maintain the system?

Let us consider these questions and indicate how each potential problem area can be handled. The point values assigned to the desirable behaviors are based on their frequency. For example, if a child performs a desirable behavior relatively infrequently, it is given a higher point value. Similarly, if an undesirable behavior occurs very frequently, a higher fine is levied when that behavior is exhibited. The total points that can be earned for desirable behavior should be greater than (or at least equal to) the potential fines that might be levied. Otherwise, the child client goes into "debt," or becomes a "welfare" client and is less likely to modify his behavior, because, as we have noted, desirable behavior is not likely to be promoted by punishment alone; punishment of undesirable behavior does nothing to promote desirable behavior.

If a child client goes into "debt," the relative point values should be changed, or a bonus can be given when a child has an especially good day or week. By so doing, the child client does not develop the attitude that "in spite of what I do, I get punished."

The parents are instructed not to "nag" but rather told to say nothing and to give no points until the desirable behavior is exhibited. When the child exhibits undesirable behavior, the parents are instructed not to reprimand, criticize, or scold. However, when the child performs a desirable behavior, they are encouraged to give praise generously.

The parents are instructed to place tallies on the chart at the time the desirable or undesirable behavior occurs. If they do not, *parents are fined* a certain number of points and these are given as bonus points to the child.

Many potential conflict situations between parent and child can be avoided if the parents make certain that a desirable or undesirable behavior has in fact been executed according to the terms originally specified. When a child performs a desirable behavior (such as completing a chore), he is required to inform the parent. The parent is asked to check whether the task has been completed satisfactorily and award points immediately. Fines may be levied only when parents have *observed* a child performing an undesirable behavior, for otherwise siblings may tattle on each other, or a fine may be levied unfairly.

Practical limits must be set on the number of times per day the child may execute specific desirable behaviors and how often he may purchase a privilege. Unless rules are established to the contrary, children soon discover that they can greatly increase their points by executing the desirable behavior excessively. For example, it is desirable for a child to brush his teeth three times a day, but fifteen times is unnecessary and excessive. Therefore, rules are set up that limit the number of times a child will receive points for such desirable behaviors. Similarly, rules are established to deter a child from purchasing an inordinate amount of a particular privilege. A child may stockpile his points and then suddenly declare that he wants to buy five hours of television time from nine o'clock to two o'clock in the morning. This type of problem can be avoided by establishing limits on privilege time per day. Also, the child client should be encouraged to spend his points on some regular basis, and a maximum should be placed on the number of points that can be accumulated.

The parents compute the point balance daily and discuss with the child the privileges he

would like to buy. Most parents find that this can best be done immediately after school or early in the evening. The child can then decide which privileges he will purchase for the remainder of the day and the following day.

Many of these problems can be prevented by typing a list of instructions which answers questions that usually arise when the program is first implemented. The parents are encouraged to place the sheet next to the HTE chart, which may be hung in a central location in the home.

Welsh and Alvord (1972) used a home token economy with three siblings (six, eight, and eleven years old) who exhibited a variety of disruptive behavior at home. Fighting, yelling, and interrupting were so frequent that the parents had little control over the children. Ten desirable and five undesirable behaviors in each child were the objects of modification. Nine privileges (television time, staying up late at night, bedtime snacks, overnight guests, etc.) were utilized as reinforcing events. Privileges were purchased by points earned for performing desirable behavior and fines were levied for undesirable behavior. The program was continued for a period of three weeks; then the parents went on vacation and the program was terminated.

The three-week modification program made dramatic changes in the children's behavior. The incidence of undesirable behavior in the eleven-year-old boy decreased from a baseline of 46 to a mean of 5.7 during the modification period. The frequency of undesirable behavior in the eight-year-old girl decreased from a baseline of 58 to a weekly mean during modification of 3. A similar change was noted in the six-year-old boy. Thirty-seven undesirable behaviors during baseline decreased to a weekly mean of 4.3 during modification. Desirable behavior also changed in a very positive direction. The eleven-year-old's baseline rate of 10 desirable behaviors increased to a weekly mean of 59 during modification. The incidence of desirable behavior in the eight-year-old during baseline was 5 and changed to 45.3. The six-year-old's 6 desirable behaviors during baseline increased to a mean frequency of 46.3 during modification.

A second baseline taken eight weeks after the home token economy was discontinued showed an increase in undesirable behavior and a decrease in desirable behavior. However, substantial increases in desirable behavior and decreases in undesirable behavior were maintained. Overall gains in desirable behavior equalled or exceeded the first baseline by 400 percent.

Demanding Behavior

Many parents seem to experience excessive difficulty dealing with the demands of their children. Rather than being able to control their children, they are controlled by them. Some children often set up their own rules, and parents appear to comply with them. One often gets the impression that the parents are afraid to get angry and consequently become objects that are skillfully manipulated by the children.

A method for dealing with parent-child problems of this type has been reported by Wahler, Winkel, Peterson, and Morrison (1965). In their therapeutic procedure, both the parents and child are involved. The mother and child are first placed in a play situation to classify the child's deviant behavior and to determine the reinforcement contingencies that maintain it. Rather than have the mother observe the therapist working with the child, she is given instructions before and after the therapy session with her child. While in the playroom with the child, the mother is signaled with a light when to respond to the child. If a signal is not given, she is instructed to sit and read a book and not respond to the child. If the mother is able to discriminate

when to reinforce or when to ignore her child, the light system is used to reinforce the mother when she responds correctly.

Wahler et al. successfully used the procedure with a six-year-old boy who controlled the time he went to bed, the food he ate, and the activities he performed in the house. Apparently, the parents were unable to refuse any of the child's demands. When attempts were made to handle the child's demanding behavior, the child's crying and shouting led the parents to concede to the demands.

Application of the methods previously described extinguished the child's demanding behavior. To determine whether the mother's new response to the child had changed his behavior, the mother was asked to reinstate the methods she had used before the therapeutic program was begun. The return of the child's demanding behavior indicated that it was the mother's behavior change that had promoted the therapeutic change in the child. However, when she reinforced cooperative behavior, the child's cooperative behavior increased to a high rate.

One of the authors worked with the parents of an eight-year-old boy who was extremely demanding—particularly when he was in a store. Analysis of the child's developmental history revealed that the parents had unintentionally taught the child demanding behavior. The child had acquired language facility at a young age, and whenever the child and his mother were in a store, he would identify objects by name. The parents were delighted by this behavior and would frequently buy the items the child requested. Obviously, his demanding behavior was reinforced.

To modify the child's demanding behavior, the parents were instructed to give the child five nickels before entering a store. The child was told that he could spend all the money if he did not make demands of the parents while in the store. Each time he made a demand, a nickel would be taken from him. He would be allowed to spend the sum that remained just before leaving the store.

On the first day the child made one demand and lost five cents. The second, third, and fourth times the child was in the store, he made no demands. On the fifth occasion, he made seven demands and lost the twenty-five cents. On the following day, he made one demand. However, from that point on, he made no further demands of his mother to buy things while in a store.

To make certain that the demanding behavior had been extinguished, a new procedure was implemented. The child was informed that if he did not make any demands while in a store, he would be given twenty-five cents when they left the store. This procedure continued until the child went one week without making any demands. At this point, reinforcement was placed on an intermittent schedule. The child was told that he would receive twenty-five cents sometimes but not at other times. To avoid a return of the demanding behavior, the parents were asked to administer the reinforcement rather frequently and to occasionally offer a bonus for appropriate behavior. The demanding behavior was maintained at a very low level.

The parents were instructed to use a similar response-cost procedure in dealing with the child's demanding behavior at an amusement park. The parents were instructed to inform the child that each time he made a request that had not been earlier negotiated, he would be required to sit and watch the other children enjoy the "fun activity." The procedure succeeded in dramatically reducing the child's demanding behavior in the amusement park. The parents utilized similar procedures to deal with other demanding behaviors the child exhibited at home.

The Wahler et al. study, as well as the case report, show that ignoring demanding behavior and positively reinforcing the child when he exhibits its opposite can often reduce demanding behavior. When the problem behavior has existed for a long time, however, response cost and time-out may also have to be combined with these procedures. Once the undesirable behavior has been reduced to a low level, an intermittent reinforcement schedule should be used to make the treatment effects durable.

Sibling Rivalry

Sibling conflict appears to be a natural occurrence in most homes. Usually the severity of sibling rivalry does not warrant therapeutic intervention, but parents often report it is a problem and are willing to utilize procedures that decrease sibling conflict.

Corsini and Painter (1975) suggest that one method of dealing with this problem is simply to avoid intervening with sibling fighting and arguing unless physical abuse is involved. They believe that bickering and arguing should be ignored by either leaving the room or by asking the children to go outside. In this way the parents do not provide an audience, and arguing and fighting are not reinforced by parent attention.

O'Leary, O'Leary, and Becker (1967) have demonstrated how parents can be taught to greatly reduce sibling rivalry. The procedures they used were somewhat unusual in that the therapist went into the home to help the parent to control the deviant sibling interactions. It will be seen how these methods might be necessary in some cases and will probably result in maximum treatment effects.

Before the treatment procedures were initiated, a baseline rate of cooperative behavior was recorded. When these observations were completed, the therapist rewarded the children with candy and praise each time cooperative behavior was exhibited. Cooperative behaviors were defined as saying "Please" and "Thank you." Also, answering each other's questions and playing together constituted cooperative play. This procedure continued for two days; on the third and fourth days, reinforcement was changed to a variable-ratio schedule. On the fifth day, the children were informed that candy could be earned only if they exhibited certain specified behaviors. The expected behaviors were carefully explained to them. For each successive day during the experimental period, the behaviors for which candy could be earned were described to the children. Also on the fifth day, the children were given check marks in addition to the candy. On a blackboard each child's name was placed in a column, which received a check mark for each instance of cooperative behavior; at the same time, the children were told who received it. Check marks were exchanged for reinforcers, such as candy, kites, comic books, etc. Gradually, the number of check marks required to receive a reinforcer was increased.

To determine the effectiveness of the experimental procedures, a second baseline observational period was initiated, executed by an observer in the therapist's absence. The results showed that the deviant behavior rose to its pretreatment level. When the second experimental period was begun, only two days were required to increase cooperative behavior to the rate obtained in the first experimental period.

At this time, the mother was taught to implement the experimental procedures. The time-out procedure was used when the children displayed physical aggression or engaged in name calling. The therapist remained in the home to instruct the mother when token or time-out procedures were to be used. As the mother became able to employ the procedures effectively, the therapist gradually assumed a less active role. Ultimately, the parent was able to administer the procedures independently.

A time-out procedure was added because the check-mark system did not appear to be effective enough to eliminate all of the aggressive behavior. The bathroom was used as a time-out

room, where the children were required to remain for at least five minutes. If the child displayed deviant behavior in the time-out room, the behavior had to subside for at least three extra minutes before the child was permitted to leave the room. These procedures proved very effective during the second experimental period, and the mother obtained highly cooperative behavior.

It is of interest to note that an older child's deviant behavior was not entirely eliminated. The child continued to display some aggressive behavior at school. However, both the teacher and parents indicated that the child had made considerable progress during the year.

O'Leary's approach may be varied by utilizing mutual penalties. If, for example, two siblings are engaged in fighting, both children can be placed in time-out. It is best to put them in separate rooms and to make certain that there are no reinforcing activities in which the children can engage while restricted. One or both children may declare that the other is responsible for the altercation and that they are being penalized unfairly. Determination of who started the dispute is difficult because each child may muster good evidence for his case. Most parents discover that it is a mistake to get involved in the complex judgment of the "guilty party," unless they have actually observed the altercation from the beginning. It is better to enforce an equal time-out penalty and inform the children it will be consistently enforced in the future. Children soon learn that it is much better to solve their conflicts in less aggressive ways.

Bedtime Problems

Bedtime problems appear to be of two types: (1) procrastination on activities before going to bed and (2) not staying in bed and going to sleep. Some parents report that these tasks take as long as an hour and a half every night.

One of the authors has modified the first type of bedtime problem. Before bedtime, all of the children are called together for a family meeting and are told the activities they must perform before going to bed. These activities are listed on a chart and the bedtime is specified. A second chart, with about twenty boxes, is also shown to the children. Paper tabs are placed over the boxes so the children cannot see what is written in them. The children are informed that each night they have completed all listed activities and are ready for bed on time, a tab will be pulled and they will be able to do or have the item written in the box. They are told that many of the boxes have "all kinds of fun things," and the game will be enjoyable for everyone to play.

Various reinforcers are written under the tabs. For example: "ten cents," "thirty additional minutes before bedtime," "a twenty-five-cent toy," "a candy treat," "a dish of ice cream," "you're doing a good job of getting ready for bed," "a meal at a favorite restaurant," "a trip to an amusement park," or other reinforcing materials and events.

The system is organized so that *all* children must complete the preparatory bedtime activities before a specified time. If they are not achieved by all, *none* of the children have the opportunity to receive reinforcement. This provision requires that all children assume their individual responsibilities. Moreover, the older siblings often assume a monitoring role and encourage the younger siblings.

The reinforcement system provides for social reinforcement also. It is a good practice to fill about four boxes with positive reinforcing statements, and the children should not be able to predict the appearance of these boxes.

The procedure can be varied. For example, response cost can be added by filling *all* the boxes with material reinforcers or reinforcing events, and—if the children fail to earn reinforcers—removing the tabs to disclose what the children *might* have received. Or, the failure

to execute the desirable behavior may be dealt with by levying a fine (e.g., an earlier bedtime the following evening or the loss of a privilege). If one child in the family is consistently responsible for all the children's loss of reinforcement, an individual penalty may be levied against that child.

Similar procedures can be used to handle the out-of-bed problem. As many of the reinforcing events are given the following day, the receipt of reinforcement could be made contingent on staying in bed.

Wolf, Risley, and Mees (1964) utilized a simple procedure to modify a disturbed child's out-of-bed behavior. At bedtime, the child was placed in his bed with the door to his room left open. If the child left his bed, he was instructed to return and go to sleep or the bedroom door would be closed. If a temper tantrum occurred, the door remained closed until the child ceased his tantrum. When the child returned to bed and stopped crying, the door was opened and remained open as long as he complied with the request.

With a little ingenuity, the procedure can be modified and used with most bedtime problems. While opening and closing the bedroom door will work, a light or a child's favorite toy may also be used; that is, a light is left on or a child may keep his favorite blanket or toy in his room as long as he stays in bed. If he does not, the light is turned off, or the toy or blanket is removed until he exhibits the desired behavior.

Check marks or points might also be used to promote staying-in-bed behavior by assigning points for the desirable behavior, levying fines for the undesirable behavior, and devising an exchange system for back-up reinforcers that are appealing to the child.

Refusal to Eat

Most parents recognize the importance of nutrition, but often their children do not comply with parental eating demands. A child of one of the present writers had a problem with eating. After some analysis, the author discerned that the problem appeared as a result of excessive negative attention to the child's eating. Consequently, a regime was instituted in which the manner of eating as well as the quantity eaten was ignored. However, this procedure did not appear to change the behavior, and a second procedure was implemented. When the child exhibited the undesirable behavior, she was dismissed from the table and placed in a time-out room. This procedure was equally ineffective. Finally, a method that employed both primary and secondary reinforcement proved to be successful.

The child was rated on a scale from one to four by the amount of food she ate. One point was obtained for merely touching the food, two points were received for eating half of the meal, three points were received for a portion somewhat greater than half, and four points were received for eating the whole meal. A reasonable time limit was given for eating, followed by an evaluation. Initially, each point earned was paired with candy. To make candy a potent reinforcer, it was withheld at other times during the day. When the child had accumulated enough points, she was able to exchange them for a small toy. The toys were chosen in advance by the child and she did not receive them until the specified number of points had been earned.

The number of points required to earn a toy was initially small, but gradually increased. Highly valued activities were also used as reinforcers. Points could be exchanged for a trip to the zoo, amusement park, etc. In addition, the child was given a small "bonus toy" when four points were earned. This "bonus toy" was always paired with praise and given on a variable basis when she earned four points for any one meal.

The child's eating increased to a level satisfactory to both parents. After the first week, the child was able to score her own eating behavior.

Although this procedure was used for the supper meal only, it had its effects on lunch and breakfast.

To determine whether the reinforcers were in fact influencing the behavior, the procedure was terminated for a one-month period. For almost two weeks the child's eating behavior was equivalent to that attained during the experimental period. The eating behavior appeared to be maintained as a result of the child's grading herself at dinnertime. During the third and fourth weeks, a sharp decline in appropriate eating behavior was noted. A reinstatement of the procedures quickly increased the child's eating habits to the level of the first experimental period. The child was eventually placed on a variable schedule and her eating behavior is now satisfactory to her parents.

A more serious type of refusal to eat is anorexia nervosa (a limited appetite for food, sometimes followed by vomiting). This problem appears to be more common with females, and it usually makes its appearance at puberty. The problem is usually not detected until there has been considerable weight loss, and hospitalization is often necessary. Anorexia nervosa has been treated in two stages. First, the client is hospitalized until sufficient weight has been gained. Second, the client is released from the hospital and preventative therapy is subsequently implemented. Behavioral procedures have been quite effective in the first stage but have not been used in a systematic way in the second stage (Stunkard and Mahoney, 1976; Gambrill, 1977).

Hallsten (1965) treated a twelve-year-old anorexic girl. When the girl was admitted to the hospital she was fifty-seven inches tall and weighed fifty-seven pounds; she was twenty-five pounds underweight. Three years before, she weighed ninety pounds and was frequently referred to as "fatty" by her peers. To decrease the child's weight, a doctor had placed her on a diet which apparently included the use of positive reinforcement. The program was effective, but the weight loss reached serious proportions. Apparently, when the child began to lose weight she experienced a reduction of anxiety about being fat. When her weight loss became excessive and she was threatened with the loss of affection from her parents and friends, she coped with it by losing weight to deal with the anxiety.

Treatment was begun by informing the girl that she could not see visitors until she gained weight. The girl was permitted to have one visitor for every two pounds she gained. After nine days, the weight loss had stopped but she had not gained any weight.

Further analysis revealed that the child had an intense fear of storms. The therapist decided to modify this fear with systematic desensitization procedures before further steps were taken to enhance weight gain. The rationale was that if her fear of storms could be quickly modified, the child would be more confident about the systematic desensitization method in altering her fear of being fat. The fear of storms was modified in one week.

Systematic desensitization procedures were then implemented to deal with the weight loss. The girl was trained in relaxation and asked to imagine different scenes involving weight gain (sitting at the dinner table eating fatty food, standing in front of a mirror observing a weight gain). These events were presented in hierarchical form and the girl reported no anxiety at any time. The evening following the first therapy session the girl ate the entire evening meal. Twelve additional sessions were held and scenes were presented in which she was intensely teased for being fat. The girl ultimately gained the desirable amount of weight.

This case study shows that systematic reinforcement and desensitization procedures can be very effective in decreasing and increasing weight gain. However, the practitioner should coordinate his efforts with medical consultation and watch for unsought consequences.

Obesity

Any parent or teacher who is intimately acquainted with an overweight child or teenager knows the distress they suffer. They are the frequent object of jokes and in their solitary moments experience much anxiety and depression. It is a serious problem to the obese individual and should be alleviated with effective therapeutic intervention.

Medical treatment and supervision should be an inherent part of the behavior modification procedures. With some children, the problem can often be effectively handled by having a physician prescribe an appropriate diet combined with contingency management procedures. For example, the authors are acquainted with one overweight child who quickly lost weight with the opportunity to play football as the reinforcing contingency. Each day the child was "weighed-in" by the parents, and his weight was posted on a chart; loss of weight was generously praised by the parents. When the weight was at the desired level, the child was allowed to participate in a football league. The maintenance of a certain weight was also a requirement for playing. Thus, periodic "weigh-ins" were required. Maintenance procedures, verbal reinforcement, and contingency management were most effective in helping the child lose weight and in preventing weight gain.

Stunkard's (1972) method for modifying adult overweight problems is applicable to children and adolescents. First, the overweight individual is required to keep daily records of the type and amount of food eaten, and the eating situation. A chart of the data provides feedback to the overweight person. Studies show that when eating occurs with reinforcing stimulus or events such as television, talking to a friend, etc., it *increases eating*. By making eating a "pure act" without these reinforcing events, one can decrease eating behavior.

To modify excessive eating, the overweight individual is instructed to eat only in certain places (kitchen, cafeteria, or restaurant). A point system ensures that the individual is reinforced for eating in a specific place, decreasing food intake, weight loss, and eating slowly. Points may be exchanged for highly valued privileges or money. With teenagers, particularly girls, the promise of new clothes after a specified weight loss can be very effective. We have not tried the method with teenagers, but it is likely Stunkard's results can be generalized.

Sloppiness

Sloppy, messy, or disorderly behavior cannot be considered very serious, but like bedtime and eating problems, it is irritating to parents. It can be unlearned if parents are given effective assistance. Patterson (1971) recommends a method used by Lindsley for dealing with such problems. The method involves the use of a "Saturday box." Parents simply explain to their children that when articles of clothing are found lying around the house they will be placed in the Saturday box. Once the clothes are deposited in the Saturday box, they cannot be worn until the box is open on Saturday.

Patterson also recommends that monetary fines be used. However, if fines are used, it is wise to specify them before the procedure is instituted to avoid any unnecessary conflict.

To make the Saturday box method work effectively, the children should be extended the same opportunity to deposit the parents' clothes in the box when found lying around. By giving the children the same rights as the parents, some of the negative aspects of the method are mitigated. As with most methods, consistency is essential. That is, if something is placed in the Saturday box, it should remain there until Saturday. This could mean that a child might have to wear two different-colored socks to school some day.

Teenagers will often scoff at this approach and indicate that their clothes are dirty and need to be washed anyway. To counteract this problem, it is recommended that the weekly wash not include the clothes in the Saturday box. The clothes in the box are returned to their owners on Saturday *after* the wash is done.

Parents can be encouraged to improvise on the Saturday box method in other ways. One such way is to give a "bonus" to a child who does not have any item in the box on Saturday. For extremely sloppy children, a daily "bonus" might have to be used for a few months before switching to the weekly method. With older children, a small fine may be used for each item in the box on Saturday.

Another approach used by one of the authors is the continual enforcement rule. The child or adolescent is told that personal belongings or used materials left in any room besides their own must be immediately cleaned up when left unattended. If a child begins to engage in another activity before cleaning up used materials, the used items must be picked up before he or she is permitted to continue in the new activity. Of course, personal belongings or play materials may be left around for some time before a parent discovers them. If this happens, a parent is encouraged to enforce the rule immediately, irregardless of what the child is doing. When a child has to stop eating or watching TV or return from a friend's house to pick up something left lying around, it is not long until the child learns to put belongings or materials away immediately after use.

Although sloppy or disorderly behavior is not a severe problem, changing this behavior greatly reduces parent irritation. Equally important, in mastering the problem, parents will have learned a method that can be applied to changing other undesirable child behavior.

Tantrum Behavior

Children's temper tantrums irritate parents and cause them much embarrassment when the behavior is exhibited in a public place. If a child has a tantrum in public, it is easier for the parent to give in to the child's demand than to handle the behavior appropriately. Parents are often sensitive to what others think about them and often reinforce undesirable behavior to avoid an "unpleasant" scene.

Most parents who realize that their child is "controlling" them through tantrum behavior will attempt to ignore it. Unfortunately, many parents ignore the behavior inconsistently, intermittently reinforce it, and thus tend to make it resistant to extinction.

Wolf, Risley, and Mees (1964) have used behavioral methods with a boy who displayed severe tantrum behavior—head banging, hair pulling, and face slapping. The boy, an autistic child, was first hospitalized to control his behavior. A time-out procedure was used when the child had a tantrum. He was placed in his room and the door remained closed until he stopped the tantrum. Ward attendants, however, unknowingly reinforced the tantrum behavior. They talked to the child and tried to explain and even apologized to him for placing him in the room. To reduce the effects of the attendants' reinforcement, a ten-minute minimum in the room was required. When the behavior was under reasonable control, the child was allowed to go home, and the parents were taught the same methods for handling the tantrums at home. A follow-up study six months later revealed no further tantrums.

Coe (1972) used a token reinforcement system to modify the behavior of a twelve-year-old boy who exhibited severe temper tantrums. The tantrums were so extreme that on one occasion he had threatened his mother with a knife. A token system was set up in which points were earned for appropriate behavior and point fines were imposed for tantrum behavior. One point was lost for each minute of tantrum behavior (up to a maximum of thirty minutes). Points were exchanged for privileges and most privileges had to be purchased.

The token system worked well until the mother violated one of its conditions. Several weeks after it was implemented, she refused to let her son buy the privilege to stay up late. Her refusal precipitated a tantrum that lasted for a considerable amount of time. Later, to counteract the mother's mistake, the boy was allowed to earn double points for appropriate behavior. However, it was stipulated that 20 percent of the points would go toward purchasing privileges around the house and 80 percent were used to pay off the debt his tantrum behavior had created. Also, each time a tantrum lasted more than thirty minutes, he received a spanking from his father.

The new contingencies rapidly decreased the tantrum behavior at home and were subsequently implemented at school. A follow-up a year later indicated that the reduction in tantrum behavior had been maintained.

Dependent and Fearful Behavior

Parents may unintentionally teach their children dependent or fearful behavior by doing too many tasks for a child, failing to provide sufficient incentives for independent behavior, punishing excessively, presenting a picture of the world as a frightening place, or modeling fearful behavior with frequent fear reactions.

The child simply learns the behavior by imitating the parent or through vicarious conditioning.

Patterson (1971) has suggested that dependent behavior can be modified by reinforcing successive approximations of independent behavior. Dependent areas and successive approximations to the independent behavior are specified, and the child is systematically reinforced at each step until the desired behavior is learned. For example, at first the child is reinforced for finding his shoes, then for putting them on. A few days later, the child is reinforced for finding other articles of clothing and putting them on, and at still a later time, for performing a variety of chores. Step by step he is reinforced for each approximation until the target behavior is exhibited with reasonable frequency.

For some children, the dependent behavior is much too strongly entrenched for such a method to be effective. A child may be fearful of leaving mother at all and be unable to involve himself in play with his peers. With such children, a method described by Patterson (1969) appears applicable. A certain period of the day is set aside to encourage the desirable behavior. The child is given a small cup and each time he makes an attempt to interact with his peers, candy is placed in the cup. At first, the child is reinforced for merely looking at his peers, later for interacting with them.

Interaction is greatly facilitated if his peers are reinforced for initiating interactions with him. When they do, a piece of candy is taken from the child's cup and given to the peer. In this way, the fearful child is encouraged to initiate interaction with his peers and his peers have an additional incentive to interact with the fearful child.

As the child begins to display social interaction, the parent gradually moves into the background. It may be best to move away a few feet at first, and then gradually extend the distance. When this is achieved, the mother tells the child that she must go into the house for a minute and will return in a short time; the frequency and duration of her stays in the house are gradually increased.

With children whose dependent and fearful behavior is severe, it is desirable to use additional procedures. Since these children cannot be "talked out" of their fear, it is necessary to teach unfearful behavior (Patterson, 1971). To do this, a child must be encouraged to perform behavior that is incompatible with fear. Patterson illustrates the concept by using an example of a child who is fearful of going into the water. It is suggested that the parents give the child candy for spending a few seconds sitting in the water without crying. Since eating candy cannot occur while the child is crying, the two behaviors are usually incompatible. To the extent that the candy is a potent reinforcer, the child, by successive steps, is encouraged to give up the fear of water. Dealing with a similar problem, Bentler (1962) had the child's mother slowly introduce the child to larger and larger amounts of water while the mother was in close contact with the child. In addition, toys the child frequently played with were present. This last procedure is a form of reciprocal-inhibition therapy, discussed in an earlier chapter.

Many fears can be overcome with the use of similar principles described by Patterson (1971) and by Bentler (1962). In a gradual manner, the parent reinforces the child's bravery for remaining in the fearful situation. At first, the child is encouraged to stay in the fearful situation for a short period of time. When he does, he is reinforced and the length of time is extended. To increase the child's desire to remain in the fearful situation, favorite objects such as a teddy bear or toy can be placed in the situation. The child is permitted to play with it as long as he remains in the situation that frightens him; it is withdrawn when he does not.

For some children, fear of separation from parents poses very difficult problems. Such a child may be assisted to conquer the fear by first being made to go outside with another adult in whom he has confidence. The mother may step just outside the door, remain for a few minutes, and reenter the house. This series of events is repeated several times the first day it is initiated. Of course, each time the child remains outside and does not cry, his adult companion immediately reinforces the child. If the child cries while the mother is inside, the mother should wait until the child stops crying before returning. This point must be emphasized to the mother, because her reappearance while the child is crying reinforces the crying behavior and not the independent behavior.

Working with parents of dependent and fearful children, the authors have found it extremely important to give praise (secondary reinforcement) to parents for efforts they make in reducing their child's dependent behavior. This seems to be necessary because the dependence of the child may satisfy some parental needs. To help the parents understand these needs and allow the child more independence may require skillful counseling.

Unfinished Homework

Most clinicians do not consider unfinished homework a serious problem, but it is an important concern to parents. They recognize that good study habits are essential to good academic progress and get concerned when children do not complete assigned school work.

Collier and Tarte (1977) emphasize the importance of certain procedures in getting children to do and complete homework. First, homework should be done at a regular time each day. To accomplish this, a timer might be started when a child arrives home from school; when the timer goes off forty-five minutes later, the child should be required to begin assigned homework. Second, to get the child engaged in study behavior, a token reinforcement system is used. They recommend a chart be made that lists the days of the week. Each time homework is completed for the day, the child receives a mark on the chart for that day. When five marks have been accumulated, they are exchanged for a treat or special privilege. Third, for children who experience difficulty completing or returning homework, the teacher should be asked to write out assignments for each day. If no homework is assigned, it should be so indicated on a note sent home. Finally, it is recommended that a time limit be set for those who procrastinate in doing their homework. At first, time limits should be liberal. However, as the child completes assigned work on a regular schedule, time limits should be made more stringent.

Phillips (1968) worked with three delinquent boys ranging in age from twelve to fourteen years, to increase their preparation for classroom assignments and homework. All were in a residential treatment center for delinquent children. The children were asked to carry with them a small index card on which their school assignments were written. The assignments were divided into five equal parts, and each part was scored independently. To earn reinforcement, the completed assignments had to be 75 percent accurate. Three types of reinforcers were used at various times throughout the experiment. The boys could earn one-fifth of the total points, money, or time for each assignment that had less than 25 percent error.

Money was first used to motivate the children to complete their assignments. The boys were given the choice of receiving the money either at the end of the day or at the end of the week. A second type of reinforcer was the earning of "late time," up to an hour of time that a boy could stay up later than usual, which, like the money reinforcer, could be used on the day it was earned or saved for the weekend. Earned points were used to obtain privileges such as riding a bike, watching TV, etc. The price of these particular privileges tended to vary, but usually one of them could be earned for completing all of the assignments with 75 percent accuracy for two days.

When the types of reinforcement were compared, the point system had proved most effective. Daily late time, though also effective, was less so, and money, interestingly enough, was least effective. At first it was thought that the ineffectiveness of money resulted from the boys' lack of experience with it, so they were given a weekly allowance for seven weeks, after which money was again used as a reinforcer. However, its reinstatement did not result in any better performance by the boys.

It would appear that clearly established rules, combined with systematic reinforcement, will likely deal with most problems associated with unfinished homework. A token system is easy to devise and use and may well be one of the more effective procedures for altering inappropriate study or homework completion.

Difficulty with Household Chores

Most parents expect children to do household chores, yet many complain that they have limited success in getting children to perform them properly. In some instances these difficulties stem from unreasonable parent expectations.

In cases in which parental expectations are reasonable but children do not carry out their chores, an approach suggested by Smith and Smith (1966) may be helpful. They suggest that for each chore assigned to a child, a reasonable time limit should be set. This may be done by specifying the time in minutes or by making it impossible to participate in a desired activity — watching TV, playing baseball, etc. — until the chore is performed. It is also absolutely essential that the chore request be enforced during the time specified. It may be desirable, for example, to turn off the TV until the child has completed the assigned task.

Corsini and Painter (1975) suggest that three conditions be instituted when a child refuses to do assigned chores. First, no one should do the child's chores for him. Second, the child should be required to do the chores before he is permitted to eat or even sleep. Third, a procedure called "work stoppage" should be implemented. Under this condition, the parents simply refuse to do their chores until the child does his. Of course, the work stoppage procedure is used rarely but should be an effective way to convey to a child that many of the things he enjoys is a result of the parents' labor.

A study by Christophersen, Arnold, Hill, and Quilitch (1972) illustrates the utility of the home token economy, as well as other procedures. They worked with two families whose children had difficulty performing assigned chores. With one of the families, a home token economy was used. The parents were instructed to specify the household chores, define their proper performance, assign point values to each chore, and impose a fine when the chores were not performed. The chores, point values, and fines were placed on a chart and posted in the house. Points earned and fines levied were also recorded on a chart for each child. Results indicated that the home token economy led to the daily performance of chores.

The procedures used with a second family involved a number of phases and treatments and are summarized briefly as follows:

1. *Basic elements of the system:* Household chores were identified and their performance was clearly specified. All chores had to be completed by 9:00 P.M. each evening. The chores were specified on a chart, and chore completion was designated by a "Yes" or "No."

2. *Baseline:* The chores were written on a chart and data were given to the children on their performance. Results: Percentage of chore completion was 0 for the son and 2 for the daughter.

3. *First experimental condition:* Children were given feedback on the number of chores completed or not completed each day. Results: Percentage of chore completion was 0 for the son and 4 for the daughter.

4. *Second experimental condition:* Stars were placed on the chart for each chore completed. Results: Percentage of chore completion was 12 for the son and 6 for the daughter.

5. *Third experimental condition:* Ten cents was given for each completed chore. Results: Percentage of chore completion for the son was 47 and 54 for the daughter.

6. *Fourth experimental condition:* Ten cents was given for each completed chore, and money bonuses were given for performance of all chores for seven consecutive days. Results: Percentage of chore completion was 87 for the son and 67 for the daughter.

7. *Fifth experimental condition:* Points were given for each chore completed and exchanged for privileges. Fines were levied for noncompletion of chores. Results: Percentage of chore completion was 59 for the son and 45 for the daughter.

8. *Second baseline:* No points were given but children had free access to all privileges they had purchased in the previous experimental condition. Results: Percentage of chore completion was 8 for the son and 4 for the daughter.

9. *Final experimental condition:* The point system (fifth condition) was reinstated.

Results: Percentage of chore completion was 47 for the son and 60 for the daughter.

The results clearly show that a monetary reinforcement system with a bonus had the greatest effect on chore performance. A point system was less effective but very successful in increasing the performance of chores. When reinforcing events were not contingent on the performance of chores, the children's motivation did not promote the desired behavior.

Brushing Teeth

A child's failure to brush his teeth regularly can hardly be considered a serious problem, but most parents feel children should learn the health habit. Behavior modification procedures can promote tooth brushing and reduce much of the hassle that accompanies it.

Lattal (1969) used contingency management procedures to increase tooth-brushing behavior in eight boys (9½ to 12½ years old) who attended a summer camp. Initially, the frequency of brushing was simply observed and recorded, but during the latter part of the baseline period, the boys were verbally instructed to brush their teeth. Contingency management procedures were then implemented to promote the target behavior. The boys were told that when they had brushed their teeth they would be permitted to go swimming after lunch. Contingencies were not used to promote brushing in the morning or evening.

Analysis of the data revealed that verbal instructions (or prompts) increased tooth brushing in some but not all of the boys. When contingency management was implemented, tooth-brushing behavior after the noon meal increased in most of the boys. No similar brushing increase occurred in the morning or evening when contingencies were not used. Apparently, when privileges are contingent on brushing, the behavior can be increased but does not naturally generalize to other situations. Therefore, contingencies to promote brushing should be used for each situation that the behavior is desired.

Proper brushing can also be increased by a simple monetary reinforcement system. Parents may place a miniature bank in the bathroom and post a chart on the door specifying the time for brushing. Each time the child brushes his teeth, the parents deposit a small sum in the bank. When the child fails to brush, a similar sum is removed from the bank. When the child has brushed his teeth three times a day for seven days, he receives an added bonus. As the frequency of brushing increases to a high rate, the child is reinforced on an intermittent basis. He is told that he will not receive money every time he brushes his teeth, but he will receive monetary surprises at various times for proper brushing. Ultimately, the behavior can be maintained using verbal reinforcement.

The two procedures we have discussed are effective, require little time, and greatly aid harmony between parent and child. Threats to obtain the desired behavior are unnecessary, and children enjoy seeing their bank accounts grow.

Procrastinating Before School

Children learn a variety of behaviors to avoid situations or tasks they do not want to face. They may dawdle when asked to do a chore, move at a snail's pace to carry out a parental request, and procrastinate about getting ready for school. It is tempting to attribute these behaviors to a "stage" the child is going through, or some idiosyncratic aspect of human nature, but, like most aspects of human behavior, it is learned and can be unlearned.

Hall, Axelrod, Tyler, Grief, Jones, and Robertson (1972) worked with a five-year-old preschool girl who procrastinated about getting ready for school in the morning. To modify the behavior, they suggested to the parents that the child be required to finish dressing within thirty minutes after the child awoke instead of her average of three hours and ten minutes. If she was not dressed and ready for school within thirty minutes, she was not permitted to watch television until 3:30 the same day. This contingency was utilized for seventeen days. During that time, it took the child an average of twenty minutes to get dressed. When the procedures were reversed and the contingencies were not used for seven days, the child's dressing time increased to one hour and twenty-six minutes. Thus, a relatively simple contingency can greatly reduce a child's procrastination about getting dressed.

With older children, the child can be required to prepare for school within a certain period of time. If the child does not exhibit the appropriate behavior, a privilege (such as use of the telephone or going out in the evening) is withdrawn for the day.

Another approach, somewhat more drastic in nature, may also be used. A child is given a specific amount of time to eat breakfast and prepare for school. If he is not ready by the stated time, he will be required to go to school in whatever clothing he has on when the time limit is up. (Of course, he would not be permitted to go to school in his underwear but would be asked to put on a bathrobe and trot off to school.) If school authorities are willing to cooperate with the plan, it will not take many trials before the child is prepared for school at the proper time.

A third procedure is to use a timer to signal the child when he should be dressed and ready for school. Each time the child is prepared at the specified time, he is reinforced with material reinforcers, reinforcing events, or points. If the child is not dressed when the timer rings, a privilege is withdrawn for that day or a point fine is levied. When the child performs target behavior at reasonable frequency, the timer is used on some days only. This alteration will not only maintain the target behavior at a high rate but will also make it much more durable.

Inappropriate Dinner Table Behavior

Many children show inappropriate dinner table behavior. When the behavior does not seriously deviate from appropriate etiquette, few parents seek help for such problems. Occasionally, parents seek consultation for a child who exhibits a variety of improper eating behaviors (e.g., cursing, fighting with siblings, playing with and throwing food) which detract from the enjoyment of a meal and should be modified.

Barton, Guess, Garcia, and Baer (1970) worked with severely retarded male subjects who were inmates at the Kansas Neurological Institute and ranged in age from nine to twenty-three years. The experimenters were interested in modifying four inappropriate dinner table behaviors: stealing food, eating with fingers, using utensils improperly, and "pigging" (eating food that had been spilled or directly from the mouth of another person). Three basic procedures were used with the different problem behaviors at various times: (1) removal from the table and loss of meal, (2) placement in time-out, and (3) withdrawal of the food tray for fifteen seconds. With most of the problem dinner table behaviors, removal from the table was used first and then combined with time-out. The results showed that all procedures had some effect, but time-out and withdrawal of food tray were equally effective. It is interesting to note that when time-out modified one behavior, it had no effect on other undesirable behaviors that were not subject to the modification procedure.

The procedures in the Barton et al. study are applicable to other children who exhibit inappropriate dinner table behavior. When a child exhibits this behavior, his plate might be removed for thirty seconds. If further infractions occur, a child might be required to eat apart from the family in a nonreinforcing room. Further inappropriate behavior might be handled with time-out and loss of the meal. If these procedures are consistently applied, the inappropriate behavior will probably be brought under control in a short time.

One of the authors worked with a parent of a two-and-a-half-year-old child who demanded that items of food be placed before him in a certain order. If his demands were not met, the child would yell or throw the food. Although the mother sometimes removed the child from the table, she would give him ice cream later to "carry him over to the next meal." The child had learned to shape his mother's behavior very well.

The author instructed the mother to arrange the child's food in the wrong order. If he behaved improperly, the child was told that he was "all through" and taken from the table. Later requests for food were to be ignored and denied. When the child exhibited proper dinner table behavior, the mother was instructed to praise him and tell him "he was becoming a big boy." Special treats were also used to reinforce the desired behavior. In three days the inappropriate behavior disappeared and remained extinguished for a week. On the tenth day the child exhibited the inappropriate behavior again, but it did not reappear after that time. A one-year follow-up revealed that the inappropriate behavior had not reoccurred.

Another child seen by one of the authors posed a different kind of dinner table problem. The child's table manners were satisfactory, but she talked incessantly. The parents and the other siblings were perturbed, because she monopolized the dinner table conversation. Two procedures were used to modify the inappropriate behavior. First, the parents set a timer at the beginning of each meal to ring five minutes later. The child was permitted to talk until the timer sounded but was required to stop at that time. After the timer had sounded, the child was permitted to ask only for food. Second, the parents placed a cup with ten pieces of candy by her plate. Each time she talked after the timer had sounded, one piece of candy was taken from the cup. She was told that, if she had five candies left at the end of the meal, she would earn ten minutes to talk with her mother or father privately. These procedures markedly reduced the child's incessant talking. Dinnertime became more enjoyable and, according to the mother, the child reduced her irrelevant chatter in other situations.

Fear of the Dark

Fear of the dark, ghosts, "bogeymen," and other imaginary fears are rather typical of preschool children. Some, however, such as fear of the dark and supernatural creatures, increase with age (Hurlock, 1964). Although most fears subside during the latter elementary years, some persist, cause distress to the child, and concern the parents.

Leitenberg and Callahan (1973) worked with nursery school and kindergarten children who were identified as fearing the dark through questionnaires sent to parents. They were then pretested to determine the extent of their fear of darkness. The children were told that they would play a game that involved going into a room and winning prizes. They were asked to go into rooms varying in darkness. The experimenters informed the children that they wished to determine how long they could stay in a room without becoming frightened. They were permitted to leave the room at any time they wished. The length of time the children re-

mained in the room was measured by a stopwatch, and all children were permitted to pick a prize regardless of the time they spent in a room. On the basis of this pretest procedure, seven pairs of children were selected. One member of the pair was placed in the experimental group and the other member in the control group. The experimental subjects were seen twice a week for a total of eight treatment sessions.

In the first treatment session the children were asked to go into a dark room and stay there until they felt afraid. If they expressed fear, the experimenter asked the child to come out of the room. The room was empty except for a chair. The only illumination was a light that could be seen under a door. The children could select a prize when they increased the time they stayed in the room. To show the children their length of time in the room, a thermometer-chart was constructed. Also, when a child increased his stay in the room, he was praised and given a prize. If his performance did not improve, he was informed that he did not do as well as on the previous trial. The sessions were terminated when a child stayed in the dark room for two consecutive five-minute trials or after eight sessions were completed.

The posttest procedures were very similar to the pretest procedures. The results indicated that the experimental group significantly increased the length of time they were able to remain in dark rooms. Apparently, feedback information and positive reinforcement can help to reduce children's fear of dark rooms.

Other procedures may equally apply in reducing children's fear of darkness. For example, a parent might devise a game of "hide-and-seek." Certain rooms in the house, lighted in various degrees of intensity, are prescribed as the only permissible hiding places. Points are given to the child who remains hidden the longest without discovery, and bonus points are also awarded to the child who hides in the darkest room. (The child is not told, of course, which room is the darkest. The illumination in the rooms is varied so that the bonus room has a different location each time.) When the child acquires a given number of points, he may exchange them for material reinforcers or reinforcing events. For each game the amount of light in each room is gradually decreased. In the eighth or tenth game, all rooms should be almost completely dark so that the child must go in a dark room to receive any points. Finally, the game is played in a backyard at night with similar rules for earning points; the desensitization of the child's fear of darkness can generalize to out-of-doors.

Oppositional Behavior

Stubborn, resistant behavior characterizes many children from two to four years of age. During that time, parental requests are often met with negativism. The behavior is observed so frequently that developmental psychologists have labeled that time period the "negative stage." Most children begin to exhibit more cooperative behavior near the end of that period, but some do not.

Wahler (1969a) worked with a five-year-old child who was oppositional at home and school. In the behavior modification strategy, the parents positively reinforced behavior incompatible with the oppositional and resistant behavior. Initially, the parents provided approval and praise whenever the child exhibited cooperative behavior, but, when the child was oppositional, he was sent to his room for five minutes. If he exhibited undesirable behavior while he was in time-out, he was required to remain in his room until that behavior ceased. Selective reinforcement of cooperative behavior and the use of time-out with oppositional behavior greatly decreased the undesirable behavior at home but not at school. Implementation of similar proce-

dures at school at a later time, however, did decrease the oppositional behavior there.

Boisvert (1974) used a token reinforcement system to work with a seven-year-old boy who was hostile and noncompliant. The parents reported that he argued excessively and was resistant to most requests. To modify the behavior, the boy was given three tokens for each hour that he did not behave aggressively. On the other hand, if he fought or behaved aggressively, he was fined two tokens and sent to his room for ten minutes. He also lost one token for each instance of arguing. Tokens were exchanged for candy and television viewing privileges.

In a six-week period, there was a marked decrease in fighting and parents reported they were more able to control their son. However, the treatment was not entirely effective in changing the other targeted behaviors.

One of the authors worked with a very oppositional three-year-old child. When the child exhibited cooperative behavior, a smiling-face token was placed on a chart; when the child exhibited oppositional behavior, a large X was marked on the smiling face. At the end of the day, the parents placed a piece of candy on each unmarked smiling face. After this procedure had been in operation for several days, a star was added to the reinforcement system. When the card was filled, the child was allowed to go to a store and buy a small toy. Gradually, the candy reinforcer was phased out, and the number of stars the child had to earn to buy a toy was increased. Each incident of cooperative behavior was positively reinforced by parent praise. Eventually, the cooperative behavior was largely maintained by verbal approval. On rare occasions when the child reverted to oppositional behavior, the stars quickly reinstated the cooperative behavior.

Similar procedures can be used with adolescents. The desired cooperative behavior must be clearly specified, and consequences appropriate for the adolescent's age must be used. Most adolescents can be reinforced with special privileges such as staying out later in the evening, telephone time, or use of the family car. Fines for uncooperative behavior may consist of allowance deductions, loss of staying-out time, and denial of the family car. Reinforcement must be given consistently, and withdrawal of privileges must be imposed regularly.

Talking-Back Behavior

Most parents are concerned about, but are not always certain about, how to handle the child's "talking-back" behavior. They often feel that the child's right of protest should be preserved, yet they fear that this kind of behavior demonstrates lack of respect and potential loss of control; thus, the parents are often hesitant to take action. Obviously, a parent must decide on the desirable behavior and enforce the appropriate contingencies. If a child is permitted to talk back and succeeds in his demands, the talking-back behavior is reinforced.

A relatively simple way to help parents deal with talking-back behavior is to instruct them to respond to the act of talking back and *not* to the child's or adolescent's verbalization. For example, if the child curses or complains and the parents believe the behavior is inappropriate, a consistent negative consequence should be imposed for each instance of talking back—not for what the child has said. By so doing, the parents are less likely to respond emotionally and to impose a consequence that is appropriate to the exhibited behavior. Of course, it goes without saying that a change agent should not attempt to modify the child's or adolescent's right to protest when parent demands are unreasonable or unjust.

One of the authors worked with a fourteen-year-old boy who harrassed his parents—

especially the mother—excessively and unreasonably. He was less prone to exhibit this behavior in his father's presence because the father occasionally used rather severe physical punishment.

Analysis revealed that viewing television and staying up late were reinforcing to the boy. Therefore, a response-cost system was devised in which the boy was required to go to bed fifteen minutes earlier for each instance of talking back. The plan was explained to the boy, and it was pointed out that while he would be permitted to discuss his feelings about any disputed issue, the parents would indicate when the discussion should be terminated. If the boy continued beyond that point, fifteen minutes would be deducted from the established going to bed time. It was also indicated that each day would be handled separately. That is, time fines could not be carried over from one day to the next.

The boy's talking-back behavior accelerated for the first three days during treatment. However, by the end of the week the inappropriate behavior had decreased markedly and was maintained at a low level from that point on. The boy was pleasantly surprised to see that his parents no longer got "emotional" on those occasions when he complained and were consistent in using the response-cost procedure. The parents were pleased with their new found ability to control their son without getting upset or angry.

As the case illustration suggests, response-cost procedures can be effective in reducing talking-back behavior. It is important to make certain that the reinforcement that is withdrawn is appealing to the client. With some adolescents, a monetary fine, loss of telephone privileges, or loss of use of the family car for each instance of talking back may also be effective. However, it should also be emphasized that reinforcement of the desired behavior is an equally important treatment target.

Parent-Child Communication Problems

There is a wise and old saying that goes something like this: "When the elders listen to the young, the young shall listen to their elders." The saying expresses wisdom because it recognizes that effective communication is a two-way street. And, the fact that it is old suggests that parent-child communication problems have been with us for some time.

Martin and Twentyman (1976) developed a program to teach parents and children effective methods of communication. Essentially, parents were taught to (1) stop blaming and lecturing, (2) avoid using power arbitrarily, (3) express feelings directly, (4) listen and paraphrase what has been said, (5) be more positive, and (6) negotiate agreements with children in a mutually acceptable way. Children are also taught to listen reflectively as well as how to express their feelings and points of view without withdrawing or being antagonistic.

Initially, parents are given practice sessions that teach them reflective listening and appropriate ways to express feelings. Parents are asked to respond to various hypothetical situations and are then given feedback regarding their performance. Then, in the presence of their child, an audiotape is played that contains examples of parents modeling effective listening and appropriate expressions of feeling. An identified problem is then presented and the child is asked to express how he or she feels regarding it. To encourage the participation of younger children, monetary reinforcement is given. A second audiotape is then played that contains examples of a child modeling appropriate expression of feeling. When this tape has been played, the parents and the child are encouraged to interact using the communication skills that have been modeled.

In the second phase, parents are asked to talk to their child without blaming, questioning, or lecturing. The child is asked to listen so that he can later state what he has heard his parents say. When the parents have concluded their statements, the child is asked to paraphrase what has been said. To encourage the child's response, points are given that are later exchanged for pennies. Once again, an audiotape is played that contains examples of a parent modeling appropriate expressions of feeling.

The third phase is devoted to training in conflict resolution. During this phase, the parents and the child are asked to provide possible solutions to an identified problem. When each person has presented all of his or her solutions, an attempt is made to arrive at a single acceptable solution. Both parents and child are encouraged to talk freely but are given assistance if they regress to ineffective forms of communication.

The training procedures appeared to be effective, although no research data is presented. The procedures seem to have been carefully formulated, and subsequent research may well demonstrate their efficacy.

Responding to the apparent need to develop procedures to reduce parent-youth conflict, Kifer, Lewis, Green, and Phillips (1974) did a study to determine the utility of teaching three predelinquent youths and their parents conflict resolution skills. The subjects consisted of two mother-daughter pairs and a father-son pair. The youth ranged in age from thirteen to seventeen years.

Before training procedures were initiated, home observations were made of parent-youth interaction. The trainers asked the parent-youth pairs to identify three major problems and discuss them for five minutes. The resulting interactions were used as a baseline to determine training effects.

During the educational phase, a hypothetical conflict situation between the adolescent and his or her parent was presented. They were asked to role play the situation for five minutes.

When the role play ended, the parent-youth pair were given a written description of the role-playing situation in which they had engaged. The written description contained a list of possible responses one could make to a conflict situation as well as possible consequences that accrue with each. The participants were asked to study the possible options for each conflict situation and note potential consequences. It was pointed out that by selecting the consequence they desired, an appropriate option to resolve the conflict could be identified.

During the training phase, the parent-youth pairs were instructed in the use of negotiation behaviors. The first, complete communication, requires that one person state an option and then ask the other to respond. For example, an adolescent might say: "I want to stay out an hour later this evening because there is a school dance. Would you have any objection if I do that?" The second type of negotiation behavior, identification of issues, requires the participants to state correctly an existing issue. For example, in discussing the prospect of a son quitting school, a parent might say: "You want to quit school and work, but I want you to continue so you can get a better job later." The third negotiation behavior, suggestion of options, requires one to make suggestions that can help resolve a conflict. For example, "Well, how about your taking one less course this semester and getting a part-time job?"

The parent-youth pairs were given instruction in the use of all three negotiation behaviors. As they practiced the skills, the trainers provided corrective feedback and reinforced appropriate responding. When training was completed, observations of parent-youth were conducted in the homes.

The training procedures were effective. Post-training observations indicated a substantial increase in the use of appropriate negotiation behaviors. Apparently, unproductive parent-youth conflict can be reduced by teaching functional negotiation skills.

Failure to Wear Corrective Devices

Most parents with children who wear corrective glasses or orthodontic devices become concerned if their children do not wear them regularly. These devices are costly and must be worn regularly to correct or mitigate the child's physical defect. Children often refuse to wear them if they are uncomfortable, detract from the child's appearance, or become the object of teasing or joking from their peers. While the child's objection to wearing corrective glasses for appearance reasons may be handled with contact lenses, this option is not available with orthodontal devices.

Wolf, Risley, and Mees (1964) worked with a three-and-a-half-year-old child with serious visual problems. He had cataracts on the lens of each eye and would possibly lose his vision if he did not wear corrective glasses. The parents' attempts to persuade or punish him had not succeeded in getting the child to wear his glasses.

The experimenters used several procedures to promote the target behavior. Because the procedures were somewhat complicated, we will summarize their main aspects. Initially, the experimenters attempted to promote the desirable behavior by successive approximation. Their hope was that by successively reinforcing the wearing of (1) frames, (2) frames with nonprescription lenses, and (3) frames with the appropriate prescription lenses, the desired behavior would be promoted. After much trial and error, however, they still had not promoted the appropriate behavior.

At this point they instituted a new procedure. By creating mild food deprivation, and successively reinforcing approximations with primary reinforcement, the target behavior was achieved. Once the child began wearing the appropriate glasses, further increase in the target behavior was promoted. Ward attendants told the child that as soon as he put his glasses on he would be taken for a walk, a ride in an automobile, given a snack, or permitted to play outdoors. If the child took off the glasses, these activities were immediately terminated. Using these procedures the child was taught to wear his glasses twelve hours a day.

Shortly after he had achieved this behavior, however, the child began to throw off his glasses. To deal with this behavior, each time he threw the glasses the child was placed in time-out for ten minutes. If he had a temper tantrum in time-out, he was required to stay there until the tantrum had ceased. With the implementation of this procedure, the desired behavior was achieved.

Hall, Axelrod, Tyler, Grief, Jones, and Robertson (1972) faced a similar problem with a child who was required to wear an orthodontal device. The child was required to wear a removable "headband" type of orthodontal device twelve hours a day. The child rarely wore it for that long, and, after many years of frustration (when the child was sixteen), the parents sought assistance, because wearing the device was now imperative.

Parent baseline data revealed that the boy wore the device about 25 percent of the time. The mother was instructed to praise the teenager for wearing the device and ignore him when he did not; the desired behavior increased to 36 percent.

To increase its frequency, the mother gave the teenager twenty-five cents each time she observed him wearing the corrective device. If he was not wearing the device, a fine of twenty-five cents was imposed. Money earned and fines imposed were recorded on a calendar, and at the end of the month he was given the money he had earned. After fifteen days with the new procedure, the boy wore the orthodontal device 60 percent of the desired time. At this point the

procedure was changed so that the teenager received the monetary reinforcement immediately rather than at the end of the month. The boy wore the orthodontal device 97 percent of the time.

The two studies we have reported show clearly that successive approximation, positive reinforcement, time-out, and response cost can promote the wearing of corrective visual and orthodontal devices. Thus, teaching parents to use these procedures correctly may alleviate a great deal of children's resistance to wearing them.

Curfew Violations

One area of adolescent behavior that is particularly problematic is the adolescent's struggle to achieve a sense of independence. The adolescent hotly contests his parents' desire to dictate what he does, where he goes, and when he should return home. To assert his independence and test his power, an adolescent often violates parent-imposed curfews. When he does, he may be faced with overly severe "grounding" restrictions. In the parents' struggle to maintain control, the imposed punishments may not "fit the crime." Although adolescents need reasonable limits and penalties, unjust penalties often incite adolescent rebellion.

One of the authors devised an effective method for dealing with curfew violations. The parent reported that her son's consistent curfew violations ranged from ten minutes to three hours. To increase the adolescent's punctuality, the following system was devised with the parent and teenager. Whenever the boy arrived home within five minutes of curfew, no consequences were imposed. If he came home fifteen minutes late, he received a fifteen-minute fine on the time he was permitted to be out the next evening or the next Saturday night; for the next fifteen-minute period he was late, he was fined thirty minutes; for the third fifteen-minute period he was late, a fine of forty-five minutes was imposed. If he was late for a total of one hour, he was fined 150 minutes (15 + 30 + 60 = 150). Hence, if he violated an evening curfew by sixty minutes, the Saturday night curfew would be 12:00 P.M. minus two-and-a-half hours, or 9:30 P.M.

To reinforce positively his keeping curfew, he was given an additional $1.50 for each week he did not violate curfew. However, for each minute of curfew violation, he lost ten cents of the bonus amount. Thus, if he was late fifteen minutes or more during the week, he did not receive any bonus. The procedure was very effective. The adolescent tested out the limits on several occasions, of course, and received the prescribed fines, but the curfew violations were quickly curtailed.

The above procedure may be varied to allow the teenager to earn extra "late time" when he goes for a week without being late. Each night the teenager is home on time, he earns ten minutes "late time," but if he is late, twice the amount of time he is late is deducted from the regular curfew time. The reinforcers the child receives for meeting evening curfews might include earning points to use the family car, bonus allowances, or dinner at a favorite restaurant.

Krumboltz and Krumboltz (1972) recommend the use of an alarm clock to deal with curfew violations. The parents set an alarm clock to ring at curfew time, and the teenager is asked to turn off the alarm when he arrives home so that it does not ring. If the teenager arrives late, the alarm goes off and wakes up the parents. Penalties are employed to deal with the violations. (It may be better for the parents to wear a wristwatch with an alarm to bed, or the teenager may come home, turn off the alarm, and go out again.)

Several variations of these procedures are possible using positive reinforcement and response cost. It is important to keep in mind, however, that response-cost procedures work best when natural consequences are used and the adolescent perceives them as fair. Remember also that behavior cannot be modified by punishment alone.

Runaways

Children and adolescents who run away from home have become a serious problem. In the United States, from 600,000 to 1,000,000 teenagers run away from home each year. The majority of these youth come from suburban homes, are often in their early teens, and 50 percent or more are female (Schaefer and Millman, 1977).

Although several factors may contribute to the problem, the runaway reaction usually reflects a threatening situation from which the adolescent feels he or she must escape (American Psychiatric Association, *Diagnostic and Statistical Manual of Mental Disorders*, 2nd ed., 1968). Therefore, the problem is symptomatic of more basic and dysfunctional relationships between the adolescent and his or her parents.

Even though adolescent runaways are a significant problem, there are surprisingly few studies of the problem and its treatment. Beyer, Holt, Reid, and Quinlan (1973) did an intensive study of a small group of runaways and found that these adolescents often came from broken homes and frequently experienced conflict with stepparents. A number of the youth had histories of absenteeism from school and poor school performance. Parent-youth conflict was also apparent regarding the number of nights out that were allowed and the time the parents required the youth to return home. The runaway reaction was often precipitated by the desire to escape an aversive home environment, or to manipulate parents into establishing a relationship that is more accepting and satisfying. Specific treatment modalities are not discussed, although the authors suggest that since the runaway reaction is symptomatic of a highly conflicted environment, parents must develop closer, more caring relationships to the adolescent and learn more effective patterns of communication.

Jenkins (1971) concurs with the observation that the runaway reaction is a frustrated response of a hurt child. And, while treatment may vary with the particular case, it usually requires intensive work with the entire family to favorably alter the home environment. If family therapy is unsuccessful, placement outside the home is indicated.

The writers' clinical experience is consistent with what has been reported. However, we have found that prevention is much better than "cure." Adolescents who eventually run away often give signs of disturbed family relationships long before they leave home. And, the first episode is often an attempt to manipulate parents to be more understanding and/or positively reinforcing. When the initial threat of running away is apparent, it is essential that parents examine their relationship with the adolescent and the behavior management procedures that are being used. It is usually important to have parents establish clear and reasonable rules and consistent but fair negative consequences for their violation.

If an adolescent does run away, the following course of action is often useful. First, the police department should be contacted and appropriate descriptions and reports completed. Second, the runaway's parents should be encouraged to contact the parents of his friends. They may be able to secure information from their children that cannot be obtained by the runaway's parents. Third, when the runaway youth returns it is important to help the parents avoid overreacting to the situation. That is, the parents may be inclined to be excessively harsh or punitive or, in the grips of guilt, they may cater to the youth's every need and act to reinforce the runaway reaction. Indeed, an adolescent runaway with whom one of the authors

worked said: "If I don't run away, my parents act mean and forget about me. When I do run away, I can count on them being nice to me for at least three weeks to a month." Hence, if negative consequences are imposed, and it is sometimes desirable, they should be fair and generally minor ones.

Two other procedures are also important. If the runaway has been involved in illegal activities while away from home and has been detained by the police, it is usually appropriate for the adolescent to experience the natural consequences of his actions. Difficulties with the police, or the fact that the adolescent has run away, indicates that family relationships need to be assessed. The adolescent and his parents should examine areas of conflict, establish more functional rules and consequences, and need to learn more effective ways of negotiating agreements and resolving conflicts.

Use-of-Car Problems

By the time an adolescent is old enough to get a driver's permit, he or she has a compelling need to own or drive a car. This point in time is greeted by parents with a mixture of positive and negative feeling. The acquisition of a driver's license happily brings the parents' role of chauffeur to an end. However, parents are also very much aware of the dangers of driving that may accompany the exuberance of youth. Cars are lethal weapons and can be used to act out a variety of urges and feelings.

Some of the problems parents may experience when they have an adolescent old enough to drive are illustrated by a case of one of the authors. The client was an extremely aggressive and defiant sixteen-year-old who had definite ideas regarding the limits placed on his freedom. When he reached sufficient age to obtain a driver's licence, he used a variety of tactics to try to manipulate his parents into signing a permit to drive. To deal with the client's behavior, as well as to provide the adolescent with the opportunity to earn driving privileges, a token system was devised.

The token system included the following elements. Five points were earned for arriving home at a specified time each evening. Three points were earned for arriving within fifteen minutes of the specified time. Fifteen bonus points were given each day that the adolescent behaved in a positive and helpful way toward family members. Fines for inappropriate behavior were also imposed. Any incident of yelling or screaming resulted in a loss of fifteen points. Also, any evening that the adolescent returned home a half hour late, the curfew the following evening was set thirty minutes earlier. The parents agreed to sign the driver's permit when 600 points were earned.

The adolescent succeeded in acquiring 600 points and subsequently secured a driver's license. However, almost as soon as he had his license, his defiant behavior reappeared. Since he had purchased his own car from his savings, he assumed that he could drive it anytime or anywhere he wished. His driving habits led to a speeding ticket and several complaints from neighbors. The parents' initial reaction was to take away their son's car, but the therapist encouraged them to modify the contingencies. Hence, the following changes were implemented:

1. Any further violations of speeding regulations as indicated by neighbors or issuance of citations would result in the suspension of the car for two weeks.

2. Any misuse of the car resulting in damage would necessitate the adolescent's repair of it before it could be used.

3. Arrival at home later than thirty minutes beyond the specified time would lead to a loss of car privileges for one day. If the son called to indicate he would be late arriving home, the parents had the option of enforcing the above penalty or a less severe one.

As might be anticipated from the case history, the adolescent violated the speeding regulation. His car was suspended for two weeks but the adolescent had previously had duplicate keys made so he had ready access to the car. To deal with the problem, the father took a decisive step. He hid his son's car and required him to earn the privilege of driving it before it was returned. Although the adolescent was most upset by his father's action, it ultimately had a very beneficial effect on him. He apparently recognized that his parents were at last going to impose consequences consistently. From that point on, the adolescent was more cooperative and his driving behavior did change.

As the case illustration suggests, token systems and contingency contracts can be useful in modifying adolescent driving behavior. Other behavioral procedures also have utility. Overcorrection was used with another case to modify the car care habits of an adolescent boy. When the adolescent did not take proper care of the family car, the parents were instructed to require the boy to wash and wax the car twice before he was permitted to use it again.

A slightly different procedure was used in another case. The father of an adolescent boy had observed his son driving recklessly. To correct the son's driving behavior, the father required his son to accompany him on three one-hour driving excursions before he was permitted to drive again. The procedure not only imposed a temporary driving suspension, but provided the son with the opportunity to observe better driving behavior.

As you may have surmised, many problems involved in adolescent car use can be avoided by anticipating situations that are likely to arise. This can be done by setting up conditions and/or contingencies regarding car use *before* a driver's license is obtained and consistently monitoring the contingencies subsequently.

Stealing

Stealing is a difficult behavior to modify for two reasons. First, the act delivers its own reinforcement because the object stolen usually has intrinsic or extrinsic value. For example, a child takes candy and consumes it himself, or shares it with his friends and gains approval; in either case, the stealing gets reinforced. Second, it is difficult to always know who is responsible for a theft. One does not want to penalize a child unless he is guilty.

Before implementing procedures to modify stealing behavior, one must develop a procedure to detect acts of stealing and find out how the stolen items are used. If a child steals to gain approval of his peer group, procedures must be devised to help the youngster obtain peer approval without stealing. Knowing when a child has in fact taken something is more difficult. One way is to indicate to the child that anything in his possession that cannot be verified as his own will be considered a stolen item. This procedure may not be foolproof, but it does convey the methods one is going to use to deal with stealing behavior.

Most initial or infrequent acts of stealing may be handled by requiring the child to return the object or to reimburse the owner for its monetary value. If this procedure does not stop the stealing behavior, or the problem is more serious, additional procedures should be implemented. For each theft that occurs, the child should be required to return the item and be charged a fine equal to the stolen object's monetary value. If the child does not have the sum needed, it should be "worked off" or be deducted from his allowance.

A slight variation of this procedure is to require the child not only to return the item taken but to give a personal toy or game to a charitable organization. The child is simply informed that each time stealing occurs, he or she will lose a favorite possession. Of course, the child should not be informed in advance which possession will be given away. If this is known, the child is likely to hide the item that is to be given away.

Positive reinforcement and response cost may be used in combination to alter stealing behavior. The child is given points for each day stealing does not occur. To make certain that one is not reinforcing undetected stealing, the child is informed that his pockets and his room will be searched periodically and any unverified object will be taken as an indication of theft. If the child cannot produce the necessary verification, the object is permanently removed from his possession, and a negative consequence is imposed. The consequence may be a large point fine, a loss of a special privilege, a monetary fine equal to the price of the stolen object, or some combination of these consequences. Points for nonstealing behavior can be exchanged for money, material reinforcers, and reinforcing events. If the backup reinforcers appeal to the youngster, the procedures will likely prove effective.

Lying

Most incidents of lying can be grouped into two categories: (1) distortion of the truth to avoid reprimand or physical punishment, and (2) "stretching" the facts to receive attention, approval, or status from an audience. With both types, the act is often reinforced. This first type is negatively reinforced (because the act avoids a potentially aversive experience) and the second type is promoted by positive social reinforcement. Both types of lying can be extinguished if the reinforcement that maintains it is terminated.

One very perceptive ten-year-old boy demonstrated how a parent unknowingly reinforced his lying. When the ten-year-old did something wrong, his first act was to tell a lie. His parents usually interrogated him vigorously, and, sooner or later, promised no punishment if he told the truth. As soon as the parents made the promise, he immediately told the truth.

Clinical experience suggests that children who lie are often subjected to expectations and discipline that are unreasonable. If a child cannot meet the expectations and fears punishment, he uses lying to hold on to parent approval and avoid punishment. The child is not likely to relinquish the undesirable behavior until parent expectations are reduced and he can receive the desired approval.

Lying is difficult to modify because it is difficult to confirm its occurrence. Each time a child succeeds in his deception, the behavior gets reinforced. When one is certain that a child has told a lie, response cost and reinforcement of the opposite behavior will modify it. For each episode of lying, a privilege (allowance, television-watching time) or valued object (bicycle) is taken from the child. At the same time, the child is reinforced when he tells the truth — and only when he is telling the truth.

Madsen and Madsen (1970) studied a boy who was observed mishandling church property. When confronted with his behavior by his father, he denied the act. To impress on the boy the inappropriateness of his behavior, the father temporarily terminated all communication with him. On one outing during this period, the family stopped for ice cream. When the offending son expressed his desire for it, the father told him he could not be certain if he was telling the truth. For the next six days, the father questioned every statement the boy made and indicated that the truth was the opposite of what the

boy said. It was not long before the boy apologized for his lying and asked to be reinstated in the good grace of his father. No further incidents of lying occurred. Apparently, the boy greatly desired his father's approval and his father's tactics impressed on him the need to be believed.

Summary

1. In this chapter we discussed methods for analyzing and modifying several problem behaviors children exhibit in the home. Four methods for analyzing parent-child interaction and conflict are: (a) observing the child and parents at home; (b) observing the parent-child interactional styles in a clinic setting; (c) instructing the parent(s) to make appropriate observations of the child's behavior at home; and (d) interviewing the parents to obtain a history of the problem behavior and parent-child conflict. Although any of these methods may be used individually, the interview is usually used with all of them.

2. Analysis of problem behavior involves several steps: (a) securing a history of the problem behavior, (b) stating the problem in behavioral terms so it can be observed and measured, (c) identifying the reinforcers that maintain the problem behavior, (d) specifying parental expectations and determining whether they are realistic, (e) specifying the type and frequency of reinforcement and punishment parents use in dealing with the problem behavior, (f) helping the parents to construct a list of reinforcing stimuli and events that can be used in the modification plan, (g) specifying the roles each parent will play in modifying the problem behavior, and (h) observing the frequency of the problem behavior before the behavior modification plan is implemented.

3. Several methods are used to train parents to serve in quasi-therapeutic roles to modify the behavior of their children. These methods vary in complexity and completeness. The behavior therapist might (a) instruct parents in the use of behavior modification procedures, (b) model the procedures for the parents while working directly with the child, (c) instruct the parents by audio-monitoring devices while the parent(s) interact with the child, or (d) train parents in the home. All of these parent-training methods appear to have some favorable effects in modifying undesirable child behavior.

4. The home token economy (HTE) is a highly effective method for modifying problem behavior at home. Like other systematic reinforcement procedures, it works because both desirable and undesirable behavior are systematically regulated by positive and negative consequences. If the HTE is carefully specified and the parents adhere to the negotiated terms, dramatic changes in the child's behavior often occur. The child learns that desirable behavior always "pays off," and parents terminate practices that previously perpetuated the undesirable problem behavior.

5. The procedures for dealing with various problem behaviors at home indicate the broad applicability of the learning principles we have discussed throughout the book. Knowledge and mastery of these principles enables the potential user to alter an infinite number of problem behaviors in children and adolescents.

We hope that your success in using behavior modification has (or will) adequately reinforce you for reading this book. We commend you for staying with us to the end.

Methods for Identifying Potential Reinforcers for Children

The first two forms described below can be used to identify potential reinforcers for children. Because stimuli and events have no inherent reinforcement property, their reinforcement property can only be determined empirically. However, the authors have found that the use of these forms do identify potential reinforcers that usually work effectively in promoting behavior change. The first form is used for younger elementary school children, and the second form is used for children in the middle and upper elementary grades. Either form may be given to a child to complete if the child has adequate reading and writing ability. If not, the forms are used to interview a child and record his or her responses.

Form I

Name: Age:

School: Grade:

Boy or Girl (please circle one)

1. If you were going into a store to buy three games, what would they be?

2. What three special things do you like to work with or play with in the classroom?

3. What are three jobs in this classroom you like to do the most?

4. If you went to a store and had twenty-five cents to spend on whatever you wanted, what would you buy?

5. What things that you did not mention above do you like to do in your classroom or while you are at school (in the building or playground)?

Form II

Name _____Age _____ Date _____

Please answer all the questions as completely as you can.

1. The school subjects I like best are:

2. Three things I like most to do at school are:

3. If you had thirty minutes free time at school each day to do what you really like, what would it be?

4. My two favorite sweets are:

5. At recess I most like to (three things):

6. If you had one dollar to spend on anything you wanted to buy, what would it be?

7. The person I most like to do things with at school is:

8. What three special jobs do you most want to do in the class?

9. If you were going to choose two students to do something real fun with, who would they be?

10. At home, the three things I most like to do are:

11. Indicate which of the games or activities listed below you most like by ranking them. Put a 1 for first choice, a 2 for second choice, and so forth until all are ranked.

_____ Playing checkers   _____ Playing a card game

_____ Arts and crafts   _____ Reading a favorite book

_____ Talking to a friend   _____ Playing pick-up sticks

_____ Drawing or coloring   _____ Being office assistant

_____ Doing a special job   _____ P.E.
for the teacher

_____ Earning time to do
what I want

12. After school and on weekends the three things I most like to do are:

13. Name the three things that people do that you dislike:

Form III
Intake Interview

Name of Child _____ Birthdate _____

Address _____

Father's Occupation and Place of Employment _____

_____Phone _____

History of Child's Present Difficulty

1. What specific difficulties or problem behaviors have led the parents to seek assistance? (Specify all problem areas: academic, behavioral, social, and emotional.)

2. When did each of these problems first appear?

    a. In what situations or in whose presence is the behavior most often exhibited?

    b. Which of the problems are viewed as most serious or of greatest concern to the parents?

    c. When or in what situations does the child display the most desirable behavior or self-control?

3. Besides the above problems, has the child ever behaved in a way that seemed especially different, unusual, or strange?

    a. Has the child ever lost consciousness or appeared as if he or she were in another world?

4. Considering the child's total development, in what areas has he or she not developed in the usual or typical way?

5. What serious and/or chronic illnesses, injuries, or deficiencies has the child experienced or does he or she have at present?

   a. Are there deficiencies in hearing, speech, walking, talking, or physiological functioning?

6. Does the child experience any problems in sleeping or eating?

7. Is the child on medication that is taken regularly?

   a. Is the child allergic to anything?

8. Does the child have any fears or phobias? (Have parents specify.)

9. What types of things are most frustrating or upsetting to the child?

   a. Under what conditions does he or she get angry and how often?

   b. What does the child do when angry?

   c. When upset, what soothes or calms the child the most?

10. What do the parents enjoy most about the child?

11. What behavior do the parents consider most desirable in the child?

12. What expectations or aspirations do the parents have for the child?

School History

1. How old was the child when he or she first started to school?

   a. Does the child like school?

2. How many different schools has the child attended?

    a. Has the child ever been unable to attend school or been out of school for more than a few days?

3. Exactly what types of problems has the child had in school?

    a. In what areas has he or she had the most success or difficulty?

4. What types of games or activities does the child enjoy with classmates?

5. Does the child have any special abilities or talents?

Family Composition and Interaction

1. What are the names and ages of the other children in the family?

    a. Which brother or sister does the child play with the most?

2. What type of discipline is most successful with the child?

3. Who is most successful in getting the child to do things?

4. Do the parents agree on child training and disciplinary methods?

5. In what areas of family life does there appear to be the most friction or difficulty?

6. Describe a typical day at home.

Reinforcing Stimuli and Events

1. What does the child do in his or her free time?

2. What kinds of food, candy, snacks, or playthings does the child like?

3. If the child had five dollars to spend, what would he or she buy?

4. Does the child have an allowance?

5. What activities, entertainment, or special privileges does the child most want or ask for?

6. What commercial games (checkers, Monopoly, Stratego, etc.) does the child most like to play?

Potential Reinforcers Specified by Grade Level

A. Kindergarten Level

Objects	Activities	Games
small doll	being read a story	Lotto
note pads	cutting pictures	dolls
candy	writing on the board	picture dominoes
books	coloring	pegs
jewelry	playing in the doll house	Playschool Match-ups
makeup kits	cleaning the sinks	Funny Faces
jump rope	playing with felt board	puzzles
jacks	listening to a record	puppets
play money	stringing beads	clay
crayons	painting	farm set
toy car	finger painting	Lego
whistles	holding the flag	Play Tiles
colored paper	building with blocks	Tinker toys
ball	pasting	
toy soldiers	going on the swings	
marbles	playing with trucks	
coloring book		
masks		
badges		

B. Grades 1–3

Objects	Activities	Games
jacks	writing on the board	jacks
candy	coloring	playing with dolls
eraser	cutting with scissors	Kaboom
pencil	jumping rope	pick-up sticks
comic books	dusting	Spirograph
toy rings	cleaning the sinks	Old Maid
small dolls	painting	Clue
crayons	making paper objects	Dominoes
coloring book	taking care of pets	Time Bomb
paper dolls	doing science experiments	checkers
water gun	kicking a ball	puzzles
small cars	swinging on the swings	marbles
toy flying planes	working with flash cards	Hands Down
rubber ball	reading	Green Ghost
whistles	cleaning the board	Slap Stick
baseball cards	going to the office on an errand	
marbles	cleaning the floor	
clay		

C. Grades 4– 6

Objects

candy or gum
pencils
comic books
teen magazines
felt pens
paperback books
notebooks
stationery
combs
plastic or paper flowers
squirt gun
model planes
popcorn
yo-yo's
stamps (for collection)
football or baseball cards
colored pencils
magic puzzles

Activities   ·

talking to a friend
making things for special
    projects
drawing
doing science experiments
being teacher's helper
solving puzzles
reading
creative writing
working with clay
using vocabulary cards
talking into a tape
    recorder
working film strip
looking at or feeding pet
looking at magazines
painting
being line leader

Games

Life
Dating Game
Go to the Head of
    the Class
Scrabble
Twister
Easy Money
Slap Stick
Spill and Spell
Password
Hands Down
Chess
Monopoly
Battle Ship
slot cars
Clue
Booby Trap
checkers
Green Ghost
Dark Shadows

D. Junior High and High School

Objects

records
teen magazines
combs
pictures of movie stars
small toys for sibling or
    disadvantaged children
paperback books
makeup
free lunch ticket
car or sports magazines
pens
psychedelic posters
candy bars
key chain
hair cream

Activities

talking to a friend
taking time in class to do
    homework
typing
looking at teen magazine
not having to take a test
helping a younger child
    learn
playing Scrabble
grading papers
reading a book
putting together puzzles
    (1,000 pieces)
getting out of class early
working on crafts or models
looking at a car or sports
    magazine
playing chess or checkers
playing Monopoly

Total Class Activities

listening to the radio
bringing in TV to watch
    special programs
having a class party
sitting by whomever you
    want to
listening to records
going on field trips
holding class debates
watching a movie

References

Addison, R. M. and Homme, L. E. The reinforcing events (RE) menu. *National Society for Programmed Instruction Journal,* 1966, *5,* 8–9.

Allen, K. E. and Harris, F. R. Eliminating a child's scratching by training the mother in reinforcement procedures. *Behaviour Research and Therapy,* 1966, *4,* 79–84.

Allen, K. E., Hart, B. M., Buell, J. S., Harris, F. R., and Wolf, M. M. Effects of social reinforcement on isolate behavior of a nursery school child. *Child Development,* 1964, *35,* 511–518.

American Psychiatric Association. *Diagnostic and statistical manual of mental disorders.* (2nd ed.) Washington, D.C.: American Psychiatric Association, 1968.

Anton, J. L. Studying individual change. In L. Goldman (ed.), *Research methods for counselors: Practical approaches in field settings.* New York: John Wiley and Sons, 1978.

Axelrod, S. *Behavior modification for the classroom teacher.* New York: McGraw-Hill, 1977.

Ayllon, T. and Michael, J. The psychiatric nurse as a behavioral engineer. *Journal of Experimental Analysis of Behavior,* 1959, *2,* 323–334.

Azrin, N. H. and Holz, W. C. Punishment. In W. K. Honig (ed.), *Operant behavior: Areas of research and application.* New York: Appleton-Century-Crofts, 1966, pp. 380–447.

Azrin, N. H. and Nunn, R. G. Habit reversal: A method of eliminating nervous habits and tics. *Behaviour Research and Therapy,* 1973, *11,* 619–628.

Azrin, N. H. and Weslowski, M. D. Theft reversal: An overcorrection procedure for eliminating stealing by retarded persons. *Journal of Applied Behavior Analysis,* 1974, *7,* 577–581.

Baer, D. M. and Sherman, J. A. Reinforcement control of generalized imitation in young children. *Journal of Experimental Child Psychology,* 1964, *1,* 37–49.

Baer, D. M., Wolf, M. M., and Risley, T. R. Some current dimensions of applied behavior therapy analysis. *Journal of Applied Behavior Analysis,* 1968, *1,* 91–97.

Bandura, A. Behavior modification through modeling procedures. In L. P. Ullmann and L. Krasner (eds.), *Research in behavior modification.* New York: Holt, Rinehart and Winston, 1965, pp. 310–340.

———. Behavioral psychotherapy. *Scientific American,* March 1967, pp. 78–86.

————. *Principles of behavior modification.* New York: Holt, Rinehart and Winston, 1969.

————. Psychotherapy based on modeling principles. In A. E. Bergin and S. L. Garfield (eds.), *Handbook of psychotherapy and behavior change.* New York: John Wiley, 1971(a), 653–708.

————. *Social learning theory.* Morristown, N.J.: General Learning Press, 1971(b).

Bandura, A., Ross, D., and Ross, S. A. Transmission of aggression through imitation of aggressive models. *Journal of Abnormal and Social Psychology,* 1961, *63,* 575–582.

————. Imitation of film-mediated aggressive models. *Journal of Abnormal and Social Psychology,* 1963, *66,* 3–11.

Bandura, A. and Walters, R. H. *Social learning and personality development.* New York: Holt, Rinehart and Winston, 1963.

Barclay, R., Jr. Effecting behavior change in the elementary classroom: An exploratory study. *Journal of Counseling Psychology,* 1967, *14,* 240–247.

Barrett, B. H. Reduction in rate of multiple tics by free operant conditioning methods. In L. P. Ullmann and L. Krasner (eds.), *Case studies in behavior modification.* New York: Holt, Rinehart and Winston, 1965, pp. 255–263.

Barrish, H., Saunders, M., and Wolf, M. M. Good behavior game: Effects of individual contingencies for group consequences on disruptive behavior in a classroom. *Journal of Applied Behavior Analysis,* 1969, *2,* 79–84.

Barsch, R. Six factors in learning. In J. Hellmuth (ed.), *Learning disorders.* Vol. 1. Seattle, Wash.: Special Child Publications, 1968.

Barton, E. S., Guess, E., Garcia, E., and Baer, D. M. Improvement of retardates'

mealtime behaviors by time-out procedures using multiple baseline techniques. *Journal of Applied Behavior Analysis,* 1970, *3,* 77–84.

Bateman, B. Three approaches to diagnosis and educational planning for children with learning disabilities. *Academic Therapy Quarterly,* 1967, *2,* 215–222.

Becker, W. C., Thomas, D. R., and Carnine, D. Reducing behavior problems: An operant conditioning guide for teachers. In W. C. Becker (ed.), *An empirical basis for change in education: Selections on behavioral psychology for teachers.* Palo Alto, Calif.: Science Research Associates, 1971, pp. 129–165.

Bentler, P. M. An infant's phobia treated with reciprocal inhibition therapy. *Journal of Child Psychology and Psychiatry,* 1962, *3,* 185–189.

Berkowitz, B. P. and Graziano, A. M. Training parents as behavioral therapists: Review. *Behaviour Research and Therapy,* 1972, *10,* 297–317.

Bettelheim, B. *The empty fortress.* Glencoe, Ill.: Free Press, 1967.

Beyer, M., Holt, S. A., Reid, T. A., and Quinlan, D. M. Runaway youth: Families in conflict. Paper presented at a convention of Eastern Psychological Association, Washington, D.C., May, 1973.

Biciling, J. P., Shipman, H., Milligan, J., and Pipin, L. Glugies, snirkles and models: Three systems of token reinforcement in the grade school classroom. *Educational Technology Research,* 1971, *14,* 1–20.

Bijou, S. Implications of behavioral science for counseling and guidance. In J. D. D. Krumboltz (ed.), *Revolution in counseling.* Boston: Houghton Mifflin, 1966, pp. 27–48.

Birnbrauer, J. S., Wolf, M. M., Kidder, J. D., and Tague, C. E. Classroom behavior of retarded pupils with token reinforcement. *Journal of Experimental Child Psychology*, 1965, *2*, 219–235.

Blackham, G. J. Strategies for change in the child client. *Elementary School Guidance and Counseling*, 1969, *3*, (March), 174–181.

————. *Counseling: Theory, process and practice.* Belmont, Calif.: Wadsworth Publishing Company, 1977.

Blackwood, R. O. The operant conditioning of verbally mediated self control in the classroom. *Journal of School Psychology*, 1970, *8*, 251–258.

Boisvert, M. J. Behavior shaping as an alternative to psychotherapy. *Social Casework*, 1974, *55*, 43–47.

Bolstead, O. C. and Johnson, S. N. Self regulation in the modification of disruptive behavior. *Journal of Applied Behavior Analysis*, 1972, *5*, 143–154.

Boudin, H. M. Contingency contracting as a therapeutic tool in the deceleration of amphetamine use. *Behavior Therapy*, 1972, *3*, 604–608.

Bower, S., Amatea, E., and Anderson, R. Assertiveness training with children. *Elementary School Guidance and Counseling*, 1976, *10*, 236–245.

Broden, N., Hall, R. V., Dunlap, A., and Clark, R. Effects of teacher attention and token reinforcement system in a junior high school special class. *Exceptional Children*, 1970, *36*, 341–349.

Broden, N., Hall, R. V., and Mitts, B. The effect of self-recording the classroom behavior of two eighth-grade students. *Journal of Applied Behavior Analysis*, 1971, *4*, 191–199.

Browning, R. M. Behavior therapy for stuttering in a schizophrenic child. *Behaviour Research and Therapy*, 1967, *5*, 27–35.

Bucher, B. and Hawkins, J. Comparisons of response cost and token reinforcement systems in a class for academic underachievement. Paper presented at the Association for the Advancement of Behavior Therapy, Washington, D.C., September 1971.

Bugelski, B. R. *The psychology of learning applied to teaching.* Indianapolis: Bobbs-Merrill, 1964.

Burchard, J. D. and Barrera, F. An analysis of time-out and response cost in a program environment. *Journal of Applied Behavior Analysis*, 1972, *5*, 171–182.

Bush, W. J. and Giles, M. T. *Aids to psycholinguistic teaching.* Columbus: Charles E. Merrill, 1969.

Bushell, D., Jr., Wrobell, P. A., and Michaelis, M. L. Applying "group" contingencies to the classroom study behavior of preschool children. *Journal of Applied Behavior Analysis*, 1968, *1*, 55–61.

Campbell, L. M. A variation of thought stopping in a twelve-year-old boy: A case report. *Journal of Behavior Therapy and Experimental Psychiatry*, 1973, *4*, 69–70.

Carkhuff, R. R. *Helping and human relations: A primer for lay and professional helpers.* Vol. 2. New York: Holt, Rinehart and Winston, 1969.

Carlson, C. S., Arnold, C. R., Becker, W. C., and Madsen, C. H. The elimination of tantrum behavior of a child in an elementary classroom. *Behaviour Research and Therapy*, 1968, *6*, 117–119.

Cautela, J. R. Treatment of compulsive behavior by covert sensitization. *Psychological Record*, 1966, *16*, 33–41.

————. Covert reinforcement. *Behavior Therapy*, 1970, *1*, 33–50.

Christophersen, E. R., Arnold, C. M., Hill, D. W., and Quilitch, H. R. Token reinforcement procedures for application by parents of children with behavior problems. *Journal of Applied Behavior Analysis*, 1972, 5, 485–497.

Clonce vs. Richardson, 379 F. Supp. 338 (W. D. Mo. 1974).

Coe, W. C. A behavioral approach to disrupted family interactions. *Psychotherapy: Theory, Research and Practice*, 1972, 9, 80–85.

Cohen, H. L. and Filipczak, J. A. Programming educational behavior for institutionalized adolescents. In H. C. Rickard (ed.), *Behavioral intervention in human problems*. New York: Pergamon Press, 1971, pp. 179–200.

Cohen, J. *Operant behavior and conditioning*. Chicago: Rand McNally, 1969.

Coleman, J. C. *Abnormal psychology in modern life*. (5th ed.) Glencoe, Ill.: Scott, Foresman, 1976.

Collier, P. F. and Tarte, R. D. *Practically painless parenting*. Chicago: Henry Regnery Company, 1977.

Corsini, R. J. and Painter, G. *The practical parent*. New York: Harper & Row, 1975.

Corte, H. E., Wolf, M. M., and Locke, B. J. A comparison of procedures for eliminating self-injurious behavior of retarded adolescents. *Journal of Applied Behavior Analysis*, 1971, 4, 201–213.

Costello, C. G. The essentials of behavior therapy. *Canadian Psychiatric Journal*, 1963, 8, 162–166.

Cowen, E. Mothers in the classroom. *Psychology Today*, 1969, 3, 36–39.

Daley, M. F. The reinforcement menu: Finding effective reinforcers. In J. D. Krumboltz and C. E. Thoresen (eds.), *Behavioral counseling: Case studies and techniques*. New York: Holt, Rinehart and Winston, 1969, pp. 42–45.

Daley, M. F., Holt, G., and Vajanasoontorn, N. C. Reinforcement menus in the

instruction of mentally retarded children. Paper presented at the Conference on Instructional Methods and Teacher Behavior, Berkeley, Calif., November 1966.

Davison, G. C. Self control through "imaginal aversive contingency" and "one downman ship": Enabling the powerless to accommodate unreasonableness. In J. D. Krumboltz and C. E. Thoresen (eds.), *Behavioral counseling: Case studies and techniques*. New York: Holt, Rinehart and Winston, 1969, pp. 319–327.

Deese, J. E. and Hulse, S. H. *The psychology of learning*. (4th ed.) New York: McGraw-Hill, 1975.

Deffenbacher, J. L. and Kemper, C. C. Systematic desensitization of test anxiety in junior high school students. *The School Counselor*, 1974, 21, 216–222.

DeLeon, C. and Mandell, W. A. A comparison of conditioning and psychotherapy in the treatment of functional enuresis. *Journal of Clinical Psychology*, 1966, 22, 326–330.

Dickinson, D. J. An operant conditioning program for children who will not complete their school assignments. Unpublished manuscript. Las Vegas, Nev., 1967.

Dollar, D. *Humanizing classroom discipline: A behavioral approach*. New York: Harper & Row, 1972.

Dollard, J. and Miller, N. E. *Personality and psychotherapy*. New York: McGraw-Hill, 1950.

Donaldson vs. O'Connor, 493 F 2d. 507 (5th Cir. 1974).

Donnellan-Walsh, A. *Teaching makes a difference: A guide for developing successful classes for autistic and other severely handicapped children*, Administrative Manual. Santa Barbara, Calif.: Santa Barbara Public Schools, 1976.

Donnellan-Walsh, A., Gossage, L. D., Lavigna, G. W., Schuler, A. L., and

Traphagen, J. D. *Teaching makes a difference: A guide for developing successful classes for autistic and other severely handicapped children*, Teacher's Manual. Santa Barbara, Calif.: Santa Barbara Public Schools, 1976.

Douglas, V. Stop, look and listen: The problem of sustained attention and impulse control in hyperactive and normal children. *Canadian Journal of Behavior Science*, 1972, *4*, 259–276.

Drabman, R. S., Spitalnik, R., and O'Leary, K. D. Teaching self control to disruptive children. *Journal of Abnormal Psychology*, 1973, *82*, 10–16.

Erickson, M. T. *Child psychopathology: Assessment, etiology and treatment.* Englewood Cliffs, N.J.: Prentice-Hall, 1978.

Erikson, E. *Childhood and society.* (2nd ed.) New York: W. W. Norton and Company, 1963.

Eysenck, H. J. and Rachman, S. *The cause and cure of neurosis.* London: Kegan Paul, 1965.

Farber, H. and Mayer, G. R. Behavior consultation in a barrio high school. *Personnel and Guidance Journal*, 1972, *51*, 273–279.

Ferster, C. B. Positive reinforcement and behavior deficits in autistic children. *Child Development*, 1961, *32*, 437–456.

Ferster, C. and DeMyer, M. A. A method for the experimental analysis of the behavior of autistic children. *American Journal of Orthopsychiatry*, 1962, *32*, 89–98.

Flanagan, B., Goldiamond, I., and Azrin, N. H. Operant stuttering: The control of stuttering behavior through response-contingent consequences. *Journal of Experimental Analysis of Behavior*, 1958, *1*, 173–177.

Ford, D. H. and Urban, H. B. *Systems of psychotherapy: A comparative study.* New York: John Wiley, 1963.

Foxx, R. M. and Azrin, N. H. Restitution: A method of eliminating aggressive-disruptive behavior of retarded and brain damaged patients. *Behaviour Research and Therapy*, 1972, *10*, 15–27.

Gagné, R. M. *The conditions of learning.* (2nd ed.) New York: Holt, Rinehart and Winston, 1970.

Gallagher, P., Sulzbacher, S. I., and Shores, R. E. A group contingency for classroom management of emotionally disturbed children. Paper read to Kansas Chapter, The Council of Exceptional Children, Wichita, March 1967.

Gambrill, E. D. *Behavior modification: Handbook of assessment, intervention and evaluation.* San Francisco: Jossey-Bass Publishers, 1977.

Gewirtz, J. L. and Baer, D. M. Deprivation and satiation of social reinforcers as drive conditions. *Journal of Abnormal and Social Psychology*, 1958, *57*, 165–172.

Gittelman, M. Behavioral rehearsal as a technique in child treatment. *Journal of Child Psychology and Psychiatry*, 1965, *6*, 251–255.

Gladstone, R. *A set of principles derived from experimental psychology.* (2nd ed.) Stillwater, Okla.: Oklahoma State University, 1967.

Goldenson, R. M. *The encyclopedia of human behavior: Psychology, psychiatry and mental health.* Vol. 2. Garden City, N.Y.: Doubleday and Company, 1970.

Goldstein, A. P., Heller, K., and Sechrist, L. B. *Psychotherapy and the psychology of behavior change.* New York: John Wiley, 1966.

Goodman, S. E. and Mahoney, M. J. Modification of aggression through modeling: An experimental probe. *Journal* of Behavior Therapy and Experimental Psychiatry, 1975, 6, 200–202.

Graubard, P. S., Rosenberg, H., and Miller, M. B. Student applications of behavior modification of teachers or ecological approaches to social deviancy. In E. A. Ramp and B. L. Hobkins (eds.), *A new direction for education: Behavior analysis.* Vol. 1. Lawrence, Kansas: Support and Development Center Follow Through, 1971.

Gray, F., Graubard, P. S., and Rosenberg, H. Little brother is changing you. *Psychology Today,* 1974, 7, 42–46.

Graziano, A. M. and Kean, J. E. Programmed relaxation and reciprocal inhibition with psychotic children. *Behaviour Research and Therapy,* 1968, 6, 433–437.

Grimley, L. K. Drug therapy and hyperactive children. *The School Psychologist Digest,* 1976, 5, 2–4.

Grossman, H. J. (ed.). *Manual on terminology and classification in mental retardation.* American Association of Mental Deficiency, 1973.

Grunbaum, A. Causality and the science of human behavior. In R. Ulrich, T. Stachnik, and J. Mabry (eds.), *Control of human behavior.* Glenview, Ill.: Scott, Foresman, 1966, pp. 3–10.

Hall, R. V., Axelrod, S., Tyler, L., Grief, E., Jones, F. C., and Robertson, R. Modification of behavior problems in the home with parent as observer and experimenter. *Journal of Applied Behavior Analysis,* 1972, 5, 53–64.

Hall, R. V., Cristler, C., Cranston, S. S., and Tucker, B. Teachers and parents as researchers using multiple baseline designs. *Journal of Applied Behavior Analysis,* 1970, 3, 247–255.

Hall, R. V., Lund, D., and Jackson, D. Effects of teacher attention on study behavior.

Journal of Applied Behavior Analysis, 1968, 1, 1–12.

Hall, R. V., Panyan, M., Rabon, D., and Broden, M. Instructing beginning teachers in reinforcement procedures which improve classroom control. *Journal of Applied Behavior Analysis,* 1968, 1, 315–322.

Hallsten, E. A. Adolescent anorexia nervosa treated by desensitization. *Behaviour Research and Therapy,* 1965, 3, 87–91.

Hanf, C. A two-stage program for modifying maternal controlling during mother-child interaction. Paper presented at the meeting of the Western Psychological Association, Vancouver, B.C., 1969.

Haring, N. G. and Phillips, E. L. *An analysis and modification of classroom behavior.* Englewood Cliffs, N.J.: Prentice-Hall, Inc., 1972.

Harris, F. R., Wolf, M. M., and Baer, D. M. Effects of adult social reinforcement on child behavior. *Young Children,* 1964, 20 (1), 8–17.

Hart, B. M., Allen, K. E., Buell, J. S., Harris, F. R., and Wolf, M. M. Effects of social reinforcement on operant crying. *Journal of Experimental Child Psychology,* 1964, 1, 145–153.

Hart, B. M. and Risley, T. R. Establishing use of descriptive adjectives in the spontaneous speech of disadvantaged preschool children. *Journal of Applied Behavior Analysis,* 1968, 1, 109–120.

Hauserman, N., Walen, S. R., and Behling, M. Reinforced racial integration in the first grade: A study in generalization. *Journal of Applied Behavior Analysis,* 1973, 6, 193–200.

Havighurst, R. J. *Human development and education.* New York: Longmans, 1953.

Hawkins, R. P., Peterson, R. F., Schweid, E., and Bijou, S. W. Behavior therapy in the home: Amelioration of problem parent-child relations with the parent in a therapeutic role. *Journal of Experimental Child Psychology,* 1966, *4,* 99–107.

Hershen, M. and Barlow, D. H. *Single case experimental designs: Strategies for studying behavior change.* New York: Pergamon Press, 1976.

Holland, C. J. Elimination by the parents of fire-setting behavior in a seven-year-old boy. *Behaviour Research and Therapy,* 1969, *7,* 135–137.

Holt, E. B. *Animal drive and the learning process.* Vol. 1. New York: Holt, 1931.

Homme, L. E. Control of coverants, the operants of the mind. Perspectives in psychology, XXIV. *Psychological Record,* 1965, *15,* 501–511.

Homme, L., Csanyi, A. P., Gonzales, M. A., and Rechs, J. R. *How to use contingency contracting in the classroom.* Champaign, Ill.: Research Press, 1969.

Homme, L. and Tosti, P. *Behavior technology: Motivation and contingency management.* San Rafael, Calif.: Individual Learning Systems, 1971.

Hosford, R. E. Overcoming fear of speaking in a group. In J. D. Krumboltz and C. E. Thoresen (eds.), *Behavioral counseling: Case studies and techniques.* New York: Holt, Rinehart and Winston, 1969, pp. 80–83.

Hunter, M. *Reinforcement theory for teachers.* El Segundo, Calif.: Tip Publications, 1967.

Hurlock, E. B. *Child development.* (4th ed.) New York: McGraw-Hill, 1964.

Jacobson, E. *Progressive relaxation.* Chicago: University of Chicago Press, 1938.

Jenkins, R. L. The runaway reaction. *American Journal of Psychiatry,* 1971, *128,* 168–173.

Johnson, D. Educational principles for children with learning disabilities. *Rehabilitation Literature,* 1967, *28,* 317–322.

Jones, M. C. The elimination of children's fears.

Journal of Experimental Psychology, 1924, *7,* 383–390.

Kaufman, K. F. and O'Leary, K. D. Reward, cost, and self-evaluation procedures before disruptive adolescents in a psychiatric hospital school. *Journal of Applied Behavior Analysis,* 1972, *5,* 293–309.

Kazdin, A. E. Response cost: The removal of conditioned reinforcers for therapeutic change. *Behavior Therapy,* 1972, *3,* 533–546.

———. Methodological and assessment considerations in evaluating reinforcement programs in applied settings. *Journal of Applied Behavior Analysis,* 1973, *6,* 517–533.

Keirsey, D. W. Transactional casework: A technology for inducing behavioral change. Paper presented at the Convention of California Association of School Psychologists and Psychometrists, San Francisco, 1965.

———. Systematic exclusion: Eliminating chronic classroom disruptions. In J. D. Krumboltz and C. E. Thoresen (eds.), *Behavioral counseling: Case studies and techniques.* New York: Holt, Rinehart and Winston, 1969, pp. 89–113.

Keller, F. S. *Learning: Reinforcement theory.* (2nd ed.) New York: Random House, 1969.

Kelman, H. C. Manipulation of human behavior: An ethical dilemma for social scientists. *Journal of Social Issues,* 1965, *21,* 31–46.

Kennedy, W. A. School phobia: Rapid treatment of fifty cases. *Journal of Abnormal Psychology,* 1965, *70,* 285–289.

Kifer, R. E., Lewis, M. A., Green, R. D., and Phillips, E. L. Training predelinquent youth and their parents to negotiate conflict situations. *Journal of Applied Behavior Analysis,* 1974, *7,* 357–364.

Kohlenberg, R. J. The punishment of persistent

vomiting: A case study. *Journal of Applied Behavior Analysis*, 1970, *3*, 241–245.

Kolvin, I. Aversive imagery treatment in adolescents. *Behaviour Research and Therapy*, 1967, *5*, 245–248.

Kondas, O. Reduction of examination anxiety and "stage-fright" by group desensitization and relaxation. *Behaviour Research and Therapy*, 1967, *5*, 275–281.

Krasner, L. The therapist as a social reinforcement machine. In H. H. Strupp and L. Luborsky (eds.), *Research in psychotherapy*. Vol. II. Washington, D.C.: American Psychological Association, 1962, pp. 61–94.

Krop, H., Calhoon, B., and Verrier, R. Modification of the self-concept of emotionally disturbed children by covert reinforcement. *Behavior Therapy*, 1971, *2*, 201–204.

Krumboltz, J. D. and Krumboltz, H. D. *Changing children's behavior*. Englewood Cliffs, N.J.: Prentice-Hall, Inc., 1972.

Krumboltz, J. D. and Thoresen, C. E. The effects of behavioral counseling in groups and individual settings on information seeking behavior. *Journal of Counseling Psychology*, 1964, *11*, 324–333.

Lafleur, N. K. and Johnson, R. G. Separate effects of social modeling and reinforcement in counseling adolescents. *Journal of Counseling Psychology*, 1972, *19*, 291–295.

Lal, H. and Lindsley, O. R. Therapy of chronic constipation in a young child by rearranging social contingencies. *Behaviour Research and Therapy*, 1968, *6*, 484–485.

Lattal, K. A. Contingency management of toothbrushing behavior in a summer camp for children. *Journal of Applied Behavior Analysis*, 1969, *2*, 195–198.

Law and Behavior. *Quarterly analysis of legal developments affecting professionals in human services*, 1976, #1, 1.

Lazarus, A. A. The elimination of children's phobias by deconditioning. In H. J. Eysenck (ed.), *Behavior therapy and the neuroses*. New York: Pergamon Press, 1960, pp. 114–122.

———. Group therapy of phobic disorders by systematic desensitization. *Journal of Abnormal and Social Psychology*, 1961, *63*, 504–510.

Lazarus, A. A. and Abramovitz, A. The use of "emotive imagery" in the treatment of children's phobias. *Journal of Mental Science*, 1962, *108*, 191–195.

Leitenberg, H. and Callahan, E. J. Reinforced practice and reduction of different kinds of fears in adults and children. *Behaviour Research and Therapy*, 1973, *11*, 19–30.

Lent, J. R. Minosa Cottage: Experiment in hope. *Psychology Today*, 1968, *2*, 51–58.

Lerner, J. W. *Children with learning disabilities*. Boston: Houghton Mifflin, 1976.

Levin, G. and Simmons, J. Response to praise by emotionally disturbed boys. *Psychological Reports*, 1962, *11*, 10.

London, P. Behavior modification. In J. C. Schoolar and C. M. Goetz (eds.), *Research and the psychiatric patient*. New York: Brunner/Mazel, 1975, 175–182.

Long, J. D. and Williams, R. L. Effectiveness of group and individual contingent free time with inner-city junior high school students. *Journal of Applied Behavior Analysis*, 1973, *6*, 465–474.

Lovaas, O. I. *Behavioral treatment of autistic children*. Morristown, N.J.: General Learning Press, 1973.

Lovaas, O. I., Freitag, A., Gold, V. J., and Kassorla, I. C. Experimental studies in childhood schizophrenia: Analysis of self-destructive behavior. *Journal of Experimental Child Psychology*, 1965, *2*, 67–84.

Lovaas, O. I., Koegel, R., Simmons, J. Q., and

Long, J. S. Some generalizations and follow-up measures on autistic children in behavior therapy. *Journal of Applied Behavior Analysis*, 1973, *6*, 131–166.

Lovaas, O. I. and Newsom, C. D. Behavior modification with psychotic children. In H. Leitenberg (ed.), *Handbook of behavior modification and behavior therapy*. Englewood Cliffs, N.J.: Prentice-Hall, 1976, pp. 303–360.

Lovaas, O. I., Schaeffer, B., and Simmons, J. O. Building social behavior in autistic children by use of electric shocks. *Journal of Experimental Research in Personality*, 1965, *1*, 99–109.

Lovibond, S. H. The mechanism of conditioning treatment of enuresis. *Behaviour Research and Therapy*, 1963, *1*, 17–21.

Lovitt, T. C. and Curtiss, K. A. Effects of manipulating an antecedent event on mathematics response rate. *Journal of Applied Behavior Analysis*, 1968, *1*,329–333.

———. Academic response rate as a function of teacher- and self-imposed contingencies. *Journal of Applied Behavior Analysis*, 1969, *2*, 49–53.

Lovitt, T. C., Guppy, T. E., and Blattner, J. E. The use of a free-time contingency with fourth graders to increase spelling accuracy. *Behaviour Research and Therapy*, 1969, *7*, 151–156.

Lundin, R. W. *Personality: A behavioral analysis*. (2nd ed.) New York: Macmillan, 1974.

MacDonald, W. S. *Battle in the classroom: Innovations in classroom techniques*. Scranton, Pa.: The Publisher's In Text Educational Publishers, 1971.

Madsen, C. H., Jr. Positive reinforcement in the toilet training of a normal child: A case report. In L. P. Ullmann and L. Krasner (eds.), *Case studies in behavior modification*. New York: Holt, Rinehart and Winston, 1965, pp. 305–307.

Madsen, C. H., Jr., Becker, W. C., and Thomas, D. R. Rules, praise and ignoring: Elements of elementary classroom control. *Journal of Applied Behavior Analysis*, 1968, *1*,139–150.

Madsen, C. K. and Madsen, C. H. *Parents —children —discipline: A positive approach*. Boston: Allyn and Bacon, Inc., 1970.

Mager, R. F. *Preparing instructional objectives*. Palo Alto, Calif.: Fearon Publishers, 1962.

Mahoney, K. The development and design of the "potty pager." Southwestern Psychological and Counseling Services, Tempe, Arizona, personal communication, 1978.

Mahoney, K., Van Wagenen, K., and Meyerson, L. Toilet training of normal and retarded children. *Journal of Applied Behavior Analysis*, 1971, *4*, 173–181.

Mahoney, M. J. and Thoresen, C. E. *Self control: Power to the person*. Monterey, Ca.: Brooks/Cole Publishing Company, 1974.

Mallick, S. K. and McCandless, B. R. A study of catharsis of aggression. *Journal of Personality and Social Psychology*, 1966, *4*, 591–596.

Mann, J. and Rosenthal, T. L. Vicarious and direct counter-conditioning of test anxiety through individual and group desensitization. *Behaviour Research and Therapy*, 1965, *7*, 359–367.

Martin, B. and Twentyman, C. Teaching conflict resolution skills to parents and children. In E. J. Mash, L. C. Handy, and L. A. Hamerlynck (eds.), *Behavior modification approaches to parenting*. New York: Brunner/Mazel, 1976.

Martin, R. *Legal challenges to behavior modification: Trends in schools, corrections and mental health*. Champaign, Ill.: Research Press, 1975.

Martin, R. R., Kuhl, P., and Haroldson, S. An experimental treatment with two preschool stuttering children. *The Journal of Speech and Hearing Research*, 1972, *15*, 743–752.

Maslow, A. *Motivation and personality.* New York: Harper, 1954.

Mattos, R. L., Mattson, R. H., Walker, H. M., and Buckley, N. K. Reinforcement and adversive control in the modification of behavior. *Academic Therapy*, 1969, *5*, 37–52.

McAllister, L. W., Stachowiak, J. G., Baer, D. M., and Conderman, L. The application of operant conditioning techniques in a secondary school classroom. *Journal of Applied Behavior Analysis*, 1969, *2*, 277–285.

McGuire, R. J. and Vallance, M. Aversion therapy by electric shock, a simple technique. *British Medical Journal*, 1964, *1*, 151–153.

McKenzie, H. S., Clark, M., Wolf, M. M., Kothera, R., and Benson, C. Behavior modification of children with learning disabilities using grades as tokens and allowances as back-up reinforcers. *Exceptional Children*, 1968, *34*, 745–752.

McNamara, J. R. The use of self-monitoring techniques to treat nailbiting. *Behaviour Research and Therapy*, 1972, 10, 193–194.

Medlund, M. B. and Stachnik, T. J. Good behavior game: A replication and systematic analysis. *Journal of Applied Behavior Analysis*, 1972, *5*, 45–51.

Meichenbaum, D. H. *Cognitive behavior modification.* New York: Plenum Press, 1977.

Meichenbaum, D. H., Bowers, K., and Ross, R. R. Modification of classroom behavior of institutional female adolescent offenders. *Behaviour Research and Therapy*, 1968, *6*, 343–353.

Michael, J. and Meyerson, L. A behavioral approach to counseling and guidance. In R. L. Mosher, R. F. Carle, and C. D. Kehas (eds.), *Guidance: An examination.* New York: Harcourt, Brace & World, 1965, pp. 24–48.

Mikulas, W. L. *Behavior modification: An overview.* New York: Harper & Row, 1972.

Miller, N. E. and Dollard, J. *Social learning and imitation.* New Haven: Yale University Press, 1941.

Mischel, W. *Introduction to personality.* New York: Holt, Rinehart and Winston, 1971.

Myers, K. E., Travers, R. M., and Sanford, M. E. Learning and reinforcement in student pairs. *Journal of Educational Psychology*, 1965, *56*, 67–72.

National Advisory Committee on Handicapped Children. *Special education for handicapped children.* First Annual Report. Washington, D.C.: U.S. Department of Health, Education and Welfare, 1968.

Nay, W. R. *Behavioral intervention: Contemporary strategies.* New York: Garden Press, 1976.

Neale, D. H. Behavior therapy and encopresis in children. *Behaviour Research and Therapy*, 1963, *1*, 139–143.

Needels, F. and Jamison, C. Educational approaches at the Los Angeles county autism project. In E. R. Ritvo (ed.), *Autism: Diagnosis, current research and management.* New York: Spectrum Publications, 1976.

Nighswander, J. K. and Mayer, G. R. Catharsis: A means of reducing elementary school students' aggressive behavior? *Personnel and Guidance*, 1969, *47*, 461–466.

Nolen, P. A., Kunzelmann, H. P., and Haring, N. C. Behavior modification in a junior high learning disabilities classroom. *Exceptional Children*, 1967, *34*, 163–168.

Novaco, R. W. *Anger control: The development and evaluation of an experimental treatment.* Lexington, Mass.: Heath and Company, 1975.

Numes, D. L., Murphy, R. J. and Ruprect, N. L. Reducing self-injurious behavior of severely retarded individuals through withdrawal of reinforcement procedures. *Behavior Modification,* 1977, *1,* 499–516.

O'Connor, R. D. Modification of social withdrawal through symbolic modeling. *Journal of Applied Behavior Analysis,* 1969, *2,* 15–22.

――――. Relative efficacy of modeling, shaping, and combined procedures for modification of social withdrawal. *Journal of Abnormal Psychology,* 1972, *3,* 327–334.

O'Leary, K. D. and Becker, W. C. Behavior modification of an adjustment class: A token reinforcement system. *Exceptional Children,* 1967, *33,* 637–642.

O'Leary, K. D. and Drabman, R. Token reinforcement programs in the classroom: A review. *Psychological Bulletin,* 1971, *75,* 379–398.

O'Leary, K. D., O'Leary, S., and Becker, W. C. Modification of a deviant sibling interaction pattern in the home. *Behaviour Research and Therapy,* 1967, *5,* 113–120.

O'Leary, K. D., Poulos, R. W., and Devine, V. T. Tangible reinforcers: Bonus or bribes? *Journal of Consulting and Clinical Psychology,* 1972, *38,* 1–8.

Parke, R. D. Some effects of punishment on children's behavior. *Young Children,* March 1969, 225–238.

Patterson, G. R. A learning theory approach to the treatment of the school phobic child. In L. P. Ullmann and L. Krasner (eds.), *Case studies in behavior modification.* New York: Holt, Rinehart and Winston, 1965(a).

――――. An application of conditioning techniques to the control of a hyperactive child. In L. P. Ullmann and L. Krasner (eds.), *Case studies in behavior modification.* New York: Holt, Rinehart and Winston, 1965(b).

――――. Teaching parents to be behavior modifiers in the classroom. In J. D.

Krumboltz and C. E. Thoresen (eds.), *Behavioral counseling: Case studies and techniques.* New York: Holt, Rinehart and Winston, 1969, pp. 155–161.

――――. *Families: Applications of social learning to family life.* Champaign, Ill.: Research Press, 1971.

――――. *Living with children: New methods for parents and teachers.* Champaign, Ill.: Research Press, 1976.

Patterson, G. R. and Brodsky, G. D. A behavior modification program for a child with multiple problem behaviors. *Journal of Child Psychology and Psychiatry,* 1966, *7,* 277–295.

Pavlov, I. P. *Conditioned reflexes.* (Translated and edited by G. V. Anrep.) New York: Dover Publications, 1960. (First published in 1927.)

Peine, H. Programming the home. Paper presented at the meeting of the Rocky Mountain Psychological Association, Albuquerque, N.M., 1969.

Pennypacker, H. S., Koenig, C. H., and Lindsley, O. R. *Handbook of the standard behavior chart.* Kansas City: Precision Media, 1972.

Perline, I. H. and Levinsky, D. Controlling behavior in the severely retarded. *American Journal of Mental Deficiency,* 1968, *73,* 74–78.

Peterson, D. R. and London, P. A role for cognition in the behavioral treatment of a child's eliminative disturbance. In L. P. Ullmann and L. Krasner (eds.), *Case studies in behavior modification.* New York: Holt, Rinehart and Winston, 1965, pp. 289–295.

Peterson, R. F. and Peterson, L. R. The use of positive reinforcement in the control of self-destructive behavior in a retarded boy. *Journal of Experimental Child Psychology,* 1968, *6,* 351–360.

Phillips, E. L. Achievement place: Token reinforcement procedures in a home-style rehabilitation setting for "pre-delinquent" boys. *Journal of Applied Behavior Analysis,* 1968, *1,* 213–224.

Phillips, E. L., Phillips, E. A., Fixsen, D. L., and Wolf, M. M. Behavior-shaping for delinquents. *Psychology Today,* 1973, *7,* 74–108.

Premack, D. Toward empirical behavior laws: I. Positive reinforcement. *Psychological Review,* 1959, *66,* 219–233.

Quarti, C. and Renaud, J. A new treatment of constipation by conditioning: A preliminary report. In C. M. Franks (ed.), *Conditioning techniques in clinical practice and research.* New York: Springer Publishing Co., Inc., 1964, pp. 219–227.

Reese, E. P. *The analysis of human operant behavior.* Dubuque, Iowa: Wm. C. Brown, 1966.

Re Gault, 387 US 1 (1967).

Reynolds, N. J. and Risley, T. R. The role of social and material reinforcers in increasing talking of a disadvantaged preschool child. *Journal of Applied Behavior Analysis,* 1968, *1,* 253–262.

Rimland, B. *Infantile autism: The syndrome and its implications for a neural theory of behavior.* New York: Appleton-Century Crofts, 1964.

Risley, T. The effects and side effects of punishing the autistic behaviors of a deviant child. *Journal of Applied Behavior Analysis,* 1968, *1,* 21–34.

Ritter, B. The group desensitization of children's snake phobias using vicarious and contact desensitization procedures. *Behaviour Research and Therapy,* 1968, *6,* 1–6.

Ross, A. O. *Psychological disorders of children: A behavioral approach.* New York: McGraw-Hill, 1974.

Sachs, D. A. The efficacy of time-out procedures in a variety of behavior problems. *Journal of Behavior Therapy and Experimental Psychiatry,* 1973, *4,* 237–242.

Safer, D. J. and Allen, R. P. *Hyperactive children: Diagnosis and treatment.* Baltimore: University Park Press, 1976.

Sarbin, T. R. Role theoretical interpretation of psychological change. In P. Worchel and D. Byrne (eds.), *Personality change.* New York: John Wiley, 1964, 176–219.

Schaefer, C. E. and Millman, H. L. *Therapies for children: A handbook of effective treatments for problem behaviors.* San Francisco: Jossey-Bass, 1977.

Schmauk, F. J. Punishment, arousal and avoidance learning in sociopaths. *Journal of Abnormal Psychology,* 1970, *76,* 325–335.

Schrupp, M. H. and Gjerde, C. M. Teacher growth in attitudes toward behavior problems of children. *Journal of Educational Psychology,* 1953, *44,* 203–214.

Shaftel, F. R. and Shaftel, G. *Role-playing for social values: Decision-making in the social studies.* Englewood Cliffs, N.J.: Prentice-Hall, 1967.

Sherman, A. R. *Behavior modification: Theory and practice.* Belmont, Calif.: Wadsworth Publishing Company, 1973.

Sherman, T. M. and Cormier, W. H. The use of subjective scales for measuring interpersonal reactions. *Journal of Behavior Therapy and Experimental Psychiatry,* 1972, *3,* 279–280.

———. Investigation of the influence of student behavior on teacher behavior. *Journal of Applied Behavior Analysis,* 1974, *7,* 11–21.

Silberman, A. Behavior modification: A new role for the elementary counselor. Video-tape presentation at the A.P.G.A. Convention, Chicago, Ill., 1972.

Silverman, I. and Geer, J. H. The elimination of

a recurrent nightmare by desensitization of a related phobia. *Behaviour Research and Therapy*, 1968, *6*, 109–111.

Skinner, B. F. *Science and human behavior.* New York: Macmillan, 1953.

———. Freedom and the control of men. In R. Ullrich and J. Mabry (eds.), *Control of human behavior.* Glenview, Ill.: Scott, Foresman, 1966, pp. 11–20.

———. *The technology of teaching.* New York: Appleton-Century-Crofts, 1968.

———. *Beyond freedom and dignity.* New York: A. A. Knopf, 1971.

Smith, J. M. and Smith, E. P. *Child management: A program for parents and teachers.* Ann Arbor, Mich.: Ann Arbor Publishers, 1966.

Solomon, R. W. and Wahler, R. G. Peer reinforcement control of classroom problem behavior. *Journal of Applied Behavior Analysis*, 1973, *6*, 49–56.

Staats, A. W. and Staats, C. K. *Complex human behavior.* New York: Holt, Rinehart and Winston, 1963.

Stone, M.C. Behavior shaping in a classroom for children with cerebral palsy. *Exceptional Children*, 1970, *36*, 674–677.

Stunkard, A. New therapies for eating disorders: Behavior modification of obesity and anorexia nervosa. *Archives of General Psychiatry*, 1972, *26*, 391–398.

Stunkard, A. J. and Mahoney, M. J. Behavioral treatment of eating disorders. In H. Leitenberg (ed.), *Handbook of behavior modification and behavior therapy.* Englewood Cliffs, N.J.: Prentice-Hall, 1976.

Sulzbacher, S. I. and Hauser, J. E. A tactic to eliminate disruptive behavior in the classroom: Group contingent consequence. *American Journal of Mental Deficiency*, 1968, *73*, 88–90.

Sulzer, B., Mayer, A. R., and Cody, J. J. Assisting teachers with managing classroom behavioral problems. *Elementary School Guidance and Counseling*, 1968, *3*, 40–48.

Sulzer-Azaroff, B. and Mayer, G. R. *Applying behavior analysis procedures with children and youth.* New York: Holt, Rinehart and Winston, 1977.

Tate, B. A. and Baroff, A. S. Aversive control of self-injurious behavior in a psychotic boy. *Behaviour Research and Therapy*, 1966, *4*, 281–287.

Thomas, D. R., Becker, W. C., and Armstrong, M. Production and elimination of disruptive classroom behavior by systematically varying teacher's behavior. *Journal of Applied Behavior Analysis*, 1968, *1*, 35–45.

Travers, R. W. M. *Essentials of learning.* New York: Macmillan, 1977.

Treegoob, M. and Walker, K. P. The use of stimulant drugs in the treatment of hyperactivity. *The School Psychologist Digest*, 1976, *5*, 5–10.

Truax, C. B. and Mitchell, K. M. Research on certain therapist interpersonal skills in relations to process and outcome. In A. E. Bergin and S. L. Garfield (eds.), *Handbook of psychotherapy and behavior change.* New York: John Wiley, 1971, 229–344.

Tucker, I. F. *Adjustment: Models and mechanisms.* New York: Academic Press, 1970.

Turner, R. K., Young, G. C., and Rachman, S. Treatment of nocturnal enuresis by conditioning techniques. *Behavior Research and Therapy Journal*, 1970, *8*, 367–381.

Tyler, V. O., Jr. Exploring the use of operant techniques in rehabilitation of delinquent boys. Paper read at the American Psychological Association Convention, Chicago, September 1965.

Ullmann, L. P. and Krasner, L. (eds.). *Case studies in behavior modification.* New York: Holt, Rinehart and Winston, 1965.

Valett, R. E. *Programming learning disabilities.* Palo Alto, Calif.: Fearon Publishers, 1969.

Vernon, W. M. *Motivating children: Behavior modification in the classroom.* New York: Holt, Rinehart and Winston, 1972.

Wagner, M. K. A case of public masturbation treated by operant conditioning. *Journal of Child Psychology and Psychiatry,* 1968(a), 9, 61–65.

———. Reinforcement of the expression of anger through role-playing. *Behaviour Research and Therapy,* 1968(b), 6, 91–95.

Wahler, R. G. Oppositional children: A quest for parental reinforcement control. *Journal of Applied Behavior Analysis,* 1969(a), 2, 159–170.

———. Setting generality: Some specific and general effects of child behavior therapy. *Journal of Applied Behavior Analysis,* 1969(b), 2, 239–246.

Wahler, R. G., Winkel, G. H., Peterson, R. F., and Morrison, D. C. Mothers as behavior therapists for their own children. *Behaviour Research and Therapy,* 1965, 3, 113–124.

Wallace, G. and McLoughlin, J. A. *Learning disabilities: Concepts and characteristics.* Columbus: Charles E. Merrill, 1975.

Ward, H. and Baker, B. L. Reinforcement therapy in the classroom. *Journal of Applied Behavior Analysis,* 1968, 1, 323–328.

Watson, J. B. and Raynor, R. Conditioned emotional reactions. *Journal of Experimental Psychology,* 1920, 3, 1–14.

Welsh, E. C. and Alvord, J. R. The home token economy—a case study. Paper presented at the Southwestern Regional Meeting of the American Orthopsychiatric Association, Galveston, Texas, 1972.

Welsh, R. S. A highly efficient method of patient counseling. Paper presented at the Meeting of the Rocky Mountain Psychological Association, 1966.

Werry, J. S. and Quay, H. C. Observing the classroom behavior of elementary school children. *Exceptional Children,* 1969, 35, 461–470.

Wetzel, R. J., Baker, J., Roney, M., and Martin, M. Outpatient treatment of autistic behavior. *Behaviour Research and Therapy,* 1966, 4, 169–177.

Whaley, D. L. and Malott, R. W. *Elementary principles of behavior.* New York: Appleton-Century-Crofts, 1971.

White, O. R. *A glossary of behavioral terminology.* Champaign, Ill.: Research Press, 1971.

Whiting, J. M. Resource mediation and learning by identification. In I. Iscoe and H. W. Stevenson (eds.), *Personality development in children.* Austin: University of Texas Press, 1960.

Wickman, E. K. *Children's behavior and teacher's attitudes.* New York: Commonwealth Fund, 1928.

Wickramaserkera, I. The application of learning theory to the treatment of a case of sexual exhibitionism. *Psychotherapy: Theory, Research and Practice,* 1968, 5, 108–112.

Williams, C. D. The elimination of tantrum behavior by extinction procedures. *Journal of Abnormal and Social Psychology,* 1959, 59, 269.

———. Extinction and other principles of learning in the treatment and prevention of children's disorders. Paper read at the American Psychological Association Convention, St. Louis, September 1962.

Williams, R. L. and Long, J. D. *Toward a self-managed life style.* Boston: Houghton Mifflin, 1975.

Williams, R. L., Long, J. D., and Yoakley, R. W. The utility of behavior contracts and behavior proclamations with disadvantaged senior high school students. *Journal of School Psychology,* 1972, 10, 329–338.

Williams vs. Robinson, 432 F2d 637 (D.C. 1970).

Winkler, R. C. Management of chronic psychiatric patients by a token reinforcement system. *Journal of Applied Behavior Analysis*, 1970, *3*, 47–55.

Wish, P. A., Hasazi, J. E., and Jurgela, A. R. Automated direct deconditioning of a childhood phobia. *Journal of Behavior Therapy and Experimental Psychiatry*, 1973, *4*, 279–283.

Wolf, M. M., Giles, D. K., and Hall, V. R. Experiments with token reinforcement in a remedial classroom. *Behaviour Research and Therapy*, 1968, *6*, 51–64.

Wolf, M. M., Hanley, E. L., King, L. A., Lachowicz, J., and Giles, D. K. The timer game: A variable interval contingency for the management of out-of-seat behavior. *Journal of Exceptional Children*, 1970, *36*, 113–117.

Wolf, M. M. and Risley, J. Analysis and modification of deviant child behavior. Paper read at the American Psychological Association Convention, Washington, D.C., September 1967.

Wolf, M. M., Risley, T. R., and Mees, H. L. Application of operant conditioning procedures to the behavior problems of an autistic child. *Behaviour Research and Therapy*, 1964, *1*, 305–312.

Wolpe, J. For phobia, a hair of the hound. *Psychology Today*, 1969, *3*, 34–37.

Wolpe, J. and Lazarus, A. A. *Behaviour therapy techniques: A guide to the treatment of neuroses.* Oxford: Pergamon Press, 1966.

Wyatt vs. Stickney, 344 F. Supp. 380 (M. D. Ala. 1972).

Zeilberger, J., Sampen, L. E., and Sloane, H. N., Jr. Modification of a child's problem behavior in the home with the mother as therapist. *Journal of Applied Behavior Analysis*, 1968, *1*, 47–53.

Zimmerman, E. H. and Zimmerman, J. The alteration of behavior in a special classroom situation. *Journal of the Experimental Analysis of Behavior*, 1962, *5*, 59–60.

Zinzer, O. Imitation, modeling and cross-cultural training. Aerospace Medical Research Laboratories, Aerospace Medical Division, Wright-Patterson Air Force Base, Ohio, September 1966.

Glossary/Index